Remember me to all the friends

CIVIL WAR LETTERS *from* **GEORGE W. HARWOOD**

Massachusetts 36th Regiment

George W. Harwood

JANET M. DRAKE

Remember me to all the Friends
Civil War Letters *from* George W. Harwood – *Massachusetts 36th Regiment*

Text © Janet M. Drake
www.facebook.com/Civil-War-Letters-from-George-W-Harwood-Massachusetts-36th-Regiment-102499675675731

Author: Janet M. Drake
Editor: Brett Peruzzi/Peruzzi Communications
Map Design: Rob Levine/Levine Design
Designer: Lisa Breslow Thompson/Lisa Thompson Graphic Design

Library of Congress Control Number: 2022901138
ISBN: 9781941573679

Published by Damianos Publishing
Saxonville Mills
2 Central Street, Studio 152
Framingham, MA 01701
www.DamianosPublishing.com

Produced through Silver Street Media by Bridgeport National Bindery, Agawam, MA USA

First printed 2022

~ DEDICATION ~

Dedicated to my parents

John W. and Marion E. Lebourveau
who began this journey for all of us.

~ CONTENTS ~

Introduction 6

People mentioned in the letters 8

Map of Thirty-sixth Regiment travels 10

Regimental flags 12

George W. Harwood letter on military letterhead 15

PART I 16

Chapter 1   Enlist and arrive in Maryland 17
             September 4 - 14, 1862

Chapter 2   Antietam Campaign, Maryland 24
             September 21 - November 27, 1862

Chapter 3   Fredericksburg, Virginia 52
             December 5, 1862 - January 7, 1863

Chapter 4   Winter of Discontent, Falmouth, Virginia 68
             January 13 - March 21, 1863

PART II 95

Chapter 5   To Kentucky 96
             March 30 - May 18, 1863

Chapter 6   Vicksburg and Jackson, Mississippi 118
             May 27 - July 30, 1863

Chapter 7   Return to Kentucky 143
             August 6 - 24, 1863

PART III 153

Chapter 8   Knoxville, Tennessee Campaign 154
                    August 30 - December 2, 1863

Chapter 9   Knoxville, Home for Recruiting Furlough 183
                    December 19, 1863 - February 21, 1864

PART IV 204

Chapter 10   Return to Virginia, Overland Campaign 205
                    May 15 - June 12, 1864

Chapter 11   Petersburg, Virginia 217
                    June 17, 1864 - March 30, 1865

Chapter 12   Petersburg, Farmville, City Point, Virginia 320
                    April 4 - April 29, 1865

EPILOGUE 332

Chapter 13   Alexandria, Washington, Mustered Out 333
                    May 6 - June 9, 1865

Chapter 14   After the War 341
                    November 1865 - June 1920

Appendix I   Massachusetts Thirty-sixth Regimental Chronology 347

Appendix II Family genealogies 351

Appendix III Bibliography 354

Acknowledgements 358

About the Author 360

~ INTRODUCTION ~

Those letters were written by my great-grandfather's cousin to his family and friends in North Brookfield, Massachusetts. North Brookfield was a farming community and the location of the Batcheller shoe manufacturing company. It is located seventeen miles north-west of Worcester. This book contains the letters he wrote home during his three-year enlistment in the Union Army during the Civil War, from August 1862 until June 1865. The letters were saved by his mother, sister, and great-niece Frances Doane Martin. Frances gave them to my parents Marion E. and John W. Lebourveau, who were both friends and a relative. They transcribed them and typed them into a legible format in the 1980s. I started with the typed collection, digitized it, and reviewed it against the original letters.

Everyone who has worked with the letters has kept the wording, spelling, and punctuation as close as possible to George's writing. I have kept a letter format similar to the originals to preserve as much as possible the experience of reading letters written from a military camp. Punctuation in the nineteenth century was not yet standardized, so often it is missing entirely. A handwritten letter also is spaced more loosely than a printed one. Therefore, when it is necessary for the reader to easily understand George's thinking, I have kept a space between words instead of inserting the punctuation which a modern reader would expect. When necessary for clarity I have sometimes added words in [square brackets]. George's letters are in roman (non-italic) font (for clarity) and my explanations and context notes are in italics.

For years it had been my dream to read the letters at a time when I could travel to the places where they were written, and place them in a larger context to learn more about the Civil War through the letters. In 2012, 150 years after these letters were written and during the 150th anniversary commemorations of the Civil War, my husband Dave and I began to study the letters and started our journey to follow the trail where they lead.

~ People Mentioned in the Letters ~

There are more complete charts of people mentioned in the letters in Appendix II. The people referred to most often are immediate family and close friends.

Family Tree

David L. Winslow - (m1) Mercy H. Dexter

***Louis** Dennis Winslow

Angeline Allen (m) George Harwood - brother of - (m2) Dolly P. Harwood

Anna, **George W.,** Ethan Allen, Fannie   David Frank Winslow (m) Edith Lord

Albion H. Doane

Jennie L. Winslow (m) Ulric J. Lebourveau

^Frances Doane Martin
(gave letters to John & Marion)

John W. Lebourveau (m) Marion E. Spencer

Janet M. Lebourveau (m) David E. Drake

*George and Louis were step-cousins who both enlisted in the Massachusetts Thirty-six Regiment. George sometimes spelled Louis as Lewis.

^Frances Doane Martin was the best friend of Bertha Johnson (Marion's mother) and a cousin of John's.

George's sister Anna was married to Freeman Doane, George's best friend. In 1862 they had one son, Georgie, born before the war, and one born in September. Albion was their fourth child. Freeman enlisted for nine months in the Massachusetts Forty-second Regiment.

George's brother Allen, later Ethan Allen, age fourteen, was in high school in 1862. His sister Frances was seven years old.

Andrew Jackson, the son of Phebe P. Harwood and William C. Jackson, was a cousin on George's father's side.

Harry (Harrison) and Henry Harwood were cousins of George's.

Lyman Gilbert and William James Haskell were two of George's best friends from home.

Moses Porter Snell, (Snell or M.P. Snell) became a close friend over the course of the war.

The Batcheller family owned a shoe factory in North Brookfield. Many townsfolk worked for them. George and Lyman had lived with and worked for them.

Map of Massachusetts ~ Thirty-sixth Regiment *Travels*

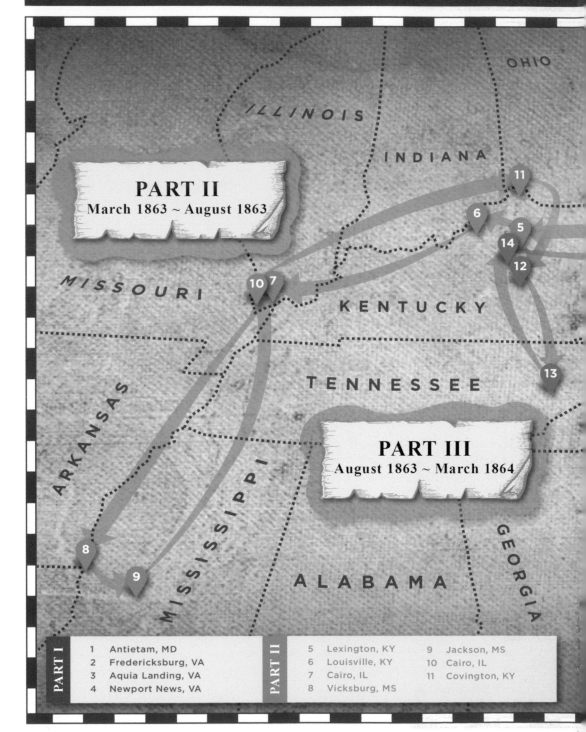

PART II
March 1863 ~ August 1863

PART III
August 1863 ~ March 1864

PART I	1	Antietam, MD	**PART II**	5	Lexington, KY	9 Jackson, MS
	2	Fredericksburg, VA		6	Louisville, KY	10 Cairo, IL
	3	Aquia Landing, VA		7	Cairo, IL	11 Covington, KY
	4	Newport News, VA		8	Vicksburg, MS	

1862 ~ 1865

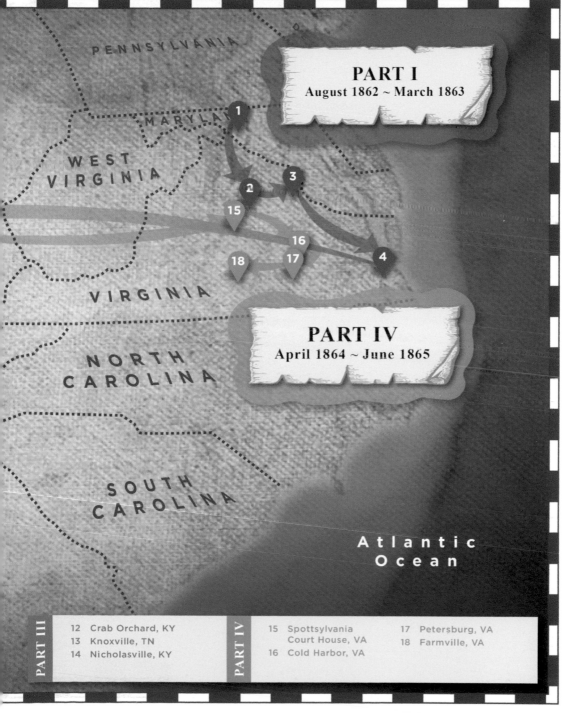

PART I
August 1862 ~ March 1863

PART IV
April 1864 ~ June 1865

PART III	
12	Crab Orchard, KY
13	Knoxville, TN
14	Nicholasville, KY

PART IV			
15	Spottsylvania Court House, VA	17	Petersburg, VA
		18	Farmville, VA
16	Cold Harbor, VA		

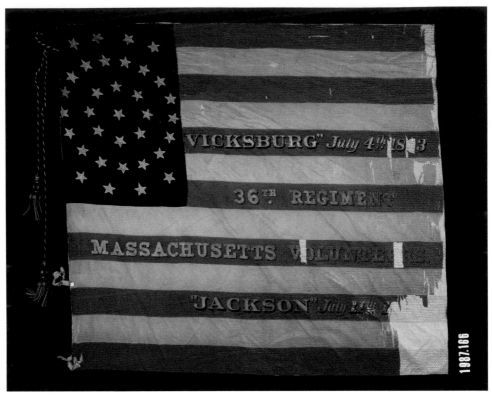

Thirty-sixth Regiment of Massachusetts Volunteers, first national regimental flag. Below is the description of this image from the Massachusetts State House Battle Flag Collection.

1987.166 Presentation National. Presented by the mayor on behalf of friends in Worcester 2 September 1862. Staff shattered by bullet 3 July 1864 at Petersburg. Received by Sergeant-at-Arms 20 October 1864. Finial spear missing. Silver plate on staff: "Presented to the 36th regiment by their friends in Worcester, Aug. 30, 1862." (Steven W. Hill, State House Flag Historian. Courtesy Commonwealth of Massachusetts, State House Art Commission.)

Thirty-sixth Regiment of Massachusetts Volunteers, second national regimental flag. Below is the description of this image from the Massachusetts State House Battle Flag Collection.

1987.198 First National. Issued 24 September 1864, received in field 7 October 1864. Received by Sergeant-at-Arms 22 December 1865. Spontoon-style finial. (Steven W. Hill, State House Flag Historian. Courtesy Commonwealth of Massachusetts, State House Art Commission.)

Thirty-sixth Regiment of Massachusetts Volunteers, second state regimental flag. Below is the description of this image from the Massachusetts State House Battle Flag Collection.

1987.171 Second State color. Issued 24 September 1864, received in field 7 October 1864. Received by Sergeant-at-Arms 22 December 1865. Spontoon-style finial. (Steven W. Hill, State House Flag Historian. Courtesy Commonwealth of Massachusetts, State House Art Commission.)

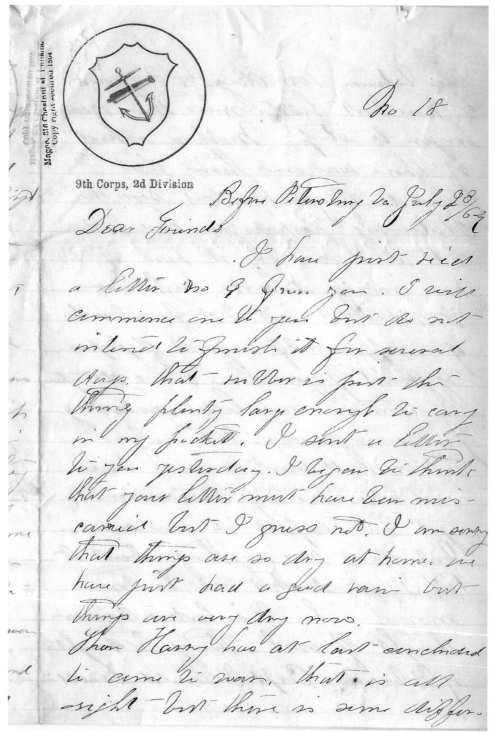

Letterhead, Ninth Corps, Second Division, letter dated July 23, 1864 (Image from author's collection.)

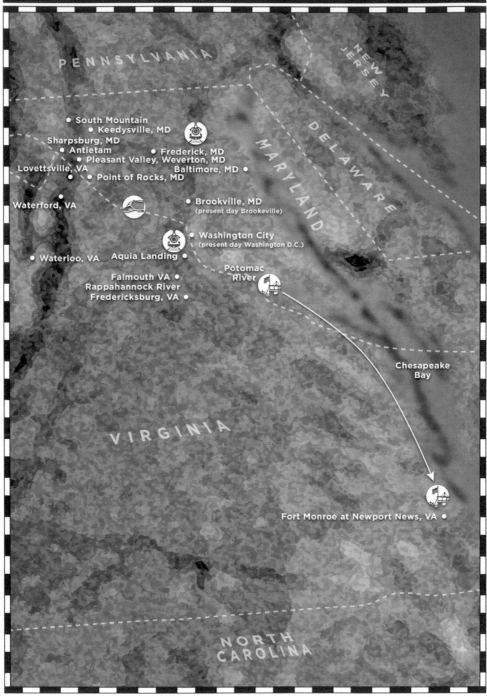

~ Chapter 1 ~

ENLIST AND ARRIVE IN MARYLAND
September 4 - 14, 1862

George Washington Harwood answered President Abraham Lincoln's call for troops in August 1862. He was twenty years old and had been working for the Batcheller Shoe Company in North Brookfield, Massachusetts. He joined the Massachusetts Thirty-sixth Regiment of Volunteers with fourteen other men from North Brookfield. After training at Camp Wool in Worcester, Massachusetts, they received their regimental colors (flags) from the mayor of Worcester. They then travelled from Worcester to Boston by train, then to Alexandria and Washington City on the US Steamer Merrimac. I think this was a side wheel steamer, launched from the Charlestown Navy Yard. It may be the steamer referenced in the Lytle-Holdcamper list of Merchant Steam Vessels of the United States 1790-1868.

Cheaspeak Bay Aug 4th [September 4, 1862]

Dear Sister Anna

     We have had a very pleasant time all has been quiet except in one case of Whiskey is 1.40 1/2 pint and hasnt to be got at that and lemons as high as .25 a peace. One man had over 40.00, so when he came on board and now he has $1.11. He bought 5 1/2 pints of whiskey and lost the rest. He has had the Deliriams Tremens badly and it took 6 or 8 men to hold him and such a site I never saw and I hope I never shall again. he thought he saw Hell and of all the cries for help I never heard. I should think it would be a warning ai [to] all who saw him. Thare are a few Lemons on board and they sell as high as 25 a peace. Thare is some Thieving going on one man has lost a watch others have lost money but I am carefull of my things and lost nothing of any account. We got on board of the Merrimac in Boston harbor about 8 o'clock and staid all night a few rods from shore, several have fell over board but I think none have been lost. I have been dreadful Sea Sick and have all the way across I vomited 10 or 12 times. The rest of the boys are pretty well I sleep on Deck and in the daytime we are as thick as we can stand and it is dirty and warm, and it looks like a pigpen, and stinks as bad. Thare is no chance for us to read our Bibles except as we take them right out in the crowd, which many of us do and I enjoy it very much even so. I think thare are many Christians on board both of the Mass. Reg and Maine. by the way the 20th Maine Regiment is on board with us, Thare are on board about 2300 persons. The Ship is about -2.90[290?] ft long 30 ft wide and it makes us thick. I never enjoyed Religion so much in my life as I have since I went into Camp my Bible is my best friend on Earth. Freeman told me that he had enlisted for 9 months I wish he was a Christian and if he has not gone from Worcester please say to him for me, to see to it that his peace is made with God before it is forever to late and while it is an excepted time and a day of Salvation. Religion will be his best friend and perhaps his only friend in time of Trouble. I am happy to think that I have many friends at home and I felt bad to leave them. I felt very bad when I left Worcester to leave Father + Freeman and the rest, but I hope I shall meet you all again before long hear on Earth but if not Oh, that I may meet you all in heaven whare thare will be no more fasting, I want to have a talk with you when I came home on a furlough but circumstances would not permit. I will close for this since I do not know whare to direct your letter perhaps I shall before I seal it up, so Good Bye from your ever true Brother

George Washington

[On the outside of the folded letter]   Mrs Anna M Doano

North Brookfield, Mass.

Present [as in to give to someone]

Delirium tremens is the condition resulting from rapid withdrawal of extreme alcohol use. The Twentieth Maine Regiment played an important role at the battle of Gettysburg. George did not know where to address the letter to his sister because she was about to have a baby and may have been at her home or with her parents.

Afternoon

Washington Sunday 7th

[September 1862]

Dear Father

    This is the first opportunity I have had to write home. We went on board of the Merrimac Tuesday night and lay at anchor a few rods from shore until morning when we started it was hardly light. The Maine 20 Reg went with us to Alexandria They have gone to join L[ ] S[ ] I was dreadful Sea Sick most all of the way. we saw a great many things coming up along Cheaspeak Bay. but we had a lonesome time of it and we were very glad to get on land again we were as thick as we could stand almost. There were 2300 [illegible] in all on board.

    We left the Ship this afternoon and are now a little way in land, but we soon expect to march on and to join Burnsides Division tonight They are about 17 miles from here. It beats all what a site of Mules and Horses there are here. The 34 Reg is within 2 miles of hear I have seen one or two of their men but have not seen Andrew [cousin Andrew F. Jackson]. We had hard Crackers and Coffee while on board. There was one man from the Maine Reg who had the Delerian Tremens dreadfully several times while on board, and of all the sights I ever saw, or heard of. Whiskey on board was as high as 3.00 and 4.00 per ½ pint and some would have it at that. some men lost money on board. Lemons were as high as .25 a peace [piece] and few at that. Where we are now there are Horses + Cattle and Hogs + Pigs + Wagons and Mules and these are no more than 8 acres of land. We had a first rate time to cross the Ocean it was so very pleasant no wind no clouds and it is clear now.

Leesbourough [Leesboro, Maryland] Wednesday Noon
We left Washington Yesterday morning and we marched with our heavy loads 12 or 14 miles and got hear at 3 o'clock about. Before we got hear at last 2/3 of the Reg fell out. but I stuck too [in] and am so lame that I can hardly move. I fell on board the Ship and received a very hard bump on the head and I am told that I was taken up for most dead but in three hours I got better and came to my sences. I do not know much about it myself but Lyman has written to Mary [his wife] all about it. The rest of the boys are all pretty well. We expect to march a few miles farther in a few days for we have not yet reached Burnside. I should like to write all about what I have seen but I cannot now. I wish you would write to me and let me know how you all do and whare Freeman is. We may not have an opportunity to write home when we get a little farther South we are within a few miles of Rebels. write soon and often and I will do the same.

From your True Son G. W. Harwood

The Twentieth Maine joined the Fifth Corps First Division, Third Brigade under Colonel T.B.W. Stockton.

Brookville, [Maryland] Saturday Sep 13th [1862]

Dear Father
As I have another good opportunity to write I think I will improve it. We left Leesborough yesterday morning about 7 o'clock and reached hear between 4 and 5. The day before we started I stood on Guard and it rained a part of the time and in the night it rained hard and when I was not

on Guard I had to lay on the wet ground and I was as wet as a dog. I am
troubled some with the Rheumatisin and my load felt heavy before I got
here but I did not leave the ranks, many did. The distance from Leesborough to Brookville is about 12 miles. [Cousin] Lewis [Winslow] is not
very well but I guess he keeps around the rest of the boys are all right. I
have not seen or heard anything from Andrew. do his folks hear any thing
from him. When we came from Washington we saw Camp Brighton the
place where Edwin spent so much time. We are about 25 miles from Baltimore and within 15 miles of the Rebels. Gen Burnside left hear day before
yesterday and is a few miles ahead of us and is expecting to have a fight
before long. I should not think it strange if we see fighting before long. In
the place where we staid at Washington the night before we left a Michigan Reg came and we left them there and the next day one of them was
shot by a scooch and they have got him in irons now. he ought to be shot.
We see any quantity of old troops pass here in all directions and they look
pretty rough. I have got over from my cold that I had when I left Worcester and I feel pretty well except the Rheumatism a little. Lyman says that
he thinks he has gained about 15 lbs. since he went into camp but I have
not, I have lost 14 or 15 if the scales agree. on our march we saw several
old Horses dead beside the road and some more that will die before long. I
have not seen but 2 passing ever since I left Worcester I believe the farms
here are old and run out. the buildings are old and some of them are log
huts and small at that. Milk is 12 cts per quart.

Sunday morning 14th

I did not finish my letter yesterday and so I will finish this morning. This
is a very pleasant morning and warm. It makes me think of two weeks ago
this morning when I went to Church in North Brookfield. We are in a
Neighborhood of Quakers - they say. they appear very friendly. We dis-
tinctly heard the roar of cannons in the N. West yesterday and do this
morning and we think that thare must be a battle or at least a skirmish. Is
there any thing new at home. have you heard any thing from [cousins]
Henry & Harry Harwood. I sent a letter to you last Wednesday mail I presume you have got that before now Give my love to my friends and tell
them to write to me and tell Uncle William's folks that Addison [Hair] is
as happy as a clam I wish that you would write often and tell me all the
news. the boys think that they shall get home in 9 months but I dont know.
I will write a letter to Anna. Please direct as I advised before

from your ever true son G. W. Harwood
Direct as follows
George W. Harwood
Co E 36 Reg Mass Vol
Washington D.C.

I wish you could let me know all the news and if any more of our friends have enlisted and what Edwin + Hubbard [Doane and] John Lampson [Lamson] think about war but I must close. I am writing on my blanket on the ground

Good bye   George

We are going after some Grapes down in the woods in a few minutes.

A sesesh or secesh (secessionist) is a Confederate soldier. The battle sounds mentioned in the letter were from the Battle of South Mountain, on September 13-14, 1862. Edwin was probably Edwin M. Tucker, who served with the Massachusetts Twenty-fourth Regiment.

Brookville Sunday Sept 14 [1862]

Dear Sister Anna,

I have just written a letter to Father and I think that I must write a little to you. I [tell?] you Anna that any one from home and deprived of the comforts of life and food which if we were at home we should think hardly eatable, but I do not complain but am thankful for what I can get with [illegible] of home as I think of the Sunday that I spent at home two weeks ago it makes me almost wish that I could spend this one thare but no that cannot be. but I hope that I can spend many more at home before long. but it is not for me to deside for Gods ways are not our ways nor his thoughts are our thoughts. Anna my Testament is my best friend and as I have not failed to read it daily since I enlisted and the communion with my Saviour is far better than the pleasures of this world. I sometimes think that it is all for the best that we are deprived of the comforts and privilages of home for a season that we may more fully realise them when we return and I hope that we shall. I intended to have a little conversation with you before I left but you know that circumstances would not permit I often think of you and pray for you. I think of all the kindness you have always showed towards me, and think that had it not been for the good example that you set before and the kind entreaties which you have made to me that

I might not have been what I now am. I feel that I have no friend on Earth that I can express my feelings to so well as you. how are you and the boys I should like to see them. has Freeman left Worcester I would that he could give his heart to God before it is to late. Are Mr Doanes folks all well. I should like to hear from them and I hope that they will write to me. Frank Jenks has just received a letter from home and he was glad to hear and so was I. We are encamped on a high hill and in a neighborhood of Quakers and they appear friendly the Rebels are not very far from hear [here] and we have heard the roar of the distant cannons yesterday and this morning I have not heard the result. I like first rate am in good health except the Rheumatism troubles me some I have lost some flesh things that we want to buy are pretty high and I buy only what is necessary. We are expecting to leave hear [here] tomorrow and getting things in order I do not know whare we are going but you can direct your letters to me as follows

      George W Harwood
      Co. E. 36 Regt Mass Vols
      Washington D.C.

I shall have to draw this note to a close give my love to the friends and acquaintances and tell them to write me please excuse this writing as I am laying on the ground and it is not a very easy posission [position]. Good Bye for this time write soon from your ever true Brother

      George W Harwood

~ Chapter 2 ~

ANTIETAM CAMPAIGN, MARYLAND
September 21 - November 27, 1862

The Battle of Antietam Creek in Sharpsburg was on September 17. The Thirty-sixth Regiment arrived September 20, three days after the battle. Here they joined Burnside's Division under General George B. McClellan.

Keedysville Sunday Aug [September] 21 '62

Dear Father and Mother,

I have not received a letter from home since I left but I think I will send another I sent one last Sunday from Brookville and one several days before which I presume you have got. We left Brookville last Tuesday morning and Wednesday we marched all day and then I had to go on Guard and stand all night and then we started the next morning and marched about 20 miles I did not carry my Knapsack for I was sick in the night and did not feel like it. Thursday Eve we reached Frederick City it is quite a large place but no very good buildings, and in fact I have not seen but few good ones since I left Worcester. We marched in to Middletown Friday and spent the night. We have seen some of the Rebels today and a good deal of their works they burned a bridge near here and it has been rebuilt and we crossed it this afternoon I have seen some of our wounded Soldiers today and they look bad. one week ago where we now stop was in possession of the Rebels. We reached Keedysville last night and found that they were fighting only a few miles ahead of us and that some of the wounded soldiers were here I have seen some of the 15th Reg David Earle is here and is wounded just above the heart the ball passed through under his arm he is also slightly wounded on the right arm I think he is on the ground now with us [Henry?] Emerson Smith is here wounded in the Calf of the leg. Charles Perry has lost his left leg below the knee I have not seen that Joseph Fretts is killed He used to board with E. M. Kittridge and wait upon Lizzie Bush. Daniel W. Knight is all right and sound I believe. Edward Russell is Lieutenant and is all right. thare are good many others that are wounded that I will not speak of A. Pellet [Archibald S. Pellett] is sick. I believe that our troops are advancing and I understand that we are to start tomorrow if not tonight. I am a little foot sore but not bad otherwise I am all right and in good health We are about 70 miles from Washington now they say. we like our Capt + Col first rate. Our troops took some sesesh prisoners yesterday and brought them into this place I should think that thare were about 200 of them they were paroled and sent back and the Rebs took a good many from us and paroled them

they have gone to Anapolis to stay a while. It seems to be the opinion of the people that they have got Jackson in a close place and I hope that they have. The boys from the 15th Regt say that [they] came from Alexandria a few days before us and that they saw the 34th Regt and saw Andrew Jackson. I have not seen or heard any thing from him. do his folks hear from him at all. Lewis Winslow is not very well but is better than he was I think. Moses P Snell is behind I think at Frederick not well and is helping in the hospital whare some of our sick are stationed This is a fine day and it seems quite like Sunday and is still for the crowd that is about here. some of the boys wish they were at home and think that they would not enlist again but I do not wish so but I do miss the comforts and enjoyments as much as any one and I guess more than some and I do wish this War was over. We live on hard bread and Coffee and not much meat - we make it go pretty well Lyman gains on it. The boys are in good spirits all of them some of us have been out and washed and we feel better. although we had to go some ways before we got thare. some of the boys have been up to the battle field and say that the Rebels dead lay in winnows on the field and they all seem to see that thare are more dead sesech than of our boys. the Rebels prisoners look hard the look is muddy like pigs. the streets from Washington to hear is all full of hogs but they are not fat to eat many of them. I do want to hear from home and hear whare Freeman is and if any more have enlisted I sometimes wish that I was with him or that he was with me have Edwin + Hubbard [Doane] or John Lampson [Lamson] enlisted. What is the news at home any way whare is Anna M. now at home or is she keeping house alone I should think that would be lonesome for her who has she got to help her is she well and the boys I should like to see them what is their little ones name, has Judson Adams enlisted I imagine[?] that he might. Father do you traid [trade] now as much as ever or more I should like to see you [illegible] I wish I could get into your orchard and get some corn and apples. some of the boys got corn and [illegible] but it is very scarce hear [here]. We have just received orders to pack up our knapsacks as quick as possible and so I will finish this some other time.   Monday 22
I will finish this letter in few words as the mail is going out in about 10 minutes and I will only say that we are about 1 1/2 [miles] from the Potomac but do not know the place we are all well and Lyman and I are cooking corn and crackers together but I must close for this time and I

wish that [you] will write all the news and let me know how you all are and Give my love to all the friends let Anna read this note and tell her to write I often think of home and wish that the time would soon come when I can return.

   Yours truly
   George W. Harwood

George's father traded cattle. The family continued trading beef cattle until the early 1900s and the succeeding owners also raised beef cattle until early in the twenty-first century. After the battle of Antietam, Confederate Generals Robert E. Lee and "Stonewall" Jackson withdrew their forces back across the Potomac River.

              Burnside Corps
           Sunday Sept 28 [1862]

Dear Friends .

   As I have a little spare time just now I will write a few lines to you and let you know that I am well and all right. This is the fourth letter that I have written home and have not as yet received any from you and I begin to think it is about time I begin to want to know how the friends at home do and whare Freeman is and what Regt he is in. The wheather [weather] out here is warm in days and cold and heavy dews at night and we have to bundle up at night. We boys miss our homes very much we miss the pantrys and the orchards we miss the enjoyment of Civilized Society and kind friends. but we hope that the time will not be long before we can again enjoy these privilages and when we do I think that we shall realise their value more than ever before. Tuesday morning we expected to march for we were called up early that morning at about half past three and stood in the cornfield two hours and then were dismissed and told to pack up and be ready to move at a moments notice but we did not go that day. Wednesday I went on Guard it rained a little in the morning but not much. Gen McClellan has been over to see Gen Burnside this afternoon and I suppose that I saw him a little ways off. Our pickets took a Rebel prisoner this morning. Several are sick in our Regt and it is reported that some have got the Black Measles too I have not seen any thing of the kind. Thursday forenoon about 11 o'clock we had orders to start at 1 o'clock and so we formed a line in the Cornfield and stood thare or sat in the dirt until four and then we were told to make our selves as comfortable as possible so we returned back into the woods and pitched our tents and staid until about noon Friday and then we marched slowly about two miles and are now in a large wheat field whare the stubbles are about a foot high a very good place to drill only a little rough. yesterday Lyman and I got some meat and cooked it ourselves and made some Coffee and it tasted good. This morning we went down to the Antietam Creek and washed ourselves. yesterday we went down to the Potomac river and washed but are now forbidden as the Rebel pickets are close to the opposite shore and we may have a fight before we know it. We are in Burnsides Army Corp third Brigade first Division. thare are more soldiers in sight of me than I ever expected to see, and I should think that it would take a large army to whip us. What do you think of Abe Lincolns Proclamation, I think that there will be a great movement about the first of January if not before. Some of the boys are talking about going home in the spring. Do Addisons folks hear any thing from him he has written this morning. I guess he writes first rate he is well. Lewis has not been able to carry his knapsack at all since he left Washington and part of the time he had to ride himself. he is not very well and looks pail [pale] and poor. Snell is behind in the hospital at Fredrick [Maryland] the rest of us are all well How is Anna and the boys I want to hear from them and from the rest of you I hope that you will write all the news soon and often a letter would do me a good deal of good. I will close for this time so Good Bye please let Anna have this and read. I will write you all more

from Your eldest Son + Brother

George W. Harwood

[On a separate piece of paper]

Monday Afternoon Sept 29 [1862]

As I did not send my letter yesterday I will write a few words more for Fannie I have just been down to the big[?] Potomac River after water and I have picked a few flowers that I will send to her I picked them on the River's Banks. I presume that they will fade before you get them. I wish that you would send me a newspaper once in a while I want to hear the news from Massachusetts the [news]papers that we get hear come pretty high and few at that. The Baltimore Clipper is almost the only one sold hear, This is a very warm day and we are almost uncomfortable in our shirt sleeves. One fellow was sun struck this forenoon on drill and they had to carry him to the Doctor the last I heard from him he was senceless.

Addison has been over to see me two or three times today to see if I have got any letters from home. he is in a great hurry to hear from home and so am I. I suppose that neither of the Parkman boys [Charles and Henry L.] have enlisted. I should like to have Mr. Bush come out hear and live a while as he said he had as leave come as not what do you think that he [would] say if he would see the maggots around on his meat as it did this morn before it was cooked but that was nothing we liked it all the better. I should like to get another peace [piece of meat] of the same kind. I guess that by the time I get home I shall be able to eat any thing or sleep any whare but I do not want you think that I mean to complain but I do not in the least. This is a good place to bring boys to a [illegible]. The 15 Regt has gone on to Harpers Ferry they say, I want you to write and let me know what Regt Freeman has joined and the letters of his Regt if you can and I may find him sometime. Give my love to all the friends. I have just received two letters from home and one paper.

Geo W. Harwood

Sister Fannie (Frances) was seven years old. The Parkman boys were Charles and Henry (Lyman) Parkman. Mr. Bush was probably Eli (age forty-three).

Letter No 5

Burnside Army Corps at Camp, Sept 30th [1862]

Dear Sister Anna

I received a letter from you and one from Father last night and also a paper from you. I tell you that I was very glad [to] hear from home I have read those letters over and over again and shall until I get another I was surprised to hear that [Henry] Lyman + Charles Parkman had enlisted what do Carrie + Elizabeth say to that? I should like to see Charles after he has marched 15 or 20 miles with his knapsack and 50 rounds of Cartridges and three days Rations in his haversack on his back. I did not think that Hubbard would come either but am glad to hear of it. I should think his Fathers folks would feel lonesome without him for he is almost always at home. I suppose that John Lamson will do as Edwin [Doane] does. Does John wait upon Eunice [Doane] now. I did not see him when I came home on a furlow [furlough]. Anna you might as well think that I felt pretty bad the morning that I left you sick in bed I wanted to say something but I could not. What do you think that I was doing when I received your letters

I had an old copper dish with some holes punched through like a pumpkin strainer and had some corn and was grinding it to make some meal. This morning Lyman made it into Hasty Pudding and then we eat it as chickens would doe [do]. Freeman wanted to know what I took that I did not need I did not take any thing and I should think that perhaps he had better take a pair of under-shirts also I almost wish that I had some. I took a change of Shirts a change of Drawers and Stockings my Portfolio a Towel and work-book and gloves or mittens and I think that I have nothing to spare. when we came to march some of the boys threw away their Woolen Blankets and some of their under cloths [clothes] and some left their over-coats but I hung on to mine, and I want that you should tell Freeman and Hubbard not to leave their Blankets for they will need them every night. Lewis is better and has done duty this morning for the first time since he left home I think. He has written to Andrew some time ago but has not heard from him and I do not [know] whare he is. He was at Alexandria last week or at least the 34 Regt was, Addison said that his wife [Ann] wrote that his Fa-ther [Samuel] had not heard from him for some time and was very anxious to know whare he was. I am sorry to hear that he has got the rheumatism for that is pretty hard. I have got it slightly now in my right shoulder I am all right excepting that, Lyman is wrighting [writing] now I think that he has sent four letters and received one. He traids [trades] some in watches and pistols he has got both, and I have got neither, and I do not want any. It makes me laugh sometimes to think how this War makes many boys get married suddenly thare [there] are several in our Company that were mar-ried just before they left. Snell for one he showed me his wife's picture. Lyman is the same boy as before how does his wife appear does she say much about that night that we met at your house just before we left. All the girls that we see out hear are as black as my boots and few at that. The houses around hear are all empty and their owners somewhare else. I do not think that I should like to live out hear. I suppose that you know how we crossed over what they call the South Mountain or whare they had their great fight near Frederick, and I had about as leave climb the old Wachusetts Mountain in Prinston [Princeton], and much rather with the company that we had that day. over

[Letter actually goes to another sheet of paper.]

I wish that you could see what I am looking at, just now. These fellows have stolen some pistols and they have been caught and handcuffed together and are marched by two Corporals back and fourth [forth] by the Officers tents. they must feel proud, I understand that their punishment is to keep marching for 48 hours with out rest they change their guard once in 2 hours. I guess that they will buy their pistols hearafter. It is my opinion that M. Duncan will not make a very good Lieutenent but perhaps he will.   Wednesday morning,
As I did not have time to finish my letter last night I will this morning. We can get no Apples or Potatoes hear and I begin to want some. Thare is a flour mill about 3/4 of a mile from hear and we can buy flour for 4 cents per lb. we got some this morning and some molasses and had a minute Pudding for breakfast. I am sorry that Mother is not quite so well and hope that she will feel better when you get home to her. I am glad that you are going home for it will be better for you and her. What is your little baby's name. does he look like Georgic I wish I could see them again about this time. I guess that Henry did not stop long at Milwalkey [Milwaukee?] do you know when he got back I did not know that he was hear before. I think that Harry will make a good Capt he is well drilled. I never expect to get any thing higher than a high private in the rear rank. I sometimes wish that I had gone in a Cavalry Company and then I could ride instead of going on foot. they use mules out hear on teams instead of horses mostly, 4 or 6 mules on a waggon and a [illegible] riding the near wheel one, some of these mules are about as big as Billy Buttin. some are as big or bigger than the Horse that Father got of Addison and look just like him he would make a good mule. I wish you would tell all the Friends to write and I will try and answer them. give my love to them all and have Father send me a paper I was very glad to get yours it seems so like home. I want to know which Regt the boys go in and the name of their company. write soon and often all of you. keep up good courage and we will be back in a little while better than when we went away. I am happy and enjoying myself first rate. you will please direct to me Co E 36 Regt Mass Vols Ninth Army Corps. Good bye for this time I will write again before long if nothing happens.

    This from your ever true brother   George W. Harwood

Henry (Lyman) and Charles Parkman joined the Massachusetts Forty-second (nine-month) Regiment with Freeman and Hubbard Doane. The Thirty-sixth Regiment trained at Camp Wool in Worcester. They were given a short furlough to go home just before they left Worcester for Boston. A haversack is a small bag with one strap which can be worn over the shoulder like a backpack. Hasty pudding is made from ground corn or wheat mixed with milk or water and cooked quickly (hastily) until thickened to a porridge. Anna's boys were Georgie, two years and Elmer, one month. Addison Hair's wife was Ann Maria Barnum.

President Lincoln and General McClellan at Antietam (Courtesy Library of Congress)

Pleasant Valley [Maryland] Oct 9th [1862]

Dear Father and Mother

    I have just received a letter from you and I was glad to hear from home, we had expected the mail for sometime, It does me more good than a meal of vituals. you say that your apples do not sell very well. I should like to get hold of some of them we can get no apples of any account and we have to pay a cent apeace [piece] for one as big as [a] small hens egg. I should like to see that colt I hope that you will keep him until I get home. Addison wants to know how that calf does that he let you have. the weather out hear is warmer hear than it is in Mass in July. We are now in a very pleasant place we left an old place last Tuesday morning. last monday I with others went up to Gen Burnside Head Quarters and Stood Guard I stood between the Gens + Cols tents and had a good chance to see what was going on, when we got back to camp we met our Regt just going out and we had to pack up and follow on several miles behind and I tell you we had a hard time, they called the role just before they got mail and out of the 1000 men they did not number more than 150. but the rest came on before night. we marched about 9 miles and over the west [illegible] or rather east path cross the Elk Mountains. It gave us such a heat that one in our Co had fitts in the night and he has now got his discharge I understand and is going home, as soon as he is able. it so happens that we most always march after I have stood on guard the night before but I think that I am good for them yet. I have lost about 10 lbs in all since I enlisted I am as tough as a whip as Lyman says, except slightly troubled with the rheumatism. Lyman gaines on his hard bread + Coffee. He has just received 3 letters. I was on picket one week ago today near the Potomac I liked there pretty well, Last Friday we had a visit from Abe Lincoln, Gen McClellan, Gen Burnside, Cox + Wilcox and about 100 others, Officers and Aids they were doing what they call a Review they looked about as I supposed they did. they were all on Horse-back. Lincoln looked just like G.B. [Gideon B.] Jenks of N.B. We are now situated between the Elk + Tenth Mountains near a Creek called Israel Cr in Pleasant Valley. I have been down to the store today about 1/2 mile from hear but I did not bye [buy] much I received a letter from Freeman a few days ago and have answered it. I was glad to hear from him. I suppose that they have not started from Worcester yet. I am sorry to hear that Ethan Allen is dead and I think that it is strange that he should make those remarks before he died. I should think that Mr. Perry's folks should feel pretty bad about Charles's death, he was a wild boy. I should think that N. Brookfield would look forsaken there are so many going to war. I hear that W. [William?] Hair is deaf. I think his deafness must have come on pretty suddenly. At least I didnt know it before, and I guess that he would get better if the War should come to a close, and I hope that it will before long things look <u>dark</u> sometimes. next sheet,

They say that they have not had any rain out hear except a few showers since last August but they have heavy dews. Father are you any worse than you were when I left home I hope that you are not. I think of you often and the tears start in my eyes often when I think of my kind friends so far away from me and of the Possibility that I may never meet with them again on Earth but then I think of that better world where thare will be no more parting, pain, no sickness, and all <u>tears</u> should be wiped away. Do not worry about me for I shall take the best care of my self that I can and I hope that the time will not be far distant when I shall return back to my old home. I am sorry to hear that Andrew is so lame and should like to see him. I hope that they will give him a discharge. I suppose that Edwin Doane has not enlisted. do they say anything about drafting now. what does Uncle David [Winslow] say about Lewis. he is in our tent now reading a paper which W. Haskell just got from home, he is not very tough, a few days ago thare was a call for men in our Regt to Vol. [volunteer] to join the Battery and to stay. thare has been a call for more to go as teamsters but I thought that I would stay whare I belonged and I guess I had better, I should ~~think~~ like to see Allen + Fannie but I guess I can wait awhile. I wish I could see home and friends. I like to ~~see~~ hear, a letter, or papers would do me more good than anything else. If I could see you I could tell you a good but I will not write much more this time, I want you should write often and give me all the particulars. Give my love to all the friends and tell them to wright please write soon and often.

This from your Eldest Son Geo W. Harwood

This is the site for the famous photograph when President Lincoln visited the Antietam battlefield in October. Because of the Union victory here, this is also where he announced the Emancipation Proclamation, which would take effect January 1, 1863. Gideon B. Jenks lived in North Brookfield. George's cousin, Ethan Alvin Allen, died September 26, 1862, at age eight of diphtheria. George's brother Allen was renamed Ethan Allen and was known as E.A. His brother Allen was fourteen and his sister Fannie was seven. Charles S. Perry, Massachusetts Fifteenth Regiment, died at Sharpsburg, Maryland on September 27, 1862 from wounds suffered at Antietam.

Pleasant Valley Friday Oct 17 [1862]

Dear Father & Mother,

As I have a little time this afternoon I will write you a few lines home to let you know that I am well and that I that I have not forgotten my friends. I received a letter from Anna yesterday and I am going to answer it and send it with this. I was very glad to hear from her and to hear that you were all well since I wrote you last I have been out on a Wild Goose Chase. Last Saturday afternoon about five o'clock which is our usual hour for Dress Parade we were called to gather as we supposed for drill, but we had orders to fall in immediately with Over-coats Haversacks + Canteens and to march we knew not whare we were hurried down to the Depot at Weaverton [Weverton] about 1 mile from hear and packed into some freight cars and sent to Frederick City. perhaps Father can imagine some thing how we looked as he has seen Cattle, Hogs + Horses packed in I suppose. at Fredcrick we got off the cars and marched up on to one of the Principle streets and then told to rest, so we laid down on the brick side walk or in the ditch until morning, and were kept near the City all day Sunday and at night we were repacked into the Cars and sent back as far as Point of Rocks thare we unloaded and took [went?] a little way from the Depot and thare were kept until morning it rained hard most of the time and was very dark I sat on a stone and leaned up against the fence and slept until midnight and then I was so cold and wet that I went with others into the barnyard in hog pen for thare were both Cows and Hogs thare and got under some cornstalk which we found in a field near by and staid until morning. We were wet through. after breakfast which we ate thare we went into a pasture nearby and staid until Wednesday when we marched back to Pleasant Valley a distance of about 11 miles. we had no blankets no tents and not much to eat and I tell you that we were pretty cold but we stood it first-rate. I did not take any cold. Lewis went with us and stood it first-rate he is pretty well now a good deal better than he has been. We went out in order to meet the Rebels at Frederick but did not. we were kept at Point of Rock's to keep them from crossing at that point. hear we could not sleep nights for it rained some and was damp and cold and we were not allowed to have a fire until daylight. we were very glad to get back again. Yesterday I stood on Guard and it rained very hard last night if you would know how it seems to go on guard, get up some night at midnight when it rains hard and go out and march up to the foot of the hill and back two hours and then lay down by side of the wall until your turn comes again. it is no fun now for me. Father do you traid much now? who did you sell that old cow to that Addison had, are you going to keep that colt until I come home. did you go to Barra [Barre?] cattle show I see that NC Frig's cattle of N. Braintree took premium and an Vaughns horse of E. Brookfield I should like to have been thare. I wish that I wish that you would write often <u>very</u> often and tell me all the particulars for they are interesting to me, a letter from home does me more good than a day's Ration. if you have a chance I should like to have some undershirts sent out I may send for some books by and by. I wish you would send out some postage stamps as we cannot get them at all times. Tell Allen to write to me I think of him and Fannie often. is Mother any worse I want to hear from home often, give my love to all the friends and tell them to write me.

> This from your true Son
> George W Harwood

Friday night

> Pleasant Valley Oct 17th [1862]

Dear Sister Anna,

I have just written a letter to Father + Mother and I will answer yours in this soon [one?]. I received one from you and yesterday and two papers and was very glad to hear. you say that you miss me at your Music I wish that I could stop in and sing a few lines with you too but I cannot now and I hope to sometime but if not on Earth may we sing sweeter songs in Heaven. you say that you think of me when you eat and that you wish you could send me something to eat I should be happy to receive something for I should like a change from what we receive. our hard bread is some of it new and good but most of it is mouldy and full of maggots 1/2 inch long some of them. Doc Tyler [illegible] the missing ones Uncle Tans's meat pies We boys buy flour sometimes and Lyman makes puddings of them. Lewis had a letter from home and Andrew yesterday. Andrew is no better I am going to visit to him soon Lewis is a good deal better so that he does duty now.   Saturday morning.

I did not have time to finish my letter last night and so I will finish this morning. We had a heavy frost last night the first that we had it is very pleasant this morning I wrote in my letter to Father about our trip to Frederick it was a sweet time. Anna you asked if we had as many prayer meetings as we used to I answer that we do not we have but very few and I am sorry to say that we have not got a Minister that I am <u>very</u> much interested in. he has had a few meetings but not many, and when he does preach it only a Lecture on Morals for he has no real Jesus Christ about him that I have heard. I wish that we had a better one but for all that I enjoy myself first-rate. my Testament is as good as ever and far better in times of trouble. I do think that when I get home that I shall enjoy religious privelage's [privileges] better than I used to. Saturday night I expected to go into a battle just as much as I expect to eat my dinner and so did the Capt but I felt ready. The Capt says that he thinks that he has no cowards in his company. I was sorry to hear that Hubbard is so sick but hope that he is better, before now. do the boys like Camp life. I suppose that Edwin [Doane] + John Lampson [Lamson] are having a good time. I wish that they would write to me. I am going to write to them. Anna I feel as though it would not be long before I shall again meet with my friends at home. ~~This was~~ for so in my opinion is not going to last forever, but we cannot tell but we must hope on, trusting that it will be all for the best. I hope that you will go home and live with Fathers folks for I think that mother will not be so lonesome Then tell her not to worry about me for I shall be as safe as any one. Sometimes I think that the nine month men will not be called out at all. I wish that there was no need of it. I understand that we are not going to drill any today but that we have this day to wash our clothes but I washed mine yesterday and so I shall have a day of rest I hope. Anna I often think of the evenings that we spent at your house and Mr Wood's do they say any thing about it. I felt pretty bad that night at your house I was sick for a while but I got over it before I went home. What a surprise we had that night did we not what do folks say about Lyman's getting married so suddenly. he hears from his bride often. if thare is a chance I want Father to send me some undershirts a pare [pair] of them. I may send home for a pair of boots and some other things would they not come by express safely ask father. Lewis sends his respects to you. I want to hear often and all the particulars I will close for I have written a long letter.

Yours respectfully

George W Harwood

Anna's husband Freeman and his brother Hubbard were serving in the Massa-chusetts Forty-second (nine month) Regiment. Edwin Doane, their younger brother, and John Lamson were still at home. Cousin Andrew F. Jackson, Massa-chusetts Thirty-fourth Regiment, was wounded and spent time in a hospital in Alexandria, Virginia. Lyman Gilbert lived with the Wood family after his father died when he was young. Doc Tyler was Dr. Warren Tyler from North Brookfield and was serving with the Massachusetts Thirty-sixth Regiment.

Pleasant Valley Thursday Oct 23rd [1862]

Dear Friends

I again take my pencil to write a few lines home to you. I received a letter from you yesterday and was glad to hear that you were all well and that Anna is going to move home. I am well and tough. I go on Guard about once in a week and it came my turn yesterday and my post happened to be over a prisoner. you will remember that I wrote to you some time ago about three fellows who stole some pistols and were handcuffed together. after their handcuffs were taken off they were set to picking stones and this is one of those fellows. he says that he is ashamed and would not have his mother know it for nothing. he insulted one of the Sargeants. another one of those fellows has stolen some money and has had his head shaved and was drummed through the Camp every little while for several days. Some laugh to see them punished but I cannot I pity them. You would laugh if you could see us in Camp. some are washing their clothes and some mending stockings + others are sewing on buttons and others are writing or cooking or all at the same time. we are full of work. We get up at 6 in the morning to roll-call and Guard-mountain at 1/2 past 7 and at 1/2 nine to 11 morning-drill at 12 dinner. 1/2 past 1 to 1/2 2 after noon drill from 3 to 1/2 past 4 battallion-drill. at 5 dress-parade 1/2 past 5 Supper at 8 roll-call and it keeps us pretty busy. thare is talk that we are going to stay hear this winter and that we are going to have some large tents. we are having pretty cold weather hear now and you ought to hear the wind howl through these window curtain tents just big enough for four to get into with both ends open. You asked how I get along with my washings I get along first-rate my stockings are all whole thare are no holes in them yet, but my handkerchiefs are getting thin I wish you would put into your next

letter a fine comb very fine so as to be sure and get the lice if they get those. I have seen none yet, Haskell + Lyman are writing home now and ordering some boots made right off so that we can send for them when we get around. and I want that you should get me some, either heavy calf or pig I think that cowhide would be to stiff when they get wet I want double sole and tap on the out side with heel and toe plates. on the heel horseshoe fashion. sise about 10 I dont care much whether you buy them ready made or whether you get uncle William to make them but have him put in some false insoles 9 1/2 are big enough but I dont think that you can get 1/2 sises but if you can do so and when I get home I will make it right all around. I can get some hear for 6 dollars not platcd only taped. Addison and others from N. Brookfield are going to send and we will have a box together before long. I wish that you would get them right off and if I never send for them you can ware them your self Yesterday I received a paper from Mrs E. D. Batcheller and was glad to hear [illegible] know that she had not forgotten me. I have written to Andrew today. The Brookfield boys are all well I believe. I should think that that boy of Uncle Bartletts was crazy to go off so I presume that Aunt felt pretty bad. he is to be pitied is he not?   Friday afternoon 24th
I did not have time to finish last night and so I will now I think that I may go to Bolivae Heights [West Virginia] tomorrow to see the 15 Regt. but do not know we may have to march I hear a rumor about camp today. it was cold last and I did not sleep very warm the ground was ~~whight~~ white this morning with frost. I hope that you will write soon and often I got a paper from you last night. I will write again before long. I don't know as you can read these letters I have to write sitting on the ground and papers as portfolio on my knees. Give my love to all the friends, so good bye.
          Yours Truly George W Harwood
hear [here] is a shilling peace that I got for change which I will send to Allen I have got one like it at home in my trunk. I will send something to Fannie sometime.

George was very specific in requesting boots because he had worked for the boot and shoe manufacturing company, E.A. Batcheller, in North Brookfield, before enlisting. Uncle Elias and Aunt Caroline Bartlett were relatives on the Allen side of the family (George's mother).

Lovettsville [Virginia] Tuesday Oct 28 [1862]

Dear Friends:

     I now take my pen to write a few lines to let you know whare I am. Last Saturday morning Lyman + I got a pass and went up to Bolivae Heights [West Virginia] to see the boys in the 15 Regt. we went up to Harpers Ferry and crossed on a pontoon bridge we looked around a while

Pontoon Bridge across the Rappahannock River (Courtesy Library of Congress)

in the villedge and then went on the boys are about 1 1/2 [miles] from Harpers Ferry they are well what few thare is left. when we got back to camp, we heard that [we] were to march in the morning and in the night it rained quite hard at four o'-clock Sunday morn we were called up and packed our things all except our Tents and be ready to start at daylight. we drew our rations and filled our haversack's ~~we~~ it had stopped raining by this time and we marched down a few miles as far as Berlin [now Brunswick, Maryland] by this time it rained hard hear we were a good many thousand of us beside Cavelry and Artillery hear we crossed on a pontoon bridge and marched up a mile or two and were turned into a field whare the mud was as high as our Ancles [ankles] and told to pich [pitch] our Tents, but not to get any rails which were all around the field but our Capt toled [told] us to go into another pasture and to take all the rails we wanted so we did by this time it was dark and we were not through for it had rained most all day hard the mud was as high as our ancles in the road and some of the time higher we crossed several brooks our feet were wet and it was cold we got a little straw to sleep on and so spent the night such a Sabbath I never spent be-fore marching all day in the rain with the wind in the N East and it was dreadful muddy all the way I don't think that we were in very good spirits that night we went to bed wet through and in the morning or about 9 o'-clock it stopped raining and we dried our things and felt a good deal better but the wind was high all day. This morning thare was a heavy frost the ground was white we expect to march on before long and perhaps before this letter gets home we shall [?] have been in a battle. you ought to see the Cannons and the many troops which are encamped about hear and the road is filled all the time day and night bound for Winchester [Virginia]. I took some cold and I guess we all did but I feell better than I expected. When I get home I can tell you things that I cannot write some of the boys wish themselves in Prison and some at home but I wish that this War would come to an end. I believe that thare is a chance now to enlist in the regular service for 3 or 5 years but I guess that I shall not bind myself any longer than this war. what do you think about this War do you think that it will come to an end pretty soon. the land hear in Virginia is pretty good and pleasant I think that I should like to live hear in times of peace. how are all the folks at home I should like to see you has Freeman gone from Worcester yet. I hear that the 34th have got their uniforms. I heard by way of Jane Wood that Josephine Lombard is married to Mr Leach. have any of the rest of the girls or old maids got married since I left. Daniel Knight says that [Dewing?] has got [illegible] how is he. I suppose that Anna has got home by this time how does Father get along with this fall work does he traid much now. have you got my letter dated 24 [letter began October 23] in which I sent an old fashioned Shilling to Allen I thought he might be pleased with it you know I have one. I have written this in a hurry and very poorly perhaps Anna can pick it out. I just wish that you would write often and give my love to all the friends Lewis is well and says what do you think our Father's would say to this I will write again when I get a better chance so good bye for this time.

Yours Affectionately George W Harwood

Lovettsville was a border town which sent an equal number of soldiers to the Confederate army and the Union army. Anna's husband Freeman left Worcester in October with the Massachusetts Forty-second (nine month) Regiment. Josephine M. Lombard married Edwin Leach in North Brookfield on October 1, 1862.

Waterford [Virginia] Saturday Nov 1st 1862

Dear Sister Anna

I have just received a letter from you and Allen and was very glad to hear from you. I am glad that Allen can write so well I could read it nicely. I should be glad to have seen Mrs + Sarah Underwood. I am rather sorry to hear that the boys [Freeman and Hubbard] have got to go to New-burn [North Carolina] but it may be all right. I was <u>very</u> glad to receive those pictures of yours they look familiar but I do not think that yours looks exactly natural. I am sorry to see you look so poor and sickly. You say that you worry about me. I wish that you would not for that will do no good I shall take the best care of myself that I can. I have not been to the doctor since I left Worcester neither has Lyman I guess that the rest of the boys have that came from N. Brookfield unles [except for] it is Addison I guess he has not. my health is very good I am troubled at times with rheumatism but not bad. I have received two letters from Freeman and answered them both some time ago. I sent a letter to you + to the ~~parents~~ Family at home last ~~night~~ Wednesday I think from Lovettsville we started that afternoon about 2 o'clock and marched until about 7 o'[clock] in the eve. we then stopped at Waterford whare we are now encamped but I do not know how long we shall stay for we hear the Cannon firing loudly now on a few miles ahead. yesterday I went on guard and had a very good [illegible] time it was very pleasant and in the air the moon shone brightly, and then I thought of home and the many pleasant evenings I had spent at home seeing others. Tuesday we had a General Inspection as they call it we were inspected by Col Welch and our Surgeons. for Supper we had a Chicken which Lyman + Haskell brought in Lyman says that he Confisticated [confiscated] it. the boys hear help themselves to hens + ducks but I have taken none. Last night as I lay in my tent and heard some of the boys singing old Methodist tunes that we used to sing together my mind wandered back to the many pleasant times we have had singing them together at home and I could but wish that I will again sing them as in days gone by perhaps never to return again on earth. I am very well contented now and we live a little better just now. Thare is a chance for us now to enlist with the regular army and Lyman says that he will go if I will but I cant see the point in that light. I do not think that this war will last many months longer for various reasons do you. I was glad to receive those postage stamps I think that we can get none except as they are sent from home. we signed the parole [payroll] a few days ago and thare is a prospect of our getting some pay pretty soon. I have not got short yet I have got over $5 dollars now some of the yes[?] many who bought more than I did have spent the last cent and are trying to get trusted [credit] Lyman has been down to 15cts but he has a little more now by selling his watch. how is mother's lameness now I often think of her, I did my washing yesterday and they look very well for cold water. Give my love to all the friends I will close for this time but will write again soon,

Yours truly George W Harwood

I guess Anna will have to read this for you as I have written fine and hasty.
Saturday afternoon brother Allen I have just written to Anna and I will
write a few lines to you I was glad to get a letter from you and you wrote
just the news that I like, about cattle I should like to go with father and get
some as I used to. I should think that apples were good for nothing at
home by your talk they are 3 or 4 cents a peace hear. I hope that Father
will keep them all until I come home. yearlings are not very high are they,
the cattle out hear are mostly no horns and the hogs are black like the people. They do their work with horses mostly. I like this country pretty well
but I do not like the stile for the hogs go into the roads in the villages. do
you think that you would like to be a Soldier I have been to Harpers Ferry
whare John Brown was hung and I thought of the Song Glory, Glory, Hal-
lelujah. I will write more sometime when I have a chance be a good boy
and I hope that I shall come home before long. I expect to go into a fight
before many days but I am not afraid. write again,

Good Bye George W. Harwood

write soon and often for nothing gives me so much pleasure as getting letters from home tell Father to write about some of his traids.

Saturday Noon
[Waterloo] Virginia Nov 8th 1862

Dear Friends,

     I now take this opportunity to write a few lines to let you know
whare we are I can hardly tell you but we are within a few miles of War-
rantin Junchin [Warrenton Junction, Virginia] We are marching hear for
them to build a bridge which the Rebels burned a few days ago. We have
had to march nearly every day for more than a week some days 4 miles
and some 20 I have got pretty foot sore and stiff. I have not felt very well
for a week past but have not left the ranks nor been to the Doctor I think I
have a slight touch of the Ganders. the Rebels are only a few miles ahead
of us they say and we have chased them for a week past. I presume that
the papers can tell more about it than I can. it is pretty hard to march so
much but if we are after the Rebels it is all right. Yesterday morning it
commenced snowing and snowed a little all day so that the ground was
white. at two o'clock yesterday afternoon we marched to hear about 4

miles in the snow it was some slippery and cold and wet piching [pitching] our tents. night before last our company went on picket and the boys hacked [?] alot of honey[,] turkey and ducks from the farm houses. Lyman [shot?] a hog. we have plenty of honey hear now as the farmers keep a lot of bees. I have no news to write in particular but if I could see you I could tell you a good deal I have seen more since I enlisted than I ever did before and if I get home I can tell some of it. I had a letter from Andrew a few days ago he is about the same he wrote me a good letter and I will write a little of it to you in his words that he used to me just before he left home I [illegible] to him the necessity of being prepared for death at any time, and in my letter to him I spoke of it again to see to it that his peace was made with God before it was to late. he writes as follows,

George I have a few words to say to you on another Subject <u>Religion</u> I mean I have thought a great deal on that subject for the past year I have prayed earnestly to God to have mercy on me and I think that he has answered them. I keep a Testament in my pocket all the time and read in it every day. I have read it through once already the Testament and Psalms and my Daily Prayer is that we may be spared to meet our Friends again at home. Pray for me Dear Cousin that I may be strengthened and not go astray in to by and forbidden paths.

I have copied his words I am glad to hear that he is seeking that better path which leads to life eternal. I want you all to write to me soon and tell me all the news. tell Allen to write to me all about the cattle and how many walnuts and chestnuts he has picked I shall be glad when this war is ended and hope that I may be spared to meet you all again at home. I look at those pictures of Free[Freeman], An[Anna], + Georgie often and am glad that you sent them to me. I have got some coins from the Rebels which the boys got out of a school-house in Berryville whare we stayed over night a regular secesh town. I am going to send them to to Allen + Fannie. I do not know whare I shall be when this letter gets to you for I expect to go on if the Rebels do not stop. I suppose that we are near the old Bull Run fighting ground. it is pretty cold hear now and it snows a little now is it very cold at home whare is Freeman has he left Boston yet. how are all the friends please write me all about them a good long letter soon and often it will do me more good than you can imagine I will close for this time, Give my love to all and particularly to Uncle Jonas Folks.

Yours Truly George W Harwood

my fingers are cold so that I can hardly write

Warrenton Junction was at the intersection of the Orange and Alexandria Rail-road and the Warrenton Branch. Today it is in the town of Calverton, Virginia. A case of the ganders could be feeling stupid or foolish as in wandering like a goose. Merriam-Webster.com Thesaurus. Uncle Jonas and Aunt Lucretia (Winslow) Harwood were beloved older family members who were mentioned often in the letters.

[undated fragment, possibly around November 8, 1862]
I have learned and seen many things that I should not if I had not come and if I get back safe and sound I shall be very glad that I came, and shall know how to value the comforts of life which I once enjoyed much better than ever before. I have seen something of the world and am desirous of seeing more, and should I ever get home I think should want to see the Western + perhaps Northern + Eastern part of the World. I have seen no place South thus far that is in Va. or Md. that I should like well enough to stay long. some of the soil is pretty good but the biggest part is rather poor, and the inhabitance[inhabitants] are a shiftless and ignorant class of people to lazy to work, getting their living by the labor of their slaves. The race of people that inhabit this part of the country are mostly of a dark complection and some of them have features similar to human beings and in some respects resemble them while others have features more like the species of animals called the Ape. that is they look very much like the pictures I used to see in the old spelling book called the Ape. They furnish us with pies and cakes at a reasonable rate and also apples. they wash our clothes for 5 cts an article and do it first rate too. but I dont think these poor creatures ought to be laughed at for they certainly cannot help their color and some of them are as bright (and quick witted) as any white men. I have written quite a number of letters lately and my papers and envelopes are getting rather short. I dont know what it would cost to send them from home. Haskell had a bunch of envelopes come for 3 cts. at paper postage and if it costs much more than that I should rather bye some hear. you can send some if it does not cost to much, and you think best. I presume that it would get dustied and jambed coming so far.

George W.

Anna what did you mean when you wrote the sentance "I think that Mr.

Wood ought to have taken him home and that I understand that he wants to hire a man."

From mid-November until December 10, the Union Army was waiting for pontoon bridges coming up the Potomac River. The long delay in getting the pontoons for the bridges gave General Lee the advantage when the battle of Fredericksburg finally took place.

Near Waterloo [Virginia] Thursday Nov 13th [1862]

Dear Friends at home,

I again take my pencil to write a few lines to you I sent one from hear last Saturday we came hear last Friday we have expected to move every day but do not know when we shall. I suppose that we are waiting for Supplies as we have had but little since we came it takes 12 or 14 crackers for one days rations and last Saturday night we drew 7 and have had none since we have had a little meat, and coffee we live on parched corn and salt which make a pretty hard fodder. I hope that we shall get something before long. Last Sunday Especial prayers was offered for Success in our cause by our Chaplain by order of Gen Wilcox I am glad that our Genl do not forget their God in their attempt to put down this rebellion. I understand that Gen McClellan has resigned and that Gen Burnside has taken his place. I dont know what to think of that. Our Col flatters the boys that this war will not last any longer than until Spring, but I have my doubts about that, dont you? I see by the papers that the President says that it must be closed then. This regiment like all others is fast dwindling away some have died one this morning many are sick and left back in the hospitals and we look like an old regt. we have not been in any fight yet but have tried hard enough I should think. Last Monday we had orders to go and reenforce Gen Pleasanton but after we had got out about 1/2 mile we were sent back. our services were not needed. I see by the papers that Thanksgiving in Mass is just 2 weeks from today. I guess that I shant come home to eat Thanksgiving supper with you this year. I will wait until next and then perhaps. I suppose that Freeman is on the way to Newburn N. C. I hope that he will not be as seasick as I was. I almost wish that he was with us. thare has been some talk of our going down to Newburn this winter and I hope that if we do I shall see the boys with whom I have spent so many pleasant hours. I presume that Mr Parkmans people feel bad to have their boys in the army. I think that the parties this winter will be few if any as the boys are all gone. I often take a look at those pictures which you sent out Anna, and almost wish I had the rest of the Family. Lewis showed me Anna Jackson which he had sent to him it looked so familiar, that I almost wanted to go home and speak to her. Whare is Edwin [Doane] now I do not hear much from him. I suppose that Judson [Adams] has not enlisted yet. Has he ever paid Father for those steers which he sold him last Spring. I suppose that Father traids as much as ever I should like to be thare and go with him some times. I shall forget the prices of cattle if I stay on hear much longer. Anna I wish that you would tell Edwin to write to me. have they done any thing towards building a new Town Hall. I don't know when I shall send for those boots and shirts for I don't know whare to have them sent. I was very glad to get that fine comb it is a nice one. thare are many things which we have to go without which would be very handy. I hope that the time will soon come when I can return home and enjoy the privilages of a [illegible] home. you said in your last letter what a blessed thing hope is I think so if it were not for this I dont know what we should do I suppose that Freeman felt bad to leave home so did I but I had fewer ties to bind me to my home than he did. What has father done with Mr Sargent place does that stand empty now and are your things thare. whare is Freemans cow does my watch run or dont you wind it I wish it was hear with me I feel lonesome without one. I bought one and sold it again and doubled my money. I bought it for 50 cts and sold it for 100 it was an old one but good for the kind. I have nothing in particular to write more. I have written to our Andrew again. I want you all to write often give my love to all the friends. tell them I am well and tough tell Allen I should like to have him write to me and I will answer it. Tell Fannie that I am coming before long if nothing happens and to be a good girl.

> Yours truly
> George Harwood

Mr. Parkman's boys were Charles and Henry Lyman Parkman, Massachusetts Forty-second (nine month) Regiment. Cousin Anna B. Jackson is Andrew's sister. Edwin Doane was the brother of Freeman and Hubbard. The North Brookfield Town House (Town Hall) had burned in a fire in 1862.

Sabbath Afternoon

Camp Fisher Nov 23rd 1862 [Falmouth, Virginia]

Dear Friends, Father, Mother, Sisters, Brother,

As I have a little time to my-self now I will commence another letter although I have written two since I received any from you the last that I received from home was a paper which I got Nov 13. We left our camp ground near Waterloo Friday the 14 and went to a little town but very noted, called White Sulphur Springs I presume you have heard about this place I think I had before I left home, and hear are some peaces of Veneering that I took from a billiard table I thought that it [would] be interesting to the children. I also got some peaces of a Marble Monument but I have thrown them a way. we left hear Sunday after and marched to Warrenton Junction we had a long hard march. The next day we started for Fredericksburg and we marched some ten miles a day and got hear Wednesday night some days they would [march] us the ten miles without much rest one day we were on the rode [road] only about 4 hours and we were nearly tired out. the rodes are as nere [nearly] full of troops and Artillery as far as you could see in each direction the last day it rained some and it was hard to cary our loads. we are now in a large field or plain. Thursday it rained hard all day and that night and hear we were in the mud a good many thousands of us. we have not crossed the Rappoehannock [Rappahannock] River but are just opposite the City of Fredericksburg which the Rebels hold, thare has been several shells thrown over that way and we are now daily and I might say hourly expecting a fight as I think that they will make a stand thare. I have stood these hard marches very well and I feel pretty well although very tired. the 15 + 21 and other Mass Regt are near hear. I have seen the boys of N Brookfield several times lately. Daniel looks just as he used to when he went away. we draw our Rations quite regularly now we have to do our own cooking which is mostly of Coffee and Meat. sometime pork and sometime beef. Next Thursday is as I hear Thanksgiving with you. I shall think of you on that day but I cannot meet with you as in years gone by but I hope that next year will find me in the Family Circle, but great changes must and probably will come to pass before that time. I understand that the boys os [of] the 42 Regt are still in Roadvill [Readville, Massachusetts] and am glad to think that they are so near their friends. is thare any news in Mass I long to hear from you. I have just come in from Devine Services but was not very much interested in the Sermon. It is quite cold hear now and we think that we want our box sent from home. I want my boots a pair of undershirts and a <u>Dairy</u> [Diary] of 1863 I should like a little bag or two to keep my coffee in about as large as a small pocket. thare are many other little things that I should like such as black pepper and Ginger and tea that you can put into the boots if you please, and any thing else that you please. you will take these things to Mr James Jenks and he will will see to or help see to boxing them up with others that will be left with him I suppose that the express will have to be paid at that end of the rout you will please pay <u>my</u> part and when I come home if we do I will make it all right. I want the Dairy to be about like the one of 1860 in my trunk about 6 inches long. thare are many things that we Soldiers would like that we can do without my clothes are in good shape except my handkerchiefs which are thin. The box will be directed the same as a letter I suppose and to some one perhaps W J Haskell that is with us. please write to me all the news and often and I will do the same this has been a pleasant day but the Sermon that I have heard does not come up to the ones that I used to [hear] and the one that I hope some of you have heard preached to day. We boys are all well and enjoying ourselves as well as we can under the circumstances. let us keep up good courage and hope for the best. tell Allen to write about the cattle and colt and the like. give my love to all, and tell them to write me a letter from a friend away does me a great deal of good. please send sometime when it is convenient the old Mass Spy that seems to give the news that I used to read and what interests me most. I will close for this time, but will write again soon. so good buy. write all about the neighbors and friends.

George W Harwood

Daniel W. Knight, Massachusetts Fifteenth Regiment, was from North Brookfield. The Massachusetts Spy *was a newspaper which began during the Revolutionary War and was published in Worcester. The Fauquier White Sulphur Springs had been a well-known resort located in Warrenton, Virginia. Mr. James Jenks was Frank L. Jenks' father.*

Camp Forbes Thursday Nov 27th

Dear Friends at home

    This a most splendid day and I have nothing in particular to do and so I will improve this time in writing to you. I am well and enjoying myself as well as I can under the circumstances. I received a letter from you last Tuesday night and was happy to get the long expected letter. I had looked for it in vain for several days. I wrote a letter to you a few days ago and ordered that box sent and in case that you have not got it I will mention the articles again I should like my boots, undershirts and a Dairy [Diary] of 1863 the box will be sent or directed to Doc Tyler as he thinks that it will come more readily Mr. James Jenks will see to boxing them up. I saw David Moulton yesterday he belongs in the 2nd [probably Eighty-second] N. Y. Regt. he has been sick in the hospital in Alexandria and says that he saw Andrew thare I hope that Mr Walker will do something for him if he can. Monday morning 60 men out of Co E were detailed to go down to Bell Plain a distance of about 7 miles and guard a train of baggage wagons, and we loaded them with hard-bread, pork and hay it was pretty muddy and the roads are very poor and several of the teams got stuck in the mud and we had to leave them thare. it took us from light in the morning until 10 o'clock at night. thare were I should think over 100 team's whare we loaded and I got sick of that business. Today we have moved our camp-ground into a better place whare thare is no mud. I presume that you have had a good supper and I have thought of you all the time. the boys have told all day what they should have if they were at home and what they are going to have when they get home but I can only tell what we or I have had in the morning for breakfast I cooked some pork and fried some hard crackers in fat, and coffee. for dinner we got some four cents worth or about a quart of meal and had a few thin cakes and a little pudding which if we were at home I should not think hardly fit for the hens but I called it good, a few beans and for Supper hardbread + Coffee. I have nothing in particular to write. I keep a hoping and so time passes quickly by it is noon before we know it and then night. the days seem short. thare has been a report in camp that Fort Darling is taken by the Union Soldiers but I hardly believe that for that is as I suppose the Key to Richmond. The weather out hear is rather cold and some rain and then the mud is over shoe deep I suppose that it is cold at home and perhaps some snow how is it? I feel happy today as my mind wanders back to the many happy Thanksgiving's that I have spent with you and the hope that I may ere another year comes I shall be in the family circle. this is the first Thanksgiving day that I ever spent away from home. I can picture in my mind just how you looked sitting around the table as I suppose that Allen

takes the corner whare I used to sit. I should like to have Allen and Father write I presume that it is hard for them to get about it as it used to be when I was thare. I should like to have them write about their traids. you spoke about your apples I wish that I could get one I have not seen an apple for a long time and then I had to pay 2 cts for one as large as a hens egg and poor at that. Thare are many things that I should like to have sent that I suppose would come in a box but I will wait until we get into winter quarters or somewhare else before I send for them. I need my boots, and shirts and Doctr Tyler thinks that they will come in his name. Do George Jackson and Anna go to school this winter I should think that you mint [might] have a good school I hope so anyway. We have not got paid off yet but thare is some talk of it I suppose that Freeman is in N.Y. or some whare else now. I hope that I shall come across him sometime. how did Mr Parkmans folk feel when the boys left. Has father sold or let the Sargent place Anna whare are your goods did you move them home, and whare is F's[Freeman's] cow did he sell her. thare are a good many questions that I should like to ask and let Allen answer them but I have no time now and I will close for this time. I hope that you will write often and all the news. please give my love to all the friends, I think of you all often and want to see you and have a good long talk. I should enjoy it, so
Good Bye   Yours Truly George W Harwood

A David S. Moulton, born in 1839 lived in North Brookfield in the 1850 census. He served with the New York 82nd Regiment. Fort Darling on Drewry's Bluff was a Confederate Fort on the James River outside Richmond, Virginia. The Union troops never succeeded in taking the fort. George and Anna Jackson were cousins ages eighteen and sixteen.

~ Chapter 3~

FREDERICKSBURG, VIRGINIA
December 5, 1862 - January 7, 1863

Dec 5th [1862]
Camp Forbes, opposite Fredericksburg Va

Dear Friends,

I received a letter from you a few days ago dated 23rd I was glad to hear from you, although nothing has happened of particular interest. I have been busy and have not written for a week I think yesterday. we still remain hear opposite Fredericksburg and Sabbath eve is just about the time I should have gone to the prayer meeting if I had been at home. Co. E + H were ordered out on Fatigue Duty and we went down to the River on a little this side and went to throwing up Earthworks for the Cannon's to opposite, and then was the time that I thought of the many pleasant Sabbath eves that I have spent at home. we shoveled by turns until nearly daylight then we went back to our camp the rebel pickets were just across the river and not more than 50 rods from us our pickets are one side and the rebels the other they can see each other, and talk together. why we are hear so long is a mistery to us. we are all pretty well that is the Brookfield boys. I have had a very hard cold and sore throat but I kept my neck done up with handkerchiefs and it is much better now. Thare are a good many sick ones in the Regt and every little while one will die. Several have got their discharge and others ought to have. I believe that nearly all that have died, have died of the Disentary caused as I suppose by laying on the ground and taking cold some mornings when we get up the ground is white with frost and we step pretty quick to keep warm. I suppose that you have all read the Presidents Message what do you think of that. I think that it would be cheaper for the Government and better for the people both North + South for us to bye their slaves and pay for them, when we can. the boys have got it into their heads that they are going home in a few months at the longest but I begin to think that we shall have to fight them to the bitter end, and if we do that 3 years will no more than do it. you would laugh if you could see us and at the same time pity us if you could look down upon us when we are getting our breakfast or Dinner, some of us with cups and some with plates a little coffee in one and a piece of meat in another and another with a stick run through his meat holding his over the fire and another with a handful of corn meal making a pudding. our cups look like old swill dippers, and we can hardly help laughing at ourselves but we keep up a continued hoping that we shall not have to live a soldier's life a great while. I should think by Addisons talk that he had got about sick of Soldiering he says that if he were at home he should stay thare unless he was compeled to come, but I have made up my mind that Uncle Sam has got me and that he will keep me as long as he wants me. I should be as glad as any one to go home and live among my friends and civilised society I do not think that the people out hear what few thare are, are any more than half civilised I have not seen a southern man for a long time except a few prisoners which we have taken. I got a letter from Freeman + Hubbard this morning and was glad to hear from them but should judge by their letters that they were almost sick of it as they look a head to only 7 months more. I can look ahead to only 32 or 33 months more with the greatest pleasure and shall be glad to get off at that. Freeman says that he has gained about 12 lbs I have not weighed me lately but think that I have gained some. Freeman says that they are not very much pleased with Lieut Duncan and have asked him to resign. it rains hard today and so I have a good time to read and wright I am going to answer Freeman today. I was glad to hear from Allen + Fannie I did not expect one from her, and I will answer them. I have nothing in particular to write but I want you to write to me as often as you can find time I presume you are busy. I should like to see you and hope to sometime. I think that something will be done before long in the Army but ware I do not know. I hope to again meet my friends on Earth but we can only say "Thy will God be done" let us hope for the best and that will be best for us. please give my love to all the friends and particularly to Aunt Lucretia, a letter from home is very cheering to a weary Soldier. I suppose that you have got my letters ordering that box. Lyman has just got a letter from home with some red peppers in it and that goes pretty well out hear and it does not cost any thing to send it.

Yours   George W Harwood

Tuesday Morning
Camp Forbes Tuesday Dec 16th [1862]

Dear Friends at home,

I again take my pencil to write you. I should have written nearly a week ago if I had had an opportunity. last Thursday morning the first thing that I heard was form into line immediately and so we took our blankets and fell in and were kept in line a little ways from camp and remained thare all day. heavy canonading commenced early in the morning and kept up all day and musketry at night. we went back into camp that night. the next morning we crossed the pontoon bridge Friday morning and they kept up a brisk canonading all day and we were kept under fire as they call it. we had no opportunity to fire ourselfes thare were a great many killed and wounded this day and one shell struck near me and killed and wounded several. we were kept hear in this City all night and you had ought to see these houses all full of holes and compleatly torn to peaces the streets were full of Furniture and such things the inhabitants had all left. nothing was left within houses but what was distroyed, chares, tables beds, books, crockery, fiddles and the like were all in the street broken in peaces. I have got a few feathers that I took out of a fan that I will send to Fannie, it may please her. such an amount of property I never saw distroyed before and hope that I never shall again until I get to Richmond. we were kept under fire as reserve all the time for five days we came back last night about midnight I do not know why, perhaps the Rebels were to much for us. such a lot of troops as we had it seems as though we could do almost any thing the 21 Reg and 15 lost a good many but none of our boys. David Moulton was killed a few days ago he belonged in a N.Y. Reg. such a rumbling as those shells made going over our heads it was enough to make our hair stand. some of the boys were considerably frightened, but before the five days were gone we got used to it. they are firing now with their cannons and I presume that we shall have to start again soon. I can give you no discreption of what I have seen within the past week and yet we have been fortunate enough to come out all right, and I think that we ought to be thankful. I presume that you know more about the result of this light battle than I do. I saw David Earle [Massachusetts Fifteenth Regiment] yesterday he is Sargent Major now. I have not seen Daniel Knight but he is well. I got a letter and papers from home this morning and was glad to hear that the box had started but I am afraid that I shall not get it at present. we have had some pretty cold weather out hear and a few inches of snow. it is mild now and very muddy. we are all pretty well except hard colds I have got a sore throat and some thing of a cough, but I guess that I shall get over it before long. last night it rained hard we got wet and had to sleep with wet feet which was not so comfortable. I begin to think that it is time to put a stop to this war. it is not pleasant Soldiering. you will please excuse this poor writing as my fingers are cold. if I ever get home I can tell you more about the past week experience and a soldiers life generally but I think that it will be sometime before this war is closed up. I will not attempt to write much more this time but will soon. I think of you all often and long for the time when I can meet you again. last Sunday we formed a line and expected to charge on a rebel battery which if we had I presume would cost many of our lives. David Earle has been in the hospital in Philadelphia and says that he had his discharge offered to him twice and I think that I should have taken it I wish that they would offer me mine I would bid Soldiering good bye but I will close I want you should write often and I will the same. remember me to all the friends

Yours Truly

George W Harwood

I do not believe you can read this letter my fingers are cold

At the Battle of Fredericksburg, the Confederates slaughtered the Union soldiers from behind the wall on the Sunken Road. At about five feet high, the wall provided good cover for the Confederate soldiers. The Confederate army was also on top of the hill above the battlefield on Marye's Heights. The Massachusetts Thirty-sixth Regiment was held in reserve on a far ridge at the rear of the fighting intending to pursue a retreating Confederate Army. The Union never broke through the Confederate line.

Log cabins with tent roofs used for winter quarters, White Oak Civil War Museum, Falmouth, Virginia (Photos by author)

Mrs [Misters] Cushing + Pelbit were here at Divine Services and offered prayers and short remarks which were very apropriate and seemed like old times.

Sabbath forenoon

Opposite Fredericksburg Dec 21 [1862]

Dear Friends,

I again take my pencil to write you a few lines to let you know that I am pretty well except for a hard cold. Nothing of much importance has happened since I wrote you last. we are having cold weather hear now. Friday morning our Regt were called upon to go on Picket we went down near the river and just back of battery and our Company and a few others were held as reserve so to support that battery in case of necessity and such a cold night I have not seen since last winter the wind was high. Haskell, Louis, Lyman + I bunked together we built a good fire and went to bed but could not sleep, and about midnight they all went of to the woods, about as far as from your house to the woods and built a number of good fires, and Louis + I set with our blankets on and put our sholders together and tried to sleep so but it was to cold for that even, and so about daylight we went down and staid thare until we were relieved and got back to camp a little before noon and found to our surprise Mr Cushing. he got hear Friday afternoon. we were very glad to see him he has gone over to the 15 Regt now but says that he is coming back we asked him a thousand and one questions and wanted to ask thousand's more. we gave him some little relicks that we took from Fredericksburg and White Sulphur Springs. he says that when he gets home he is going to have a large meeting and I hope that some of you will be able to go and hear him he says that we are as fat as hogs. he says that he had a prayer meeting in our hospital and that our sick appeared to be very glad of it, and he asked us if I thought that that they had many and I told him that I thought not unless they had got a Minister, for we were so unlucky that we had got none. Our Chaplain does not have a prayer meeting from one months end to another and only a few remarks on the Sabbath I should like to have Mr Cushing preach us a sermon before he goes back. he offered a prayer in our tent just before he left for the 15th. he said that the thought he should preach thare today. Now I will describe our tent it is built like a log-house with the ends locked. it is five logs high, the logs are about 6 inches through about 10 ft long 7 wide

2 1/2 high then we put our fly tents on for eaves. we can just stand up in the center. five of us live hear Haskell, Wheelock, Gilbert, and a fellow by the name of Wood he is about 23 years old, he enlisted in Munson but then belongs in [New?] York state. we have Family prayer hear before going to bed and sometimes prayer meetings. we enjoy ourselfes pretty well but long for the time when we can go home. Doc Tyler came in to see us this morning and said that we had got a good house. by the way we have got a fire place the whole bigness of one end and it looks a little like the old fireplace in the back room. it is made out of sods and mud this soil is good for plastering almost as good as clay. I am waiting very patiently for that box as my shoes are <u>very</u> poor and when we go out on picket as we did the other night I suffer I think that I never suffered so much in one night as I did that night last Friday and I shook good. when we go into battle or form a line or drill Louis stands nearer to me than Lyman. Haskell and I are together, Lyman near the rear of our company and I at the head, and Louis in the rear of the company ahead of us. Mr Cushing asked us a good many questions and when he gets home he can tell you more than I have ever written some of the boys say that they do not want to go so near the canons again as they did in their last fight. it appears by Mr Cushing report that the union loss was great, much larger than I expected and I am sorry to say that I think we did not accomplish any good but we must expect some defeats I think that our Regt were exceeding lucky in not going into a more active part of the fight. I do not see much prospect of this War's closing at present and at times I feel disheartened and blue but then we must put up with many things not pleasant but all these trials and troubles and sufferings are but short when compared with eternity and will work out for good in the end I hope. Gods way is not our ways nor our thoughts his thoughts. "A few more fears a few more tears and sorrow and sighing shall forever flee away". we know that first trials then blessings. let us be of good cheer and have faith to believe that we shall have grace given us from on high if we are his followers. I will not write much more now, and will answer Allens letter some other time I shall be glad to hear from home often. Mr Cushing gave us boys 1/2 lb of black tea a little soft bread an apple <u>each</u> and a bottle of rum and water which will do us good sometimes. I dont know as you can read this it is so fine but perhaps you can I will write again soon if I do not now. we have got to go out to Divine Services now in a few minutes and I wish that Mr Cushing might be

hear and he said that he would be if he could I will close, remember me to all. I remain yours truly.   George W Harwood
Mr Pelubit [Francis N Peloubet] of Oakham is with Mr [Christopher] Cushing.

"A few more fears a few more tears and sorrow and sighing shall forever flee away" could be from a hymn based on a passage from Isaiah 35:10 or 51:11. Mr. Christopher Cushing was the associate minister from the Congregational church in North Brookfield. Doc Tyler was the physician from North Brookfield who was serving with the Massachusetts Thirty-sixth Regiment. Myron R. Wood was from Monson and served in the Massachusetts Thirty-sixth, Company E. Mr. Francis Nathan Peloubet was a Congregational clergyman in the 1865 census for Oakham, Massachusetts.

Monday Morn [December 22, 1862]

Dear Friends

As I did not send my letter last night and have received one from you this morning I will just write a little more. Mr Cushing took supper with us last and spent the night. we had for supper fried pork and hard-tack. he broke his tooth eating hard-tack, and did not sleep much in the night because he was cold. we had a prayer meeting hear last night and a good one to. I guess that when Mr C - gets home he will have a good long story to tell and one which will interest you all. he has gone now to visit some of the hospitals and Haskell has got excused and is going with him this morning a little while. David [Edward?]Russell + David Earle of the 15th came over yesterday with Mr Cushing. I [illegible] that our Reg went on Picket last Friday and they have gone again today. you said that you hoped that our box had reached us before now but it has not and I do not know when it will. I am afraid not at present. you may think strange that I did not go on Picket today with the rest but I got excused today for the first time, on account of my poor shoes and a sore heel. my shoes are all gone and my great toes are out of both Shoes + stocking and every time I step my toes go on the frozen ground and Doc Tyler said I ought not to go on Picket. I have tried for several weeks to draw a pare of shoes from the Government and the Capt says that he will do the best he can for us. thare are a good many in the Reg in like and <u>worse</u> manner. I need the box very much and hope that it will come thare are but very few boots out hear and they are 10,12 dollars a pair. when we crossed the river I went with my feet wet all the time and I took cold and have a sore throat now you said in your letter that you supposed that Fredericksburg was in our possession and that it was a compleat licking on our part but you are mistaken it was a total failure. the worst defeat that we ever had and the greatest victory to the rebels that they have ever had, and Fredericksburg is today in the Rebs possession, and as to our loss we had not less than 15,000 killed and wounded and so we are so many precious lives weaker and nothing accomplished times look dark, darker every day, and I fear that this war will never end until the last drop of blood has been shed, unless it be by the direct hand of God Almighty. Little do you at the North know how this war is conducted and the little simpathy a sick or wounded soldier gets, we may write to you but we can not discribe it. those only know who are the sufferers or eyewitnesses. I am thankful that I have been blessed with such good health. I have seen cases in this company whare men have been sick and not able to take care of themselves and hardly able to get up and but little care was taken of them and one man was discharged when he could not get up alone and when he got to Washington he died and who cared. I have got in my tent with me today a sick young man who is hardly able to take care of himself and his brother has gone on Picket. I shall do the best I can for him to make him comfortable tonight. Many are the trials, the sorrows, the sufferings, the temptations, the privations, the discouragements of a Soldiers life. we are dishartened at times, and were it not for the precious promise of Gods word, sad would be our feelings, but kind friends these sad experiences which we are called upon to pass through are for our Spiritual good and "we shall reap if we faint not" in some future day. these trials are alike intended to humble the Soldier and the friends at home, let us be reconciled to the will of God whatever it be, let us be prepared to live or die and at last to receive the crown laid up for us at the right hand of our Saviour God, thare to join with the redeemed ones in singing the blest songs of Moses and the Lamb. I hope that I may be spared to meet you all again and then live before long. I am glad to hear from you often the oftener the better. I wish [cousin] Anna Jackson would write me I shall be glad to answer it, and [cousin] George [Jackson] and all of the friends I have. I hope that Andrew will get home soon, I should want to if I were in his place, I think that your dresses are going to be about the things and am glad that you have got them. I received a paper some time ago with some tea in it. I was glad to receive it. I got a paper from Mrs E D Batcheller a few days ago and am glad that she has not forgotten me. I have written a long fine letter and do not know as you can read it but Anna used to be good for picking[?] out poor writing. write to me often one and all and I will do the same unless battel [battle] or the march prevents it. something has been said about our going into winter quarters. Have you heard anything from Uncle Joseph [Harwood] of late. I should like to see him. I am as fat as a hog and feel pretty well generally. yours hastily

    George W. Harwood

Before they enlisted George W. Harwood and Lyman H. Gilbert lived with and worked for Mr. and Mrs. Ezra D. Batcheller making shoes. Uncle Joseph W. Harwood was in Illinois with his wife Cordelia C. Selfridge and children Amelia and Charles.

Christmas Morn
Camp Forbes Dec 25th [1862]

Dear Friends,

    I now take a little time this morning to write to you. I am well and hope that you are all the same. I received a letter from Cousin Anna [Jackson] this morning and have answered it and was glad to hear from her and should be glad to hear from many others of my young friends and acquaintances. you will notice that I do not direct or address each of you indivually [individually] in all of my letters but I hope that you will receive them the same, for when I say friends I mean the family circle since I last wrote you which was last Monday nothing of much importance has happened Tuesday we had a general inspection or rather review, and we had a muddy place to stand. the mud was ancle deep and we had to stand thare an hour or more and I found it pretty tedious with my old shoes. the water run write ~~into the~~ under my toes, but never mind I drew a splendid pare of army shoes yestoday. the express boxes or a load of them came hear day before yestoday but none for the Brookfield boys. the weather hear is mild now and I shall not suffer if it does not come just yet. thare is a report in camp hear that we are going to move soon but I do not know, some say to Washington to do Provost Duty I hope we shall. Mr Cushing left hear for Washington yestoday I was sorry to have him go but presume you will be glad to have him return. he does not know much about Soldiering yet and he said that he should tell as favorable story about us he could, and when I come I will tell the rest. since I commenced this letter Doc Tyler has been hear and says that he has received a letter from Mr Walker stating that our boxes were thare but could not be forwarded as that all boxes that arrived thare after the 11ᵗʰ must could not be forwarded at present or not until some other way was provided. I have not heard anything from Edwin [Doane probably] yet. have you heard anything from Freeman since you wrote me last. I should be glad to know whare they are. Mr Cushing seemed to think that war would not end at present or that the North would not back down but fight it to the bitter end if need be. When the boys go on picket they have a good time to talk with the sesech pickets. they asked our boys the other day if they would swap Gen Burnside for one of their Corporals. they asked if we would kill off our leaders if they would. our boys asked them how long they thought it would take the privates on both sides to settle the matter and end the war. they said about 1/2 hour. they would shake hands bid each other good bye and go home <u>and so would I</u>. I am quite fleshy but do not know how much I weigh. I wish I could send you my picture with my uniform on as you have not got it. ~~but~~ I can get it taken in Falmouth by paying a dollar and as we have not got paid of yet my dollars are not very pleanty [plenty]. I look at those which you sent to me often and they are certainly comfort to me. Anna, does'ent Mr Doane feel lost almost without Hubbard. I should think he would. David Earl [Earle] is hear now and says that they boys in the 15ᵗʰ are all well. [Francis?] Amasa Walker wrote to Doc Tyler that he intended to come out and see us. I hope that he will. David Earl [Earle] says that he was never discharged until since this fight at Fredericksburg and now things look dark to him he says, and so they do to me now but you know that it is always darkest just before daylight. I think that in one week from now we shall be neary [nearer] Washington than now. As Earl [Earle] says we retreat that way because we cannot go towards Richmond. I will close as thare is nothing more for me to write that I know of I hope you will write often and all the particulars. Remember me to all the friends if you please send a few more postage stamps and keep an account of what you send to me and sometime I will repay it, if I live I guess that we shall get paid of before long but dont know. I will close hoping for the best and <u>wishing you all a merry Christmas</u>. Good bye, truly yours

George W Harwood

Tuesday Morning
Camp Opposite Fredericksburg
Dec 30th [1862]

Dear Friends,

I again take my pencil to write a few lines. I am well and hope you are all the same. we are having very fine weather and the ground is not frozen. I think by the appearance of things that we are going to move soon but whare I do not know. yestoday all our sick were sent to Washington, and thare is no little stres among the troops concentrated hear. the pontoon bridges or rather boats and other articles to make bridges of is all loaded and ready for a start, and I understand that we are to have three days rations packed up ready for a start. I have not had a letter from home for some time. I think that I have written three since I have received any. I have no news of much account to write. Last Sunday we had a Grand Review by Gen Burns, and Burnside was a spectator almost every Sunday we have Inspection or some thing of that kind to interfeir [interfere] with Divine Services and so we had none last Sunday. we have prayer meeting every few evenings somewhare in the Reg. Haskell had a letter from Doc Porter a few days ago, and he said that he expected that Andrew was on his rode home. you know that Austin Porter is in the 34th. Some of the 15th are over hear every few days and we expect Daniel W. Knight + Amasa Kimble [Kimball] over today. You would laugh is [if] you could just see us when our rations are delt out. yestoday those we drew three onions for our tent of five persons one small one and two large ones so we cut the large ones in two and the pieces were not of a sise so we drew straws to see which should have the biggest pieces. I thought that looked big for five men drawing straws for an onion. I hope that if I ever get home I shall have enough to eat for once. I am quite sorry that the box did not reach us and I do not expect it now, at least not at present. Addison inquires of me every little while if Father says any thing about that calf he wants to know if it grows well. do you keep that colt yet I hope that you will keep it until I come home. make her grow as fast as you can. last Saturday I was quite unwell and got excused from duty. I had such a sore throat and ear ache that I felt poorly. what is the news about home. I should like to go with Father on some traid as I used to. what does Uncle David [Winslow] think about war now. Louis is a little unwell but not much the rest of the Brookfield boys are all right, only we want to get home as soon as we can. do you hear any thing from Freeman lately I see in some papers that they had gone down to N Orleans is that so. I am feeling in good spirits and am contented as well as when I was at home but I suppose it is because my health has been good. if I should be sick then I should want to get home, I know. I dont see how this war is going to be settled except by fighting and that will take a long time. do they have prayer meeting in the school-house now. I should like to call in some evening. whare does Judson Adams live now I should think Edwin [Doane] would be lonesome as I can think of but few boys of his age about thare. when I get home I want to go out west and then I guess I shall be contented to stay at home or somewhare in Mass. I dont think I should like to live hear very well. has Mr Wood got so that he can drive his colt yet. I should like to see him try it. And this year has almost gone. time flies rapidly does it not, but I will close. Wishing you all a Happy New Year and hoping ere another year is past and gone that I may be with you.

Yours Affect Geo. W. Harwood

Charles Austin Porter from North Brookfield served with the Massachusetts Thirty-fourth. George had two uncles named David, David Winslow and David Allen.

Jan 2nd [1863]
Camp Opposite Fredericksburg Va

Dear Friends,

This is a most splendid morning and I will improve a few moments in writing home. The long expected box has arrived. We came off Picket yestoday forenoon and all heard that the boxes were coming. Mr Walker + Frank were hear a few days ago but I did not see them I was on picket as soldier supporting the first Con [Connecticut] battery. Thare I saw Bob Clark + Joe Williams. late last evening a little before midnight we were aroused up by the arrival of our express boxes. they got here just in season to be to us a New Year's present. We were very glad to get them Louis + I took ours out last night they came in pretty good shape, but Louis had a bottle of Whistleberry jelly I should think by the looks. the bottle broke and run all over his vest and one of my shirts got a little stained. the pies were all mouldy unfit for eating. we ate a part of the inside of the meat pies and threw the rest away his bread was spoiled our apples were all right and my cakes were all right. my boots fit good, but I wish the legs were a little longer. Lyman's boot legs come up above his knees. his are as much too long as mine are too short. he had to cut out the back side so that he could set down. I think Louis has got some good ones. we were very glad to get the other small articles they seemed like home. what did my boots cost I should like to know. I like my shirts to I want you should keep track of what money you spend for me, so that I may repay it some-time. I was glad to get that paper + envelops for they cost high hear and poor at that one cent each. I paid a cent for this sheat of paper. Addison has got his box to. Henry Bowin [Bowen] has cut or split his middle finger so that he has to keep still he traids watches very often, and makes money he sent home by Adams Express 40 dollars at one time. he has traides with Addison 3 or 4 times I think that Addison is a good custermer [customer] for Bowin [Bowen]. this is the first letter that I have written home since I have received one from you. Do you write? or not I understand by Louis + Lymans letters that Father + Uncle William have been out to see An-drew. I am sorry that could not get him. Louis said that he had changed! in what respect has he changed. Mary wrote to [her husband] Lyman that it was reported thare that I was dead, but I guess that they are mistaken as I should have heard of it before. Haskell is Sargent now. I understand that the 42nd has arrived in New Orleans they are a good ways off are they not. I expect that we shall move from hear before long but whare I do not know some think across the river others have different opinions we can see the Rebs digging earth works all through the streets and banks of the river but our Genl's think that they are evacuating the place, and doing this for a show, but time will tell. I will not write much more this time but hope to get one from you soon. I am thankful to you for those articles in the box. Remember me to the friends and write often, for I am anxious on the arrival of the mail to hear Harwoods name called.

Yours Truly George W. Harwood

Robert H. Clark, First Regiment Connecticut Volunteers, is listed in the Histori-cal Record of Soldiers and Sailors, North Brookfield, 1886. NPS.gov, Soldiers and Sailors database lists both Robert H. Clark and Joseph Williams in the First Regiment Connecticut Heavy Artillery. George's father, also named George and his Uncle William C. Jackson had gone to visit his cousin Andrew who was in the hospital in Alexandria.

Opposite Fredericksburg Jan 7th [1863]

Dear Friends

  As I have a few moments leasure now I will write to you. I received a letter + paper from Mother last Friday Jan 2nd and one from Anna Jan 4th I was very glad to get them for it had been sometime since I had had any. I receive a paper from Mrs E D Batcheller every little while and Lyman + I got a letter from her night before last. she spoke about Mr Cushing lecture and though [thought] it was very interesting were any of you thare? I wrote a letter home I think last Friday morning I received the box New Years night, and I was very glad indeed to receive it. My boots fit well but dear me they do ware my stockings so fast. I do not like this pen and so I will take my old pencil again I like my boots pretty well except the legs and they are rather short. by the way who cut them out and bottomed them and what did they cost. My little diary is just the thing I should like to send my old one home. the dried apple came in play first-rate and I wish that I had four times as much more. the cake did not last long as you may well suppose. those bags are just the things for me. I told you in my other letter that one of my shirts got stained with Louis jelly but it washed out in good shape. I am well pleased with them also. Anna wrote me that you were intending to have Demming Smith + G [George?] Stoddard. have you had them yet. did Stoddard stay until morning. Anna you spoke of Lydias having the tooth-ache. it makes me think of a tooth which I had drawn a few weeks ago after it had ached long enough I walked down to Doc Tyler. it was tight but decayed and came hard. it was all I could do to keep from holloring but I thought that if I could not have a tooth drawn I shurly could not undergo what many wounded Soldiers have to. I am sorry that Andrew could not have his discharge how do his Father + Mother now. I should like to hear from Freeman + the boys first rate. I understand by the way of Haskell that Mr Hebart does not like first rate as he says he should like to eat out of some swill barrel in N.B. I have thought so at times but we live better just now. we have to drill two hours and dress parade which takes one half hour more. yestoday we had a Grand Review by Genl Burnside himself it rained a little but it was a pleasant time. when we gave him 3 times 3 cheers he took of his hat and showed his bald-head, which looked like a full-moon. his head is more bald than Fathers, and I suppose you know how his whiskers look in his pictures. they look like him. Henry Hairs death was very sudden was it not. does Judson live thare now. Oh Judson had a large party I wish I could have looked down on them I think George Stoddard done [?] his past dont you Isnt Jane getting girlish in her old age it is about time for her to commence. I dont know as I have anything of much importance to write more, but this cooking [every day?] and laying on [illegible] than dirt isnt what it is cracked up to be. We are having very fine weather now a days it rained a little yesterday and is cooler today. I am going to write to Mrs E D Batcheller before long as she says that she considers Lyman + I as members of their family still. I wish I could see you and then I could tell you much more than I can write, and I hope that the happy day will come when I can meat [meet] with the loved friends at home, but if in the Providence of <u>God</u> we are <u>not</u> permitted, let us so live that we may all meat around the great white thrown [throne] in heaven whare parting is no more, thare to enjoy each others presance <u>forever</u>. Remember me to all the friends and write often. yours affectionatly

George Washington Harwood

please put in a few postage stamps as this is my last one, and they are hard to be obtained hear, and I will see that these expenses and favors are in time <u>if I live</u> compensated.

~ Chapter 4 ~

WINTER OF DISCONTENT, FALMOUTH, VIRGINIA
January 13 – March 21, 1863

Jan 13 [1863]
Camp opposite Fredericksburg Va

Dear Friends,

I have just come of Picket and will now try to answer this letter
which I received from you Last Sunday eve, yestoday morning we went
on picket on the Banks of the Rappahannock and came of this noon. yestoday was a fine day and last night was not very cool and so we got along
very well. I stood three hours last night from 1/2 past 9 to 1/2 past 12 and
then is the time when one will think of his home and friends behind. the
river whare we stood is about 30 ft wide and the Rebel Pickets are just
across our boys went across this morning in a boat and exchanged papers
with them. I was very glad to get your kind letter as I always am, and
nothing does me so much good as a letter from home. I saw Louis today
he says that they got a letter from home and that Andrew is not better + I
do hope that he may get his discharge and that too before long. he said that
he received a night-cap but I have not seen it. they are very good things I
think. this is the second letter that I have written with ink for a long time. I
have borrowed Lymans Gold pen and like it pretty well. Lyman + I went
over to the 15th a few days ago and on our way back we called on Mr F. A.
Walker at Genl [Darius N.] Couch's headquarters and had a very pleasant
call he appeared glad to see us and said that he should be glad to do any
thing for us that he could at any time. we thanked him and bid him good
bye. he is a fine looking young Officer. Today we have drawn dried apple
for the first time and that was poor and wormy. you said that Father was
going to write me a whole letter I hope he will. you spoke in your last letter about the young man that he, Mr Cushing, referred to the other Sunday.
I knew who he ment for I well remember addressing those words to him,
and I can truly say that I feel safe in the hands of my <u>God</u> for I know that
he will do all things for the best. I feel that these trials and hardships
which I am called upon to endure are but slight, yea <u>nothing,</u> when compared with what our Savior suffered for me and [illegible] mankind. I feel
that death has no terrors to me, and that if by my sufferings and <u>death</u>
even, I should be the means (through God) of converting or leading my
friends to seek that better past which shall never be taken away from them
neither in this world nor the world to come. I would gladly spend the three
years in Soldiering, and my <u>daily</u> <u>ernest</u> <u>prayer</u> to <u>God</u> is that <u>you</u> Dear Fa-

ther must give your heart to God, and spend the remainder of your days in the vinyard of the Lord, knowing that soon at the longest we must meet around the thrown of God to render up our account for the deeds done heare in the body whether good or evil. let us dear friends so life that we may hear our blessed Savior say with us in the last great day of Judgment, come unto me ye blessed of my Father, enter ye with the joys of your Lord. I feel that if I should live to come home again that I should be a different person for I have made up my mind that if a man gain the whole world even, and lose his own soul it profithith [profiteth] him nothing. I hope that you will all write to me often and tell me all the news. I wish you could see the old horses and mules and the like out hear at one time I saw about 20 dead horses and mules in a pile. a few days ago the men buried about 40 at a time. the houses and barns and all the property in this vicinity is distroyed and decaying and large wood lots are cleared off. Hundreds of acres are clear which a few months ago were heavily wooded with white Oaks and other hard woods it will be a sorry looking country when this War is ended. what do you think of the war at the present time. I am sorry that the boys were so sea-sick for I know how to pity them. I feel sorry that [H.] Lyman [Parkman] is so poorly of and hope he will be better before long. I will close for this time expecting to hear from you all before long. Give my love to all and accept this from me. your eldest son and brother,

George W. Harwood

Sergeant Major Francis A. Walker from North Brookfield was on the staff of General Darius N. Couch.

~~hear is another piece of that billiard table that I took at White Sulphur Springs for Fanni to look at if she wants~~. [Written at the top of this letter and scribbled out so perhaps he did not include it.]

Jan 19 [1863]

Camp opposite Fredericksburg

Dear Friends,

I received a letter from Anna + Allen last evening and was very glad as usual to hear from home. Nothing of importance has transpired since I wrote you last. I expect to go on picket again before long if I stay hear. Last Friday night we had orders to be ready to march the next morning and had rations delt out for three days, but we have not gone yet and last night there was rumors in camp that we were going to start in the night for Aquia Creek, and thare take a transport for Washington or Richmond but we did not go, and our Capt says that he thinks we shall stay hear some times yet. we have drilled this morning and things look like staying for the present. I am pretty well and am very fleshy. I weigh 180 without my overcoat and no vest, a thin blouse. Allen says that he ways 120 I think that he grows fast. he will be larger than I if he lives. we are having pretty cold weather now and before morning we are sometimes cold, but I do hate to mend the stockings. I got Mr Cheaver [Moses A. Cheever] to do my washing last week for 10 cts he boiled them good. I do not see any prospect of this war coming to an end, and I sometimes feel a little blue and I do not feel like writing today. I should like to see you all. I wish you could see us hear in this hut or pig pen, and some times when we think of our condition it makes us feel sad and homesick, and I guess I feel a little so this morning. yestoday was a very fine but cool day we had no Divine Services at all, and I could not but contrast my privlages now with what they were then when I was at home and with what I presume you are enjoying every Sabbath. I begin to want them to [illegible] this War through and let us go home or else kill us off. the 42 had hard luck I think but I understand by the papers that the company that F[reeman] + Hubbard are in are safe as yet. I should like to hear more from them. I hope that Lyman Parkman is better than when you wrote your last before this. we boys are scattered all over the South and it will take a long time if ever to bring us all back safe and sound. I hope Andrew will get his discharge soon, and I guess he will. Allen wanted to know if I carried my Gun on my right shoulder or changed it. we are expected to carry our gun on our right shoulder but we do change sometimes without leave. we did not cary our knapsacks over to Fredericksburg but carried our blankets and tents in a role. we had 60 rounds of cartridges and our guns loaded + caped and half cocked all the time. Father do you think it is safe to send money home in a letter, if we should get paid off soon I should want to send my money home some how. how high are apples now with you. they are 5 cts a peace hear and small at that, 16.00 per barrel. I buy some but they cost to much, flour is 30.00 per bll. [barrel?] hear in Falmouth. they ask 15 cts for a loaf of bread as big as a [illegible] dish. candy is 10 cts a stick. I have bought none of that for I cant see the point. milk 20 cts a quart, coffee 2 cts per pound, and other things are as high accordingly. It is pretty cold out hear, and it makes our hands + cheeks red to go down to the brook and brake open the ice and wash every morning. we go back double quick sometimes. What is is your baby's name. I didnt know until you wrote about Elmer and so I concluded that must be it. I should like to see those little fellows. I received a letter from Mrs E. D. Batcheller and answered it a few days ago. write often and remember me to all the friends. I dont know whare I shall be when this letter reaches you but I guess not hear.

Yours Affect

George W Harwood

Aquia Creek was a major supply station for both the Union and the Confederacy. It changed hands several times during the war. The troops took the train from the campground to the river. Today it is a very pretty park.

Jan 22 [1863]

Camp opposite Fredericksburg Va

Dear Friends,

Again I take my pencil to write a few lines to you. I received my cap and toillet a few days ago. I like my cap very well it fits good, and I am very much obliged to you Anna for it. I can have my picture taken but don't know as it is best at present. I should to see it however, I suppose that you have heard that the army of the Potomac is stuck fast in the mud. we have a good deal of rain hear for a week or two past and it is quite yes very muddy. Last Tuesday we had an order to have three days rations and be ready to start the next morning, to we knew not whare. it rained hard all that night and at 11 o'clock we were called up for a ration of beef, and again at 2 o'clock to roll our blankets and be ready to fall in, and again at 4 to put on our equipments. our tent leaked and we got some wet and dreaded to start off for battle for that was what we expected, but we did not have to go in to battle for the order was countermanded and we had to go on Picket I had not felt very well for several days but I though[t] we had got to fight and I wanted to go, and had not been to the Doc at all. it rained hard all the morning but I went with the rest on picket, and stood in the rain a few hours around a smokey fire. by the way our Company was held as reserve, and I told the Capt that I did not feel well and would like to [go] back to camp. he told me to go. I came back and had a good night's rest but the rest of the boys had to tough it through with a little or no sleep.

it rained hard all night and they were pretty wet. on my way back I met the drummer boy with Whiskey for the Co, which the Capt delt out to them. The next morning after they got back to camp we had some more. I was not thare but they drew my ration and put it in the tent for me, as I was not very well I took it for <u>Medecine</u> at night we had some more delt out and they said it was to be delt out daily for the present, but that was the last, and I am glad of it. although it had no bad effect upon <u>me</u> I saw the effect upon some others to my sorrow and I told the boys that I had taken the last drop I should unless ordered by the Surgeon. whether the whiskey done me any good or not I feel a little better today, but not very well. perhaps when I get home I will tell you more about the whiskey, but will not write it. it rained again last night. Things look dark now and our Capt says they never looked darker to him, I fully agree with him. we have again been defeated in our plans to overthrow this rebellion. these last movements cost a great deal, some lives and many horses, 21 in one battery and the cannon's had to be left fast in the mud. the Rebs have got it painted and stuck up on a post: <u>Burnside stuck in the mud.</u> they say that they will come over and help us get our cannons out and place them any whare we want and they can whip us then. Father don't things look dark to you now? do you traid much now? how does Judson Adams get along with the place has he paid you for those steers? do you think that they can pay the rent. Freeman and the rest of the boys are a good ways off. I should like to see them or even hear from. I would write but I dont know how to direct. you spoke about sending some more paper and envelopes I am not very short and thare is no great hurry but whenever thare is an opportunity I should like some. The boys out hear have taken it into their heads to whittle some make pipes and some make rings and so I thought I would whittle out one and send it home that I might see it if I ever come back. it is <u>not</u> a good one and I mean to make a better one. I have nothing more in particular to right this time I hope that you will write soon and often Remember me to my many friends. I suppose that Andrew has not got home yet I intend to write to George [Doane?] soon but my time is pretty much taken up in drills, Inspection, and Review and mending my cloths + reading + writing +s [etc]   Yours Truly

George W Harwood

Major General Ambrose Burnside planned to cross the Rappahannock River and march on Richmond beginning January 20. By January 22 because of heavy rain

the effort, which came to be called the "mud march" ended in failure. Burnside was relieved of command on January 25 and replaced by Major Joseph Hooker.

Jan 30 [1863]
Camp opposite Fredericksburg Va

Dear Friends

I received my handkerchief and a letter from you last Monday night I'm much obliged to you for the gift. it is a good one I think. I got a letter from Andrew at the same time he seems to be in good spirits. I'm sorry that he can't have his discharge. we have had several rany days lately and last Tuesday morning we had to go on picket and it rained all that day and night and in the morning it commenced snowing and we had a sorry time I assure you all we could do was to spread my rubber blanket over our shoulders and stand and take it. we got no sleep at all but very wet. I suppose that is the beauty of Soldiering. we Soldiers have some rough times. it snowed hard all that day and night, and in the morning thare was from 6 to 8 inches of snow. the mud out hear is very deep and slipery the wheels go in up to the hub. Each company details one or two men and sometimes more each day to do the extry duty such as choping wood, and bringing water for the cooks or on guard at the commisary and such like. it came my turn yesterday to chop wood. we choped yellow pine for that is the only wood near hear and it took 8 mules to bring what one could draw on in good traiding. In your letter you said that thare was a re-port thare that Burnside had again crossed the Rappahannock he intended to I suppose but the rain hindered he has resigned. I'm sorry. things look dark. Mother said she was affried [afraid] that I did not get all the letters. I think I have got them all now, night-cap + handkerchief, but no papers for some time. she spoke about Andrew's not changing his cloths for 4 weeks. thare are some among us that go as long as that and even longer, but that is more than I can go. I washed last Monday 2 shirts + drawers, stockings + swaths [socks?] what we boys had furnished us when we left home. the[y] look well but it has rained so much since that they are not fully dried yet. I have got so that I can mend equil to any old woman, but I hate it. I've pached my sock with old socks legs. I like my boots first rate. [Lyman] Gilbert sold his he got into another of his fits such as he used to have at home you know if he wanted any thing he would have it at any price and if he wanted to sell any thing he would <u>sell</u> it at any price. it was so with him hear, because they hurt his ancles a little, and away they went. I guess that you had better not send any socks at present for if these give out I can draw from the Government for 26 cts a pair and they will last a while. I'd like another box perhaps I shall send some time and then I'd have cheese, dried apples and such like as that, a little pepper, or tea would come with a sheet of paper without extry postage. I guess that the report that the 36 is to be divided is all nonsense, but I had rather be in a battery than any whare else. Then Mrs Bisco is dead I'm sorry but what is our loss is her gain for to depart and be with Christ is far better. Is Mrs Stoddard any better or does she grow worse. Mother does your lameness get any better. I wish it might. I often think of your pains and sufferings but dont know as I can do any thing to help you. you say that I am not out of your mind, day nor night, but dont worry about me for that will do no good. I'm doing well but I must say that it is rough, but I shall not have to follow it always I hope. I wish you could just look in and see five men in a pig-pen I wish you could send me Uncle Jonas hog-horn and then I'd be satisfied for the present. I wish I could hear from Freeman and write to him his time is most half out, good for him. Anna how do your little boys do. The beef cattle out hear are a good deal like Fathers meadow hay cattle in the spring. I guess they live on fathe[?] or nothing, perhaps as father used to say on moonshine and fog, but I can't write much more <u>now</u>. I hope to meet you all at home again some time but if not, I do hope to in that in that heavenly world whare parting is no more. this world is full of trouble + trials but it will be short at the longest I hope Aunt Lucretia is better before this time. please remember me to her, and the rest of the friends write often. I am feeling pretty well, but I should think that we should all die lying on the ground and getting wet and no good chance to dry, nor warm food to eat. I should like to see you all and then I could tell you more than I could write in an age. tell Freeman to write to me I will write to him when I know how to direct.

This from your obedient Son and brother G. W. Harwood

Do you hear any thing from N. A. Powers to know whether he is dead or alive. you know that thare was a report that he was dead.

Eunice Whipple Rice Bisco died on January 17, 1863 leaving behind her husband Foster Bisco and a housekeeper Marietta Greene.

Feb 3rd [1863]

Camp opposite Fredericksburg Va

Dear Friends,

I received a letter from you last night and was very glad to hear from home once more. I thought that perhaps Father would have got ready to write by the time I received that, but I was mistaken but I suppose that it is just as hard as now for him to write as it used to be when I was at home. you spoke about my being dishartened, but I think not bad but who can help it. that is a Soldiers privelage to find <u>fault</u> and feel <u>blue,</u> and for a man to lay on the ground and live as we live with the prospect ahead which we have now. looking at it in a worldly point of view but trusting in <u>God</u> and hoping for the best is all we can do. I think that all will come out right in the end, but I must confess that things look dark at the present time. the Soldiers are sick of this life and long for the close, but Mr Cushing says that the people in the North dread the end of this war on account of the Demoralization of the Soldiers, and I think that that will be true to some extent for the influences of camp life tend to degrade a man. even professed christians become worldly + profane. one has to be constantly on his guard or he will be led astray. I often think of what Dea [Deacon] Morse said in a prayer meeting in school-house No 6 that christians should pray that soldiers might be kept from the Demoralizing influences of camp life. he is an old soldier you know and has had experience. M. P. Snell has just arrived since I commenced this letter. he looks well and is fleshy, and I have bought 1/2 quire of paper of him. what do you think? can we conquer the enemy or not. I think it is doubtful. the weather is cold hear now and I think that this is a rough life for one to live and at times I almost think that the shorter such a life is the better. I have written to Mrs Hair for Addison he is sick and is in the Hospital. he wants a night-cap like mine, and not like Freemans he likes mine first rate. he wants his wife to see Anna about [it] and will pay for it. Mother says that Father had rather I would be in Andrew's place and on some account I should as leave for I think I could get my discharge. if not I could see my friends with out paying so much thare is a chance for some to get a furlough now of 10 days one man is going [to] start for home on a furlough in a day or two but we shall have to pay our expenses both ways and that will be rather rough what do you think about it? it will take half of the time to go and come. we expect to be paid off before long we have sined the pay role. we boys tell what we will do if they do not pay us soon but that is all the good it will do we can talk but U.S. has got us fast and we shall await his money. he is a hard master if you deal with him honestly but the Col say says that check is essential to the service. (Soldiering) Anna I think that verce you sent is a very good one particularly al [all] aplied [applied] to our case. truly 'tis all for the best that we have the bitter with the sweet but it is hard for frail human creatures to realize that fact, and I fear that many think to much of this life and not enough of that life which awaits us in another world. In a moment the dearest ties that binds man to this world may be cut asunder and they will be ushered into the presence of their final judge. whether prepared or unprepared it is all the same with them. "he that is un-just let him be unjust still. he that is gilty let him be gilty still, and he that is righeous [righteous] let him be righeous [righteous] still" [Revelation 22:11] as a man leaves this world so he will enter the next. surely it be-comes us so to spend these days + years hear on earth so that we may be prepared to die at any moment and under any circumstances, and hear our Saviour say unto us in the last great Judgement day "Well done good and faithful servants enter ye into the joys of your Lord"[Matthew 25:21] I will not write more this time and will answer Allens at some other time I think. please write often and if convenient send a few postage stamps when I get my pay I will make it all right. remember me to all the friends.

Yours Truly   George Washington Harwood

A quire of paper is about two dozen sheets of paper all the same size. Mrs. Hair was Addison's wife, Ann(a). She asked George's sister Anna about knitting a night-cap for Addison.

Feb 6th [1863]
Camp opposite Fredericksburg

Dear Friends,

I received a letter from Freeman last night and [he] wanted me to answer it but I do not know how to direct. please write and let me know. yestoday I went on picket and came of this morning and had another old fashioned N. East snow + rain storm. this is the 3 or 4 time that I have been on picket when it rained hard all day + night, and I have got about sick of this life. I had a talk with the Rebs this morning and they appear very friendly and say that they dont want [to] fight us any more. they say that it seems like fighting their own kinsfolks and that if it could be left to the privates then it would be settled at once, and they wish that the officers could have a chance to fight it out by themselves. they are as sick of this war as we are, and are willing to treat us like friends. yestoday our Regt got paid off up to the first of Nov my bill was 21.66. I will send a check to Father and he can draw the money from any bank in the U.S. I will keep a little myself. We are under marching orders now and this Corps is going to Fortress Monroe and from thare to N. Carolina probably soon. I dread to leave this lovely muddy <u>State</u> Va. the mud is ankle deep all the time almost and when we go on picket we have to stand around a little smokey fire with our feet in the mud, but I do dread to go down South. I am afraid of seasickness. Freeman and the boys are all well but they did not tell me how to direct. I shall write them in a few days. I hope that your baby is better than when you wrote me a while ago! F.[Freeman] and the rest say that they wish I was in the Regt + cos with them and I wish so to, but wishing does no good but we may meet down south, but doubtful. Addison is a little better I believe. I dont know but I had a leave go down South or stay hear and travel around in the mud. I am very fleshy now but I fear that it will whittle my flesh off some to go into a warmer climate and on board those old transports. I weight 180 Freeman says that he weighs 173 I thinks. I wrote in the note to Allen that they were giving furloughs but I understand that that has played out, I understand. How is it at the North now is thare plenty of change is thare any silver I have seen none for some time, no silver we use Government shin plasters so called among soldier's and 5 cts is the Cast [value]. I suppose that the Green backs are not worth near a dollar in gold, but they will pass as well as any thare will they not? they do hear. The Rebs Pickets told me this morning that they thought that war would not last longer than June or thare abouts that thare was a fare prospect <u>of Peace</u>. in the letter that I received Hubbard [Doane] & Charles Parkman wrote also they appeared in fine spirits I wish that I was with them. This money that I send Father can use if he wants as I do not want to use it hear if Mother wants to use any she can have some for herself or Fannie she can have it and welcome. I have nothing more to write of importance this time but presume that I shall be some whare else when this letter reaches you. perhaps hearafter I shall not have a chance to write so often as I have heartofore, but I shall write as often as I can and want you to do the same. I had over 2.50 when they paid me and I will send a check of 22.00 and have left 2.25 I do not have to spend much and if I get short I will send for a little at a time. the Adjutant, Sargent Major + Capt advised me to send a check and not the money for you could easily draw the money yourself or endorse it and send it to be collected, and if the check is lost I can get another. they owe me over 3 months pay now. I have not felt very well for a week or two and have had the Rheumitism in my knees fore sometime more or less and it doesent do me any good to lay on the ground and get wet. write often. Snell visits with and we have a very good + agreeable times.   Good By

Truly Yours

George W. Harwood

Before the Civil War the US issued currency in silver and gold coins. State chartered banks printed their own paper money. Some state banks accepted paper money from another state at face value, others at a discount. To finance the war, Congress passed several National Currency and Banking Acts, instituted Federally chartered banks and printed a national paper currency with green ink on the back (greenbacks). This became the currency we know today. Shinplasters were temporary paper notes used when silver coins were unavailable.

[undated, between February 6-12, 1863 Falmouth Virginia]

[no salutation, probably to Anna]
I have just received a letter and 2 papers one with paper, and a paper last night one from Mrs [E. D.] Batcheller and a letter from Mrs Bush + Jenifer [Jennie?] I enjoyed. I was very glad indeed to get a letter for it is [several illegible words] a letter ever is I am feeling a little down hearted and desponding. I am sorry that your little boys have been sick but hope that they will get better. I think that Father's + Mother's are getting in the way of enjoying life, going to an oyster supper. I should like to sit down to an oyster supper and I think that the [several illegible words]. you say that it is cold weather in Mass but it is quite warm hear. You spoke about Allen's pretending to sit up and keep Fannie [?] company while F. + M. [Father + Mother] were away to the oyster suppers. I can readily imagine how he looked as I have sat up in the same way and should like to again. I think that Elmer is a very pretty name you may have written to before but I have never received a letter stating his name before I should like to see him little chap you said An [Anna] that you rec'd a letter from F [Freeman] so did I a while ago but he did not give me directions and I am going to an-

swer it as soon as I find out how to direct. I am going to write to Uncle Joseph [Harwood] when I get time. I should like to have Henry + Harry [Harwood cousins] write to me. I suppose that Edwin [Doane] + John [Lamson] are having a fine time this winter. they have both written to me and I expect to hear from them again. If Father does not write to me pretty soon I shall write to him <u>personly</u> althoug[h] I don't think strange for he never writes unless he is obliged to. Mother wrote that F+ [Father] thought I had better not send my money just yet but I have sent a check long ago I hope it will reach home in safety my boots go nicely I like them much. I am sorry that Andrew [Jackson] does not get home. I dont wonder that he feel a little home-sick or lonesome at times, and I must confess that I do feel at times lonesome and wish that I was with Freeman and wish that I could do this or that and when I am on picket in a storm I almost wish that I had not enlisted but I don't know as I <u>am</u> nearly sorry, because I feel that these privations are for my best good and that I shall return home again in due time, if it be the will of God that I should not return. I have the blest assurance that my name is written in the Lambs book on high, were it not for that hope I should at times almost dispair. If I am better prepared to enter that Hevenly world now than I shall be in a few years hense and it be the will of my Heavenly Father to take me hense without permitting me to return home. I feel that I could with joy say "Thy will o God, not mine be done," and it is my daily prayer that I may be prepared for life and prepared for death and for the Judgement seat of Christ that I may render up my last account with joy and not with greaf [grief]. This is a hard place for a man to live a good upright christian life. Thare are temptations hard to be resisted, trials hard to be boarn, but we must remember that No cross no crown, and he that endureth until the end <u>shall be saved</u>. I written a good long letter this time. they are going to give furlough they say to Married men first and they fell into line to see who should go a man from Grafton was the lucky man. I couldn't draw because I couldn't sware that I <u>was</u> a married man. I shall expect a letter from home often and long ones two. I take great comfort in reading them. I suppose that we are not in the Army of the Potomac now, but you will direct as usual.

Yours affect + etc
George W Harwood

George often mentions oyster suppers with his sister Anna. He mentions religious feelings in letters to her more often than to anyone else.

Feb 12 [1863]
On board the steamer S. America

Dear Friends,

As I have nothing in particular to occupy my time just now I will improve them by writing to you. the old boat rocks so that I can hardly follow the line. We left our camp opposite Fredericksburg Tuesday about 2 o'clock in the afternoon marched down to the Depot about a mile distant and took the cars about 4 o'clock and reached Aquia Creek about 6 o'- clock came on board the South America about 7 o'clock and left the next morning about 7 we came around into [___ Lorings?] bay this a m + here about 3 P.M. we started again this morning about 7 and sailed down into the Chesapeake bay and anchored on account of the Fog and our old Steamer is an old rotten dirty, filthy thing hardly safe for a thousand men and baggage. our Regt and apart of the 100th Penn are on board. the remainder of the 100th and the 45 Pa are on board the John B Warner and are in sight of us. it rained yestoday in the afternoon and last night, and is some foggy today. I said that we anchored this morning but we remained so only an [h]our or two the sun came out. thare is only one <u>woman</u> on board and she is a Darky she cooks for the Officers. the sailors are mostly darkys. we are packed in pretty thickly and it is a tremenderous nasty place the floor is covered with tobacco spittle and water and clam shills. the old thing leaks some. Last night our Capt and 4 of the men went out in a small boat to the shore and got some clams we boys opened the shells and swallered them without any ceremony whatever. those were the first raw clams I ever ate or rather swallered. we amuse ourselves by whittling out rings and hearts and such like things. those of us who have more of a taste for that, than we have for playing cards and reading dime novels. some are writing and a good many telling stories and smoking and traiding watches, Pistols + knives money is very plenty now with the poorer class, and the most shiftless, some of which have spent most of their last 2 months pay for which they can show but little. have you received the check I sent in my last letter dated Feb 6th. When we got to Aquia Creek we found several Ex [Express] boxes our tent mate [Myron R] Wood had one I bought a slice of cheese which relishes good with hard-tack. we have to pay 10 cts for a cup of coffee hear or the same for the privelage of setting our cup on the coals. I was a little dizzy when I first came on board and do not feel just right now. it's a filthy stinking place hear to make the best of it. I expected to have received another letter from home before I started but did not the last I received was a paper with mustard, much obliged.   Feb 15th.

We reached Fortress Monroe about 7 o'clock Friday night and anchored a little ways from shore and spent the night in the morning we went on to Newport-News whare we landed and went up the river a little ways and encamped on a large level plain, a very fine place and sandy. Saturday morning we went to work to fix up our tent and a little before noon we were ordered on picket and we have just been relieved we were stationed on a large dung heap in the midst of a large, what was corn field but now is a field of weeds nearly as high as my head. it looks to me as Father says the prarie of the West do. I think that it is a great deal pleasanter hear than it was in Fredericksburg although I dread to go much farther South. the last day I was on board the Steamer I was quite dizzy and unwell. I am quite fleshy but do not feel as well as I look. that is have not for the past week or two, although not sick. We can buy things hear quite cheap we can get apples for 2 + 3 cts each, and bread, reasonably. we have soft bread delt out to us hear, one loaf per day. I had about as leave have good hard bread a part of the time as the soft bread is a little sour, but I am very well satisfied with my living and do not mean to be understood to com-plain about my living when I am well I can eat them with relish I sent home to much of my money I guess I wish I had kept 2.00 dollars more (next sheet) [switches from pencil to ink]

I have a little more time and I think will improve it by writing to you, my kind friends far away. often on a long hard march does my mind wander back to the scens [scenes] of my childhood, to the happy bygone days, to the many priveledges which it was mine to enjoy, beyond many of my fel-low creatures and to day being the Sabbath day my mind runs back to my <u>home</u> so different from my present circumstance. would that those happy days mint again be mine to enjoy. the weary soldier thinks of his home as the dearest spot on Earth to him. thare is no place like home! we are all hoping that this war will soon end and we be permitted to return home again in safety made better by having been separated from our homes and friends and all better society. We have prayer meetings when we are en-champed [encamped] occationally [occasionally] I am not as much inter-ested in his services as I am in the 100 Pa. we go over thare often their chaplain is a good sound minister, preaching the truth the whole truth and nothing but the truth. he is very interesting, wholy engaged in his work. their officers are men of better principle I think then ours as they take part in their meetings, and ours are hardly ever present. I understand that our Col. was once a Supurentend in a Sabbath school but now he is a different man. he is a profane ungodly man. many a man who was a <u>christian</u> at home is something else now. happy is that man who can endure unto the end, who can live a christian life and still be a soldier. write often and all the news and remember me to all the friends.

Yours Affect[ionately]

George W. Harwood

George was using lined stationery and switched from pencil to ink.

Newport News Va. Feb 20th [1863]

Dear Friends,

I received a letter from you a few days ago and a paper and also a letter from George H. Jackson. I have written to uncle Joseph. we have had a rainstorm for the past few days. yestoday I went on guard. we have got these A or wedge tents so called, five of us in a tent Gilbert, Snell, Wheelock, Haskell, and I we like them much better than we did those old shelter tents. I have written to Freeman + Hubbard we have got to drill 4 or 5 hours per day hear. we live better than we used to we have more potatoes and onions and fresh beef. we can buy things more reasonable hear than any whare else since came out to Virginia I did not keep but little money with me thinking that I should not need much but I am getting rather short and I wish that Father would send me 2 or 3 dollars. they will not take any thing but green backs, and tharefore I wish you would send them, if convenient send in 50 cts peaces + 100 peaces instead of sending in one large bill. I dont think that the Rebel term of Peace are any thing at all. they want we should give up all and come under. I dont think much of that. I think that Judson has done pretty well to pay so much dont you? Louis had a letter from him a few days ago. he is the same old boy. we have got a very fine place hear for drilling and we have got concidrable of it to do. we have got to ware a small peace of blue flannel about 2 inches square on side of our caps. we are building a side walk in front of our tent about 3 ft wide made out of pine logs split with the split side out and the road or street is turnpiked equel to any high way or city street, and things look as though we were going to stay hear for a while at least. our Guns + Equpments have got to be kept in good order and our brasses scoured, and every thing in tip top stile and that is what I like for thare are some who are slack and those who are prompt have to suffer for the whole in many cases. I think that we shall have a floor out of logs and cover it over with bows but I dont know. It is very pleasant to go down to the shore or beach when the tide is out and gather little shells and pebbles I have gathered some just for curiosity sake and I will send a few to Fannie. I dont know but they will get broken before they get thare. this is a very fine day but we have had some very hard days it rained about 48 hours in a steady streach and we had nothing but our shelter tents and they were not raised at all. the old things leaked and our blankets and coats were just as wet as water could make them we had to lay in bed day and night most of the time. it is a wonder that we do not catch cold more of us so exposed. oftentimes when we wake in the morning we have found our feet in a puddle of water, but now we have got the new tents I hope that it will not be so. I understand that the people of N. Brookfield have voted to build a new Town House worth 13,000 dollars. how is that? Rather steep is it not? but I must close and go to work. please excuse this poor writing as I have written this in a terrible pucker[?]. don't forget the money. remember me to the friends and write often and oblidge your eldest son + brother.

George W Harwood

Shelter Tent, Farragut Museum,   **Wedge Tent, 22nd New York near Harpers Ferry,**
Farragut, Tennessee (Photo by author)   **West Virginia (Courtesy Library of Congress)**

Shelter tents were for two men; each had half of a tent which they buttoned together. Wedge tents slept six men, four comfortably, and were closed at one or both ends. The piece of blue flannel worn on his cap was the corps badge. General Hooker had these put on his troop's caps.

[post script upside down at top of the next letter] Mother who did you refer to when you said that some of our Town men had returned from the Army with disgrace upon themselves and upon their friends.

Newport News Va. Feb. 26 [1863]

Dear Friends,

It is very convenient for me to address you all in one word, Friends. I am very glad you Anna are at home so that I can write to you all in the same letter. It gives me much pleasure to read a letter from home and am glad to have you all write although oftentimes a little repetition of the same news. I received a letter from home and also from Freeman last night. he said he was on guard that day. I received a letter from Andrew a few days ago. I think I wrote in my last letter that I had written to Uncle Joseph. I have aslo [also] written to Charles Parkman. Yestoday we had a General Review by Gen Dix. I think, we have got a very fine place hear. the ground is very hard we have to drill several hours each day. we have our cooking done for us now coffee and all. I like the new or rather old arrangements pretty well. we draw soft bread altogather. I have sent home in my last letter I think, for some money. I shall expect that along before long. I guess that 2 or 3 dollars will be all I shall want. a few days ago Lyman and I washed our cloths and left them on the poll [pole] to dry. we left them out as the other boys have over night alongside of our tent and some one borrowed my old stocking and left me with one pair. the most that I care about it is I hate to cheat anybody so bad. they took them in the night for a good home made pair of stockings I suppose but they were far from that the heels and toes are all gone or nearly so. I shall draw a new pair as quick as possible. we have just come in from battalion drill we have had a rather hard time it was warm and we were drilled by the Senior Capt as the Col is at home on a furlough the Leuint. Col. has resigned and the Major who came out with us has also resigned and our present Major is off on other business. our head Surgeon is also at home on a furlough unwell I understand. It seems that some of the Officers can get a furlough of them are unwell or other good reasons but we privates can get a discharge sometimes the day before they die and sometimes the papers are made out after he is dead and buried. one man in our Co. was sick, an old man and they kept him around until he couldn't get up alone and gave him his discharge and he got to Washington and died. they huried him off at last for fear he would die before he got off their hands. Then you think that Aunt ~~Dolly~~ Lucretia + Uncle Jonas are disposed to look on the dark side of the question, but it is not so with me. I feel like looking on the brightest side if thare be any. I presume that I have written before M. Porter Snell had got back and tents with us he is a private now and is well and quite fleshy. When Mr Cushing was out to see <u>us</u> near Fredericksburg Va. <u>he</u> [Snell] was in Frederick Md. and did not see Mr Cushing at all. Mother spoke about going down to C. R. Stoddard. I should like very well to get hold of a good large Turkey I could make something of hole myself I think. I suppose that C. K. is the same man that he was of old when I was thare. I dont know what Mr Foster Bisco will do if Marietta [Greene] leaves him, now his wife is dead. How long has Mrs David Prouty [Caroline] been crazy. I dont know as I have heard of that before if I had I had forgotten it. I remember you wrote that their son Jonas was ill. has Roswell Biscos son [Hiram R.] enlisted. I have forgotten his name, is Father going to let the Sargent place in the spring or take care of it himself. I suppose that he has given up the Idea of traiding Mr. Jason Wilson for his farm. March 1st which is close at hand U. Sam will owe me 52 dollars. time flies fast soon our three years will be out, and we shall be our own men again. some say that they would not enlist again, but I do not know whether I should or not, but guess not as a private

[on a separate piece of paper] a few words more as I have time.

You said Anna in one of your letters that Aunt Lucretia came down to hear my letters read. I dont know as I have any objection to that, only please say to her that I write what comes in my mind first and do not stop for much meditation and of corse do not compose them so correctly or take the pains that I should if they were going out of the family I am often in a great hurry and a crowd bustling around me. Anna how is it with you do you like to sit down and write to a stranger or to one whom you know or feel is your superior. when I have a letter to write to my superiors (and they are mostly of that class) I always dread it. I have overcome that in a measure since I came into the army. I have found out that those who thought themselves to be <u>somebody</u> are nothing but human beings this is the best place in the world to learn human nature or man shows himself right out to be with him daily situated as we are. I am greatly disappointed in some of our boys but will not write any thing about that now if I ever should get home I should to tell you some things, but I must draw this to a close. I like to write and have a good <u>Gold</u> pen but am a poor writer. I have no time to take pains for I am always in a hurry but it isnt half the work for me to write that it used to be. I have written a long letter after all. I did not think of writing half so much and I hardly know what I have written and shall not read it over to see. good Bye.

[on a separate piece of paper]

Thursday morning a great change in the weather since last night. it has cleared off cold and very windy the wind blew down our chimneys so that we can hardly stay in our tents, and it is so cold that in order to keep warm I have got on a pr of heavy buckskin gloves and this steal pen makes this writing look pretty bungling. I can write fast enough with Gloves on but not so fine as I can without. I will not write any more this time. I look for a letter tomorrow morning.

Good Bye.   Very Aff Yours   George W Harwood

Hiram Roswell Bisco served with the Massachusetts Sixtieth Regiment.

[upside down at the top of the letter] Hear are some rings that I whittled out of Beef hoof when I was back in Fredericksburg

Newport News Va. March 5 [1863]

Dear Friends

I received a letter from you last night and the money and was very glad indeed to get it. Yestoday we followed the remains of a Soldier Brother, and as we have reason to hope a Christian Brother to the grave. His name was Manard [Solomon R. Maynard] of Paxton he is the first who has died with the [illegible] in our Co. he was sick but a little while, about 8 or 10 days with the Typhoid Fever, and was crazy most of the time during his sickness. he was about 23 years old and several inches taller than I am. we intended to send his body home but could not get a coffin that was suitable. he may be taken up sometime. I have not heard a word from Addison since I left Fredericksburg. he was then at Aquia Creek in a Hospital. I dont know whether he has got his cap or not. Fan [Fannie?] asked me Mother if Mr Wheelock [Joseph B?] was a professor of religion. I answer he is not but is or says he thinks a professor he uses no profane language and says that he likes to hear us talk and I have talked with him. he thinks he is a Christian. Yestoday afternoon we had a Brigade drill three regiments of us together, and are to have another this afternoon. they are 3 hours long and are rather hard. I can hardly find time to write a letter without being disturbed. I wrote a letter to Freeman a few days ago and was interrupted 4 or 5 times. I received the letter that Father wrote one sheet. I am very glad indeed that Cousin Andrew has got a furlough and wish he could get his discharge. I should like a furlough first rate but thare can not be at present. Tell Andrew to write to me before he goes back if he has time. We have to have our boots blacked every day and our Guns kept bright and are to have some white gloves the Capt says and we have a piece of blue cloth on our left cap button. we have the blacking [lice?] found us, and are to have our hair trimmed up closely. soon after I left Washington last fall I had my hair cut short, shingled close to my head but it has got out some now. I shall have it clipped off close to my head again when it is a little warmer. Haskell received a box a few days ago ~~and~~ (day before yestoday) and Snell one yestoday one came through in 6 days and the other in 7 they come through very quickly now. they had cheese + butter pies and cakes &c. &c. they came through nicely, except some bottles which broke. Anna you spoke about writing fast. I guess that I shall learn to write fast, that is Short Hand or phonography [stenography?]. Gilbert and I are both studing it a little when we get time. Snell can write it as fast as he can talk almost. Yestoday when we buried one of our Co. the Capt chose 8 men to fire the salute over the grave. I was one of them the rest of the company marched behind without guns. it was a solumn time and before I enlisted should have thought very interesting, but I have got so accustomed to it now that I think but little about it we are not very well pleased with our Chaplain he never was made for a Chaplain in the Army I think. I'm sorry that we haven't a better one. I am well that is pretty well I have not felt first rate for a week past. I dont see as thare is any bright prospect of this war's being ended at present perhaps not until my three years are out, be that as it may. if I live to get home happy shall we be, and if I fall on the battle field or in the Hospital, will it not be all far better for me to die first and be with <u>Christ</u> then will my soul be at peace, and the trials or perplexaties of life be to and end. Happy shall we be in that upper Jerusalem! that city of our God! thare to be bright + shiny lights Jesus + us. Remember me to the friends and write often.

Yours Affectionately George W. Harwood

1863
Newport News Va. March 10th

Dear Friends,

    I came off picket this morning and found a letter from you + a paper from Ezra D [Batcheller]. we went on picket yestoday morning and had a very fine day and night, but it commenced raining hard this morning and we got wet through. I have not received Addisons cap. I had a letter from his wife a few days ago and she wished me to write to him if I had not got it, and so I did. You spoke about stockings. I had rather draw them from the Government, and have no trouble about making or sending. Lyman has sent home for a box and has ordered 1/2 rhyme [ream] of paper and says that he will sell me some of that and envelopes to go with it, so that you will not need to send any. as for postage of stamps, I can buy none out hear, and I wish that you would get a little money of Father and send out some, quite a lot of them, and, charge it to me. I wish that you, some of you, would keep account of what you have to pay out for me and sometime I will make it all right if I live. I am very glad that Anna Jackson has got so nice a present, for I think that she deserves it. I [am] sorry that Andrew is no better and should like to see him. Anna I shouldn't think that you could write with your little boys all over the table, and in the ink bottle. little chaps I should like to see them. you must think every thing of them. what does Father think of them he used to think a good deal of Georgie. I am expecting a letter from Freeman about this time. I have learned one thing within a few days, and that is if a man has got monied friends, that have a great deal of influence they can get a discharge easily a few days ago one of our Corporals who has not seen a sick day since he came out, his name is Blanchard of Boston about 21 years old, his uncle who is the Chief of Boston Police came out and and went to the Secratary of war and got his Discharge papers, and our Col and Capt were obliged to sine them, although thae [they] both refused at first. they were made out on the Ground of Promotion, but his Father wanted him in some business in Boston. he is a wild boy. Anna, [Lyman] Gilbert + I are studing Phonography [stenography?] when we get time. (which is not very plenty) I like it pretty well and can write it some but not very fast. you know that Mr Pickard wanted us to learn it. Snell can write it as fast, nearly as a man can talk. he offeres to learn us for nothing if we want. I dont know but you will think that I had better learn to write long hand first. my fingers are so cold now that I can hardly hold my pen. it rain hard and the tent has wet through and leaks some, besides my cloths are wet through, and we have no fires as it is warm most of the time. I have got a very good pen now a Gold pen and Silver holder and so has [Lyman] Gilbert, [William J.] Haskell, [M. P.] Snell. I like to write first rate and can write much better and easier when I take panes, than I could. I should like to hear from Mr Tinkhams folk very well, and know whare the boys are. Thare is not much more of importance that I will write this time, although thare is much more that I could, and if I could see you, I could tell you much more. we are closely inspected now when we go on Guard or Picket. yestoday morning we were inspected 4 times that is Guns + E[q]uipments and have to have our boots blacked and look as slick as though we were going to Church or Mass. I suppose that Doc Tyler has got home. he is sick. I did not know that he was going until he had gone. Our Chaplain went with him, they say, but I hadn't missed him. I think thare are some things about this war that looks encouraging and others that look dark, but I cannot but think that it will be brought to a close before another winter. I hope so at any rate. write often and remember me to the friends.

Yours P. Affect George W.

Newport News Va. March 17 [1863]

Dear Friends,

I received a letter from you night before last. I received one from Andrew and Aunt [Anna L.] Bartlett [Allen] at the same time. perhaps I never told you that I wrote to her sometime ago. I thought it might please her. I also received one from Uncle Joseph [Harwood] a few days before. he seemed to be very glad that I wrote to him and wanted me to write again. he said that he would like to see me out West. he said that when this war first broke out he had a idea of enlisting but that he had given up long ago, as the hardships of camplife were more than he wanted to encounter. I guess by what he said that he isn't doing much this winter. he didnt say any thing about his wife or family. I do not feel much like writing to day I am not drilling today but am on water duty. every day they detail 2 men to bring water for the cooks. it is about as far as from our house to the head of the lane. it is warm and pleasant today but yestoday + day before were cold dreary days we had a heavy frost this morning or rather last night. The Officers horses have to be guarded nights and night before last I had to go on at half-past 7 and stand until 11, 3 1/2 hours I had 7 horses another fellow had 4 another 3 it commenced raining about 1/2 past 9 and rained hard most of the night. the other fellows got pretty wet but I got in between two horses that had a little shelter over them and did not get much wet. I tell the boys that I know when it is going to rain, for it hasn't failed raining for 2 month but once when I go on. the weather hear is quite changable it may look pleasant in the morning and rain before night or when you go to bed at night the moon and stars shine but before morning rain hard and clear off again. Louis had a letter last night from home. he says that he has a box coming and something for me. I shall be glad to receive it. Lo-[Louis] is as fat as a pig and stands it better than I expected. I suppose that you remember about the frigate Cumberland. she was sunk about a year ago. we can just see her mast. thare are several old [w]recks in sight. thare are quite a number of Gun boats right hear in sight. I think 2 Moniters. The boys are building a frame to put a wreath on in the front of the center of company the width of the street which is about the width of any common road. we have got little trees stuck into the ground each side of each street, and things look pretty nice. I hope that we shall stay hear all summer. the Offisers are having furloughs right along and some privates in other regiments and I am hoping that we shall have a chance pretty soon, but perhaps not privates arnt of much account any way. I am glad that Andrew [Jackson] is having such a good time and hope that he will get his furlough extended or a discharge I am glad that Allen goes around some. I should have laughed to see Allen, Ellen and Jonas + Emma I should think that they would get lost in the sleigh. Docs Father expect that Judson [Adams] will stay thare another year. the first of April is very close at hand. will Bush stay with E. D. Knight. I suppose that Mr Cunningham doesn't say any thing about buying the Sargent place. I do not think of any thing that I will write this time. I dont think our army is doing much any whare at the present time, and the prospect is quite dark for a settlement at present. Is it so? Snell had some books come to him yestoday that he sent for to give to the little black children. we went over to one of the houses and gave three little boys some, and they were very much pleased. we are going again tonight. write often and remember [me] to the friends

                Yours with love [some sort of symbols xoxo?]

The Frigate USS Cumberland was sunk by CSS Virginia (Merrimac) on March 8, 1862.

I did not have time to mail this letter at Newport News. We left Sunday afternoon. I am now sailing down the River Ohio and will mail this at Cincinnati
Ohio with money. I will write again soon. March 27th

Newport News Va. March 21 [1863]

Dear Friends,

I have just received a letter from you and also a paper with black
pepper. I am very glad to receive them and been expecting a letter for a
day or two. I sent a letter to Freeman yestoday but have not heard from
him for some time. Lyman had a box come last night which started last
Tuesday not quite 4 days. Louis expected his but it did not come 4 or 5
boxes were stolen at the landing when they were unloaded, by the 27 New
Jersey Reg. perhaps that was one of them but we do not know. I have
drawn a pair of socks and can get along very well for a while if those you
sent do not come I bought a quire of paper of Lyman and wrappers to go
with them, at the same time I can use more as I have got several letters to
answer and I intend to write more. I live [like] to write and can write much
faster and easier then when I left home. Our things are packed up and we
expect to move, and have expected to for several days we are liable to
move any moment. we should have gone before if it had not stormed so. it
commenced snowing day before yestoday and has snowed and hailed +
rained ever since and has not cleared off yet. our orders are to start when it
stops storming. we are going to Baltimore and from there to Tennessee to
join Genl Rosecrans army, so report says. if that is true we shall of course
have a rough time among the hill + mountains. we may well expect long
hard marches and perhaps desperate fighting, be that as it may. we are in
good heart now and I think pretty well prepaired for either. thare are quite
a number of men in our hospitals hear very lame with the rheumatism
some have been discharged, and more ought to be. I have not been to the
Surgeon but once since I left Worcester, and then I was not not very sick
then, but I did not feel much like going picket that morning Lyman has
not been either. he is better than when he was at home, and fleshy he
treated us on his wifes [Mary] broken hearts + amputated fingers which
she sent in his box. he was very glad to get it. Louis is fat and weighs 171
lb. with overcoat on. You asked me Mother if I had written an answer to
Mrs Bush's. I have not answered it yet but intend to she wrote me a good
letter. I consider her a very fine woman. I think that I wrote in my last that

I had received a letter from Uncle Joseph. Anna have you ever written to Mr Tinkhams people I should be glad to hear from them. I am intending to write to Henry + Harry [Harwood] when I get time. Have any of you seen Doc Tyler since he got home. I heard from him today by the way of Haskells wife [Orril]. did any of you see our Chaplain or hear him preach. I understand that he preached a sermon to the people of N. Brookfield. I hope that they were interested. I saw our Chaplain when he came back and that is all I have seen or heard from him since. he makes a very good postmaster. Mr Cheaver [Cheever] is not very well he is most to old for a soldier this sleeping on the ground is pretty hard business for the men. we all feel it more or less. I get up some of these cold damp mornings rather stiff. the rheumatism troubles me in the back and knees, but not much. we shall be old men before we know it. I am very glad that Andrew has got his furlough extended I wish he could get a discharge and have it done with. I think he will never be fit for a soldier, but hope he will get over it. it does seem bad that so many should get crippled for life, but if I get out of this with one leg or one arm I shall concider myself comparatively lucky. I hope to get home safe and sound and feel almost sure that I shall. I feel perfectly safe and did in the affairs at Fredericksburg. (another sheet) Sunday morning. I did not have time to finish my letter last night and have a little time just now. it has cleared off. nothing has been said about moving. Father did you ever know Elijah Dean of Oakham he is dead I believe now. he had two boys in Co K. 36th about 19 + 21 years old. they are both dead now. the youngest one fell behind the regiment on our marches and said he was going back to a hospitals a few miles back. he was sick, but he has never been seen and a body was found side of the road I understand near whare he stopped. marching hurts men more than any thing else, without it is the bullet. I understand that it is good sleighing in Mass. it is very sloppy hear. this snow is not going to last any hear. it is a fine time to snow ball and the boys are improving it, without any regard to the day of the week <u>as usual</u>. I am very glad that Father has let the Sargent place, although it does not pay the interest. who pays the <u>taxes</u>, which of course will be several dollars. I feel just now more encouraged about the affairs of our country, than I have been for a long time before. I do think that this war will be brought to a close before many months. I dont know as thare is any one thing in particular that I think of, but things pretty generaly look favorably. I expect to see some hard fighting first however. It is reported hear that we are going to be paid off soon or by the time we get to Balti-more, up to the first of March I hope we shall if so I intend to have my picture taken if I can get a good chance. George T. Fisher of East Brook-field was over hear last Sunday from Fortress Monroe. he is not enlisted but is a clerk in a Clothing department he is about my age, and appears very Gentlemanly. he came out about the same time I did. Father how is your arm now it used to be lame is it any better or does it grow worse. Mother are you as well as you was when I left. I often think of you and your suffering and wish that I could do some thing for you. I dont think of anything more to write this time although I could fill several pages if I had time. I should be glad to see you all and think I could talk some. I dont know as you can read this as I am pretty much crowded and doubled up, and am a poor writer at the best. I was glad to receive those stamps as I had borrowed several and had none.

This from your true son + brother,
George W. Harwood

Postal stationery wrappers were issued by the Post Office from 1861-1934. They were sheets of paper large enough for wrapping a folded or rolled newspaper and were imprinted with prepaid postage. It seems they may have been used to wrap letters as well as newspapers. Elijah Dean's sons, Daniel W. and his brother Isaiah from Oakham, Massachusetts served with the Massachusetts Thirty-sixth Regiment.

OHIO

ILLINOIS

INDIANA

Ohio River

Covington, KY ●

● Vincennes, IN

Centralia, IL ●

Jeffersonville, IN ●● Louisville, KY

● Lexington, KY

● Nicholasville, KY

● Cairo, IL
Mississippi River

KENTUCKY

MISSOURI

Island Number 10
(New Madrid, MO) ●

ARKANSAS

● Memphis, TN

TENNESSEE

MISSISSIPPI

Yazoo River

● Canton, MS

● Snyders Bluffs, Milldale, MS
(present day Redwood)
Big Black River
● Vicksburg, MS ● Jackson, MS

ALABAMA

Southern Railroad of Mississippi
(line runs east west through Jackson and Vicksburg)
Great Northern Railroad
(line runs north south through Canton and Jackson)

~ Chapter 5 ~

TO KENTUCKY
March 30 - May 18, 1863

Statue of Henry Clay, Lexington Cemetery, Lexington, Kentucky
(Photo by author)

Lexington Ky March 30 [1863]

Dear Friends

It is pretty cold today but I will try to write a few lines but perhaps not finish my letter. One week ago I was 1000 miles from hear. we left Newport News Sunday afternoon [March 22] went on board of the Kenebec and reached Baltimore before daylight Tuesday morning we stayed on board until afternoon then we took the cars, for we knew not whare. we stopped at Harpers Ferry in the morning and took hot coffee + soft bread which was waiting for us. we run to Cumberland and took supper on coffee + bread as before. the next morning we stopped at Grafton and got bread + coffee we reached Parkersburg just before dark whare we unloaded and took the Steamer Boston and got coffee + hard-tack. we left late in the evening. at daylight we had gone nearly 100 miles. we passed by several very pleasant places such as Portsmouth, Mayville &c we reached Cincinnati just before dark, but did not get off. in the morning we crossed over to Covington and marched up to the Depot a mile or so, and waited until nearly dark for the train to come to take us to Lexington the distance is about 90 miles which we run in the night. the next morning we unloaded, stacked arms, and waited for further orders, which came soon after noon when we marched up into a very fine pasture near by and pitched tents, and are expecting to stop for a while as we hear that Col. Leasure commander of the brigade has command of this post. We had a very pleasant trip although rather hard + tiresome, as our accommadations were rather poor. in the cars we were packed in so thickly that we could not all lay down, and freight cars at that. From Harpers Ferry to Parkersburg the country is very Mountainous and rocky. we passed through some 20 tunnels and some of them were long ones. the people ran out of every hut + house and waved their hats and handkerchief and appeared glad to see us. the land is much better than in eastern Va. As we passed down the river ohio we had a good chance to see the land on both sides, and the inhabitance ran out and waved their handkerchiefs and Union flags particularly the women. the land on both sides is <u>very</u> good and hear in Ky. it is first rate - I think I should like to live hear in times of peace. They have got a beautiful Cemetary hear in Lexington in which are many fine monuments and among them is that of Henry Clay. I think that it is not all marble. it is said to be 132 ft in Height about 45 ft ~~in width~~ square at the bace.

the cost is said to be about 50,000 dollars. the the statue on top I think must be marble and is 15 ft in he[i]ght. it is in plain sight of this camp ground. Thare are a good many secesh hear they say. the Rebel Genl. Preston house is ~~in~~ close by, and Col Morgans he belongs to a band of Gurillars, Gen Breckenridge and other noted rebel officers. thare is a large Insane Asylum within a few rods of our camp. The sine of Abel Harwood dealer in boots + shoes can be seen. it has never been taken down. I have not seen it myself but Haskell has. a citizen told him that he did not know whare Harwood was but had heard that he was dead. ~~thare can be no mistake as to~~ Whare does Mr Young live that married ~~Lucretia~~ ~~Lucricha~~ Lucrictia Tomblin [Lucrctia Tomblen]. is it not in Georgetown Ky. that is ~~6~~ 12 miles from hear. if she is thare I should like to see her. I write in such a hurry today that I make a good many mistakes and some pretty poor spelling. I did not intend to give you much of a discraption of our trip from Newport News to Lexington that would take to long, only a few particulars. It is sadning to see how little control some men have over themselves. at Baltimore a good many of our men got drunk, and some fot their Officers so that they had to be tied and others guarded. at Cincinnati some went ashore in the evening and come back or rather were brought back by the guard before morning dead drunk, and some were left at these places drunk and couldn't be found. at Covington whiskey was as free as water and as we had to lay thare a good part of the day a great many of our men got dead drunk I think that perhaps full 1/2 half of our regt drank some, and several in each company got clear down. it took about all the sober ones to take care of the drunken ones, privates, Corporals and sargents were all aligk [alike?]. thare was a good breakfast provided for us at Cincinnati, but the soldiers acted so bad in other regiments that had landed that we could not go and get it. when <u>we</u> stop in a place it is no uncommon thing to see a man rolling around in the mud utterly helpless, or to see one Officer leading a man back to his company One ~~of~~ man in our Company got so drunk in each of these three places that couldn't go alone, and took several to handle him. at one time it took two men to guard him with guns. at another 3 or 4 could hardly keep him in the cars, so that the Captain had to take hold himself. he is a young man about 21, naturly bright + smart. another man about the same age in another Co. acted so bad that the Col. himself took him down in a hurry. thare are several in regt little boys 16 or 17, 2 or 3 of those were so bad that they couldn't help themselves at all.

Last night one company had 4 men under guard for the same offence. it is sickning to me to see such work, but this drinking is not confined to the men. the Officers do the same thing although not so openly. I have never seen any of the officers in our regt drunk, but I have seen them when a little more would have tipped them over. a man told me that he saw one of our Docters drink 9 times in one afternoon. I dont write this for you to tell off but mearly that you may know what soldiers do, and the influence which surround them. I had rather you would not ~~share~~ speak of these things to any outside as I am not in the habit of reporting the ill conduct of any of my fellow soldiers. I could write many more things equily as bad that have transperied [transpired] in days before will not and perhaps I have written already too much, but a man is not fit for a Soldier if he does not use tobacco, drink whiskey, play cards, and use profane language. many a night have I been to bed when the occupants of the tents around were playing cards and swaring, and on board the boats, one night in particular whare 3 or 4 groups of men + boys with [several illegible words crossed out] 3 or 4 in each group were playing + cussing when I went to sleep, on each side of me, but these things and such men have nothing to do with me nor I with them. Whiskey + Cards have been passed to me but I couldn't see the point as we say. We are expecting a mail as we have been down for a week or more, and we have come to a stopping place. they say that we shall get paied off soon. I hope we shall. you will direct to me as usual unless I write to the contery I sent a letter to you from Cincinnati which I wrote in Newport News. this a long letter and so are all that I write to you. Wheelocks box came to him on board the boat but Louis has not got his yet. Lyman was left back on duty at Newport News, to help load + unload baggage and he has not come up yet we expect ~~him~~ them soon thare was 10 in each company. remember me to all the friends. I guess I shall write to Aunt Lucrucia [Lucretia] if I ever get time.

Yours Affect George W Harwood

The Lexington Cemetery has the graves of many of Lexington's citizens and distinguished social and political families. One section is the National Cemetery for Union soldiers. Next to it is a section for Confederate soldiers. In most places cemeteries do not have both Union and Confederate soldiers. George's Great Uncle Abel Harwood had moved from North Brookfield to Lexington, Kentucky in the early 1850s where he had a boot and shoe store. At this time, he was living in Bloomington, Illinois. Lucretia W. (Tomblen) Young is the granddaughter of

Jonas and Lucretia (Winslow) Harwood of North Brookfield. They are referred to often in the letters as Uncle Jonas and Aunt Lucretia. Granddaughter Lucretia married Daniel P. Young. She and Daniel are buried in the Lexington, Kentucky Cemetery.

Camp Dick Robinson [Lancaster, Kentucky]
Apr 10 [1863]

Dear Friends

I should have written to you nearly a week ago but have been so busy that I couldn't. Last Sunday afternoon we had to pack up and go to Covington as thare was to be an Election in Cincinnati the next day, and they expected trouble but as it happened all passed off quietly. H. P. Wilkes of Boston was in Cincinnati at the time and he came over to see us he brought pies + cakes to us and as it was a cold chily day and poor rations his treat was very acceptable. He looks just as he used to. Hear Doc Tyler camc to us and we were very glad indeed to see him we ~~came~~ started back to Lexington ~~Monda~~ Tuesday morning. Wednesday morning we left Lexington and reached Nicholasville just before dark. after we had fallen into line in Lexington Mr Young + wife [Lucretia Tomblen] drove up, hearing that we were thare came to see us. they look natural we saw only one minute thay told us to go to his Fathers in N-[Nicholasville] and we did so, and had a good time a good supper. Louis I couldn't find so he didn't go. they appear like good folks. the next morning we started again and came through to hear, Camp Dick Robinson a distance of 15 mile, about 27 from Lexington, and Lexington is 99 miles from Covington, which we rode in the cars and Covington is just across the Ohio River, near opposite Cincinnati. I dont know how long we shall stay hear, only a few days I think. they say that we shall have our pay this afternoon or to-morrow we have had no mail since we left Newport News. we are very impatient our feet are all blistered and we are lame and stiff I never felt so miserable in my life. I never fell out on a march in my life until yesterday. I couldnt go I put my knapsack on ~~the~~ a waggon, and then I could hardly move, so I told a teamster that he mint go on foot and let me drive his team. he did and so I mounted a mule and drove the team of four mules the rest of the way 5 or 6 miles I think. Louis and the rest of boys got ~~on~~ (as many as could) on the waggons. we got hear at last a ~~d~~ tired lot of us. I never was so near used up in my life, as I feel now. I hope this war will close soon some how. if I could get a little rest I should feel better I think. I reckon that if I were a commissioned officer I should resign at once, but I suppose that thare is a good time coming if I only wait a little longer. when I enlist for a Soldier again I shall be older. some think that they shall get home in 6 or 8 months, and I hope we shall. I almost wish that I was in the 42nd and run my risk at that. I would like to give 200 or 300 dollars if I have it, to be my own man again. The Farmers hear are busy ploughing they have got about ready to plant. I like to see them plough hear with 2 horses or mules on a plough some have 5 teams in one field. I like this State so far first rate, and think I should like to live hear. Thare is much that I could write if I had time I should like to see you and if I ever do I presume I shall talk some. I am very anxious to have a mail from home. Doc Tyler asked me the other day how I liked this life. I told him he ~~must~~ mint make out my discharge and I would go home. They say that we shall have to go on 125 miles or more to Cumberland Gap I think that we shall have a rough time this summer some hard marches. then men are not used so well as mules hear in the army and the quicker a man gets out of it the better. I hope you will write often and I shall do the same. Uncle Sam has caried us about conciderable the past 2 or 3 weeks and now we have got to cary ourselves, but never mind. When we got hear last night thare was only 6 men to stack arms in Co. E. and the other compansni [companies] about the same. I will not write any more this time. my head aches and I am going to lay down. Whare is Andrew. do you hear any thing from Free-man. Remember me to the friends as usual

Yours Affect George W. Harwood

~~Thare~~ You will direct to me differently

George W. Harwood

Co. E. 36th Reg. Mass. Vol.

Burnsides Department

Via Cincinnati.

It beets all how many liquor shops thare are all along the road hear in Ky. every day some body gets intoxecated yesterday and day before I saw lay-ing beside the rode I should think 6 or 8 men strung along beside the rode, some fighting their Officers and other[s] to drunk to. it is very warm hear today the roads are very hard + dusty. I think thare are good many Sesesh hear in Kentucky and thare are some good Union people. One thing I dont like and that is the Hogs run in the streets in all the Southern + Western

Cities + ~~Towns~~. Thay have warm weather hear in the day time and cold damp nights. you know I have been talking about going West I begin to think I am going don't you, but before I forget it The graves of William + Loren Ranger are in Lexington I suppose that you knew that they were dead. One of the DeLands I think his name is Charles lives in Lexington but I didn't seen him. I wish we could have ~~seen~~ staid thare in L.[Lexington] and done provost duty. Thare are a good many Mass people in Cincinnati. If I ever get home I can tell you more than I can write I have a chance to see a good deal in my travels but I have to pay pretty dear for some of my sights. I should lik[e] to have uncle Sam take me down to New Orleans and back and show me the Country and take me home as soon as he can make it convenient. [M. P.] Snell thinks we shall get home in 6 months. I dont. do you? I didnt think of writing only one sheet but I hardly know when to stop, when I am writing home Who caries on the Adam [Adams] place this year?
　　　　　　George W.

Camp Dick Robinson was a temporary camp situated on the Robinson Farm and used mostly for recruiting. It was later replaced by Camp Nelson at the end of a railroad line just south of Lexington, Kentucky. President Lincoln would have liked to send troops through the Cumberland Gap to Knoxville, Tennessee but did not have the resources to do this yet. Freeman Doane was in the Massachusetts Forty-second (nine month) Regiment. The $200 or $300 George would like would pay for a substitute to serve in his place.

　　　　　　　　　　　Camp Dick Robinson
　　　　　　　　　　　Apr. 11th [1863]

Dear Friends,

　　　　I have just received a mail of 4 letters and 3 papers 2 of the letters were from home. Mother spoke of sending a paper with pepper and another with ginger. I received the one with pepper. I suppose that it is not lawful to send such things in paper nor over 3 words in writing, besides the mail to cheer us the paymaster is around and handed me 52.00. I have got a check of 40.00, and if I want to send any more I will send the money at some other time. I was very glad to receive the mail + money. when I got up this morning I felt sick and have not felt very well all day but feel a little better tonight. I have had little or no appitat [appetite] for a week past. I had some beens [beans] for dinner and have got some apples for supper It is quite warm hear much warmer than it was a few days ago. I guess my bowels are a little out of tune, but I guess I shall be all wright in a few days. you said that Freeman spoke about the drunkenness of the Soldiers + Officers in New Orleans. every day I see men drunk, and yesterday and today they have had a man hand-cuffed to a large battery wheel. he got drunk and charged bayonets on his Lieut. and now they have got paid off they will drink worse than ever. I wrote a letter to you and sent to you yesterday and wrote most of the news of importance. I expect we shall move from hear before many days perhaps tomorrow as it is Sunday and that is the day for Army opperations. I think that the prospects look dark for a speedy close of this war the boys are some of them quite discouraged and begin to think that they shall have to stay with U.S. their three years out. others are more hopeful, and I am among that number. thare is a great deal said in the papers about the sufferings ~~in~~ of the women + children in the rebel states, and of the neckedness + filthiness of the sesech soldiers. I know this to be a fact nearly every day while we were in Lexington our army brought in reb. priseners and they were filthy, ragged fellows, the worst looking soldiers that I have seen since I came out and I have see[n] conciderable many. they used to take several hundred at a time, and thare are loads of starving women and children coming in to ~~the~~ the larger places ev[e]ry day for food, coming of the mountains whare they have been hiding. many of these newspaper reports I know to be true, and some I presume, yes, I know to be ~~fake~~ faults [false] but I will not dwell upon this subject longer. I see many sad sights that I have not time to mention if I would. I shouldn't be surprised if we were called into battle before long we are liable to at least, but be that as it may, I do not fear any thing. if we have got any fighting to do I want to do it and then if spared return home, whare I may enjoy a good deal, but I hope that if I am not permitted to, I may enjoy a great deal more in a mansion which my Saviour has prepared for me in his Heavenly Kingdom, seen the trials of life will be over and we shall be at ease in a better world I hope. If it were not for that hope I dont know what I should do. As Mr Cheaver [Cheever] says, no cross, no crown, but it is getting dark and will close and will write again ~~tomor~~ soon. I write in my letter yesterday how to direct to me I will write again for fear you may not get that.

Co. E. 36 Reg. Mass. Vol.
Burnsides Department

Via Cincinnati

write often and I will do the same. I intend to write to Freeman tomorrow. I will write to Allen + Fannie soon

This from your son + brother George W Harwood

April 18 '63

Dear Brother Allen

As I have a little time I will write a few lines to you. how are you these days and what are you doing. farmers hear are ploughing and getting to plant what has Father got to do his ploughing with this spring a pair of short-horns as usial. I suppose that Addisons mule has gone hasn't he. do you remember that I wrote in a letter when I was in Pleasant Valley that they had shaved a boys head and were then drumming him through the camp for stealing money. he had the word thief pin[n]ed on his back. he has been stealing money and buying whiskey, ~~in the Capt~~ and he is now going through the camp with a hole cut through the top of a barrel large enough to put his head through and rest on his shoulders with the word, thief on the barrel. he is under guard. this is the third offence that he has been under guard for, but he dont care much about it. he is about 18 years old. they have got 3 men arrested for getting drunk and then going to sleep on their beet while on guard they have got hand-cuffs on and to ~~the~~ a wheel. thare is a very heavy battery carriage down beside the Col. tent and all who get drunk or insult their officers or any thing of the kind, have to join that battery, and there are a good number of them, some days 6 or 8. intemperence and other vices abound among the soldiers. how does that colt do I hope that Father will keep her until I get home. I believe that I shall bring a mule with me when I come. I dont know as you or any body else can read this the boys are all talking, and I have got my knees about as high as my head.   Good Bye   George W. Harwood

Apr 18th [1863]
Camp Dick Robinson

Dear Friends,

I have just had my picture in 2 postures so that you can see which you like best they are rather dark, and in fact I am badly tanned. the 2 cost 1.25. I will send them in 2 different letters, and shall start them both today if nothing happens. I received a letter from home and one from Freeman night before last. You spoke of receiving a letter from me mailed at Lexington but nothing about the one I mailed at Cincinnati ~~and~~ which I wrote in Newport News the day I started, March 22nd I got the paper with pepper. you will not need to send any more pepper nor ginger as I dont use them so much and have a supply, on hand. I have never heard any thing from my box but can get along well without it. I have yarn left yet. I wrote to Aunt Lucretia a day or two ago. In my last letter dated 11th I sent a check of 40 dollars which I hope you have got. Addison is not with us and I dont know whare he is. I have not heard from him for some time. I should think that Aunt Phebe [Jackson] would feel greatly releaved now his [Addison's] wife is out of the neighborhood. We are having very fine warm weather hear now and things look nicely. we received a company letter from Mr. Tomblin [Orin A. Tomblen] telling whare his Daughter [Lucretia W. Tomblen Young] was and whare his (Mr Youngs) Father [Robert Young] lived, but we had got ahead of his times. we have to have a pass signed by the Col before we can go for water or any whare else we are under very close restrictions, on account of some few the whole Reg has to suffer. four men have had their heads shaved and hand-cuffed together and then to a battery-wheel for ~~sleeping~~ getting drunk and then going to sleep while on guard and at their post. another for stealing has carried a barrel on his shoulders 3 or 4 days this is the third offence of the same crime. once before he had his head shaved and drummed through camp but all this does no good as he is past shame. he is about 18 years old. 8 more are under arrest for gambling I guarded them one day, and several others for different offences. Louis had his picture taken the same as I and sent them yesterday I think that they are good ones. Lyman [Gilbert] had his taken in Covington sitting and hear standing, so that you will know how Soldiers look. I am coming home next fall if nothing happens, or rather somthing happens. it is the opinion of some hear among us soldiers + citizens that this war will play out before many months perhaps it will, I hope so, but fear not. They have had our address changed I wrote you before but not right please direct

Co. E 36th Reg. Mass Vols.
1st Div. 9th Army Corps
Via Cincinnati

Enstead of by Washington, but they will come either way, Via Cincinnati a little quicker they say. I have nothing of much importance to write more, but I have <u>got</u> a very hard headache to day for the first time for some time. perhaps my pictures show it my face is very red and the pictures look black. I blacked my boots but not my face as the sitting picture indicates. Freeman seems to be in good spirits and I am glad he is. I wrote to him a few days ago. I have written a little [to] Allen which I will send with one picture. I will write to Fannie when I get more time. have you read about the drying up of a spring near Fredericksburg Va. I presume you have. I believe in it. do you? I have got nearly out of postage stamps again as I had [written] a good many [letters] lately. please buy me another Quarters worth and send as soon as you can make it convenient. remember me to all the friends and write often. a letter from home is cheering. Snell tents with our orderly sergent and one of his colledge chums as he did when he first came out before he was sick as four is about enough for one tent and he was an odd one.

Yours Affect. George W Harwood

Louis D. Winslow
(Tintype and photo in author's collection)   *George W. Harwood*

The picture of Louis Winslow is the one referred to in the letter. The picture of George was taken later when he was a sergeant. Aunt Phebe was George's father's sister, who married William C. Jackson.

Camp Dick Robinson 1863
near Bryantville Ky. Apr. 22nd

Dear Friends,

I will commence a letter to you althoug[h] I do not intend to finish it today. I sent a letter to you only last Saturday and my pictures with it. Saturday is the afternoon I began to feel sick and dizzy and went into my tent and laid down the next morning I went to the Surgeons he told me that I had got a hard cold and must be careful or I should have a Fever I was very feverish at that time. he gave me some ~~physee~~ salts, and then some powders I have not done any duty since. today I feel quite lonely as nearly all the regiment have gone out as we expect a scouting expedition they took most all the men that were able ~~that were~~ to go the Col wanted no others but what could stand a long march. It is warm and very pleasant. Every thing looks beautiful the trees are leaving out. the peach trees are in blosom. the grass is green and shining. When a man feels sick he will think of home and almost wish that he had never enlisted. if wishing had done any good I should have [been] at home several days ago. a board for a sick man is a hard bed you know.

Thursday. I will write a little more today. it is cooler today and begins to rain. the weather changes very sudden hear we have April showers quite often. everything is in a thriving condition. We have got 2 more regiments in our brigade now. the 27 Mich. and 8 Tenn. so that it makes a large brigade. thare are a good many troops near us who belong to this Div. it seems to be the opinion of citizens hear that the war will not last a great while longer, and I am trying to think so too. I feel a little better to day than I did yesterday but have a small appitite. I had left off my under shirts and was wondering what I should do with them as I couldnt cary them very well. when a chap came along and gave me 1.50 for them. I gladly let them slide.

Saturday - I guess I will finish this letter this morning. I received a letter from home last night. I am feeling better than when I commenced this letter but do not feel well. I am glad that Andrew has got his furlough extended but it seems foolish not to give him a discharge and [be] done with it. I'm sorry that Fathers arm is so sore and lame. I wonder how much rent Mr Parkman expects to get out of his tenents   what will Charles do when he comes back (but he hasn't got thare yet). I understand that cattle are very high in Mass. how is that? Whare is Harrison Brewer now I haven't heard any thing about him for a long time the last that I heard from him he was at Fort Warren. I spoke about the boys going off they have got back all right I dont know what they went for. I have written in several letters how to direct to me they will come any way and you may direct as you please they will come by the way Cincinnati quicker than by Washington. Kentucky is a beautiful farming country and thare are some good people hear. they all talk differently from us at the North. the other day a large Omnibus full of Ladies came from Danville up to see us thare was 28 or 30 of them Danville is about 10 miles from hear. I have a chance to see a great deal hear in the army but when we come to march it takes all the fun off. I will write a little on another sheet to Allen. write often and all the news.

> This from your affectionate son and brother.
> George W Harwood

April 25th [1863]

Dear brother Allen,

I found a sheet in my last letter from you I am glad that you can write so well, and hope that you will write often. can you read my writing yourself or does Anna have to pick it out for you. Allen do you remember a boy by the name of Adams that used to live with Mr Spooner and run away with Bill Jones. he went to school to Anna one Summer. he is hear in the 36 I did not know it until yesterday he was telling that he knew Doc Tyler before he came out and I asked him whare [he] lived and then he told me. he is a trifle nut I guess. I bought me a watch yesterday and sold it again before night made 1.50 cent in about one hour. I dont like this paper it dont write good this paper is intended for short hand and is fit for nothing else. tell father not to sell that colt if it is a good one. I should think you would get sick of rabbits + doves as you did not have very good luck last year. I should have thought father would have used that horse of Addisons instead of bill. Our whole regiment have got white gloves and at night when we go on dress parade we ware them, and black our boots, and polish our brasses and look quite slick. we live mostly on peas and pork the bread that we draw is so sour that the hogs wont eat it. I live on Ginger bread mostly. I will write again soon. write often.

From your affectionate brother
George W. Harwood
(hear is a ring that you may have if you want.)

Anna taught school probably during 1857-1859. Bill was a horse. The Adams boy could be Joseph P. Adams, who served in the Massachusetts Twenty-first, Thirty-sixth, and Fifty-sixth Regiments as a musician. He was from West Brookfield. George was writing on a pad of lined paper which measures 5 x 7 3/4 inches, smaller than his usual stationery.

[Undated fragment, not on lined paper, possibly sent with the April 25 letter to Allen.]

Last night we had a Brigade Dress Parade and were intending to have a Brigade Review + Inspection ~~with~~ of Guns + Accoutrments also Knapsacks, Haversacks + Canteens, but it is so rainy that we cannot. I suppose that before this you have got the picture I sent you of myself. You can fill my Album with ~~them~~ my own picture if you dont have enough of your own. good Bye for this morning

Ever Aff. Yours
George W. Harwood

~~April 28th~~
~~Camp Dick Robinson~~
Stanford Ky. May 1st '63

Dear Friends

I came off picket Wednesday morning and found a letter for me from home. We had a dispatch about midnight that [we] might to go on and reenforce Gen. Carter. we left in the morning about 7 o'clock and marched on to Stanford a distance of 18 miles, got hear about 5 o'clock P.M. I guess we shall not go on today, not before afternoon any way, as we have just had orders to cook 2 days rations. Over-coats and clothing ~~was~~ are of very little account on a march most of them threw them away. I shall not cary my Overcoat much farther it is so warm. Yesterday was fast day I suppose, and I thought we went pretty <u>fast</u> some of the way. you asked in your letter who went to Mr. Youngs with me Doc. Tyler the Chaplain, Snell, Haskell + Wheelock. the Doc + Chaplain staid over night. I wrote a letter to Aunt Lucretia [Harwood] a while ago I wonder if she ever got it. Lucretia [Tomblen Young, her granddaughter] knew me as quick as I told her my name but not before she said that I looked like the Harwoods a little. old Mr Youngs folks fancied they saw a look about me like the Harwoods you know they have seen Abel and Mr [Orin A.]Tomblen + Lucretia. Mrs Young [Lucretia Tomblen] said she thought every thing of Mrs Abel Harwood [Mary D. Batcheller] almost as much as a sister. they used to visit often. Lucretia seems to think [illegible] of this country and so do I. it is decidedly beautiful. everything is lovely. it is very warm today the sun is burning hot. I did not intend to finish this letter today in fact I think we shall leave before night.

> Sunday noon
> Middleburg May 3rd

We left Stanford about 2 o'clock Friday afternoon and reached Hustonville about 6 o'clock a distance of 10 mile and stopped over night and started at one o'clock the next afternoon and reached hear about 6 or 6 1/2 o'clock last night about 10 miles more. this is just no place at all very few buildings but good land. Our last marches were short but rather hard and quite warm. most of the boys stood it first rate but it came tough for me I was very tired + foot sore. I have seen a family of East Tenneseeeans this morning that fled from their homes to save their lives. more than a year ago a man, wife, three girls and one boy the man has been wounded and one of his daughters had her eye put out with a rebs bayonet trying to save ~~his~~ her fathers life. She is a beautiful looking young lady about 20 years old. they told a long sad story which we have reason to believe is true. I received a letter from Aunt Lucretia yesterday was glad to hear from her we are now about 65 miles from Lexington. we expect to go tomorrow today it is warm and showery and we are in a rather muddy place. I dont know as I see any signs of crushing this rebellion at present some are hopeful and others are gloomy Lyman says that I look upon the dark side and I tell him he looks upon the bright side altogether if he thinks we shall get home in 4 or 5 months, but I shouldnt think strange if we get into a fight before many weeks and go home by that way. Im getting rather tired of carting my house and furniture and tools all on my back. it makes me think of the Italian organ grinders I used to see around home. how is Andrew [Jackson] I have been expecting a letter from him for some time. I have not had one from Freeman for a long time, but I will close for now.

> good bye
> Yours &c
> George W Harwood

East Tennessee is in the Confederacy but about half the people there are Union sympathizers. The area is near Knoxville and was occupied throughout the war by opposing sides. At this time, the Confederacy was occupying Knoxville and many citizens had fled.

Camp Near Middleburg May 7th '63

Dear Friends

I have just received a letter from you dated April 27th stating that you had received my letter with my pictures. I am glad that [they] reached home safely. this is a cold rany day and not very pleasant writing as my fingers are rather cold + stiff. since I last wrote which was last Sunday I we have moved our camp, Monday I think about a mile and while moving we were caught in a heavy shower which wet us through in good shape. I dont know when we shall move from hear as I understand that we are not wanted at present to reenforce Gen Carter, but I suppose that we are to keep in supporting distance. I had rather go into a fight than take many hard marches. marching is the worst part of Soldiering for me. I expected to get a letter from Father this time but did not. is he able to write or is his arm so lame that he cannot use it. I should think that he would want a pair of old oxen to do his work with as he is getting old and lame. The news has just come into camp that Hooker has captured Lees army, and how the boys did cheer and hurrah. I had heard of the death of Mrs Wright. she was very low last fall when we left you know. I have received the letter from Aunt Lucretia [Harwood] was very glad to get it. I am very glad to receive the present from Ellen R. Doane and will answer it perhaps to her directly. The ~~War~~ war news is quite encouraging now and I earnestly hope that the time will soon come when men will learn to war no more, when rebbellion will cease to exist, when peace and prosperity shall again bless our land as in years gone by, and the stars and stripes again float over land and water throughout these once United States, and that we may be again a happy and united people, a <u>peculiar</u> people whare <u>God</u> is the <u>Lord</u>. You at the North have great reason to be thankful that you are so far from the scen[e]s of strife, and that the hand of destruction has not swept from you the comforts of this life, like as ~~they~~ it has hear or farther south. I would that you could travel through Virginia and other parts of the south, and sea the ruins caused by this war. <u>War will end</u> and our cause <u>will</u> come off <u>tri-</u><u>umphant</u>. it may take years, but it <u>must</u> and <u>will</u> come off triumphantly at

<u>last</u>. the sods may cover the remains of many a brave true soldier before that end is accomplished, but come it must. many a brave son of the North has gone. many more may go to their last resting place while in their countries service but when can dust be consigned to dust so well as when in the defence of its countries rights, its home, its all. Should I be permitted to return home safe + sound, the school which I am now passing through will prove to me valuable I cannot but hope but that I shall again return to the home and friends Ive left behind me. I hope you will all write often and all the news you can think off I should be glad to hear from Father directly but I understand he is lame and am sorry I have commenced to write to Allen but dont know as I shall send it this time I intend to write Freeman before long perhaps today. I think that the book mark which Ellen [Doane] sent to me is very pretty. it is a good fit for my testament and I trust that I shall move it each day at least one leaf, and that my eyes may rest on the encouraging words "hope on"

Yours Affect. George W.

(Anna please hand this <u>billet</u> to Ellen)

In late April, Major General Hooker had some success in driving General Lee out of Fredericksburg. It had looked like he would be able to continue on to Richmond. Ellen R. Doane is Freeman Doane's sister.

May 11 '63
Camp near Middleburg

Dear Friends

This is a most splendid morning and as I am not very busy I will commence a letter to you. Yesterday was a beautiful day, and together with that blessed day came the glorious news that Hooker had recrossed the Rappahannock with heavy reinfercements, and that Stoneman had been reinforced by Dix and had captured the City of Richmond, that the stars + stripes now float over the rebel capitol, that den of iniquity, that hell on earth. such a cheering I never heard before. such beating of drums was almost enough to raise even the dead. we formed torchlight prosessions and marched around the camp and through the different Regiments in the brigade and they returned the same, every man with a candle lighted in his bayonet. the 100 Pa. put a lighted candle into the muzzle of their guns and formed a star such splendid sights I never saw. the boys went up to the top of a high hill in front of the camp and built large fires in the woods and we all got candles and put them on the tip of our tents of officers and soldiers. such illumination was never seen in the little town of N. Brookfield. such lively demenstrations of rejoicing could hardly be equiled. the news reached hear just before dark in the midst of our prayer meeting but prayer meeting was of no account then and the Chaplain was left alone talking to the wind. Patriotic speeches were made by Capts. Warriner, Smith, Sawyer, Lieut[s]. Brigham, Gird, Adjutant Hodgkins the latter came out as private in Co. B he now ranks as Lieut. the Col. made a few remarks and joined in the cheering. we kept it up until 10 o'clock, and then retired with sore throats. the old tunes of Dixies Land, Yankee Doodle, and Marching along, &c were never played with more life and animation. you would have thought if you had been hear that we were all going home immediately, and some went so far as to say that [they] thought that the rebellion was nearly crushed. would that it were even so. we feel much encouraged it at the receipt of such good news, and if we could have a few more glorious victories I should feel that this war would soon be over. if this news be true we shall be encouraged to go forward with more energy, and if necessary fight till the last armed foe expires. gladly would the gallant 36th have met their enemies face to face last night. gladly will they meet them when called to do so. I wrote a letter to Freeman Yesterday I have received those tracts and read them. I dont know how long we shall stay. I think not long. I have not attempted to give you much of a discription of our actions last night, neither could I if I would for no [thing?] could express this. no pencil paint them. I understand by the way of Denis Wharton [that] Andrew has got his discharge. write often

Yours Affect. George W. Harwood

Captains Stephen C. Warriner, James B. Smith, William H. Sawyer, Lieutenants William F. Brigham, Joseph W. Gird, Acting Adjutant William H. Hodgkins, Colonel Henry Bowman. Burrage, pages 321-323. Cousin Andrew Jackson was discharged in May 1863. I don't know who Denis Wharton was.

Middleburg May 15 [1863]

Dear Brother Allen,

I will write a few lines to you as I have a little time to spare. do you remember how I used to tell you that soldiers would walk like old Moses Hill when they were tired. I find that it is so, when we get foot sore do you remember the time we came out of our Meadow with a load of hay last summer and got caught in a shower and how we had to take it. I told you then that I presumed that soldiers had to stand just such showers and could get no shelter nor dry cloths I find that to be so our whole regiment got caught in a shower equil to that the other day and wet us all through and such a shouting and singing you never heard. we were on the road moving our camping ground. that is the way with us soldiers when it rains or snows or when we have to go through a river or a large mud puddle or see any thing amusing. I have seen a jack and jennie they are the worst looking creatures that I ever saw. thcy have got ears as big as rabbits have in proportion to <u>their</u> size. have you been a swimming this year I have been in today. I have been out to the brook and washed all over every little while ever since I left home, all through the winter. The boys had some fun today trying to hold a wild mule 3 or 4 would take hold of the rope and then the mule would start and run through a crowd of boys and run over some and drag some more, and at last get away. we have some fun out hear 40 or 50 boys going in swimming together or playing ball and other amusements. at the same time it is harder work than farming. soldiering is a lazy lousy life. sometimes we get a lot of darkeys to dancing and it is fun thare a[re] plenty of Violins and fifes, bugles and drums and a plenty that can play them. three darkeys will collect a larger crowd than the same number of ministers. The corn and potatoes out hear are large enough to hoe. they look well. I will not write any more this time.

From Your Affect. Brother
George W. Harwood

I hope that you are getting better of your lameness. that colt causes some trouble, dos'nt she!

DEAR SISTER FANNIE, I WILL TRY AND WRITE YOU A FEW LINES BUT SHALL NOT STOP TO MAKE THESE LETTERS VERY GOOD. YOU HAVE NOT WRITTEN TO ME FOR A LONG TIME. I have made all these marks that I want to for the present, and Anna will read the rest. We have had orders to be ready to take our arms at a moments notice, as Morgans Cavalry is sead [said] to be in the neighborhood and we are liable to be attacked any moment. I suppose that you are going to school this summer and I hope that you will learn a good deal, so that before I get home you will know how to read and perhaps write. kiss Georgie + Elmer for me I wish I could see them. good bye George W.

A jack and jenny are a pair of donkeys. George writes to Fannie in ALL CAPS because she is seven and learning to read. General John Hunt Morgan was a Confederate Cavalry Officer. He conducted many raids in Kentucky against the Union. Georgie and Elmer were the toddler and baby sons of George's sister Anna and Freeman Doane.

Camp Near Middleburg May 18 [1863]

Dear Friends,

I do not feel much like writing today. I suppose that you will be expecting a letter from me about so often. I wrote a few days ago a full sheet to Allen + Fannie and I will send that with this. for several days we have been expecting Gen Morgans cavalry to make a raid through this portion of Ky. I came of picket night before last. I guess that thare is no danger we were ordered to have our guns whare we could lay hands on them at once. I received a letter from Freeman some 2 weeks ago. I have written to Henry + Harry. I have written considerable many letters lately and have only 2 stamps left that you sent a few weeks ago. You asked me Mother if I had any dress coat. I have none we have never had any. I should have been glad to have been up to Uncle ~~Alvens~~ Alains [Alvan's] with you first rate. I have been expecting a letter from Andrew for some time. I am glad he has got his discharge. Addison has got back to the Reg. but is not very tough. We have a roll call every 2 hours all day this roll call was instituted because some few poor shiftless <u>dogs</u> go off and get drunk and get into trouble, and one got his arm shot very badly. every man not present at these roll calls are at once reported to the Col. Lyman has gone on another detail to Stanford I dont know what for. I dont think of much more to write this time. I have expected a letter from you for several days. almost every Farmer hear has got about 12 hogs and from 4 to 15 hounds the men all drink whiskey and both men + women use tobacco. we have some quite interesting meetings hear now, and a good degree of interest taken in them. Hooker was defeated was'nt he? bad for us. I guess that they will have to try another Genl. wont they? Write often.

    this from your affect. son + brother George W Harwood

Uncle Alvan (aka Alvin) Allen. The battle of Chancellorsville, Virginia took place between April 30 and May 5, 1863. General Hooker was unable to force General Lee out of Fredericksburg and Chancellorsville and retreated in defeat. Confederate General Stonewall Jackson was fatally wounded by his own men. The troops in Kentucky obviously had originally received false information on the outcome of the battles.

~ Chapter 6 ~

VICKSBURG AND JACKSON, MISSISSIPPI
May 27 - July 30, 1863

Camp Near Columbia May 27th '63

Dear Friends

    I received a letter from you one week ago today and one from
Freeman at the same time. We left Middleburg last Saturday and marched
8 miles we rested over Sabbath and Monday 14 + Tuesday 14 [miles].
yesterday morning we started at 4 oclock, and the morning before at 5,
making 36 miles in all. I didnt feel very well and so it came quite hard for
me. We have just had orders to be ready to march tonight 3 days rations,
and guns in good shape and take blankets as not, what we call light marching orders, 60 rounds of cartridges. I do not expect to finish this letter
tonight I shant have time as we start at 7 oclock. we hear that the rebs. are
near with quite a force. thare is no great rest for a soldier march march, but
this time we expect a brush with the enemy. thare are large blisters on my
feet now before I start on this trip but if it will do any good I am willing to
go and fight them. I am glad to get letters from home so often should like
to hear oftener thare are those in the Co that haven't had a letter for a long
time. thare are men hear who don't write to their wives for weeks at a
time, but those are men of hardened feeling and they show it. I saw by the
papers before you wrote that Josiah Doane was married I wonder if the
town expects to provide for their little babies. Then Lyman Parkman has
become <u>Father Parkman</u>. Some are dreading this march for fear of a fight
others are ready to go, and that is the case with me but something seems to
say that if we go into a fight I shall get wounded.

Sunday May 31st

We got back from our scout at midnight last night. we got into no fight.
our Cavelry took a few reb caverly and that was all. we went a round
about way of 25 miles to get 15 ~~and~~ we came back another way. the first
night we went about 12 miles and stopped about one o'clock in a moving
whare the grass was nearly a foot high in the morning we went into a
large woods nearby and remained until 9 the next morning it rained hard
all night we made a shed of rails and covered our rubber blankets over it,
and got through the night pretty well by sleeping on the bare ground. after
marching about 12 miles and the most of that in the rain we halted again
and sent Co. E. out on picket but it so happened that we had a good place
the resurve in a school-house and the outpost in a meeting house. about 5
last night we started for ~~home~~ camp and reached hear at midnight. the mud

was ankle deep and we marched very fast we got covered with mud and had to cross several rivers up to our knees, on the whole they gave us a hard one. I did not feel well when we started and do not now. they would not let me do any picket duty although I told them I could. they told me to go to bed and rest up and so I did that was the first house that I have slept in for sometime. I wish this war was over for I am sick of it, an[d] tired of marching. Addison is better. Lyman has come back to the Co. and has gone on picket today. I dont know as will write any more this time. remember me to all the friends and especialy to Aunt Lucretia I shant always be a soldier. <u>thare is a rest for the weary</u>. I should have written a week ago if I had had time but we have been on the move so that I couldn't.

good bye Yours &c. George W Harwood

Josiah M. Doane married Polly Ann Steele on May 12, 1863 in North Brookfield. (Henry) Lyman and Mary E. (Bush) Parkman had a baby, William Henry on May 13, 1863.

[upside down on the top of the next letter] We are now in Louisville it is about 12 o'clock Sunday night [June 7] and I can send this from hear

Jamestown Ky. June 2nd 1863

Dear Friends

I will commence a sort of diary and in a few days send it. I wrote in my last letter that we got into camp at midnight Saturday night [May 30]. at midnight Sunday night they called for 120 more men out of the 36 [Reg.] for picket I was one of that number but every thing passed of quietly we were relieved in the morning. in the afternoon orders came to march at 1/2 past 4. at that time we fell in knapsacks and all, for a long march, and at sunrise this morning we were unslinging knapsacks in Jamestown we rested a few minutes every hour and once we stopped an hour and made coffee. we marched full 20 miles it was a light moonlight night. this was the first night that I ever marched all night. I stood it pretty well. Just as we had unslung our knapsacks and and were unrolling our blankets for a morning nap, firing was heard on the Cumberland river road by our picket and they came running into alarm the camp we fell into line at once and loaded our guns and marched in line of battle up to the edge of a woods near by and sent out skirmishers. the other regiments 3 or 4 of them also fell in. we find that thare was only 3 companies of reb. cavelry. they crossed the river which is only 4 miles from hear and dashed in upon

this place, but saw that we were to much for them so they put back. I believe that they took 3 of our pickets and we took one of theirs. he fell off of his horse and couldnt get away.   Wednesday evening.
It rained hard a good part of last night. at three o'clock this morning several Companies from the brigade were sent out as scouts two Co's from this regiment they have not returned yet. we lay last night with our guns loaded and by our sides, but no alarm was given. We are now in the first brigade instead of the third as we always have been. this brigade is commanded by our Col. Henry Bowman, acting Brigadeer General 36 mass, 45 Pa, 27 + 17 Mich regts. this will make no difference in the directions of letters. This has been a beautiful day.
Hamilton Friday 5th We left Jamestown yesterday noon and came back to Columbia we got thare at 9 oclock in the evening and at 6 o'clock this morning we started for Lebanon a distance of 40 miles we have marched 20 miles today we got hear at 5 oclock rested an hour for dinner made coffee. we have had a rough march we are doing big things now at marching. we are going to take the cars at Lebanon for Louisville, and from thare to Suffock Va. or else to Vicksburg I dont know which.
Saturday the 6th
We had roll call this morning at 1/2 past 2 and fell into line at 1/2 past 3 o'clock and took another march of 20 miles we reached hear Lebanon about 2 o'clock this afternoon a footsore tired lot of us. we have marched (I mean the brigade) 60 good long miles and I think more in 50 hours and carried our knapsacks, and so you see that we have not had much time to rest. the past 8 days we have marched 120 miles and I have been on picket 2 nights and one day. they keep us pretty busy, but I am about played out for the present on marching. we are to take the cars tonight I understand at 8 o'clock for I know not whare. I expect to Louisville. we are all pretty well worn and need a few days rest. We have signed the parole [payroll] tonight and shall probably get paid off tonight or in the morning 2 months pay. we are very anxious to know whare we shall go when we get to Louisville. I will write on another piece of paper. I will not write any more this time.   George

It was June 1863 and General Ulysses S. Grant had decided after several unsuccessful attempts to take Vicksburg to surround the city with a siege. For this he needed as many troops as could be made available. The regiment received orders to go to Vicksburg to reinforce General Grant's army there. They went with

Major General John G. Parke and served under General William Tecumseh Sherman's Fifteenth Corps. Both Union President Abraham Lincoln and Confederate President Jefferson Davis stated that Vicksburg was the key to ending the fighting which began in April 1861. United States President Lincoln said "Vicksburg is the key. The war can never be brought to a close until the key is in our pocket," and Confederate President Davis said "Vicksburg is the nail head that holds the South's two halves together."

Jeffersonville Ind June 8th [1863]

~~Louisville Ky June 7th~~

Dear Friends

I sent a letter out last night from Louisville stating that we had got paid off. We started from Lebanon about 3 o'clock yesterday (Sunday) afternoon and reached Louisville about 9 in the evening and laid around the depot until nearly 12 o'clock and then received 2 months pay. We laid around. I stood guard a part of the time and made coffee, and about 3 or 1/2 past we started for the river about one mile. we crossed over to Jeffersonville and got ~~thare~~ hear just at sunrise, and stopped thare until about 9 o'clock, and started at 1/2 past 10 hear we had a chance to spend our money. Louisville is a splendid place beautiful large blocks of buildings 5 + 6 stories high. one of our boys got knocked down and robbed of his money knife and every thing else worth any thing.

Cairo Ill. June 10th

After leaving Jeffersonville Ind. we run to Seymour and thare got hot coffee for dinner, and then we went on until midnight or one o'clock and then stopped for a while in the cars at Washington the people brought out pies and bread and water and gave us freely, and several times on the road when we stopped for a moment they would give us food + water. they treated us like friends all along the road. at daylight we stopped at Vincenes [Vincennes] and took bread + coffee. we changed cars at Sandoval at 12 o'clock about one we stopped at Centralia and took hot coffee, bread + rost beef. we crossed the line, at river Wabash about daylight that divides Ind. from Ill. it took about 10 hours to run from Centralia to Cairo we reached hear about midnight and came down on ~~and~~ board the Steamer Melivn [Meteor], and have not started yet I dont know when we shall I like the looks of Ind. + Ill. first rate Ind. is best for grain. we saw many large fields of wheat + rye. Ill. is more leavel and they have good cattle, hogs + horses. we have a chance to see a great deal on the road. I did not see many good fields of grain in Ill. I shall not attempt to give any discription of our journey for I have not time to write. if I ever get home I can tell some things. some of our boys got left when the cars stopped they would run into the store or saloon and be behind. one boy in Co C got tight and fell off the cars when they were in motion and broke his arm. I went out this morning and got a good warm breakfast and I feel better.

Thursday 8th [11th]

We left Cairo about 1/2 past 4 yesterday afternoon and run until dark and then stopped for the night. the water is low and they did not dare to run in the dark. we stopped near Island No 7. We started again this morning about daylight and after we had run some hour and one half we came to Is-land No 10 we halted ~~hear~~ thare just a moment. thare is quite a force ~~hear~~ thare. they have cannons on each side of the river. The Mississippi is not so wide and deep as I supposed it was I should'nt think it was over 1/2 or 3/4 of a mile wide. thare is not much to be seen on the Missouri side but woods. it seems to be one large forest of heavy timber, very little cleared land in sight. (A few hours later) We are now sailing down the river be-tween Tennessee + Arkansas and it is all woods on both sides. thare is a ~~sight~~ lot of wood dying hear and young wood is sprouting up. little did I think one year ago, that I should sail down the Ohio + Mississippi rivers. I have often spoke of going into the Western States, and I have thought I should like to go into some of the Southern States. I am now on my trip through the Western States.

[Letter unsigned]

Cairo is at the confluence of the Mississippi and Ohio rivers; a strategic spot for control of the river and railroad shipping. General Grant's headquarters were here before the Vicksburg campaign.

Memphis Tenn. June 13th '63

Dear Friends

I sent a letter to you yesterday morning from this place, with 10.00 enclosed I have some fears that it may not reach you safely, but shall not worry about it a great deal I dont think. We reached here as I wrote in my last [letter] about 9 o'clock night before last we lay hear all day yesterday and so far today. I dont know when we shall leave. this afternoon we all went ashore, and had the old Steamer cleaned and then we came back.

This is quite a large place, and I think that considerable business is going on hear now. it is a dirty place like all other Southern + South Western Cities and villages. ~~Yesterday~~ About 2 or 3 weeks ago the 46th N. York Reg went down and some of their men got drunk, just as they do in this and all other reg. and 9 of them fell overboard and were drowned. you know that a body will rise ~~after~~ in 9 or 10 days, and yesterday and today they have been floating down 3 or 4 each day. they have turned black and are bloated. some of them have been drawn ashore and 20.00 a good watch and pistol was taken from one but his name was not ascertained. it seems hard to think that a man should get drunk, fall overboad, get drowned and after 9 days float down and at last be robbed, and after laying around until he stinks and the flies eat them half up, he is <u>chucked</u> into a hole to get rid of him, the same as a dog or a mule. nobody cares any thing about him. Oh, he is nothing but a dead Soldier. We have to drink the water after these men + hogs and all manner of filth. I think it is some as Doc Tyler says. he dont see any thing nor has'nt for a long time seen any thing worth sacrificing his life for. Our present and I think for a while our future prospect does not look very bright, but Im bound to look on the bright side if thare is any. I could write things from now until tomorrow at this time and even longer that transpire among us daily, that you who are not accustomed to such things would think were terrible, but I will only speak of one. A part of the 27 Mich are on the Steamer with us, and some of both regts were drunk or partly so one of the 27 who was the worse for [illegible] insulted our Luent. Cols Hostler by words and by opening a scuttle door which was forbidden and let his horse partly through. after some words the hostler picked up a stick and rapped the 27th over his head. he fell and in a few minutes was a dead man. this was done in the morning day before yesterday, hardly a word has been said about it, and what was done with the man I do not know. the hostler had a dinner given him by Col. [Henry] Bowman and nothing more was done about it, to my knowledge. no friends present to mourn. nobody cared. I expect they called it self defence and I presume it was. When we were coming on the railroad I dont know exactly whare, one of Co A who was drunk and sleeping on top of the cars, we expect rooled [rolled] off his hat + blanket were thare in the morning, but he has not been seen or heard of since. he was most likely killed, a sad death to die. several of our men we expect deserted coming through Ind. + Ill. they had a good chance. A Steamer has just come in from Vicksburg with sick + wounded soldiers, a good many of them have lost ~~their~~ an arm or leg others are wounded more slightly ~~but~~ and it looks sad to see them but I have seen so many that I dont think so much about it as I used to, but I pity them just as much. I know not but that I too may be placed in the same circumstance. I have just learned that thare are 400 of these sick + wounded soldiers who came in tonight and they are now unloading them this has been a very warm day a great deal too warm for comfort.

[letter unsigned]

Memphis is on a bluff overlooking the river where the Battle of Memphis was fought in June 1862, giving the Union control of the city. It was one of several large hospital towns. Warehouses, hotels and large homes in the vicinity were used as hospitals. The city was also a major supply depot for Generals Grant and Sherman. A hostler is a groom or stableman responsible for looking after the horses.

Sunday about noon
Memphis Tenn. June 14th 1863

Dear Friends

As I have plenty of time to write, I will write a little more today. Last evening thare was a call for men to help unload those wounded men and so I went. I wanted to see the hospitals they had got them mostly unloaded before we were called for, but darkness overtook them and thare were a few who were so lame that they could not be caried in the Ambulances. I did not have to go up but once, and then I helped cary a young man who was wounded in the knee and he was so sore that the least jar made him groan. we had to cary him more than 1/4 of a mile on a streacher. I went around in the hospital and looked the boys over some, some with a leg off, some with an arm off, others wounded in the head, hip, shoulder &c. &c. they looked bad, but most of them seemed to be in good spirits. I inquired of one of the attendants how many hospitals thare were in the place. he told me that thare were 9 certain, and would accommodate from 700 to 900 men each. they are not all full but thare are a good many in each   he told me that the hospitals were all about the size of the one we were then in and that was as large as the Adams Block. We are again on the move, sailing down the Mississippi. we started from Memphis at 6 o'clock tonight. We are bound as we suppose Vicksburg. I know of very few who are much pleased with the Idea. We went ashore again today and staid about 2 hours most of us went into the river and had a good wash. several of the last Steamers that have been down the river lately have been fired into by a kind of Guerrilla. 50 men have been detailed tonight to ride on the upper deck, and watch for the same. This has not seemed much like the Sabbath day. it has been noise + confusion all day long. everything that I see or have seen for a long time are entirely new everything seems changed. the only thing that looks familiar to me is the bright blue sky above and the red sun just setting in the West. I have not had a letter from home for a long time not since I was at Liberty or Middleburg. in fact we have had no ~~male~~ mail for a week.

Tuesday June 16th 1863

We are now sailing down the Mississippi we are now passing Columbia Ark [Arkansas]. we stopped yesterday afternoon about 4 o'clock near or at Island No 72 8 miles above Nepolian [Napoleon] Ark. and thare 2 Gunboats joined us, so it makes quite a little fleet, 3 large steamers + 2 Gunboats. ~~We have~~ last night thare was a falts [false] alarm given, several guns fired. about 11 o'clock we all got up and took our guns, but it was nothing but a cow going through the brush. we have been fired into from the Ark. side several times this morning and we have fired back, both Artillery + Infantry. no damage has been to us so far several bullets struck our Steamer they fired high appearently at the Pilot. We expect more firing they say that we have not seen the worst of it yet.

Wednesday 17th

We stopped last night a little before dark at Providence Lou. and spent the night thare I went on guard. we started again early this morning. we are now near the mouth of the Yazoo river. we can hear the roar of the distant cannon plainly. we are now up the Yazoo river 8 miles. I expect that we are going to unload here they say we have got to march 4 or 5 miles, but I dont know. I will write again soon. Addison has not been very well for a few day but is a little better now. he wants to know how that calf is getting along. I want to know how that calf is getting along and whare she is. remember me to all the friends. I wrote or sent a letter to Freeman yesterday. I have written this last in a hurry.   Good Bye

Yours Affectio George W. Harwood

The Adams Block is the commercial district in North Brookfield. It is a two-story building with three to four stores on the first floor. The regiment was in Liberty and Middleburg, Kentucky on May 23. Columbia, Arkansas no longer exists. It

was just upriver from Chicot Point. Erosion by the river washed it away by the 1870s. Napoleon, Arkansas also no longer exists. It was a hospital town at the mouth of the Arkansas river across from present day Rosedale, Mississippi. It too suffered from river erosion and was finally destroyed by a flood in 1874.

The following letter was to George's brother-in-law and best friend, Freeman Doane. He completed his enlistment with the Massachusetts Forty-second (nine month) Regiment in August 1863. The letter covers the same time period as the previous letters written from May 27 - June 14-17.

On board the Meteor June 15th 1863

Dear Brother Freeman

It has been some time since I have written to you and now as I have a little time I will improve it. We are now sailing down the Mississippi River. I cannot give you much of an idea how I have spent the past month. We left Middleburg Ky. May 23rd and marched 7 miles to Liberty the next day was Sunday we rested Monday (and started) 1/2 past 4 in the morning and marched [illegible faded script] until morning we started at 4 and [illegible faded script] making 35 miles from Middleburg [illegible faded script] Wednesday we policed the quarters [illegible] we had orders to be ready to move in light marching order this is 3 days rations + blankets, 60 rounds of cartridges. at 7 p.m. we joined a lot of cavlry and marched until one oclock or went about 12 or 14 miles in the morning we went into the woods and staid that day while the cavlry went on that night it rained hard we had no tents and so we got a slight soaking. the next morning we started again and marched some 12 miles more it rained hard a good deal of the way [several illegible words] then our Co had to go on picket I was unwell but went. the next night about 4 1/2 we started back to Columbia 16 mile and we got thare just midnight. we took a round about trip in all about 40 miles, mud ankcle deep. The next day (Sunday) I received a paper from you + washed my cloths. at midnight that night they called up 120 more men for picket some alarm was given. I was among that number. I came in in the morning. at 5 o'clock that afternoon we started knapsacks, and all for Jamestown a distance of 20 miles we marched all night and reached J. at sunrise. just as we had unslung our knapsacks and were unrooling our blankets for a morning nap, when we heard the firing of guns on the Cumberland river road and the pickets came running in with the reb cavlry close behind them. thare were only 3

companies of rebs. not knowing that we had so large a force thare, they made a dash into the place on seeing us they put back taking 3 of our (the federals) men. we took one of theirs. we fell into line at once, and loaded, and sent out skirmishers but it did not amount to much. Wednesday we rested. The next day at 12 N[oon] we started back for Lebanon 60 miles in a hurry. We reached Columbia at 9 o'clock that evening the next morning at 6 we were off again went 20 miles more stopped at Hamilton. at 8 1/2 the next morning we started a sore lot of us 4 Regts. our brigade, and reached Lebanon about noon or soon after, making 60 miles in 48 hours and caried our knapsacks. we signed the parole [payroll] that night (Saturday), at 3 o'clock (Sunday afternoon) we took the cars for Louisville. we reached hear about 9 in the evening a distance I think of 65 miles hear they commenced to pay us off, 2 months pay up to May 1st about midnight I got my pay. hear we got bread + coffee and some of the boys got some thing else and one of Co C boys got knocked down and robbed of his 2 months pay, and every thing else he had. we lay around no sleep until nearly day light when we marched to the river about a mile from the depot. we crossed the river into Jeffersonville Ind. on an old flat concern for the business. we left hear about 10 P.M. at noon we stopped and took coffee at Seymour [illegible words] whare we took supper. about midnight we stopped at Washington Ind. and [here?] the people brought out food and water for us and treated us kindly a good many of them were young ladies, (by the way one of them a young miss of some 18 years handed me her name) at daylight we stopped at Vincends [Vincennes] and took bread + coffee, at noon [stopped] at Centralia and took rost beef, bread + coffee
	another sheet

[on top of the next sheet of paper] Freeman I hope you will excuse this little dirty sheet of paper but my paper is getting short just now.

at one o'clock we changed cars at Sandoval hear some of our boys left us. we reached Cairo about midnight and came on board the Steamer Meteor. we left the wharf about 4 o'clock the next afternoon. the river is so crooked and snaggy that they did not dare to run [at] night we stopped for the night near Island No 7. after running an hour or two the next morning we halted at Island No 10, only a short time. they have cannons placed on each side of the river. I think it would be a hard place [to] pass without leave. we reached Memphis Tenn. about 9 o'clock in the evening. we lay hear all the next day loading on coal and the like. a few weeks ago the 46 N. York reg went down the river and some of the men got drunk and 9 of them fell overboard and were drowned. today several of them came floating down and were hauled out hear. they have turned black and are bloated to a puff. from one of them was taken 20 dollars a good watch + pistol. his name was not ascertained the next day we went ashore and had the steamer cleaned and went in swimming more of those drownded soldiers and some dead hogs floated down today and I saw some dead hens in the water and we have to drink it yesterday (Sunday) we went ashore again and had another wash and at 6 last evening we left Memphis as we suppose for Vicksburg. night before last 400 sick + wounded soldiers came up to Memphis from Vicksburg I helped cary one poor fellow to the hospital and thare I had a chance to see a good many wounded men, and a sad sight it was to see them. You will see that we marched about 160 mile in little more than a week we have had a chance to see a good deal, ~~coming down~~ going through Ind + Ill and then coming down the river a short time ago we passed down by Heleana [Helena] Ark. on both sides of the river we can see the ruins of towns that have been destroyed. Some of the boys got drunk coming from ~~Cairo to Me~~ Louisville to Cairo and one of Cos A fell off the cars in the night and his hat + blankets were found on top [of] the cars in the morning. he has not been seen or heard of since. I expect he was killed another in Co C fell off and put his arm out others deserted. a part of the 27 Mich. who are this brigade are on board this steamer with us and one of them got tight and had some words with our Lieut Cols waiter [hostler?] he lifted a scuttle and let the Cols horse through and after a few more words he the Hostler picked up a stick and rapped the 27th over his head. he dropped and in a moment was a dead man. what was done with the man I never knew. they called it self defence. The hostler had a dinner given him and nothing more done about it. We boys are all pretty well except Addison Hair he is quite unwell. I have got the rheumatism some, and today it troubles me conciderably. I wish I could see you and then I could tell you some things that I cannot write I had a letter from Edwin about a week ago. I ~~understand~~ hear that Lyman Parkman's wife has got a little boy. (Papa Parkman) what does he say about that. I have not time or room to write to Hubbard [S. Doane] or Lyman [Parkman]or Charles [Parkman] but remember me to them. Louis [Winslow] + Lyman [Gilbert] send their love to you + the rest of the boys I dont know whare I shall have a chance to mail this letter I will write a word on this letter then, that you may know whare I am. write often and please excuse this pencil my ink is gone. my pencil is poor, my paper is dirty I'm in a peck of trouble. I wish my time was as near out as yours. I expect to spend 3 years in the army, bully for the man that can stand it that long. from your brother [in-law].

George W. Harwood

June 16th We are now in Providence Lou. and may stop awhile 75 [miles] above Vicksburg

William Henry Parkman was born May 13 to (Henry) Lyman and Mary E. (Bush) Parkman. Hubbard and Freeman Doane, and H. Lyman and Charles Parkman were in the Massachusetts Forty-second (nine month) Regiment.

Snyders Bluffs. Miss. June 19th 1863

Dear Friends,

I sent a letter home last Wednesday just before we left the Steamer. we were then up the Yazoo river about 12 miles instead of 8. we landed about noon on what is called Snyders Bluffs about 2 miles below Haynes Bluffs, which are not occupied by our troops now it is a place of not much importance. we marched nearly east about 3 miles on the road leading from the Yazoo to the Big Black river. we are about 14 miles in the rear of Vicksburg. The water hear is not very good the water in the Yazoo river is unfit to drink and is concidered poison. I saw no Aligaters but they say that thare are plenty of them thare. a few days ago one man got eat up alive as it were by one others have lost an arm or leg. thare are Aligaters in the Miss. they say but I saw none. Snakes + lisards and the like are numerous here as well as bugs and mysquetoes. We do not expect to have any thing to do about taking Vicksburg. we understand that Grant has men enough thare. Johnston is said to be within 8 miles of us. we have got out a good many pickets and are ready for him. I wish you could see the cannons down near the landing that our men took from the rebs a few weeks ago they are very large and weigh 13,000 lbs some of them. I dont see how we ever took them. These bluffs are covered mostly with trees. one as beautiful as any is the Magnolia. it is grown in the north in hot-houses the same as the Fig + Orange. thare are plenty of Figs growing hear, but are not ripe yet. these valleys or ravines are full of ripe black-berries, and we have picked a good many of them. thare is a kind of moss that grows on these trees light colored, and hangs down 2 or 3 feet, and looks pretty.

Today Lyman + I thought we would have some greens for dinner, and so we went into a field near by and picked a lot of parseley, and boiled with pork, then added salt + pepper + vinagar. it went first rate. we are now together under a large Tulip tree writing just back of our camp, away from the noise + confusion. Thare are plenty of peaches, grapes, plums, figs, [pospeises?], apricots, cherries &c growing hear, that will be ripe soon. the weather here is very warm, and in the middle of the day, it is so warm that I dont feel like moving. I think that I have seen as warm weather in Mass. but I must say that it is uncomfortable. As Snell says, we are away down south in the land of traitors, rattlesnakes + aligaters. thare are rattlesnakes and another kind called copperhead here I have seen none. I like to hear the old band strike up on the tune Dixies Land. I believe that when I come home I shall fetch a few bamboo + cane fish poles. thare are plenty of them here, and they cost high in the north. the swamps here are full of fine ones, splendid long nice ones. I have seen some good corn here, some 10 ft high, well tasseled out. squashes are as large as my double fists. Since I commence this letter I hear that one of our boys has just killed a rattlesnake with 14 rattles making him 17 years old. I understand that they do not have rattles until they are three years old.

Sunday afternoon June 21st

Yesterday in the afternoon we moved camp about 3 miles round on to the road leading to Vicksburg. From hear to V. it is 10 miles but only 8 to our line of forces. we are here I expect to guard this road and we are on Picket today. yesterday morning about 1 or 2 o'clock we heard cannonading and they kept up a continual roaring until about 9, and towards night they commenced again. today they are at work some, only a little compared with yesterday. we hear that the rebs tried to get out of Vicksburg, and so Gen Grant began to shell the City. I hope that he will make a clean thing of it, and it is thought he will. we are here to attend to Gen. Johnston who is said to be some 8 miles from here. (another sheet) Thare are plenty of the nicest of blackberries + plums ripe hear. this morning just after day light Lyman + I (and 40 more) went a few rods from camp and filled our [illegible] cups with berries, and our caps with plums. we had just all we wanted. This has seemed the most like Sunday to me of any for a long time. on this post thare are only 11 or 12 of us, and we are all busy reading, or writing or asleep. we have not much to read now as we have had no mail for 3 weeks and have seen no papers for some days. It is now about time for the afternoon service to close with you. methinks I can see you all seated in the old church as ~~in~~ you used to. I can follow you home and after supper if some of you do not go to the prayermeeting, I fancy that Anna will play + sing a few tunes. O! I would that I could join this evening in singing these good old tunes as I used to sabbath evenings. Lyman has got a revival melodies, and when we get time we love to sing together. one tune better than any other is found on the 23ʳᵈ page Revival Melodies. "Forever with the Lord" the tune is beautiful and the words seem particularly adapted to us as Soldiers. we nightly pitch our moving tent a days march near home, to our home on earth or heaven. Anna I wish you would find this piece and play it and see if you dont call it good. I ~~im~~ enjoy myself down here as well as could be expected and I guess better I have only a little more than 2 years more to stop in uncle sams service, time passes rapidly. then if not before I hope to meet you all around the family fireside. I suppose that Freemans time is nearly out, but I am getting down into his neighborhood as it were. I hope we shall go round through the Gulf of Mexico home. we are all pretty well. Addison has been sick but is better. remember me to all the friends. write often, and all the news you can think of.

Yours Affectionately, George W. Harwood

There were two lines of trenches surrounding Vicksburg. One was facing the city and the other faced outward against General Joseph E. Johnston's Confederate forces which were expected to arrive to support the troops trapped inside the city. When the Massachusetts Thirty-sixth Regiment arrived another Union regiment moved to the inner trenches and the Massachusetts Thirty-sixth assisted with reinforcing the outer trenches. The rear of Vicksburg was the northern side of the city along the Mississippi and Yazoo rivers. The Confederate troops in Vicksburg expected General Johnston to come to their aid from Jackson, Mississippi. He never came. Freeman Doane's regiment, the Massachusetts Forty-second (nine month) was in Louisiana. The tune "Forever with the Lord" by S. M. Double in New Revival Melodies, J.W. Dadmun, Boston, 1860 page 23.

In rear of Vicksburg June 23 1863

Dear Friends

It is now about sundown the pleasantest part of the day. It is so warm here ~~thare~~ in the middle of the day that one dont feel like writing or doing any thing else. I have been sick all day. I took cold on picket and I feel sick and lame. we are expecting to have a brush with Johnston, should not be surprised if we were called out any moment. Every morning and evening they are shelling Vicksburg one continual roar. just before daylight or sunrise we can hear their rifles plainly. I should think that they would give up the contest, for I think we must be to much for them. we have got rifle pits all around us. a squad of our boys went out and washed this afternoon.

Saturday June 27th

I came off picket this morning. we have to go on picket or building earth works about every other day. [ink smudge] careless boy (blot. blot.) when we go on picket we have to go about one mile. we have a very good place in the woods except the mosquitoes and gnats and they bite terribly. I am nearly covered with their bites. some of us go berrying or pluming every day. I eat a good many of both. the Doc. says that they are good for us. The Doc [Warren] Tyler, [William James] Haskell + [Lyman] Gilbert and some others got a pass and went down to Vicksburg or rather to our forces this side to see the fortifications. I thought that it would not pay to go 8 miles to see them. Thare has been one continual roar of artillery + muskitry day + night for a week past. I have got so used to it that I hardly notice the noise now. I did not feel very well a few days ago, but I feel pretty well now it is quite warm hear and in the forepart of the night it is so warm that we can hardly sleep. a small mail came in last night but nothing for me. I have been expecting a mail for more than 2 weeks. the last letter that I rec'd was in Lebanon Ky. 3 weeks ago today. that was from Edwin Doane and I should say that Anna directed it. It has been nearly 4 weeks since I recd a letter from home. this is the 6th that I have sent since I have received any.

Tuesday June 30th 1863

I will write a little more tonight. a small mail came in this afternoon and thought that I should surely get a letter, but no. I feel quite disappointed. we have been kept pretty busy lately. they kept some of us on duty 3 nights + 4 days at one heat. This has been a very warm day and I have had no duty to do. I have got quite badly poisoned with Ivy. my ankles wrists + hands and it hangs on good. I use salt + water pretty freely. This morning Lyman + I thought we would have some milk so L. went to a plantation nearby and got a little of[f] a darkey only 20 cts a quart. we can get some green corn, and make sause of Green apples I dont eat much of this green fruit and vegetables such as squash and cucumbers &c. I would'nt live hear in Miss. if they would give me the best plantation in the State. about all this state is good for is to raise cotton. I suppose that it is profitable business, but I dont want to live whare the ground is so warm as to blister your feet, barefoot. I have not heard any thing direct from Vicksburg for a few days, but they have not kept up so constant a cannonading for the past few days as they did. It is thought that we shall not stop long in this state I hope we shant. I had rather be in Virginia I think. I think that if I were in or near Washington I should apply for a furlough of 20 or 30 days, but I am now to far away for that. I guess we shall have to stay our 3 years out fast enough, but I could'nt see it when I enlisted.   (another sheet)

In rear of Vicksburg July 3rd

Dear Friends

     I seat myself this morning to finish this letter that I commenced a few days ago. I came off picket yesterday morning. yesterday was the warmest day I think that we have had, burning hot. A fellow in Co. C. died night before last and was buried yesterday. this is the first death that we have had in the regiment for some time. several have died in hospitals away. we left quite a number of sick on our rout[e] from Ky. to Miss. several deserted 5 from our Co. Henry Bowen for one. Thare is nothing going on hear very new, same old story day after day picket about every other day. I dont hear much from Vicksburg this morning. it is reported hear that tomorrow the 4th of July he is going to have some music. I hope he [Grant?] will take this city. I dont like this state very well, for I dont feel so well here. I have a kind of sick head-ache and lame back and side-ache, &c. ~~Thare is~~ a small mail comes in every day nearly, but I have received none. Lyman rect one from Mesiak [his cousin Harriet?] Wood yesterday that came through in 13 days, but I expect to have a pile of it soon. I think that I shall stay at home or go on picket tomorrow the 4th Im not going to ride around and spend my money foolishly or for fast horses this year. I have got a 20.00 dollar bill, confederate script if Allen wants he can have it. it will do to look at. I suppose that it is about time to commence haying. I have'nt seen any mowing ground down hear they pasture the whole and poor at that. I guess that the cattle get their living out the year round. I should like to see you all, but I dont know when I shall have a chance. when a man feel unwell down hear he will think of home. I wish that this war would come to an end, but I dont see any very bright prospect, do you? this war will come to a close some time that is certain. I hope that I shall be permitted to return home to my friends, but if I shouldnt, I feel that I have reason [to] hope for a better life to come. I hope that you will write often. I intend to write about every week and sometimes oftener. Remember me to all the friends and write all the news. keep me posted.

> Good Bye. my head aches
> This from your son + brother
> George W. Harwood

On July 4, 1863, Vicksburg surrendered. The day before, July 3, the Confederates had been defeated in Gettysburg, Pennsylvania. That evening the Massachusetts Thirty-sixth Regiment began a forty-eight mile march to Jackson, Mississippi to complete the destruction of the railroads and ensure the Confederates would not re-occupy their state capital. The Union could now resume shipping goods along the Mississippi river. The residents of Vicksburg were given food by the Union occupying forces. All Confederate troops were paroled to return home after surrendering their arms. Vicksburg was an occupied city for about 10 years.

> July 13th '63
> Near Jackson Miss.

Dear Friends,

I received 4 letters from home July 4 and a paper or two and I wrote a little on one sheet the 6th but did not have a chance to send it as we started July 4th ~~and~~ from Snyders Bluffs and have been moving ever since day before yesterday we left our knapsacks and took only a blanket and met the Enemy some 3 miles from Jackson and at once sent out skirmishers the 45th Pa. and then formed a brigade line and marched forward through swamps over ditches and through woods. they fell back a mile or more and then they came to this entrenchment and the rebs began to through [throw] grape and canister. Cos. A + F relieved the 45 ~~in~~ the next morning with some of the Mich. boys, and at night, Cos E + K were sent in to assist as ~~the~~ our men were falling back. we went in and we were relieved yester[day] morning by the 2 Div. we came back to the rear 1/2 or 3/4 of a mile within supporting distance. the 27 Mich had several wounded and one or two killed and so did the 45th Pa. the 36th Co. F had 7 I think wounded and two killed, C 1 wounded E had 2 wounded slightly I happened to be one of them a spent ball or rather grape shot took me in the leg just above the knee but did not brake the skin only brought the blood to the surfice it is swelled up and is quite sore so that it is hard for me to walk, but I shall be all right in a few days I hope. the Capt. says that I must stop hear in the Hospital if they are called to advance today. we have got one of the best of Capt. a brave man, so if you see my ~~kname~~ name in the papers among the wounded you will know that it is slight and of corse wont worry about it. Lyman is detailed as cattle guard and so he was not in the skirmish I was very lucky to get off as slick as I did but we have'nt got through yet. they are busy now. we went to the front saturday night about 5 oclock I wish you could have heard the balls zip into the ground all around as thick as hail stones. we would lay behind stumps and trees and any thing we could I was laying behind a stump, and the balls struck the stump close by my head zip. zip. they go. I was behind a stump when I got hit, and had been thare all night with my gun in my hand laying on the bare ground. I began to think I was sent for, but still I felt safe, ready to live or die I felt that my maker was just as able to keep me then + thare as any whare if he chose. I dont know as we have anything to fear if we put our whole trust in God. oh, I wish that you Father was a christian and my daily prayer is that you may <u>seek</u> and <u>find</u> that Saviour who is able to sustain you through life, and salt your pillow in a dying hour. dont take christians altogether for a guide ~~for to~~ for we are all pail [pale] creatures, but take the Bible and Christ for an ~~guide~~ example and you will be happy hear and hereafter. Mother you asked me if I was willing that Allen should ware my boots once I have no objections. take any thing he wants of mine. If I ever get home thare will be time enough to get things for me. I dont know when I shall have a chance to send this letter I presume not until after the battle is closed. I may go in again before that time, perhaps to come out no more alive Remember me to all the friends and particularly to Aunt Lucritia + Uncle Jonas. I have written a little to you Anna respecting Andrew and left it in my knapsack I will send it when I get it and will write again soon I may get my knapsack before I send this. we are now living on half rations for a few days. News came last night that Port Hudson was ours and that Lee had been driven from Pa. <u>good.</u> I borrowed this sheet of paper and am writing on the back side of my tin plate and sitting on the ground in the woods. it rains a little. we have to drink rain water out of mud puddles most of the time as springs are scarce.   Good bye for this time

Yours &c. George W Harwood

Port Hudson, Louisiana is south of Vicksburg; it surrendered on July 9, 1863. This is one of the sites where the United States Colored Troops (USCT) played a significant role.

Mildale July 23rd 1863

Dear Friends

I wrote you last in or near Jackson the 13 and received one from you the 15th Jackson was evacuated the 17th. we started that morning and marched up toward Canton about 10 miles and stopped over night the next morning we started and came back some 4 miles and turned to the right and went a few miles and to the Miss. Central railroad, and stopped over night. the next morning (Sunday) we were routed at 3 oclock and at 4 we went to tareing [tearing] up the track and burning the sleepers and bent the irons and in the afternoon we marched back to Jackson. Monday we started for Snyders Bluffs and came from 18 to 20 miles. this next morning I with others was detailed to cary a stretcher. thare were 6 wounded men so bad that the Doctors thought that they could not ride in an Ambulance. 12 men to a stretcher we brought them all that distance, on and a harder job I never had any thing to do with. it was burning hot and dusty and I was all tired out. they were a great deal heavier than a large knapsack. the Docs hurried us and fretted because we could'nt go faster. we were all worn out and my feet were sore and chafed my side ached the blood all rushed to my head and I felt very bad. just before dark I told them that I couldnt carry any farther and so did others but he said we must we went a few rods further and turned up into a mans door yard and sat them down and laid down near them and stopped over night without blankets or any thing else. early in morning they sent Ambulance and took them in. that day when we stopped for dinner and one poor fellow died he was wounded through the neck we buried him and went on. that same day one of Co Es. toughest men got hot heat through and dropped down and died soon after. evry day men, young men are marched until they die. the next day I road in a baggage wagon and got along better we reached big black river that night the next day we rested nearly all day. this morning we started at 4 oclock and came back to our old camp at Milldale or in rear of Vicksburg. we are going up the river as soon as they can get transportation. we are very glad to get back to our old camp ground for all the while we have been gone we have lived on 1/3 + 1/2 rations and have marched hard and our water was very poor we had to drink out of mud puddles and dead water that had stood for weeks. several mules died drinking the same water. our Capt was in this 7 days fight before Richmond about one year ago you know they said had poor water then but he says this is worse and in the while as hard or harder than that campheyn [campaign] but not so much hard fighting we are all worn out one day thare was only 3 guns in this our Co and no Capt. our Capt. is a man about Fathers sise [size] shape and all about 200 lbs. when he falls out we know they are marching hard. more than 1/2 half of our living for the past week has been roast corn + salt but we hope to get enough now. I understand that we are ordered to report to Cincinnati. [Lyman] Gilbert is on cattle guard but we expect him back to the Co. soon. Haskell had a lame knee and staid hear all the time. Joe Walker + Frank Jenks are sick with the Fever one Lieut in this Reg died with the Small pox and one Capt and 10 or 12 men are sick now with the very o'loid [varioloid] we have all been exposed to it. Louis fell out on ~~the~~ these marches and has not come up. I expect he with the teams. I am pretty well rather thin in flesh we have marched here in Miss over 100 miles within a short time and had some fighting to do. I will tell you how I have spent a few of my past Sundays last Sunday I ~~lugged hard all day under a stretcher from 4 in the morning until dark~~ tore up railroad and marched in the afternoon. sunday before in the morning I lay behind a stump shooting at rebs then went back and lay in the woods. sunday before marched to Big Black [River]. sunday before on picket. I will go back no farther. I'm tired of Soldiering. I should like to get home. my leg is most well now the swelling has gone down it is some sore and a little blue. I have seen just all I want to of Miss and long to get back. I never saw so much corn in my life as I have in this state I have seen fields after fields from 10 to 50 acres of corn higher than my head. talk about starving them, the rebs, out. I dont see why this war may not be closed before many months. you ought to see the amount of property that is distroyed hear daily. 1,000 upon 1,000 of dollars [illegible] houses are burned to the ground. I know something what it is to go into battle now I have had bullets enough ziping by my head and striking near my feet it is no fun I assure you I shall not attempt discribe it if I ever get home I can tell you more about it. I think I am lucky to get off so well a good many of us men were wounded badly and some died. A few days ago we were halted in woods and rested. we sat down ~~on~~ in the brush and trees one boy heard a noise or rattle he looked down behind him and thare lay a rattle snake all coiled up ready to leap. the boys killed him I saw him. We burnt the dwelling houses on the road to Jackson and we suppose the house of Jeff Davis + his brother Joe good if we have, but I will close. 2 men were buried last night and one this morning 2 from Co H. Louis Co.

write often good bye George W Harwood

[Undated fragment from around July 23]
We have had but little sleep since we left here we didnt get to bed until 10 or 11 and got up from 1 to 4 2 crackers and 2 cups of coffee a days rations. if I ever get whare thare is any thing to eat except fresh beef I shall have it we have enough of that this a great state for peaches the plantations are covered with peach trees which hang full but are not ripe thare are some apples + pares. I have worn these boots most of the time since they came Jan 1 one of them is good now the other will hve to go a while longer my shirts are pretty good will last until cool weather I think. My stocking are very poor. I wish I had time and [illegible] that I could give you more of an Idea of what we soldiers do and what we pass through I wish you could se us sometimes after a hard Thunder shower or a long hard march we have got so that we can lay down on the bare ground with no blankets all night a few nights ago we got caught in a heavy shower and were soked through but we slept well and came out bright in the morning. it is a wonder that we dont all catch cold and die we are used more like beasts then like men and I shall be glad when we get home. I suppose Freeman has by this time. Good Bye George.

Union troops from Vicksburg converged on Jackson, Mississippi from July 10 to July 16. After General Johnston evacuated the city, the Union took control on July 17, 1863. The seven days fight a year ago was during the Peninsula Campaign. The Union had attempted and failed to capture Richmond, the Confederate capital. Varioloid was the common name for smallpox, variola major (also minor) during the nineteenth century. The Davis family plantation may have been Fleetwood, owned by Joseph Davis near Bolton, Mississippi. It was burned after he left in July 1863. Miller, page 500.

[upside down at top of the next letter]   Aug 1st
I have just rec't 2 letters from home + one from Freeman mailed 8 + 15th
F. [Freeman's] the 10 we have not started yet

Milldale Miss July 27th [1863]

Dear Friends

I sent a letter home last Friday but will commence another today as I have nothing to do. yesterday seemed the most like sunday of any for a long time when I awoke yesterday morning it was still and warm and the sun shone brightly I thought of home at once and if I have been homesick since I enlisted it was then I rearly [really] wanted to ~~come~~ go home. since we came back from Jackson we have had very little duty to do and are getting rested some. I feel a good deal as I used to after we had got through haying. I want to sleep day and night. I feel pretty well except tired. Thare was a small mail in last night but none for me. I hear that drafting has commenced in Mass. I am anxious to know who and how many come from N.B. I dont fear the draft. I suppose that the 42nd has got home before this time. I suppose that Henry + Harry [Harwood] are subject to this draft. Andrew + George [Jackson] are both exempt arent they. why did Charles Knight come home? was his time out? You have'nt written any thing lately about the Town House are they building one or going to soon. Father are cattle high now, and is thare plenty of money in circulation. I understand that wages are high and help is of corse ~~searse~~ not very plenty. some of you wrote a while ago that the colt had some bunches on his hind legs. how is that? is she spoiled. we had a heavy shower here last night the rain fell as fast as I ever saw it before in my life. We are expecting to take Transports soon. I have seen enough of this beautiful state. I am now passing through a grand schooling but it costs pretty dear sometimes I think that one term will fit a man for any business, or at least one term will be enough for me. does Freeman want to try it again if he does come into the 36 and try marching, the 9 corps keep on the move.

Wednesday July 29

As I have nothing in particular to do this afternoon, I will write a little more although I have nothing new to write as I know of. yesterday I answered the letter that Mrs Bush wrote to me a long time ago. we have but little to do now. We are waiting for transports to take us back up the River. night before last we had a prayer-meeting for the first time for a long time. often are we called to lay a fallen soldier in the grave thare are a good many sick, besides the wounded so the hospitals are pretty full Frank Jenks + Joe Walker have both had the Fever but are getting better and begin to want to eat. The war news which we hear of late is quite favourable I think all round and we begin to think that we shall get home about Thanksgiving or New Year. Anna have you received an answer from Mr Tinkhams people if so whare are the boys. I should like to hear from them. A small mail came in yesterday and one the day before, but thare was nothing in either for me. the last letter that I rec't from home was mailed June 30 one month ago. Does Marietta Greene live with Mr Bisco now. you said that she talked of living [leaving] last Spring. how is Mr David Prouty's son (Jonas is his name) you wrote a while ago that he was quite unwell, his mother also. I never saw Louis look better at home in my life than he does now. he is rather tired the same as the rest of us, but says he feels well. Lyman has come back to the Co. he has been on cattle guard. Sweet Potatoes are getting ripe. we like them pretty well and have dug most all we can find.   another page

Thursday 30th [July 1863]

I will finish this letter this afternoon I think. last night papers came from home to some of the boys, with the names of the drafted men from the various towns. In N.B. I saw many familiar ones, E Doane + J. Lampson [Lamson] E. D. Knight C. D. Hendrick J. Batcheller, R. Babcock, &c. It will come rather hard for some to hire. What will E D Knight + Hendrick do with their farms? I can't think. I suppose of corse that L. Olmsteadt will pay the 300, and not come, but they cant all do that. I saw by the same paper that they have had quite a riot in New York city sad times this war makes. I hope that the 42 have got home before this. how do you get along with your haying and who helps you. does Allen mow this summer I will remember the team Father had when he commenced haying last year Charles Ks steers how they ran across the field back of the barn. then the little stags were not much better + came near braking ~~his~~ their necks. I dont like such teams for haying and I hope you have a better one this season. What will Jonas Prouty do of Spencer I think I saw his name in that list. Who is Augustus Prouty I should like to know. I wish that Edwin [Doane] + John [Lamson] could come here to this Reg as I understand that the old regs are to be filled up. We expect to take Transports tonight or tomorrow morning. I shall be glad to go. it is quite warm here. we are to report to Cincinnati I understand. we shall be much nearer home then. I dont care how near home we get if we get ~~thare I~~ back to Washington I shant object. I dont rearly see as they want us any whare. I am glad that I volen-

teered instead of being drafted. if I had been at home I should have been drafted I presume just my luck, but I will close for this time. I should be glad to see you all I hope I shall when <u>war</u> is over.
(my leg is most well)   George W. Harwood

Cousins Henry and Harry (Harrison Jr.) Harwood were born in 1841 and 1843, probably subject to the draft. Cousin George Jackson was born in 1844, perhaps too young for the draft. Charles W. Knight served in the Massachusetts Forty-fourth. He may have been wounded. The Town House (Town Hall) in North Brookfield burned in 1862. The town rebuilt it in 1864. Bunches are horse spavins which look like bumps or growths and cause a colt to be lame. Horse Review, page 762. The New York City draft riots were July 13-16, 1863. On March 3, 1863, President Lincoln had signed the Enrollment Act of Conscription which required every able-bodied man in the Union to be drafted. In New York City names were being called by lottery beginning July 11. Many were protesting the provision that wealthy men could pay someone to serve in their place.

~ Chapter 7 ~

RETURN TO KENTUCKY
August 6 – 24, 1863

On board the Hiawatha Aug 6th 1863

Dear Friends

Day before yesterday (4th) we had orders to pack up and come down to the Landing. we did do that but had to wait over as the steamer had not got thare ~~the Steamer came~~ but came ~~in~~ that night, so at 2 o'clock we were routed and packed up but did not get on board until 3 o'clock ~~that~~ in the afternoon that is military to get us all [up] in the night when they dont want us. that is the way they did on our trip to Jackson they got us up every night nearly while we were gone once or twice. ~~in the night~~ that is the way they have always done, but it did not make much difference night before last for we were all awake and jawing for the flies + mosquitoes were so thick that no one could sleep. I never saw such mosquitoes as they have here in Miss and the little black gnats are worse than they are. We were all very anxious to get out of Miss. it seems as though we should all burn up. the men are all faint + week [weak] and now we are packed on this one transport 3 reg of infantry 27 Mich. 45 Pa. 36 Mass. and Benjamins battery [Second US Artillery Battery E] with all the horses and we are so thick that we can hardly sit down much more lie down. we started about 4 o'clock last night for Vicksburg after forage and some other loading we went in sight of V. and met an Express bringing the loading to us. so we went no farther. that made several miles extry for us to ride the distance from the mouth of the Yazoo down + back. A few days before we left the bluffs we received an order from Gen. Grant expressing his thankfulness to us (the 9 corps) for ~~our~~ the valuable services we rendered him in taking Vicksburg + Jackson. he says we held a responsible place in rear of V. and were ready for an attack from Johnston at any moment had we not been thare he (Johnston) might have made bad work at Jackson we were in front and done well. he says that he will cause to have the victories of Vicksburg + Jackson written on the several flags in the 9 Corps. (Good) so you see that the 36th will have some praise after being in service for a year.

Friday 7th

Yesterday was Thanksgiving I did not think of it when I was writing. I think that it very appropriate to [describe?] our day to thanksgiving after the recent victories. I think that the hardest of our fighting is over, but we dont know that seems to be the opinion of many, but time alone will tell and we must wait. It is the report that we, this 9 Corps are bound for

Fortress Monroe or Newport News others say to Cincinnati, but that is also uncertain. I dont know as I have any desire to go back to the army of the Potomac. We are slowly winding our way up the river only about 6 miles per hour we are so heavily loaded that our old craft is unable to go faster. both sides of the river are are covered with woods or nearly so. on either side we can occationaly see beautiful large plantations. we amuse ourselves by reading whatever we can find to read the Chaplain distributed a few papers among us. some play cards and smoke + tell stories others sleep, any way to pass of time. one can spend a good deal of time looking off to either bank. I have seen a good many cranes + turkey buzzards, wild geese &c. I found it very pleasant last eve to sit from sunset until late in the evening until all were laying down and many of them asleep, with my feet hanging off the upper deck whare our Co are quartered. all was still except the splashing of the fish in the water far below me. my mind wandered away to my home so far away I could hardly realize that I had sailed down and was now sailing back up the Miss river a soldier armed and equiped to do battle for my country. I can only say that I [two words crossed out] hope the time will come and that at an early day when such services will be no longer needed. I dont know as you can read this thare is such a motion to the boat that I cannot draw a strate [straight] mark.

      Good Bye   George W.

On July 31, 1863, by Special Order No. 207, General Grant wrote:

"The endurance, valor, and general good conduct of the NINTH Corps are admired by all, and its valuable co-operation in achieving the final triumph of the campaign is gratefully acknowledged by the Army of the Tennessee.

Major-General Parke will cause the different regiments and batteries of his command to inscribe upon their banners and guidons "Vicksburg" and "Jackson."

Burrage, pages 73-74.
The flags of this and other regiments are in the collection at the Massachusetts State House. A hologram version of some are on display in the Hall of Flags.

In Proclamation 103 dated July 15, 1863, President Lincoln called for a "day of national thanksgiving, praise and prayer" to be observed on August 6 in grati-

tude for the recent victories of the Army and Navy on land and sea. Among the victories to be noted are Gettysburg, Vicksburg and Port Hudson. He set the annual celebration of Thanksgiving which we still observe as the fourth Thursday in November later that year. Today there is a National Park surrounding Vicksburg. There are statues for all of the Union and Confederate states who sent regiments to the Vicksburg campaign. Remains of the trenches are still visible and the views from the bluffs overlooking the river show the importance of this city to railroad shipping and river transport for the entire country.

Aug. 9[th] '63
On board the Steamer Hiawatha

Dear Friends,

I sent a letter yesterday from Memphis, which p[l]ace we reached about 9 o'clock yesterday forenoon. we all went ashore and had the Steamer cleaned pretty thoroughly. we left Memphis at 3 or 4 P.M. We had a chance to buy bread + cakes and some fruit. we hope to reach Cario [Cairo] as soon as noon tomorrow. It is quite warm here and particularly when we are on the hurricane deck. quite a number of men are sick. one died last night and thare are more that will not live long. one man has got the [two illegible words]. we all feel rather dumpish + sleepy. They tell me that today is Sunday. how time flies, and here in the army it is rather difficult to keep the run of the day of the week. one can see no difference between sunday and any other day, just as much traiding, just as much noise and confusion, and this morning almost the first thing I done was to stump [?] a man to traid knives. we did so neither of us thinking that it was sunday. I felt sure that it was saturday, and it seems now as though it was. I suppose that Freeman has got home sure before this time. Snell had a letter from his father a short time ago. he seems to think that this war is near its close. I hope it is. Porter [Snell] is very much pleased to think that he has a little brother and wants to go home and see him. It is so warm that I'm not going to write longer this time.

Covington Ky Aug 13th
We reached Cairo Monday morning about 9 o'clock and went on board the cars about 4 in the afternoon we reached Sandoval about noon we had bad luck and were delayed the engine got out of repair we changed cars at S. and took the Ohio + Miss railroad and reached Cincinnati about 4 o'clock last night, and took supper and about dark we crossed over into Covington

Ky. whare we are now in barracks. I understand that we are to be paid off
here. I have been sick for the past 3 days I am all worn out and a very bad
diarhea. I havent felt so bad since I have been in the Army. I have been
betting upon getting back up here whare I could get things to eat and ripe
nice fruit but I have no relish for any thing. I should like a better place that
these boards to lay on. I have just received a letter from home dated the 5th
thare is a back mail somewhare that I have'nt got which we expect now
we have got here. I should think by your writing that you none of you [are]
very well I sorry that Father dont get along faster with his haying he
ought to have help. I think that it is strange that they dont lett the 42 come
home you spoke about Mr Thomas falling out of bed. I should like to try
it and see whether I could stay in bed all night or not. I dont blame Edwin
[Doane] + John [Lamson] any for not wanting to come, but Roswell Babcock didnt need to pay for I dont think they would take him. I shall write
but little more this time for I feel so sick and faint, rather feverish, my
tung is coated quite thickly. I should like to get a furlough but I dont know
as I shall try. I wish that the war would close. I should suppose that they
would let this 9 Corps rest a while now after having such a hard time we
have been on the move almost constantly ~~for~~ ever since we came out one
year ago. I know that for one I ~~kned~~ need rest. Lyman + Louis are neither
of them very well they are tired and worn also. I will not write any more
this time if we get paid off I shall send some home. Good Bye
    write often. Yours &c. George W Harwood

*Moses Porter (M.P.) Snell's new half-brother was Thomas Elisha Snell, born July
22, 1863, to Thomas Snell, Jr. and his second wife Mary Wilcox Fish. Roswell H.
Babcock was about thirty when he was drafted. Evidently he paid the fee for a
substitute to serve.*

[No. 1]   Covington Ky. Aug. 16th 1863

Dear Friends

  I will improve a few moments towards the close of another Sabbath day in writing to you. I have not felt well for some time and I do not
now far from that. thare are a good many sick in the Reg at the present
time. they sent away to the Hospital in Cincinnati, today about 50 from
among them were F.[Frank] Jenks + L.[Lyman] H. Gilbert Lyman + I
were taken about the same time with Chronic Diarhea + billious rather
feverish too. he lost flesh faster than I and perhaps he is worse a little. he

told me this morning that he felt a little better. we shall be around again in a few days I guess. Today a man came from the City and preached to us he said he was settled minister in Brookfield in 1856 I don't know who he is or what his name is he is a native of N. Hampshire. a good many are going home from here on furlough. I think I should have tried if I had not been that I was exposed to the very o'loid [varioloid]. one of our Co came down with it several days ago. If I do not have it after 8 or 9 days have expired I shall not at all. I have been exposed 40 times. I care nothing about it myself but I might cary it among children who would take it. it would cost to go + come about 50 to 60 dollars. do you think it would pay, situated as I am, or do you think that my large family need it all my wages. we have had orders to be ready to move we shall probably go tomorrow. we are going to Hickmans bridge, about 15 miles from Lexington. it may be a little more. The boys all say that thare is no danger of giving the small pox and they would go home if they could get a chance. I dont know as could get one. don't say any thing about my coming for I may not try. I should like to first rate. I hear that the 42nd are at home. good for them.

Camp Nelson 18th

Monday forenoon we left Covington and started for this place we found ourselves in Nicholasville and came down to here about 4 1/2 to 5 miles. we have a very fine camp ground and a nice spring or water not far away. we expect to stay here several weeks to rest up. I presume I shall go over and call on Mr Young's people. I should like to first rate. I feel a little better now than I did. Haskell is sick now with Fever we expect to be paid off tonight. Louis has just left me I spent so much time talking with him that it is too dark to write more tonight. (thare be time enough in the morning) Wednesday afternoon. I will now see if I can finish this letter. We got paid off this morning up to the first of July. I will not send the money home this time for I may take a notion to come myself before we get paid off again if I can. the boys are going in for furloughs, pretty strong. they say that thare is no danger of the small-pox now. I am glad that we have such a good place to camp. I have just sent my cloths off to be wash pants and all. I feel pretty well today. thare are a great many sick in the reg. several cases of Fever. out of our 1000 men that we left Worcester with only 250 are fit for duty and they are hardly fit. we can buy some things here and I shall some I bought some nice butter this morning to mix in with our army rations. Money circulates pretty freely today. You spoke about thare being

909 men in the steamer with Freeman if they all belonged that Reg I think it must be pretty full. they must have lost but few. we have left all our sick and feeble ones and what thars [there are] left are of strong constitution naturely some days on our marches we could'nt find more then 100 men in the whole reg. What does Father think about this war does he think that it will end before the 3 years are out. that is 2 years more I sometimes think it will and then again I doubt it. I dont see as the Rebs have much to fight for now or rather whare they can make much of a stand to fight, with much of a force. I believe that I have been a soldier about as long as I want to be for the present. I should care if I could only stay in the City of Washington and do provost duty. it is this hard marching that kills the men. such Officers as we have in the army are enough to mad [madden] any body they dont seem to care any more for a man then they do for a mule. Our Col. and Lieut Col. have both resigned and gone home. our Major has gone home on a furlough. our senior Capt has command of the Reg now and he dont enough to last to him to bed without running. this Regt has pretty much run out it dont look much as it did when we left Worcester. I well remember that time. the last that I saw of you was Father + Freeman looking after the cars as we started off. I felt bad <u>very bad</u> it was all I could do to control myself and keep from crying. thare stood Mrs [Sarah W] Wood, Etta [Harriet?] + Mary Doane [Gilbert] all crying   that was a trying hour to me. little do we know or how much we think of friends + home until the [day] of separation comes. thare is much in this life that is trying. no one knows how much they can stand until the hour of trial comes. often have I heard men in our Co tell how they could go into battle and what they would do, how bold they would be and so on and when we were called in at Jackson they were the first to hang back turn pail [pale], and show them selfes cowards by being so frightened that [they] couldnt load their guns. some shirked out entirely. the men that say the least I find are our best men. When we first came out we were on guard one day Mr Cheaver [Cheever] was on he was at one end of his beat and a man crossed on the other Mr C. run after him crying stop, stop, or I'll run my gun through you he thought that he could run his gun through him because he had a bayonet on the end of it. he makes an awkward soldier. he is cook now. Addison is cook now in his Co. I shouldnt like that business at all. did I understand that Charles Parkman [Massachusetts Forty-second] was the regular Co cook. how does Freeman feel does he want to

reenlist or has he seen enough of it. Anna you asked me how far I helped cary that wounded man on a stretcher we caried him 18 miles, and a hard job it was. I must draw this to a close for the mail is about going out and they are calling for the mail Good Bye write often

Geo W Harwood

Camp Nelson in Nicholasville, Kentucky was a large camp in Major General Burnside's Ninth Corps. It was a supply depot, repair facility for rolling stock and wagons, and a hospital facility. It became well known for its later role as a refugee center for enslaved persons and a major recruiting and training center for the United Stated Colored Troops, the USCT. The regiment rested here for eleven days, August 16-26, then it was on the move again.

[No. 2]   Camp Nelson Ky. Aug 20 '63

Dear Friends

I received a letter from you last night. It was mailed July 29 an old one. I also received the letter that Freeman wrote just before he started [for home]. I wish that I could have seen him. I received a letter from him sometime ago in which he told me not to write again for fear he would not get it before he went home, but now he has got home I am going to write as soon as I get around to it. Mother asked me in that last letter how my cloths were. my shirts are a little thin but will ware some longer I have mended them a little in several places, since I came back I have drawn some new socks and had my shirts and pants washed so I look as slick as when I first came out. I have got one good boot the other is run over badly but will ware a while longer. You said that it wouldn't be very strange if Father came out if we should stay around Cincinnati. I wish he could come and it isnt far to come from Cincinnati to Nicholasville and we are only 3 or 4 miles from thare on a good road. I intend to get a pass before long and go and call on Mr. Youngs people and I may have a chance to see Lucretia [Young]. I should like to first rate. It dont seem to me as though I was a great ways from home, and in fact I am only 2 or 3 days ride from thare. I think that Kentucky is a pretty good state but it dont seem like Old Mass. You spoke and often do speak about the sermons that you hear preached. I wish that I could hear some of them for I have hardly heard a decent ser- mon since I left home. we have got a post master who talks to us once in a while. our Chaplain makes a better post master than Chaplain. our best meetings are the prayer-meetings which we sometimes have evenings we

have one or two ministers and I believe three in our Co. I suppose that
Freeman remembers Mr Gupper he saw him in Worcester he is the oddest
man I ever saw. Mr Cheaver [Cheever] speaks to us occationaly he is a
good harted man. he tells the same story every time. did you ever hear him
speak in meeting? thare is but little interest taken in religious things
among us now. the men dont seem to care much about any thing. they are
tired and worn out, but we hope to get rested now. nothing seems to cheer
us up like mail if I had not the privledge [privilege] of writing and receiving letters how sad + lonely I should feel. thare are several men in our Co
that cannot write nor read writing and so once in a while they get some
one to write a few words for them and if a letter comes for them get some
one to read it to them. that style of correspondance would afford me but
little satisfaction. such men as these cannot enjoy but little of this life com-
paritavely. take away from me my Education limited though it is, and you
take away a large portion of my happiness. we have but little reading matter except Newspapers as we cannot cary books with us on a march we
sometimes pick up books when in camp and when we move leave them. I
shall be glad if the time ever comes when I can have the privledge [privi-
lege] of keeping some choss [choice] books + papers I sometimes like
some poetry that I like. the other day I was reading in a book of Longfellow Poems. one piece in particular I liked and so I thought I would copy it.
I will send it in this letter perhaps Anna ~~will~~ would [like] to read them. I
sent a letter yesterday but I felt like writing again today. I miss Lyman +
hope he will get back soon. I tent with Wheelock + Haskell as usual.
Haskell is a little better I think Remember me to the friends.

Yours &c Geo. W.

I do not have the copy of the Longfellow poem.

[No. 3]   Aug 24 '63
Camp Near Nicholasville Ky.

Dear Friends,

I will commence to write a few lines to you. I came off guard this
morning. I do not feel very well yet. Doc Tyler I understand is in Cincinnati sick, about 25 out of 35 or 40 men in our Co are sick. we have had orders to be ready to move down to Crab Orchard some 20 miles from here.
I think that it will be hard marching us. Louis is on guard today. he says
that he is tired, and we all are. it is quite warm here. I should like to see

Father here first rate. I should like to see you all some think that we shall all get home in less than another year. I wish that it could be so but am fearful. what do you think about it. I suppose that Freeman is at home thare with you isnt he. I expect every day a letter from Freeman + Hubbard how are the Parkman boys. I almost ~~wish~~ had been among the 9 months men, and then again I dont care, but when this <u>war is over</u> if I return I in good health I shall never be sorry I came. I am quite fleshy now but I feel like an old man, just after haying in the meadow 7 or 8 weeks. I dont know as I have any news in particular to write this time. I had a letter from Lyman a few days ago he is Camp Dennison Ohio Ward 27. I feel rather lonely without him not feeling well myself, and we have been together so much you know, but we need not think that we can always be together. I would that I had Freeman with me if I could, but I am glad that he is out of the service and hope that he will never enter it again. I hope that the Government will not need his services any more. What are the young people all doing I should like to know. is John Lampson [Lamson] teaming I think you told me he bought the big team at Newtons auction. How are Mr Bushs folks I have'nt heard any thing from them for a long time. Sometimes when I feel sad + lonely and look at our Reg now when compared with what it was, and think of the many that a little while ago were as well as I was, that are now laying in the silent grave. they have gone to their last resting place. then I think that it is more than probable that I shall never see home + friends again that I shall be called hence to be here no more long before my 3 years expire, but when I feel well I look forward to the expiration of my time with strong hopes. I often ask myself shall I ever be better prepared ~~of~~ for death than I am now. I answer never. I think I told you in my last letter that we had got paid off up to the first of July. I think I have sent home 72.00 in all since I came out I have got now nearly 30.00 I intend to save at least 100.00 dollars a year. I shall not send any this time. I expect to save some on my clothing acct. How is that colt you wrote me some time ago that it had bunches on her feet is it going to spoil her or not. Father how are you on it for stall stock how many cattle have you? I should like to look the Farm over and see how things look, but I think I will close for this time. I want you to write all the news you can think of. Remember me to all the friends. does Allen go to the High school this term does he ware my boots how tall his [is] he ~~how large is he~~ he must be large if he can ware my boots.   Good Bye G W Harwood

INDIANA

OHIO

WEST VIRGINIA

• Nicholasville, KY

Crab Orchard, KY •

KENTUCKY

VIRGINIA

Cumberland Gap, TN •

Beans Station, TN •   • Rogersville, TN

Blains Cross Roads, TN •   • Morristown, TN
(present day Blaine)

Strawberry Plains, TN •   • Greenville, TN
(present day Greeneville)

Knoxville, TN •

Campbell's Station, TN •   • Erins Station, TN
(present day Farragut)   (present day Bearden)

• Lenoir Station, TN
(present day Lenoir City)

NORTH CAROLINA

East Tennessee and
Georgia Railroad
(runs between Chattanooga
and Rogersville to Virginia)

TENNESSEE

• Chattanooga, TN

SOUTH CAROLINA

GEORGIA

~ Chapter 8 ~

KNOXVILLE, TENNESSEE CAMPAIGN
August 30 - December 2, 1863

[No. 4]   Aug 30 '63
                                           Crab Orchard Ky.

Dear Friends

     I will try and improve a little of this day in writing to you. We left camp near Nicholasville Thursday morning and marched to Camp Dick Robinson that day the next to Lanchester [Lancaster] and yesterday to here making 30 miles in 3 days. out of the 101 men in that left home in our Co. thare are 9 of us left, Snell, Wheelock + I from No Brookfield Snell is 8th Corporal acting Sargt. It is quite cold today and clear. I received a letter from you last Monday, M marked No. 1 I think that I got all of your letters. I got a letter from Henry Harwood Wednesday. he wrote that Freeman + Anna were thare that day I am expecting a letter from home next mail, which I guess will come tonight Thare is not much news going on that I can think of today. I do not feel like writing but I thought that you would like to hear about this time. I have a hard head-ache + pain all over. a good many of our boys have got the fever + ague. I have had a slight touch of it. some have got the mumps and almost every thing else. I do not know how long we shall stay hear but I presume that we shall have to go on down to Tennessee. I should like right well to see Father + Freeman out hear. I wish that they would come. I would come home if I could on a furlough, and to be honest about it I should like a <u>discharge</u> better. I dont see any great prospect of this war's coming to a close at present. Father has'nt written much about his traid but I suppose that he traids the same as usual. I have seen some good cattle here in Ky. and fine horses. horses are pretty high here a fair kind of a colt is worth from 40 to 50 dollars at 4 months old. when we came down through Ill. I saw some working oxen such as would have brought 90.00 at home. when I left they told me that they would bring about 54 thare as for the price of stock in Miss. thare was none. the man that got his hands on an animal first owned it. You wrote that Uncle Harrison had saved 600 dollars in case his boys were drafted. it seems by that that [they] arnt so fond of military as they used to be, but it is a different thing to be a soldier than what it is to drill a little after work toward night. the novelty of soldiering has worn away with me. it has now become a stern reality. I hear that Mr Benjamin Dean has raised a new mill whare the old one stood. Didnt you know it or did you forget to write that he was building. you never have written any thing about it. Do you know whither Lymans wife hears any thing from the hospital or not. I have heard from him once. Haskell we left at Nicholasville he was quite sick. Doc. Tyler was with the sick thare he came the day before we left. I did not see or hear any thing from Mr Youngs people when I was in N. the last time that is since I came from Miss. but I will draw to a close for this time and when I feel more like it I will write again Good Bye this dont seem like sunday but I suppose that it is. I have been policeing this forenoon. My clothing bill amounted to 31.38 so you see I shall save some this year. Remember me to all the friends and write often + all the news.

Yours &c &c

George W. Harwood

No 5

Crab Orchard Ky Sep 3ʳᵈ [1863]

Dear Friends

    I have just received a letter from you marked No 2 I enlisted the 12 of Aug. and so I shall have to number this No 5. I am glad to hear that Mr Jenks has gone to see Frank for when I saw him last he was sick and farely cried he said he wanted his Father to come and get him. Frank is with Lyman in the Hospital 125 miles from here. you spoke about sending a box. I dont think it is best to send a box at present. I hardly know what I want, as for socks I dont want any I have drawn two good new pairs all I want is a pair of boots and a shirt by + by before cold weather comes on. we may not stay here long and I dont want to cary any more load than I have got if a box should come through. you say that Doc Russell thinks this war will end ~~in~~ before six months thare are a good many that think just so and I wish I could think so too but I cant. 2 boys from this Co started home on furloughs of 20 days last night I think thare were 2 from each co. Im thinking that the 50 or 60 dollars that it would take to go + come would do me a good deal of good should I come home to stay in the corse of a year. you said you thought I did not get 1/2 half your letters I guess I got them all I got one about once a week. do you write often? I do some times. I am very glad that Allen goes to school I hope he will learn fast what does he <u>study</u>. I felt quite unwell when I got up this morning and I went to the Doc and got a large dose of Magnesia Sulphors and I hope to feel better soon we have had conciderable policing to do since we have been on this ground and they have commenced to drill today. some of the sick that were left at Nicholasville when we came off, came up yesterday but Haskell did not come I dont know how sick he is. I do not get many papers now or lately do you send as many. I sent a Cincinnati Daily Gazette to you yesterday thare was no news in particular in it but I thought you might like to see a Western paper once in a while. the Reg is now out on battallion drill I hope that they enjoy it but I guess that thare is some swaring among them. there is only a little handful of them. I see by your writing that Father has not got done haying yet I should think that it is about time. he has had a long siege this year. I hardly anticipate staying here another year but if I should + should live to pass through what I have for the past year I shouldnt be sorry that I came for I see + learn much every day I understand that we are to be paid off again the 15 of this month if we do I shall recieve about 38 dollars I have heard Father ~~tell~~ talk about boys spending their money foolishly and not knowing the value of a dollar and so on I have seen enough of that I know of boys in this or that have spent every sent [cent] of their bounty + years wages thare are those who do not pretend to send home any money who have friend yes families that need their earnings. the Government allows us a certain amount I think 42 dollars at the end of the year they settle up with us they are going to settle up to the 27 of Aug the time we were sworn in as a Reg. Those who have taken up more than that amount of clothing have it taken from their monthly wages those who do not draw that amount have the balance paid them in money. some boys who are careless and tear their cloths out fast have drawn 80 + even 90 dollars worth. I have drawn 31.38 that is the difference. Freeman how did you + the Government come out on the clothing bill. I suppose you had a settlement. Do you ever see any thing of C. R. Stoddard these days I should like to see him [for] but 3 or 5 minutes just for fun. I suppose that all kind of business is good and wages high how is it are the taxes pretty high. I suppose it aint quite time for the droves of cattle to come in is it. I should like to go + get a drove if I was thare, I would. what has Father got for horses now anything besides the pony how is the colt getting along. it is cold + damp tonight and looks like rain. I dread much of a storm. ~~what rain~~ are the Parkman boys getting any better. how is Lizzen + Louis + Jennie. I suppose that Hubbard and Edwin are all right. I am going to write to them before long but I must close. good Bye Remember me to the Friends.

George W Harwood

George numbered his letters from the date the Ninth Corps rejoined Burnside's Army of the Ohio after returning from Vicksburg where they had been assigned to General Sherman's Fifteenth Corps of the Army of the Tennessee. Magnesia sulphors may have been sulphate of magnesia (Epsom salt), a purgative used to treat dysentery and other ills. Lizzen, Louis and Jennie might be his Winslow cousins Frank (ten), Jennie (nine), Lezette (eight), and Henry (four).

[No. 6]   Crab Orchard Ky. Sept 8th '63

Dear Friends

      I have Just recd a letter from you. I received the bottle of Balsam that Father sent me a day or two ago Mr Jenks gave it to Joe Walker and he to Haskell and so at last I got it. I was glad to get it for it was just the thing I needed at that time for I had a hard pain in my bowels the day it came I took some and it done me good. Anna you asked me if [I] had recd the Photograph that Anna Jackson sent me. I have I rec'd that a long time ago it is a good one. I rec'd a letter from Andrew a few days ago and answered that this morning. you have never written to me before that our Father had had Ethan put on to our Brothers name I am glad of it so I suppose he will go by the name Allen as usual but I shall call him Ethan I dont like the name Allen. When I write to you and address you as I most always do <u>friends</u> I mean the whole family and I want Freeman to understand I mean him as will as well as though I addressed him personly but if I have time I shall write him a few lines in this letter. you spoke about Frank Jenks refusing a discharge I think he must have altered his mind since I saw him last for he said he wanted his Father to come out and get his discharge if possible. We have just got orders to be ready to move in a few days to Knoxville Tenn. a distance of about 165 miles over mountains + through valleys I do dread the march if I ever did once ł our reg is in poor condition to move many of the men are sick the sick that we left back at Nicholasville have come up but are not fit for duty yet. I had hoped that we should remain here long enough to have got thoroughly rested but no, and now I have given up all hope of rest until this war ends, or I am called away to my last resting place which will come first time alone can tell I would like to come home after I have done here but it is not for me to choose. You spoke about that man Smith + wife from N York. Lymans wife wrote to him about it some time ago and he told me. I think he done will to keep away from his friends so long. How odd it seems to think of

Martha Smith (or she that was) and George Dewings wife and a dozen others if I could think of them little girls with children. what kind of a Journal does Allen keep like the one I used to keep when I went to the High School or a common Diary. I wish that I could go to school and keep a daily Journal as I used to. I'd say I could'nt keep a better one. tell Ethan to keep a good one. does he go to school on foot or do he + Freeman ride. I should think that would be the handiest way for both, but I'm writing this so fast and take so little pains that you will hardly be able to read it. I write a good many letters nowadays that is more than I used to. I will put in .50 in this letter so that you may send out a few postage stamps as I have got but 2 left and am going whare they ain't so plenty. I wish that Father could have come out and see me before I left here. thare are and have been several men + women out to see their sons + brothers + husbands. Addison says that he shall get a furlough as soon as he can cost what it will, but perhaps war will end in 6 month and that will do for me, and shant have to come back. I will draw this to a close for this time. write often. Please remember me to all the friends.

so Good Bye

George W Harwood

Tell Father he had better let the old meadow go for this year.

Balsam is from balsam fir, used to treat asthma, colds, cough and as a laxative. Allen was George's mother's maiden name. His brother, born Allen, renamed Ethan Allen was known as E.A. Harwood. Cousin Ethan Alvin Allen died in Sept 26, 1862, age eight from diphtheria.

I forgot to number the other which would have been 6   No. 7

Ky. Sept 17th 1863

Dear Friends

      I will now try to write a few lines to you I dont know when I shall have a chance to send it. we are now 10 miles from Barbarsville [Barboursville] Ky. and 20 from the Cumberland Gap thare is nothing here but an old grist mill. I rec'd your letter No 4 and the Valuation + Taxes a few days ago and was glad to get them. We left Crab Orchard the 10 and have marched every day except Sunday. some of the way the road was rough and hilly but a part of the way was good we start in the morning at 5 o'-clock get up at 1/2 3 and march from 10 to 16 miles and then turn in marching comes pretty hard for most of us. we have left a good many be-

hind. we are resting today and are to be paid off. I shall send a check of 40 dollars I believe that will make 112 that I have sent home if I have kept acct. I shall save 12.50 on my clothing acct this year. some run over from 30 to 40 dollars a few have 20 dollars due them. thare dont seem to be much news to write it is the same old things over + over. I do not feel well at all but I intend to keep up good ~~courage~~ cheer for I think that this war will play out before many months or I shall I think sometimes a few days ago we met 25.00 [2500?] prisoners that were taken down to Cumberland Gap a short time ago. it is quite warm here now and rather dusty. we started with 8 days rations on our backs of Sugar + coffee + hard-bread, and some meat so you see that we had a big load with knapsacks guns + equipments and the teams are as heavily loaded ~~so~~ a good many wagons have been broken on this trip I shall be glad ~~to~~ when we get to Knoxville Tenn. for I shurely think we must rest thare. Addison has gone to Mass. to guard out conscripts I dont know whether he will have a chance to ~~come~~ go home or not. Im sorry if Lyman Parkman has got the chills for I have had a touch of them and know they are hard. I see that they have taxed a good many persons that were not in time on the first of ~~may~~ May but were in the army and some that have been in for 2 years but I suppose they wont pay it [to] them. Father do you think that it is any safer to send a check than it is the money. is it much trouble to get the money or the check do you have to pay any thing. I pay 25cts for the check. we have pretty strict orders in the march if we fall out without leave we are to be severely pun-ished and non commissioned to be redused to the ranks. the Doc has to write a pass for you. I should like this business if they would use us like men and not so much like beasts. I dont think that they use us as well as they mint if they would. a man here isnt to be judge of his health they have a surgeons call every morning in camp and the sick must go ~~to~~ if they excuse you all right but if they dont you must do duty any way. I should rejoice to have this war close, <u>pride would have a fall</u>. I am going to write to Freeman some and guess I shall direct to him this time. I did not know that that Hill boy that was shot had ever enlisted, <u>poor boy</u> I was surprised to hear that Mary Ann Earl was married what kind of a man has she got for a husband, but I must draw to a close and write to Freeman a word I cant much for thier want to run. I suppose that Allen has a good time going to school I will write again when I have an opportunity. write often
Good Bye George W Harwood

I shall not write to Freeman in this letter

Because Union control of the Mississippi river was restored, President Lincoln had enough troops to take back control of the strategically important railroad city of Knoxville, Tennessee. On September 2-3, 1863, the Union Army under Major General Burnside re-took Knoxville from the Confederates, who had occupied it since May 1863. The prisoners George refers to were probably from General Frazier's Confederate troops who were guarding the Cumberland Gap and surrendered on September 9, 1863. Massachusetts real estate taxes were and still are due on May 1. Mary Ann [Parkman] Earl[e] married Timothy Keefe in early September 1863.

No 8

Morristown Tenn Sept 25th '63

Dear Friends

      I will write a few words today but dont know when I can send it. we have been on the move every day since I got paid off and sent you the check we came through the Gap last Sunday and reached here (instead of Knoxville as we expected) Tuesday that day we forded two rivers and came ~~of~~ over two mountain[s] 22 miles in all it took from 5 in the morning until 8 in the evening a rough hard march. the next day we started to guard a large wagon train to Greenville we went out 10 miles that night and then had orders to come back the next morning. we did so. by the way the rest of the Div. took the cars here and went to Greenville and were ordered back and to Knoxville so that they had a ride ~~to~~ from here to G. + back and we had a walk of 20 miles for nothing. they have gone on to K. and we expect to go tomorrow I dont know whether we shall go on the cars or not the wagon train that we were guarding has gone on and thare is a battery left with us. I like the looks of East Tenn pretty well better than I expected, but thare is one thing that I cant tolerate and that is the women all smoke + chew and aint thought much of in society if they dont.

Knoxville Tenn Sept 27th

Sunday afternoon. I will now finish this letter as I understand that thare will be a chance to send tonight last night about 10 o'clock after we were all in blankets orders came to pack right up. we went on board the cars very thickly packed on top and reached Knoxville about 3 this morning we were pretty cold having no overcoats and that air was keen. the moon shone brightly we are now in the woods about one mile from the Depot.

the report is now that we are to move in the morning but whare to I dont know. The news ~~thare~~ here today is that Rosecrans has taken 62 [12?] thousand prisoners, killed + wound 6 more I dont know how true it is. thare are a great many troops here, and any quantity of Cavelry + artillery things look as though something had got to be done. Knoxville is quite a place I have'nt been into the center of the place but can look on from these hills. since we left Crab Orchard we have marched some 175 miles and rode in the cars more than 40 more if we had come directly from Crab Orchard to here we should have save[d] some the distance is 165 miles I here [hear]. we are having very fine weather cold nights and warm days. some say that we are going to N Carolina I see that they are bound to show us the country the different southern states but not much rest. I understand that Gen Burnside says that he will give us a chance to go home in 3 months I hope he will we seem to be victorious at all points now, for which success we should be thankful. I feel as though the end of fighting was not far off. I feel better than I did a few weeks ago. my feet are quite sore and marching comes hard. Louis is quite well except sore feet. I have been talking with him this morning he (like me) has seen enough of the <u>sunny south</u>. This being sunday and at this hour some of you are most likely at church. (<u>2 o'clock</u>) oh, I think of you and well do I remember the many pleasant sundays I have spent with. I long to be with you again and enjoy those precious priveledges again. I feel that thare is a good time coming for me soon. ~~I~~ if I come home I shurely shall enjoy it, but if I leave this world thare is still greater joy in store for me. had I time and sun I mint write many things that I shall not attempt. we have climb[ed] some large mountains and seen some yes many things worthy of remembrence. I will write again soon and send when I have a chance. remember me to the friends. if you dont here from me so often dont worry for it is difficult writing on the move.

Good Buy from George W Harwood

Knoxville was occupied by opposing forces throughout the war. President Lincoln wanted to obtain it for the Union because the area was primarily pro-Union and several important railroad lines went through there between Virginia, West Virginia, Nashvillle and Chattanooga. The Ninth Corps kept the Confederate forces from returning to Knoxville. In the Battle of Chickamauga, Georgia on September 19-20, Confederate General Bragg defeated Union Generals Rosecrans and Thomas who then retreated to Chattanooga, Tennessee.

Knoxville Tenn Oct 1st '63

Dear Brother Ethan,

I will write you a few lines this morning and send you a paper that you may see the style of a Southern paper this is it full size. thare is no news in particular. I am glad that you go to school + like so well you say that it is hard for you to write in your Journal it used to be for me and I guess that my old Journal will show that by its looks, but I am glad that I was obliged to write in it, for I think it is a good thing, and I hope you will try and keep a good one. we are still in Knoxville and I dont know when we shall move. thare is said to be a rebel force near here. Gen Burnside rode around in our camp night before last he is a pleasant looking man he said he was glad to see us. the last time I saw him was at Falmouth Va. last winter when he was in command of the Army of the Potomac I shall not have room to write much more this time. I hope you will write often and send with the rest if it is only a few words or lines be a good boy + study hard.

Good Bye from your brother George W Harwood

George was kidding with his brother, he wrote on a scrap of paper about three by four inches. These two letters were kept with a copy of The Knoxville Daily Bulletin, *dated Wednesday, September 30, 1863. The paper is ten by thirteen and three-quarter inches, printed on two sides.*

Knoxville Daily Bulletin, September 30, 1863 (Image from author's collection)

No 9
Knoxville Tenn Oct 1st 63

Dear Friends

I will commence a letter to you today but dont know as I shall finish it. yesterday was a fine day we policed our quarters and had our streets laid out &c + pitched our tents in perfect order. we are encamped in a fine grove not far from town and good water pretty handy. thare is not much here that we can buy and so we shall not be likely to spend so much money. cheese is .75 cts per lb + butter can hardly be found at any price things are very high + scarse. It commenced raining about 2 o'clock last night + has rained ever since and now it rains hard I feel pretty good this morning and like writing so I commenced this letter I wrote last Sunday + to Ethan [Allen] this morning. I received a letter from Lyman H. Gilbert a few days ago he says he isnt getting along very fast. at the same time I rec'd a letter from home + Hubbard. I think that I numbered my last 2 letters 7 the last one should have been 8 making this of corse 9. I am now sitting in the middle of my tent on my blankets the rain sounds good striking on the shelter over my head but I dont like quite so much spattering through on my paper and if it rains much harder I shall be obliged to stop. Thare is but little news for me to write that will interest you nothing of much importance has transpired since I wrote last. Gen Burnside + staff rode through our camp night before last he looked natural. if you have ever seen his picture you know how he looks. the men all like him and would go a good ways any time to see him.

Knoxville Tenn Oct 15th

The reason that I have not written before is this. Saturday the 3rd we were ordered out in light marching order. we took the cars and run up as far as Bull Gap Station about 1/2 way from Morristown to Greenville the next morning (Sunday) we marched on some 4 miles and done picket duty until the 10 we then advanced on as far as Blue Springs some 5 miles whare we attacked the enemy in the forepart of the afternoon and about 2 hours before sundown we had it pretty warm. the balls flew like hailstones but we pressed them back of their entrenchments and came up on a open field whare they had full view of us, and they commenced throwing shell at us. we all fell flat to the ground the shot + shell just passed over our heads as we lay with our faces almost buried in the dirt. our batteries meanwhile were not idle. here our Lieut. Col. was wounded 2 Lieut. and several others. we lay in this position until dark and then spread our blankets and remained thare over night. when we first attacked them ~~they~~ their skirmishers were in one piece of woods and are in another some 40 or 50 rods apart. it was a dangerous piece of business to cross the the open field but we did it, but few were wounded as we pressed them we saw their dead and wounded laying in the woods we took some prisoners. the next morning ~~the~~ we found that the rebs had all gone and we followed on 20 miles that day but did not over take them but Gen Foster did and had quite a brush with them at or near Rheatown (that is as far as we went) he killed + wounded conciderable many, took some prisoners 2 pieces of artillery, and some baggage wagons the old muskets lay along side the road plenty of them and some dead men + horses we stopped over one day at or about 1 mile beyond Rheatown and our men buried some 30 of their men thare that were laying dead around in the woods. one man had one half of his head taken off by a shell. his brains all run out on the ground, "sad sight". our men buried in all 100 or more of their men I dont know how many prisoners they took. We left Rheatown for Knoxville the 13 (Tuesday) leaving quite a force thare under Genl's Foster + Wilcox we came back to Bull Gap Station 30 miles in 2 day and took the cars thare about dark last night and reached here at 12 or midnight. the citizens were almost frightened to death for fear the rebs would get them and flocked to-gether by hundreds with all the old guns they could find. several hundred of them enlisted at that time. if I had time or could see you I could tell you all about our battle at Blue Springs maybe I can sometime, but I can never ex-press my feelings to you, that I experienced that day. it was the most trying time in my life I think. Louis was unwell and did not go. he has rec'd a letter from Anna + Freeman. we lived on half rations most of the time. I am sorry that I have not given you a better discription of our little fight but I have not room nor time. I recd letters 6 + 7 today and papers and was very glad to learn that you were all so well, and that F + A [Freeman & Anna] have con-cluded to remain at home for the present. I think that it will be much pleas-anter for you all. you spoke about going to cattle show. I should like right well to have been thare and gone also. you spoke about having fruit I wish I could get hold of those fall Greenings + grapes we have but few apples here that a person can eat and they are high. our living is rather poor now it is hard to bring supplies through the Gap from Crab Orchard a long hard road. the weather here is pleasant but cool nights. I sometimes wish I had an over-coat but I shall draw a new blouse in a few days and an overcoat by + by.

[originally on same sheet as Ethan's letter, paper appears to have been cut with scissors]

Gen. Burnside went up with [us] to Blue Springs and Rheatown. he sent on a lot of mounted infantry from the 23 corps ahead of us the morning before we attacked the enemy. they went up most to the enemy and left their horses and went to skirmishing but did not succeed in driving the rebs Burnside stood back and looked on a while. said he I have got some men back here that can do it but I hate to let them go in. my 9 corp will do it (said he) and we went in and relieved the cavalry men and when we had gained the point that I speak of whare we hugged the ground so, the Genl sent word to our Brigade commander Col Morrison. said he, Col your men have accomplished in five minutes what 5,000 men have failed to do in all day. he complimented us very highly. he thinks a good deal of his 9 corps and the 9 corps think a good deal of him. I wish you could see him he rode up last from Greenville on the Engine he looks so pleasant I wish you could see him. the cars were heavily loaded and going up a rise of ground they got stuck he got off and said get off and push boys but they went on without their help I must close I will write again soon please remember me to the friends and write often. I have not written half enough. Good Bye

       I am well now first rate.

       George W. Harwood

The Battle of Blue Springs was October 10, 1863, northeast of Knoxville along the railroad line towards Greenville in East Tennessee. Skirmishes in Rheatown (now Chuckey) and Bulls Gap were on October 11 and 13. Fall Greenings are a variety of apple.

No 10

Knoxville Tenn Oct 18th '63

Dear Friends

      As I have a little time this afternoon, I will write a few lines to you but shall not send them today. it rained hard all the forenoon and is cloudy and chilly now. I have attended Divine Services this afternoon for the first time for a good while the 79th New York Chaplain preached he is a young man not over 28 years a little bigger than Mr Peters of N. B. but he is smart he has got some good ideas into his head. it seemed quite a treat to listen once more to a preacher of sound doctrine. I have heard only one or two preachers since I left home that interested me very much. I expect this man will be our Brigade Chaplain. I hope he will. As I read my Testament and meditate on its sacred truths and know what it [is] to be a follower of my Saviour by experience. I long to have my friends + companions become the followers of the same Saviour, and let me urge upon each of you in the family who have not already sought that better life, to think of these things. Christ is waiting to receive you, delay is dangerous, today is ours, tomorrow we may be in eternity, standing before a just God, prepared or unprepared. can we render up our last accts with joy? let us not be deceived. let us not trust to much to good morals for they wont save a man. good works alone wont save a man, but let us strive to follow an example, Christ, and all will be well with us. what a blessed thought that when we have done with this life, its trials, its temptation, its discouragements, its hardships, that we have a hope in Christ, that we have the blessed assurance that we shall go to dwell with blessed Saviour eternal in the heavens, whare we shall be free from sin + sorrow, pain + sickness, and whare thare will be no change but from Glory to Glory. Yesterday morning my Capt told me that thare had been a call for men to go into E. Tenn recruiting and that he had sent in my name I expected to be called upon at once but have not as yet and perhaps shall not be. still I may be before I send this letter and so not have a chance to send at present as I may be gone several weeks. you all have read a great deal about Parson Brownlow of Knoxville Tenn. I have seen his house but I have not seen him. some of the boys have [heard] he is going to start a paper, as you have seen by our northern papers I presume. It is rather cool and I will not write much more this time. Monday 19th. I will write a little more this afternoon we have had a Co drill this morning and are going to have a battalion [drill] this afternoon and dress parade tonight. this is a very fine day warm + clear. I rec'd your letter last night No 8 dated Oct 7th I am very glad that Freeman + Anna have concluded to remain whare they are. it will be so much pleasanter for Anna + Mother. you spoke about Father traiding I should think by talk that he traided conciderable, but what about having a to have a lisence to traid. I never heard of such a thing. has every man got to have a lisence if he wants to traid sheep or calves for [or] geese please explain more about this lisence business next time. I am glad that Freeman has got enough to do. how is John Dexter [Lamson] now is he getting along well? Do you think that Frank Jenks will ever come back to the Reg. I have not heard from Lyman directly for about a month. I should like to have him come back on many accts but I dont feel very homesick. Joe Wheelock

(another page)

+ I tent together and have pretty good times he + I are all that are left in this Co from N B. Louis tents about 3 rods from me I can speak to him any time Alvin Thompson [is] about as far the other side. I can see him any time by just looking in that direction without getting out of my tent, and that is all in the Reg from our town at present. Cummings is driving team[s] now. there is a rumor in camp that we are all going to move in a few days down to Loudon Bridge I dont know how true it is. we are waiting they say for cloth-ing to come up. I expect to draw a new blouse and drawers + I dont know but a pair of socks. my shirts are getting thin quite so, and I shall draw a new one before long. if I were near home whare I could have a box I would rather have some new ones like my old one if they cost 3 times as much, but I cannot get a box hear but I will make these old ones go ~~with~~ under an army shirt this winter. I should like a pair of boots but I have got a good pair of shoes. I shall not draw an overcoat at present ware two blouses when it is cold. Does Mr Holman live on the old Ludden place where he did last year. How much are apples worth per lb. I think I saw in the Mass Spy that they brought in Worcester market 2.00 apples here [they] are very poor + not very plenty 20 cts per doz for little small apples, pretty high. cheese 50 cts butter 62 1/2 writing paper is very high little papers of pepper 15 cts, a hank of black linnen thread 15 cts poor at that, a bottle of ink 15 cts. every thing is as high and the sutler has plenty of cans of oysters + jellies of all kinds from 50 cts to 2.00 per can. so you see that 13 dollars per month dont go far with those that purchase these things, that is jellies + canned fruit to gratify the the taste only. I like dried fruit + jellies but shall not buy unless I am sick + in need, a little cheese + butter make hard tack and <u>sour</u> soft bread relish. we are not living very high now, not quite as well as I should like we draw mostly soft bread but it is a little sour, fresh beef is plenty. you say that Henry has got out as "chief of staff" in the medical department. I judge by that he must have a commission or is he only a clerk, but I must draw this to a close tell George Jackson I have got his letter and will write when I get time. remember me to all the friends. you say that E D B [Batcheller] + Wife are going to write I hope they will. write often + keep me posted. I like when Freeman writes for he tell all the new in the village + shop.

Good Bye from your son + brother George W Harwood

Parson Brownlow was a nationally known and controversial figure from Tennessee. He was the owner of the Knoxville Whig *newspaper and a circuit rider for the Methodist church. To help finance the war, Congress passed the Internal Revenue Act on July 1, 1862. One of the provisions was to require an annual license for horse dealers, and cattle brokers. Frank Jenks received a discharge for disability on October 21, 1863. Henry E. Smith served with the Massachusetts Fifteenth and was at Chester Hospital in Pennsylvania where he was "commander of guard" and also assigned to "receive and care for rebel prisoners" after Gettysburg. Temple, page 334. A suttler or sutler was a travelling salesman who sells food, stationery and other small items to individual soldiers.*

[No 11]   Greenville Tenn Oct 23 '63

Dear Friends

     As I am not very busy this afternoon, I will commence a letter to you. We left Knoxville Tuesday (20th) about 9 oclock in the cars and reached Greenville about 4 in the afternoon we slept out on the Depot platform that night. the next morning we went up into the center of the place and took possession of a building on the corner of Main + I guess there is no name to the other St's. we have a very good place thare are 12 of us in all 1 Capt. 1 Lieunt 3 Non-com 7 privates. yesterday we bought 1/2 bushel of potatoes + 2 beeves [plural for beef] livers + ham had a gay time eating. we have got a long table long enough for us all thare are two fire places in the room. today we have drawn rations flour, sugar + coffee + beef, and we had a good chance to buy some nice butter and so on bought 12 lbs 25 cts per lb. we got our flour baked here ~~in the~~ at one of the houses. today we put out our ~~postages~~ Notices <u>Recruits wanted.</u> we are having a fine time 1 man from each Co. today it rains hard, and as I think of the Reg on the march or in a fight for ought I know the 9 corps left Knoxville the same morning that we did and went towards Chattanooga ~~way~~. I understand that they are having trouble thare I think that this squad is very fortunate to be in a house, a hotel + store opposite. chestnuts are selling for 20 cts per nut apples 10 cts per doz.

                               Sunday Oct 25th

I will write a little more today, a mail went out this morning but I had not mine ready. I dont know when it will go again. I think in a few days. yesterday it rained all day some of the time quite hard. I had another turn at the chills + fever yesterday afternoon which lasted the chill an hour or more + I was feverish all the rest of the afternoon and evening. I feel quite well today.

I have had only 2 turns at it since I came here every other day they come on. I have been to church this morning. we had a very good discorse text was from Mark 12-28 last clause [12:28-34]. I think that I have not been in to a church before since I left home, and sat in <u>pew 110</u>. it seemed a little like home, but should a good deal rather have been in N B whare I hope to be some day, but the war news of late that we have ~~been able here~~ heard is rather discouraging, but we must expect some defeats as well as all <u>victories</u>. as I told you in the beginning of this letter we are nicely quartered and are having the easiest time that we have had since we left home I expect that the Reg is down to Loudon Bridge but we have heard nothing from them since we left Knoxville. We have got a pretty good crowd of fellows I think. four of us are writing on this table. this is the first table that I have written on for a long time. I can write better [than] to sit down on the floor and write on my knee. It has cleared off and is quite warm + pleasant the most of the boys have gone out and it seems really like Sunday. there is no preaching in the place this afternoon I dont know why. thare are several churches. the people of East Tenn. are a very shiftless lazy ignorant set. I dont think we shall get many Recruits and none of us are very anxious to but at the same time we shall try and do the best we can. I think I shall enjoy stopping here if the chills will let me alone. I will write a little more on another sheet before I send.

Tuesday 27th

I will finish this letter this morning I guess. yesterday was a very fine day, but it rains a little this morning. yesterday I had the chills again but not so hard for I took a dose of Quinine a little while before they came on, and am going to take another today. some of the boys went into the old post office and found a lot of reb envelopes and news papers. I cut of[f] some stamps to send you perhaps some of you have never seen any of them. I should like to have you see these papers. they are reb. all over. We have not got any re-cruits yet and we dont feel very bad to think we have'nt. Capt says that we could get more in Worcester Mass. and we boys all think just so. I should like to get home and get some good apples the apples that we buy here are poor + smell are thare plenty of chestnuts + walnuts this year. I should like all I could eat for once. it hasnt seemed like soldiering the past week. we have had no roll-call no guard and we go whare we please and come same no guard can stop us.

I must close. Write again soon

George W Harwood

[Note upside down at the top of the last page] Here is a Reb envelope pretty poor dont you think so

This letter included a blank piece of lined paper labelled "Rebel writing paper". Greenville, now Greeneville, was a pro-Union town. It is the town Vice-president Andrew Johnson was from. President Lincoln was anxious to support East Tennessee and keep it in the Union because of the pro-Union sentiments there and the strategic railroads which connected West Virginia, Tennessee, Georgia and Alabama. The chills and fever he experienced on alternating days probably indicated a case of malaria. Mark 12:28-34, when Jesus was asked which commandment is the greatest, he replied, "You shall love the lord your God You shall love your neighbor as yourself." Revised Standard Version.

No 12
Greenville Tenn Oct 31st '63

Dear Friends

     I will commence a letter to you this morning as I have nothing else to do. I rec'd a letter from you last night, was very glad to hear again from my home + friends. We are still in this great village of Greenville and having a very easy + pleasant time we have had nothing to do since we came here but eat, drink + sleep we have all got passes so that we can pass the guards and all patrols at any hour in day or night. we go out nearly every evening and call on the young people here in the place. we have some good times a few evenings ago we went to a singing school + are going again before long if nothing happens. they sing old pieces that I never heard before. they have got some pretty good singers, some pretty decent looking young ladies, but they dont come up to the Mass girls. Night before last we heard a rumer that the troops above us were falling back and were going to fall back as far as Bull Gap and so of corse if they did we should have to go with them a good many citizens fell back and we packed up ready to start but did not go. before night it was all quiet again. I sent a letter to you a few days ago from this place. I do not intend to finish this letter today. I have sent in for an overcoat but have [not] got it yet I should like some new boots + shirts from home but I should'nt dare to have one (a box) sent. I have not heard any thing from Mr. W. [James] Haskell since I left Crab Orchard he was quite feeble then and down spirited he wanted to go home his sister died but a short time ago. I knew a long time ago that George Davis was married but I did not know that he lived in N.B. before. Then John Dexter [Lamson] +

Eunice [Doane] are rearly [really] going to be married soon I did not expect so soon. I thought surely Edwin would get married before Eunice. Hubbard ought to be reminded that its about time for him. by the way what is Judson about that he has'nt got married before this time. I thought 15 months ago that his day was not far distant.   Sunday Nov 1ˢᵗ

I will write a little more this pleasant Sabbath afternoon the first day in the week + month it is warm + pleasant. I have been to church this morning but thare is no preaching this afternoon and so I will spend a part of the time in writing we had a very good sermon but I have heard many better ones I suppose that some of you have been to church today and as I think back upon the old church + congregation, I fancy I see you seated in your accustomed places. 14 months have expired since I left the scenes of my childhood. it seems but a short time to look back to that time, but when I stop and think on what I have passed through it seems longer, but I hope that ere another 14 months passes over my head I shall have returned to my home and this war honestly ended time alone will tell and all we have got to do is wait. yesterday we were mustered for our pay we polished our Guns + equipments in fine style and put on our white gloves and blacked our shoes and went out into the street looking pretty slick we went through the manual of arms a few times and made a few wheels and [there] came in quite a crowd gathered around. they have got some Ind. boys here doing guard duty (6 months men) they are a green pack dont know enough to salute an officer. but I must draw this letter to a close I am getting near the bottom of the page I expect that we shall return back to our Reg before another week comes round but I am in no hurry. write often and I will

Good Bye yours &c George W. Harwood

Sarah Elisabeth Haskell Wilson died in Stoughton, Massachusetts in August 1863, the last of W. James Haskell's siblings to die. Eunice A. Doane married John Dexter Lamson on November 3, 1863.

No 13
Morristown Tenn Nov 9ᵗʰ '63

Dear Friends

I will write a few lines this morning and send out. I commenced one to Anna before I left Greenville. We left Greenville Friday night just before dark. The troops were all ordered to fall back to Bull Gap Station, on acct of the fight at Rogersville that day (Friday) we marched that night about 13 miles and then turned into an old barn about 1 o'clock and started again about 7 the next morning and came down to the Station and staid thare until 3 in the afternoon and we heard that the cars were not coming up thare that day so we took a little truck car and put on the Officers trunks and all of our things and then we pushed it whare it would'nt go itself. Capt, Lieunt + 10 of us men and a darky we had a fine time it took us 3 1/2 hours, 13 miles. the 45 Pa were thare [at Bull Gap Station] recruiting and they came down on another car and if we didnt have a fine time where it was down grade we did slide in good shape. the 36 + 45 Pa. agree first rate you say a word against one Reg and you hit the other. the 45 have got orders to report to their Reg and have gone on but we have not and are at present in an old Store unoccupied as such now a very good place. Our Capt has gone on to the Reg on business so we shall remain here a few days at least. I understand that our Reg has gone into winter Quarters have made good houses, but I had a rather remain in the recruiting business as I have no duty to do that is hard, and we have a good warm room. we are having fine weather rather cool some of the time. I am quite fleshy I weigh 175 lbs. thinly dressed. I dont know as thare is much news to write this time. in the fight at Rogersville last Friday we lost some men about 1000 in all prisoners a part of 2 Regs of mounted Infantry and one battery 4 guns. I received one letter from home, since I left the Reg. while at Greenville I expect another when the Capt returns from the Reg. I will write again soon. you spoke about sending a paper to me I have not got it yet. I shall next mail I presume Remember me to all the Friends I am as ever your affectionate Son + Brother

Geo W. Harwood

I thought I would not write anymore today but I altered my mind and am going to write a little more. I want to say a word about the sufferings of the citizens as well as the soldiers here in East Tenn. When we left Greenville the men women + children in town (the Union I mean) were frightened half to death many of them packed up and left whole families some men left their ~~wife~~ wives & children and fell back with the army some sons left their home for fear that if the Rebs should come into Greenville that they would hang them or distroy their property. many a union man has been hung in and around Greenville and many a boy, because he would'nt tell whare his Father was women have been shamefully abused. thare is one old negro woman that lived close by whare we stopped that had her <u>nose</u> shot off by a reb soldier some months ago. she done some ~~washed~~ washing for him and she asked him for her pay. he went off and afterwards he shot at her in the street and took her nose off without damageing her other ways. I could mention several cases had I room I have thought a good many times that I should much rather have you all whare you are away a thousand and more miles whare I could see you but a few times ~~in~~ and even not at all ~~than~~ in the corse of my 3 years than have you here exposed to the enemy as they are here in Tenn. or Ky. you dont know what the people have to suffer whare the soldiers of both parties are all the time in possession running into your house pulling down your fences stealing any thing that they could get their hands on. You have great reason to be thankful that you are away from such scens [scenes]. It is saddining to see such distruction as this war makes all over this part of the land I should think that a few years more of war would ruin them altogether. it is all the people can do to live here now and I dont know what they will do this winter and next summer they have'nt sown but little wheat this fall for they want the wheat to use <u>now</u> and I dont know what they will do another summer.

George W. Harwood

The fight at Rogersville, northeast of Knoxville, was on Friday, November 6, 1863. The Confederates took the town by surprise and held it until the end of the war. Winter quarters were near Loudon just west of Knoxville. The letter was written on ledger paper, seven and three-eighths by twelve and a half inches.

[Note at the top of the next letter] (Alvin Thompson is missing we dont know whether he was killed or taken prisoner or what became of him.)
No 14   Knoxville Tenn Nov 18th 1863

Dear Friends

      I will commence a letter this afternoon. I dont know when I shall have a chance to send it. this is paper that I took out of a large acct. book in Morristown. I left M- and joined my Reg Tuesday the 10. I found them fixing for Winter Quarters. I worked on the tents until Saturday morning. we had got up some good log-houses. we have our food at Loudon Bridge here attached. we went up thare that after noon in the rain for it rained hard all day and the mud was deep. we lay in line of battle that night and just before daylight we retreated back to Lenoire [Lenoir] Station whare we had our tents Quarters built. the rebs followed us up so that we had to burn up the officers baggage and distroy the baggage wagons and almost everything, a sight of stuff distroyed. that night we had to lay in line of battle within 40

rods of the enemys line of battle, our guns loaded + caped [capped], bayonets fixed no blankets spread but knapsacks slung all night. it was cold and I
never suffered so much from cold in my life. we all shivered like a lief
[leaf]. and the enemy charged on us once or twice in the night but a volly
from our guns checked them. after a long sleepless night, we retreated just
before light and fell back towards Knoxville before breakfast, the rebs close
upon us and continuously firing upon our rear. when we got to Campbell
Station about 15 miles from Knoxville we were obliged to make a stand the
9 corps and a few [from the] 1 Div of the 23 [Michigan] were engaged they
came up on 3 sides of us. we the one our Brigade were in the center and and
thare we had a fight. I understand that the General said that he didnt expect
to see our Div again. we had'nt been engaged but a short time when a bullet
knocked my gun out of my hands and took me on side of my neck + throat
almost taking the breath from me it fairly stunned my left arm for a few
minutes. one of the boys took me and helped me back to the rear, and thare I
found a good many wounded we all had to run as fast as we could more
than a mile, the our men falling back as fast as they could our Brigade es-
caped being taken prisoner and that was all. by this time the batteries got
into posision and our men were relieved I fell back to whare the cooks
were. the Doc told me to do up my neck, or rather bath it in cold water. I did
so. I heard that the troops were all going to fall back in the night to K. so I
went on 6 or 7 miles and then crawled into an old barn but a friend of mine
from Co H detailed on the Brigade Commissary came along and heard that I
was thare he gave me some supper for I had none and it was dark. he took
some of my things and we came on we reached Knoxville about 9 oclock,
23 miles from Lenoire [Lenoir]. we marched that day 24 miles and fought 7
hours. I staid with him that night. before morning the troops all reached K.
yesterday they skirmished all day and flung up rifle pits and breast works.
today they have been fighting pretty hard, both infantry + artillery + cavelry
I am now with the cooks in an old oat field, feeling pretty sore and my neck
is + throat is swelled up some conciderably. our reg is now supporting the
skirmisher Our Capt was wounded in the foot slightly day before yesterday
our only Sergeantt with us was wounded in the leg and we expect taken prisoner one other man is missing from our Co. My old tent mate Wood our
loss that day was quite heavy about 40 killed wounded + missing from our
Reg I hear. Louis had a ball go through his cartridge box and just scrape his
arm, but is with his Co. one Lieunt one private killed shot through the head,

and never knew what hit them. I was glad to get out with a slight wound as I hope it will be nothing more, but I have suffered a good deal this afternoon. it pained me a good deal of the time. I understand that Gen Sherman is in the rebs rear I hope he is if we do not have help from some sorse we shall all be taken prisoner I fear. I received a letter from Lyman this morning from Portsmouth Grove R.I. I was very glad to hear from him. I got the paper you sent me a few days ago. I will close and eat my supper it is most dark. Oh that this war was over. they are fighting very briskly now. I pitty the pickets tonight.

     good bye, from George W.   Tea is 4.00 per lb. here in the City Sunday Nov 22 I will continue this letter this afternoon as I feel a little like writing. I wrote on the other sheet the 18. the 19 they all fought all day hard the rebs worked around on our right and are trying to surround us I should judge. 20 I came back to the regiment and am now with the rest of the sick + lame on the left of the Reg it looks like rain and does rain a little. the 17 Mich of the 3 Brigade went up to the front and charged on the rebs sharp shooters that kept picking of our men and burned 3 houses + I believe more. about 9 o'clock evening the rebs then shelled us, killing one of the Lieunt in the 17 it beet all the 4 of Julys that I ever saw, but no fun for me we all had to go into the rifle pits for an hour or so after that all was quiet that night. yesterday it rained hard all day ~~we went into a~~ but they kept fighting that is the skirmish-ers kept it up. we were relieved toward night and went into a house. this morn-ing the reg went back into the pits but the sick + lame + sore are in this house. we have all got guns + equipments furnished us to use in case of necessity. this is a very fine day they are fighting some today. I think not so hard. I under-stand that reinforcements have reached here today but I dont know how true it is. my neck is quite lame but is doing well I think. we have been reduced to very small rations a very small piece of bread + meat with a little coffee + no sugar. I think we have reason to feel a little downharted. we are all thinly clothed. I expected to draw cloths long ago but the clothing did not come and thare is none in the place. I have no overcoat a very poor blouse my shirts are quite thin, + rather holey, my pants are old + socks also, but never mind thare is a good time coming sometime I hope, but I dont see how we are going to get out of this affair without help. Oh! I could tell you some things that I will not <u>write</u> could I see you, and if I ever do I ~~will~~ think I will, but my patriotism is not quite all gone yet but runs low at times, such times as these. sometimes I want my discharge and then again I would'nt take it.

Thanksgiving morning [Thursday Nov. 26] It is with feelings of sadness mingled with pleasure that I think of my home this morning and then think of what I have undergone lately and what I am likely to undergo before we get out of this campaign we are surrounded or nearly so by our enemy. [At the top of the other side of the paper] (bottom side up careless) Monday morning I took a gun and joined my Co in the rifle pits. thare was some sharp fighting that day. I went on guard that ~~day~~ night. In the morning the Co went on pickets or as skirmishers. today the 2nd Mich lost heavily in a charge on our right some 60 killed + wounded in so small a Reg yesterday morning when the Co came off Picket we went back of the pits + into an old building to support a battery. about the middle of the afternoon there was sharp fighting on the left and the rebs fell back with much loss. we worked in the afternoon + evening until about 9 o'clock throwing up a breast work for another cannon. we have splendid moonlight nights and are in fact having fine weather. we are still in this building I am now thinking of what again I [will have for supper?] I can tell you how we live. we draw a small piece of bread about 3 1/2 or 4 inches square wheat + indian [corn-meal], a piece of meat not more [than] half a meal, sometimes pork at other times beef, a little coffee + sugar <u>daily</u> and that is all. it is less than quarter rations just enough to keep us from starving, but I will not complain as it is the best we can do. I shall feel thankful if we can get out of this at that. many men expect to get out with being taken prisoner. I am a little fearful. this letter may never be sent you it is well that the friends at home dont know our situation at present and many past times. my neck is much better but is quite sore yet. my thanksgiving supper will be 3 or 4 mouthfuls of bread + fresh boiled pork <u>fat</u>, such as would have turned my stomac at home. I now crave it.

Afternoon. It is now about time for you to sit down to your supper. I have just eaten mine. I had more then I expected. thare is a darky boy who cooks for a Capt in our Reg who gave me some tea grounds that made me a good cup. I steeped them over. I managed to send out and get 10 very small biscuits for 25 cts. it is next to impossible to buy any thing. I have got 10 cts left over the pay master is waiting to pay us off as soon as this fight is over, and if we have to give in he will burn his money. The Gen. sent out a guard and picked up all the darkys that they found floating around the City and set them to work digging rifle pits they have been at work several days Thus far today it has been very quiet no very brisk firing but at it all the time a little. today is the 13th day that we have been fighting everyday the wounded are brought into the hospitals. I shall be glad when I can receive a mail I have received none 2 weeks from home. I will close for this time. I hope you will all enjoy your Thanksgiving Supper.   George W.

The Battle of Campbell's Station was November 16. The town had been a stop on a stagecoach route. At this time there was a railroad line here. Later the town would be renamed for Admiral Farragut, who was born nearby. Lyman wrote from the Civil War general hospital at Portsmouth Grove, Rhode Island, at the tip of Aquidneck Island. There were a series of battles and retreats at Lenoir and Campbell Station from November 13-15. As Major General Burnside's troops retreated east towards Knoxville, they pulled General Longstreet's troops further away from Chattanooga. By November 18, the Union troops were inside Knoxville. Alvin Thompson was captured and died at Andersonville.

Wednesday afternoon.   No. 15.   Knoxville Tenn Dec 2nd 1863

Dear Friends at Home,

        I will write a little this afternoon hoping I shall have a chance to send sometime. I have written a little scetch of most every day since this fight commenced. the last I wrote was Thanksgiving day. the next day Friday we signed the Paroles [payroll] (but have not got our pay as yet.) thare was some picket firing but not so much as on days before. Saturday we had a heavy thunder shower in the morning and it rained a little all day until towards night. thare was some skirmishing or picket firing through that day, and about 1/2 past 10 or 11 that evening the rebs charged on our Fort, [Fort Sanders] (I was on guard at the time) and lost very heavily in killed + wounded between 300 + 400 we took that night some 600 prisoners. our batteries shelled all night and the next morning, (Sunday) they had a hard artillery fight not much infantry. about 9 o'clock they sent in a flag of truce and so did we that both parties could have a chance to bury their dead and provide for their wounded. the wounded prisoners were exchanged I understand. our loss was slight not more than 50 or so wounded. thare was no more firing until night that afternoon we were ordered back to the reg and went into the rifle pits. it was very cold + windy that day. the next morning our Co went on picket it was a pleasant but cold day, not a great deal of firing. plenty of rebs in sight we had to keep down behind some small entrenchments that we threw up in the night and if we stuck our heads up they would fire at us. in the night we had to throw out videtes, [vedettes] that is go out in front of the pickets and close to the enemy very carefully and see if we can hear or see any signs of a movement. I stood three hours within a few rods of the rebs, could hear them talk and cough and see them put on wood and make a fire. I dont like such jobs very much but can do it. at the point whare we go on picket our pickets are no more than 15[?] rods from the enemies. we can see their features plainly in the day time by looking through some crack. we relieve our pickets mornings at 5 oclock before light. Yesterday morning after we came off picket we fixed our rifle pits so that we can have a small fire in them and lay down. we do not get much sleep. during the 24 hours that we are on picket we cannot sleep a wink night nor day. not a man of us. when we are in the pits we have to keep awake one third of the time, in case the pickets get into trouble, to wake the rest of the men. some nights we have to shovel last night I shoveled 2 hours and stood guard 2 hours they are putting some sharpened stakes into the ground in front of these pits leaning toward the enemy to hinder them, about 4 ft high. we have got a wair [wire] a few inches from the ground clear around in front to trip them up. many of our men fall over it without thinking. Col Morrisson acting Brigadeer fell his whole length the other night. today I have done nothing but I shall have to [illegible] guard some of the time tonight and shovel some I expect. we drew yesterday a little corn meal for our ration of bread and had a pudding. the same today. I had a little pudding for breakfast and have had no dinner, nothing but a cabbage stump that I picked up, and a small piece of ginger bread that I bought and paid dear for it. I expect to have a little more hasty pudding and a little molasses for supper about one small meal in a day ration, but these things are'nt all ways going to continue. I can put up with it under these circumstances. last night we got the new[s] some way that Gen Grant had whipped Gen Bragg handsomely and that he (Bragg) was in full retreat for Delton [Dalton] Ga. after losing 6000 prisoners 52 pieces of artillery &c. I hope it is so. Gen Burnside seems to be in good spirits I see him nearly every day. he praises us for our bravery in the later fights, for our patients [patience], suffering as he said from cold, hungar, hard fighting + long marches. <u>Bully for Gen Burnside</u> Saturday 5th. day before yesterday morning I went on Picket after working the evening before on works in front. it was pretty quiet not much firing until towards night. thare was one or two alarms in the night but it did not last long. yesterday new[s] came that we had 10 days rations coming to us. Gen Sherman is at Lenoire [Lenoir] Station whare we had our Winter Quar-

ters built with 30000 men Gen Granger is here in this place came yesterday. yesterday in the afternoon our men opened on the rebs, stirred them up
a little.

[top of next page] continued

It is evident that the enemy is leaving as fast as possible. they are going
round on our right and probably bound for Va. but Sherman I understand is
after them. Gen Sherman captured some cars and ammunition at Lenoire
[Lenoir] but the rebs run 30 cars and 3 locomotives of[f] into the river at
Loudon. about midnight last night the rebs all left our front pickets and all
so that our men have been over into their old camp this morning and so of
corse it is quiet here today. we have come out of our pits and ~~piched~~ pitched
our tents. it rains some is very muddy. Louis has just been in to see me the
boys are in fine spirits Louis is in as tough as a whip. I cannot begin to
write you the half of the news and what is going on here daily. I shall not attempt it I have noted down only a few things. you will and have heard by
the papers all about this fight. the rebs loss was more than I expected they
admit a loss of 1500 prisoners and all but I hear that their loss is larger still.
Gen Longstreet issued an order to his men to take from our men overcoats
and shoes + boots or any thing they wanted, and then sent in to Gen Burnsides to serrender but Burnsides sent word back that he couldnt see it, but
that he had got his old boots and he could have them if he could get them.
Gen Burnside is a nice man. the other day he went up to a cannon an[d]
sighted it as he wanted it, and then ordered it fired he looked to see the effect and then said he wanted about 3 more in the same place. he was as jolly
as any of them. he laughed + talked with the men. thare is a report here that
Gen Forbes is going to take command of this department, that Gen Burnside
is going to the Washington and will be likely to take the 9th Corps with him
I hope he will. it is cold and I will not write any more now. it is much to cold
to write much out doors in Dec. without a fire. I shall be glad when the mail
comes do you get all my letters as I number them I get all of yours. I recd
the paper you spoke about that Jennie Livermore sent me. I suppose that
Ruth must be quite an accomplished young lady isnt she?

Sunday Dec 6th

I will try and finish this letter today and send as soon as I can a mail went
out last night or this morning under escort but I hadnt my letters quite ready
and no time to finish them is reason to send. this is a cold rough day we had
a Co inspection this morning. It seemed good to hear the Church bells this

morning the first time for a good while. it seems pleasant to be so quiet again after the fight and now I long to get a mail from home, and I presume that you are as anxious to hear from me but dont worry about me for I am all right my neck is much better nearly well all the trouble is over. I want a little more to eat and a few cloths to ware, both of which we shall have in a short time I expect. Our men took some more prisoners yesterday. I think we have used Longstreet pretty rough a few more such fights will clean him out. his men hollered to ours one day <u>Vicksburg</u> they thought that they had got us shure and would starve us out if they had to starve themselves doing it, but as it proved it was no Vicksburg to us. we expect our pay soon but I shall not send any home until I think it is safe. is thare plenty of money in circulation now? I have written to Lyman I suppose that he has been home before now. it is quite a priviledge for him to see his Wife and his friends I should like to visit you a few week if no more but I shall have to wait awhile, hoping that our all wise Providence will permit me to do so sometime. I know that I have great reason to be thankful that my life has been spared through the many dangers seen + unseen which we have been called to pass through the past few weeks in particular. many have gone to their long [?] homes never to return many have been crippled for life. it seems sad to look upon so many men dead + wounded as thare upon a battlefield. I did not go up to the Fort [Sanders] last Sunday after the fight but those that did say that it looked very bad men piled up in all shapes almost like a winnow whare our shells mowed them down, but I cannot write much about it. I can only say that I had no idea what it was to be a soldier or what a soldier has to pass through. I will write a little on another piece

I know well that the folks at home have a very ~~small~~ poor idea of soldiering and it is well that they do not, for if they did they would ~~have~~ be likely to worry more about us. thare are times when a soldier gets along pretty easy and does not have much to do, and thare are some who have no friends or home that they care anything about that like the business, but thare are none I think but that dread a fight. I for one have seen enough of soldering and shall be glad when I can return to my own home and engage in the peasful [peaceful] pursuits of this life. I am just anxious to hear from you as I have not for several weeks. I understand that Col [Henry] Bowman is on the road hear to again take command of this regiment ~~again~~ I hope he will. I wish you would send me a Dairy [diary] larger than the one you sent last year I would like one large enough to put a common sized letter in envelope (I reason [?]) I believe that they dont keep such things as Dairies here I have seen none I guess you can leave the ends open and not have it cost much to send it. I suppose that Ethan + Fannie go to school this Winter who teaches? does that young man work for Father now? I suppose he has got his fall work done, long ago, and nothing to do but do his chors. I hope he will take good care of the little colt and if possible have a good horse out of it. I should like to step into your pantry + celler a few minutes about this time well do I remember when I used to find fault with good warm brown bread + butter and jonny cakes &c. when my days ration ~~consists of~~ is now a small piece of <u>brown bread and a piece of pork,</u> no coffee no sugar no [illegible] no buns or any thing else. this is learning me a good lesson. I wish I could see you, as I cannot write half enough I have written two long letters but have not written any thing yet. I guess you will think that I have given you a poor acct of the late fights and so I have but I did not intend to when I commenced for I have not time nor room. I will close now my best wishes to you all. please remember me to all the friends. I am well + all right Good Bye from your son + brother

George W. Harwood

A rod measures five and a half yards so at fifteen rods the opposing troops were about eighty yards apart. A vedette is a mounted sentry stationed in front of an army's outposts to observe the enemy. The military engagement in Knoxville from November 19–December 3 is referred to now as a siege. Technically it was not one as Burnside's troops were able to forage for food supplies north and east of the city. On November 25 Generals Grant and Sherman defeated General Bragg at Lookout Mountain and Missionary Ridge in Chattanooga. The Confederate forces under Longstreet tried to circle around and take Knoxville but were not successful. Longstreet retreated from the city of Knoxville on December 3 but stayed in eastern Tennessee for the winter. General Sherman arrived to reinforce Burnside's troops on December 6. My husband and I attended a re-enactment of the battles of Campbell Station and Fort Sanders in Knoxville in 2013. President Lincoln gave the Gettysburg Address on November 19, the same day that the siege of Knoxville began.

~ Chapter 9 ~

KNOXVILLE, HOME FOR RECRUITING FURLOUGH
December 19, 1863 – February 21, 1864

No 16   Near Beans Station Tenn
                                         Dec. 19th 1863

Dear Friends at Home,

      I left 2 letters at Knoxville with one of our men that was unable to come to send Nos 14 + 15 I expect he sent them but do not know. have you got them. We left K. Monday 7 in light marching orders. we have followed the rebs up as far as here they have captured some of our wagon trains of late and we have taken some prisoners + artillery. no new of much importance has transpired since I left Knoxville. I wrote all up to thare in the other letters. we have had a cold time a part of the time and it has rained some. my portfolio is in my knapsack. this is a piece of paper that I borrowed or rather a chap gave me. the knapsacks are ordered up I understand. my fingers are so cold that I can hardly write so that I can read it. we have just made out a requisition for clothing I put down for a whole suit. thare is a report here that we are going to Washington with Burnside but I can hardly credit it. I hope we shall for we are having a rough time of it at present on such short rations (1/2) and we are all thinly clad but we stand it remarkably well. my tent mate Joe Wheelock is quite sick with the Chronic Diarrhea I hope he will get better soon. I have received 4 letters from home within a few days. then John + Eunice are rearly married ~~good~~ a pretty good match I think. you spoke of Joe Rich death and the funeral services I think perhaps Mr Cushing was a little plain. its his way, but for all that it may do no harm. I think you Anna must have had a splendid time with your Brother + Sister at your Oyster Supper. I would that I could have been present, I can imagine how you looked and that is some comfort isnt it? I think that they are offering a pretty large bounty to Volunteers at the present time and if money is any object they had better come and help finish crush out this rebellion. I dont think it will be many months longer, about the time my 3 years are out, I reckon. what Reg is Nat Foster going into or don't you know yet. You spoke of George Stoddard's marriage. I could'nt help laughing to myself when I read that. I used to see this girl every day when I lived with Ezra I guess she is pretty smart and fair looking but I must say his taste differs from mine in choosing a Wife. I should think that the young people were all getting married at home I had a letter from Hubbard a day or two ago he think he shall wait until after war is ended and I have come to the same conclusion with regard to myself. I should think that they were putting up a rather expensive Town Hall, perhaps none to much so, but isnt the bill pretty heavy. ~~you~~ I should like to have a short furlough and come home as Lyman did. it must be pleasant I should like to see him better than ever. I want to ask him a few questions about the people in N Brookfield. I should have laughed to have gone by Mr Doanes Thanksgiving day and seen all of you men + women (for such you were) out playing ball + I Spy + such but it is all right I hope you had a good time it must have reminded you of old times when you ~~that would go [illegible]~~ were little school children, but I say go in while you are young. Most that I have written thus far seems to be directed to Freeman + Anna as they have done a good portion of the writing but I mean all. I am sorry that mother's lameness is no better this winter but Allen must help her all he can and Fannie too, and I presume they do. I am convinced that if I were to live my life over I should do more to help my dear Mother when I could I can see now whare in I failed to please my mother at all times and do all I could for her, but it is too late for that now I can only ask her forgiveness and strive to be a kind + oblidging son here after. Yesterday we received 2 months pay all up to Nov 1st soon they will owe us 2 more. my fingers are nearly stiff with cold and this paper is about full I shall try and write a little more before I send. Yours with my best wishes + prayers

George W. Harwood

Sunday afternoon The knapsacks have just come up and we can send a mail if we will get it in in less than 10 minutes I am well and will write soon the letters that I left in Knoxville with my friend have been sent I hope you will get them. remember Nos 14 + 15 write if you ever get them I cannot stop to write any more this time so good Bye George W Harwood

Nathaniel H. Foster served with the Massachusetts Twenty-fifth. George Stoddard married Catherine G. Finessey on November 28, 1863. Many regiments were being offered bounty money to re-enlist.

No 17   Near Beans Station Tenn
                                                     Dec 22 '63

Dear friends at Home,

    This is a very fine day and I will write a little while to you I shall have to write with a pencil this time for my ink is about played out. I have but little or no news to write this time. I sent a letter to you day before yesterday the 20th. I did not know that the mail was going out until 5 or l0 minutes before it went I guess you will think by the look that I was in a hurry, and now I must tell you what I was doing when word came that a mail would go out. I was frying thin cakes as you would call them, but they will hardly do to be called by so good a name. we draw flour and eat it the best way we can with salt and water. I understand that they intend to give full rations of bread or meal soon. the 9th Corps are expecting to be relieved by the 8th Corps the Gen Commanding the 8th has already arrived in Knoxville I hear, (we are 18 miles from K) and the troops will be here soon. we are expecting to go to Washington or Baltimore I guess that thare is no doubt about that as those that ought to know say it is so. then I shall expect to see some of you out thare with a box from home. I have sent in for clothing but I shall want some shirts + socks + boots from home I guess I can tell better when I get thare. the army shirts are cheap corse concerns and I dont like them and the socks wont ware but a few weeks. we have not had a chance to change our cloth very often the past 2 months and some of the boys have worn their shirts 8 or 9 weeks without changing them. I have changed mine much oftener and have had one washed today but they are both pretty well worn out. I wrote in my last letter that we had been paid off. I guess I shall hang on to my money for the present. our Officers are making out the Muster and Paroles [payrolls] again today I presume we shall be paid off again before many weeks. they will owe us 2 months more the first of Jan. how quickly the past year has passed away but how great the changes have been many a brave son of New England is no more. many have been crippled for life, but it is all for their country. we have great reason to hope at the present time that this rebellion will soon be crushed out everything looks encouraging. at nearly every point our armies are victorious, and if they do as much the next year as they have the past what will be left of rebeldom! prisoners that we take from time to time here in Tenn. all tell the same sad story. they are all suffering from starvation and cold many of them are shoeless except what they can pick up. they strip our dead of almost every thing and of our men that they take prisoners they take a large portion of their cloths, and leave them to suffer. I hope I shall never fall into their hands.

Thursday 24th I will now try to finish this letter that I commenced day before yesterday. I have just finished my dinner. this forenoon I bought a quart of wheat meal for 25 cts it looked a good deal like oat or cob [corn?] meal and tasted about the same. I fried it griddles cakes I would eat one while the next one was cooking. for breakfast I had a piece of beef a cup of coffee (no sugar) + parched corn. this is a very fine day rather cool, but no colder than I should expect this season of the year. I am quite well + fleshy the boys all look pretty well concidering what we have passed through the past month. I wrote in my last letter that my tent-mate Joe Wheelock was quite unwell he has the Chronic Diarrhea pretty badly, but I hope he will be better soon. I see by a paper that some of the boys got that the 9 months men are liable to be drafted this call. what do they think of that arrangement rather into them as we say. I have been thinking that perhaps Freeman ~~would~~ will have to come again ~~but~~ I hope not for his sake, but am anxious to have the rebellion put down and to raise men to do it with. I understand that nothing short of 800 dollars will clear a man this time. thare is a good deal said about the 9 Corps going to Washington all manner of stories afloat some say that all those who have not served in the army 2 years are to be left in the Department of the Ohio, and the rest to go to to Washington or Baltimore but I cant see the dividing the old Corps any such way. I am anxious to get back a little nearer somebody

I will write a little more on this piece of paper as I have room enough to send it and I never get tired of writing home whether I have any thing to write or not. Anna you wrote in one of your letters some time ago that Freeman had sent me a paper you also spoke about some verces in another or the same one but they have never reached me paper + bundles dont come so readily as letters they are almost sure to come No 14 was the last letter I have got all up to the 15 we are expecting a mail before long. in looking over my things today I find a pair of shoestrings that I found on a shelf in Greenville what used to be a Post Office or Store. I took them thinking I would send them to Fannie + as thare is room I will send them just for the fun of it. she may like them coming so far from home as they do + among rebels. I got several things of no acct a few old reb papers that I brought along I should like to go to the Singing School in N Brookfield a few evenings this winter I hear Mr Sumner teaches I suppose that Ethan will be a great musician before I get home. my time is most half out I hope I can spend the last half in some easier place than we have the first if we dont go to W- I shall wish that we had never heard any thing about it. it only makes us uneasy, but we mint as well talk about that as any thing else. the biggest part of our Co are [in] Ky or some other state in Hospitals some of them are sick + some are playing off. Our Capt says that we ought to go back and take their places. he thinks they are the best able to do duty at present we have only 12 guns left in the Co out of the 100. ours is the smallest Co in the Reg. none have over 30 I guess. Tomorrow will be Christmas I suppose, but I shall have to draw to a close I think that would be rather rough if those 9 months men are drafted I guess I am about as well off as any of them, in for 3 years by the time they have expired I reckon war will be played out.

write often, Yours Respectfully
George W. Harwood

General Henry H. Lockwood was in command of the Eighth Corps from December. 5, 1863-March 22, 1864.

[No. 18]   Dec 30th '63

Near Blains Cross Roads [Blaine's Crossroads] Tenn

Dear friends at Home,

This is a splendid morning and as I am not very busy I will commence a letter to you. nothing of much importance has transpired since I wrote you last. it has been some time since I rec'd a letter from you. we remain in Tennessee living on little or nothing but parched corn, but I am growing fat on that so the boys say but I dont see how I can. Last sunday it rained hard all the afternoon and we moved camp it was very muddy whare we were and uncomfortable getting around. when I wrote you last I some expected that we should be in Ky. when I wrote next but not so. thare is some talk about our going to Washington but I dont know how whether we shall or not. I must say that we are living pretty poor and I believe poorer than thare is any need of, and thare is no chance to buy much and what we do we have to pay pretty dear for. I bought a little butter a few days ago at 75 cts per lb. we are getting pretty ragged. I am dressed the poorest + thinest now that I have been at any time since I left home, but the weather is fine + not very cold except mornings which are frosty, no snow here as yet. Col [Henry] Bowman has got back to the Reg he came last week we were glad to see him I dont know whether he is going to take command of the Reg or not. he hasnt as yet. The old Reg's are reenlisting pretty freely all who have been out over 2 years can have a furlough of 30 days and receive the 400 + [illegible]. some are being mustered out and in again today and their 3 years to commence now. I have talked with some of them they dont think that the war will last that time, + I hardly think it will. every thing looks brighter to me and I rearly hope they will continue to. Since I commenced this letter the cooks have drawn rations 1 lb of flour to a man, more than we have drawn at any one time for a good while + a piece of pork so I shall have one good meal for supper.

January 1st 1864

I will try + finish this letter that I commenced a few days ago. I would not write today but I suppose that you will be looking for a letter about this time. it is a week ago yesterday since I wrote. yesterday we were mustered for our two months pay in the forenoon + in the afternoon it commenced raining and kept it up all night + this morning it snowed a little but it has cleared off now + is cold + windy and the most uncomfortable day we have had this winter it smokes [smoky mountain fog or mist] so bad that we can hardly see any thing but I think that it will be warmer in a day or two. I am writing this letter with my woolen mittens on + I guess it will look bungling enough. I am laying down in my tent, portfolio on the blanket I am resting on my elbows with my feet out doors by a little fire in front of my tent. The old Reg are enlisting over again for 3 years from this time 30 days furlough 30 days more to recruit in the State + a large bounty. thare is some talk that the 36th will have the same chance and if they do I presume that at least 2/3 of them will reenlist it is a great inducement to them and if we have a chance I should'nt think strange if I went in again as I have no very strong desire to quit the service while the war continues. the rebellion has got to be put down + I am just the man to help but we havent got a chance yet. Father what do you think of reenlisting. I will close this wishing you all a "Happy New Year"
good Bye Remember me to all the friends.

Respect yours George W.

I guess I didnt number the last should have been 18.
No 19   Jan. 7th [1864]
Near Blains Cross Roads [Blaine's Crossroads] Tenn.

Dear Friends at Home

It has been nearly a week since I wrote you last, but I have not recd one from you for a much longer time. we have had pretty cold weather for the past week and our old cloths were hardly enough to keep us warm. yesterday I bought me a nice Vest, and have mended my other cloths so that I feel pretty comfortable. I have also bought a pair of Drawers. we have not drawn any clothing for a long time and do not expect to at present but we some hope to go whare they have got some. we live on 1/2 rations of bread the same as usial [usual] no Rice, Beens, or anything of the kind. The 21st have left here and are going to start for Mass tomorrow. I have been pretty busy for a few days past this forenoon I have mended my pants + Blouse. night before last the Capt called me down to his tent and told me that he proposed to appoint me Sergt and for the present Orderly, our orderly + 2nd Sergts are back sick. the other 3 they have reduced from continued absence from their Regt when they were able to come up. I presume that Freeman will remember Fupper, the minister he was 2nd Sergt. Kup + Haskell the Sergt that was wounded + taken prisoner is now in Knoxville, I guess doing will [well?]. I was a little surprised that he appointed me Sergt skipping 8 Corpl + three Sergts, but he said that he should like to do better by me but could not at present. he said he should like to see me hold a commission. I have of corse some more to do than I had before clothing acct, + sells to keep mail to get details to make morning report to make out &c &c. I wish I was whare I could get my watch for I need one now I had one a few days ago + sold it for 20.00. I should like a few more stamps as I am out. I dont know as I shall finish this letter tonight. No more at present.

Sunday morning Jan 10th

I will continue this letter this morning we have just come in from our usual Sunday morning inspection. Yesterday + day-before we fixed up our tent + built a chimney it works very well. we are having pretty cold weather here at present some snow on the ground and it looks like more snow. thare is no news in particular as I know of. yesterday I bought a little writing paper it cost pretty high 3 cts a sheet 2 cts for envelope 3 for stamp so you see that every letter that we send costs 8 cts, but I shall write just about so often, cost what it will. we expected a mail yesterday but it did not come. I hope shure that it will come today, for I have'nt had a letter for a good while the last that I did get was mailed Dec 3rd I think. Whare is Lyman H Gilbert now. I should like to see him pretty well. I understand that Mr Cheaver [Cheever] is at home on a furlough I am glad to hear it I hope that he will get a discharge for he isnt fit for a soldier, to old

+ clumzy. When we left Crab Orchard, Haskell wanted to get a furlough pretty badly but I guess he has'nt as yet. Snell is in Crab Orchard now I hear. Clark in some hospital, he is 8th Corpl. now instead of 3 Sargt as he was when he left Camp Wool. has N. Brookfield filled up her Quota for the last call. I hear that they have in some parts of Mass without any trouble + I am glad of it. I guess that the 36th wont have a chance to reenlist at present. I hope not for it would be just like me to go in again. Louis had a letter from H. G. Harwood some time ago. I suppose that he is at home before now is'nt he? has Lyman Parkman got over his chills + fever or any better? Henry + Harry Harwood like military so well that I should have thought that [they] would have been in the Army long ago, but perhaps they dont like it so well as they did. I like some parts of it first rate and some I dont. I see that I have got most down to the bottom of this sheet. I will not write any more this time. I hope to get a mail soon. Please remember me to all the friends.

> Affect. Yours
> George W. Harwood

We have drawn a Cow-Hide to make into moccasins [illegible] that are the present off [offer] for shoes. What do you think of that?

By the end of the war 247 men from North Brookfield had served in the Civil War, twelve more than the town's quota. Schouler, Volume. 2, page 659, also Temple page 300. I did not find any mention that the Massachusetts Thirty-sixth Regiment was given the re-enlistment offer.

No 20   Jan 15 '64
> Blans Cross Road [Blaine's Crossroads] Tenn.

Dear Friends a Home

I will improve a few moments this morning by writing to you although I have nothing new to write. I find that I have a little more duty to do since I commenced to act Orderly, but no guard on fatigue. we have drawn a little clothing today. I got a pr of Boots. this is the first time that we have drawn Boots. we expect more in a day or two when I hope to draw something more. We expect to move tomorrow or soon to Strawberry Plains 8 miles from here I dont know when we shall go over the [Cumberland] Mountain if at all. all we drew yesterday for rations was a piece of pork day before yesterday and day before that a piece of pork (small) and a gill of flour we cannot buy much and so we go pretty hungry. we have drawn nothing as yet today and it is already past noon. I had 1/2 ~~hear~~ ear of corn parched for breakfast + coffee thare is but little complaining among the men as we know that it is the best that we can do at present, or at last they tell us so. we are told that thare are plenty of rations on the way. Rev Mr [Thomas B.] Fox of Boston is visiting all the Mass Rgts in the Army of the Cumberland both in the field + hospitals by order of Gov Andrews. he called on us day before yesterday + addressed us in words of encouragement + praise for our undaunted courage + bravery + patinec [patience], suffering what we have for the past few months and even at present from hunger + cold. he says that thare is superabundance of provisions + clothing in Mass. (we are glad of that we didnt know before I suppose he thought) and that nothing should be withheld from the soldiers from Mass that were within reach. I do not speak of our short or <u>no</u> rations with any intention of finding fault far from it. only to let you know that we are short and can realize what it is to be hungry what many a man in Mass cannot say <u>with truth</u>. I used to think that I was hungry when at home, but I was deceived in myself. the boys dont have much duty to do + are in pretty good spirits, look quite fleshy. I have got a little cold just now and my throat feels a little sore this morning but I am quite well. <u>Good</u>! they say we are to draw a little flour soon + you may believe that wont go bad at the present time. I made me a pr of Moccasins a few days ago but I shall have no use for them. they were pretty hard looking things. I cut them out + made them in about an hour they were warm hair in but too heavy to march in, just the things to take a sleigh ride in. have you sent the Dairy that I spoke about some letters ago one of our boys recd one last mail a large one postage only 4 cts. I heard a few days ago that Haskell had gone with others to Portsmouth Grove RI. do you know anything about it. Louis rec'd last mail a Photograph of his Father but in one hand hammer in the other it looked just like Uncle David himself. I should be pleased with a Photograph of Father + Mother + in fact each of the family. I should prize them higher than almost any thing else. I have written this in a great hurry as my writing shows without my speaking of it. I wish you would send me a hank of black linen thread as I am entirely out and cannot buy. I guess you will think that I am full of my little vents but never mind I'll make it all right sometime. We are now in a land of nothing. the thread will come in a letter I guess. they tell us that thare is a big mail not far from here which we hope to get soon. I am anxious to hear from home. I shall have to close for this time I think Louis says that George Spooner has enlisted + Mr Maxwell [Nathaniel B Maxwell]. my love to all write often.

From your son + brother Geo W Harwood

A gill is a teacup, one quarter of a pint, one half cup or four fluid ounces. George R. Spooner and Nathaniel B. Maxwell served with the Massachusetts First Regiment Heavy Artillery.

Uncle David L. Winslow, Louis' father
(Photo in author's collection)

No 21   Jan 17 '64   Strawberry Plains Tenn

Dear Friends at Home

      This is a fine Sabbath morning and I will commence a letter to you. yesterday we left our camp or the Cross Roads and marched over here 8 miles, whare we expect to stop for a while. it was warm and the ground thawed a little just enough to make it very muddy and hard marching. we changed camp I suppose on acct of our supplies the cars come up as far as here. late in the evening we rec'd a large mail, a back mail more than a month old, in which I rec'd 2 letters from you 15 + 16 I was very glad to get them as it has been sometime since I rec'd one from home. I was sorry to learn that you had worried so much about me Mother asked if the skin was broken on my neck. it was taken off about as large as a quarter of a dollar thare is something of a scar left now. 2 months ago yesterday it was done. my gun went into the hands of the rebs the ball stroke [struck] the gun first. She also asked who I tented with. I tent with Joe Wheelock and have ever since Lyman went away. he has been sick but is now quite well. Anna you spoke about staying at home from church and having for supper pork soup + dumplings, meatpie + doughnuts. I should like right well to have been thare. I told Wheelock what you had for supper, said he tell them I wish I had been thare, and thare would'nt have been any left if we were as hungry as we are now. You say that Henry Harwood sais [says] he that he is going to elect Butler for President I think he would make a good one, but <u>Abr Lincoln</u> will make a better one or at least good enough. I go <u>for him</u>. I was surprised to hear that Caswells Wife was dead. Srgt [Lucius L.] Merrick + I and I think others whose names were in the papers as wounded rec'd letters from New York with Circulars in the[m] I had 6 all alike and I will send one of them to you. they got in a hurry I think.

                                     Afternoon

I have just been down to Divine Services we had very ~~in~~ a very interesting discoure [discourse]. I am glad to have a chance to attend once in a while if no oftener thare is but one Chaplain in the Brigade. he is quite young but a good preacher very smart + I like him much. after services he said that he was authorized to say to the men that we should have more ration soon as they were certainly on the way. we drew today [a ration] of flour to make a desert flour gravy, about one gill with a very small piece of Beef, but we are all gay + happy still. we all think of our homes and long to be thare, with the ever dear friends of this Earth. the name of Home of Father, Mother, Sister + Brother are cheering to us. thare is nothing in which a soldier delights in more than in talking of their friends + home Oh! if we could get home we say, but while we think so highly of our homes + friends on Earth, thare are some among us who bare in mind that we have a home beyond the skys, and a friend also ever constant, ever true, with whom we can hold sweet communion at any time + under all circumstance, who is never far from us and whith whome we may hope to dwell when we have done with earth's pilgrimage.   Monday noon I did not finish my letter last night as I had to make out a new requision [requisition] for clothing. we have already drawn some I have drawn a dress-coat + have got my stripes or shivrens on. last night we had orders to be ready to march this morning at 7 but we did not go it commenced raining this morning and rains now. I am glad that you had Mr Bartletts family with you Thanksgiving they must have enjoyed it. how are they getting along this winter dose he get any work to do. Joe Wheelocks brother lives in his house so Joe says. I think [Joe] is a much better man than his brother. he is in the tent with me now. he says that if I cant find anything else to write I may send his respects to you. he is always around to hear the new[s] if thare is any when I get a letter from home.

Good Bye for this time. Yours &c
George W Harwood

Addie (Adelaide) A. Caswell died of epilepsy on December 12, 1863, in North Brookfield. She had married Wilder Caswell on September 1, 1863.

No 22   Jan 26 '64
                                                  Near Knoxville Tenn.

Dear Friends at Home
          It has been a little more than a week since I wrote last. I sent a Knoxville Whig a few day[s] after. we left Strawberry Plain Saturday morning I think. we fell back with the enemy firing into our rear a part of the way but no great damage done to us thare were some commissary stores distroyed that the 23rd Corps left and as our Div were left to cover the retreat we had a chance to get some Over-coats + Shoes. I got me a good Over coat for nothing and have drawn other clothing so that I am pretty warmly dressed. the weather is fine + spring like we are now 6

miles west of Knoxville on the Kingston road pleasantly encamped, as we hope the last camping ground in Tenn. we are near the rail road. we have just had orders to clean up and be ready for a Review they are turning over some of our teams and things look like our going north soon and it is the opinion of all. I hope that we shall. I have seen about enough of Tenn. we are getting about 1/2 rations now of Bread + meat sugar + coffee. small biscuits are 60 cts pr Doz here in Kn [Knoxville], no larger than a hens egg I bought 90 cts worth last night after supper and eat them all up + was hungry then, but that is all right.

Jan 27ᵗʰ I will write a little more today and perhaps finish my letter Capt Warrin [Warriner] is absent on 3 day lieve of absence he went night before last last night the C Major ordered a Co inspection and as thare is no Commissioned Officer in the Co now, I am left in Command and of corse had to inspect them, and today he ordered a Co drill of one hour and in-spection, so I gave the Co my first lessons in drilling who knew as much about it as I did. I am pretty busy now writing and one thing and another. I had to write in a diary for one man who is sick + a letter for another who cannot write at all this morning and then comes the morning report + Sergeans [Sergeants] call + police call in thare turns all of these the first Sergt has to attend to, but it is such work as I like to do I some expect Sergt Merrick up he is in Knoxville much better he will then act Orderly. I have been expecting a mail for some days + they say that it is coming near here somewhare. we have splendid weather now and I feel first rate. I have cloths enough now for the present. I have got a new suit right through, <u>am fat + tough</u>. It is now nearly night we have just rec'd a mail I got one letter from you in which you said you had sent a diary + paper I have not got them yet then Andrew [Jackson] is rearly [really] married is he? I was greatly surprised to hear that. I guess he has got a pretty good little woman for a wife dont you? Tell Hubbard not to get behind the rest of the boys or rather <u>young men</u> for such indeed they are, but I [am] going to see this <u>war</u> ended before I attend to those things. I am afraid that we shall not see Lyman here in the Reg again at present if ever if he has gone back to R.I. I like this service pretty well better than I used to. you asked what I had got for Gloves I have got a pr of woolen ones that will do for the present and if we should'nt ~~com~~ go North all I shall want. If we do + want I [will] send. we are having very fine warm weather here at present warm enough to go shirt sleeves all day. I suppose that Charles K.[Knight] is the same man he used to be. I guess if you are going to read my letters to the Public I shall have to spend a little more time + take a little more pain with them. I never stop to premeditate or hardly ever read them over to see what I have written for I am always in a hurry and have time enough to if I would take it.

[undated]

I wish that I could have my picture taken and send home. I dont ~~know~~ believe that you would all know me I have altered a great deal in looks + actions since I left old Mass. I have I mean to get a furlough if we ever get North + can and my Capt. will do all he can for me any time now if I should ask him. he is good to me + in fact all the boys one of the best officers in the Reg. he dont say much but that is enough he means a good deal, + all mind at his command but I will close for tonight tell Andrew + wife to favor me with a good long letter and I shall be pleased.

Good Night   Sergt G.W. Harwood

George received his promotion to sergeant on January 1, 1864. Cousin Andrew F. Jackson married Sophia P. Livermore on December 31, 1863, in Brookfield, Massachusetts.

Sergeant George W. Harwood
(Photo in author's collection)

No 23   Near Knoxville Tenn Jan 31ˢᵗ 1864

Dear Friends

  I will commence a letter to you this afternoon but dont think I shall finish it. The 29ᵗʰ Mass. Vols. start for home tomorrow morning and those who did not reenlist joined our Reg. this morning, 7 to each Co I think 3 of our boys came up a few days ago that were left back sick, so we have got a desent Co. again. We had to drill 3 hours per day last week but I understand that this drilling has played out for the present day before yesterday I was pretty busy writing making out the <u>monthly return</u> of Co. E. we dont know when we shall ~~come~~ go North if at all the teams + Regimental horses are to start soon. forage is very scarce we are having warm weather now with a little rain yesterday.

Feb 3ʳᵈ I commenced this letter some days ago but have not had time to finish it. day before yesterday we were getting ready to go out on inspection when orders came to fall in at once in light marching orders. we went out about 7 miles post haste. it was then after dark we stopped over night. the next morning drew some rations expecting to go on, but we soon learned that the 23 Corps got frightened so we had the order <u>about face,</u> and came back to our camp. yesterday we had an inspection of Camp + Garrison equipage. today we have had a Regimental inspection of guns, equipments + knapsacks by our Brigade inspector. tomorrow we are to have a few drills I hear. thare is no news of much importance furious camp rumours but it is pretty evident that we are to go north before long. we are all quite anxious to do so, hoping that if we do we shall have a chance to see some of our <u>friends</u>. Should we get as near as New York and that is the talk, I shall expect to see some of you out thare. I shall also apply for a furlough. I feel a little down tonight my bowels are out of tune I guess. I dont get much mail of late it takes a letter from home to cheer up a soldiers drooping spirits. when I feel tired + things dont go right, and I feel sad + lonely or meet with any disappointments (as we often do you know) I think of these virses [verses] that I write from an old paper. "Thare is a Land" by: Francis B. [D] Murtha

    "Thare is a land whare sunshine dwells
      And sorrow never is.
    A land brighter and more beautiful
      Aye, sweeter far than this;

Whare music floats upon the air,
And all is joy and pease,
No gloomy shadows linger thare,
All strifes and discords cease.

A heaven for the worn and weary,
For those bound down with care,
A place of rest and quietude,
'Mid angles [angels] bright and fair.
No knawing sorrow at the heart.
No griefs nor tearful eyes.
But all is radiant as the stars,
'Tis thare - beyond the skys."

Thursday the 4th   I will write a few lines more this morning. I have just received a letter from W James Haskell from Portsmouth Grove R.I. it is a little cooler today and quite windy. I have no news to write. I have been expecting a Diary which you sent. I hope to get it soon. I cut out a few pieces from an Knoxville Whig for the fun it I think Parson Brownlow talks pretty plain dont you. He tell[s] who can live in East Tenn. after the war and who cant. <u>he cant for one I'm sure</u>. Remember me to all the friends and tell them to write I should be glad to hear from all of them, especialy <u>Andrew + wife</u>.

     From your obedient Son + Brother Geo. W. Harwood

Francis D. Murtha wrote a number of songs which were set to music by Stephen C. Foster in the 1860s. I did not find this particular song.

No 24   Erins Station Tenn Feb 10th '64

Dear Friends,

     I have no news to write of importance. we recd quite a mail today but none for me. I expected to have recd a Diary and several letters before this time. the last letter that I got from home was mailed the 13th of Jan. but many of the boys recd their[s] today up to the 25 + 26 I hope I shall not have to wait much longer. I have not felt well the past week but am better now. Do you know whare Lyman H. Gilbert is a letter came to the Reg for him today from his Wife. She directed it to Camp Dennison Ohio, but they wrote on it returned to duty. we have been expecting for a long time to start over the [Cumberland] mountains North but have not started yet. rumours are that we do start soon. I hope if we do get North we shall receive our mail more regular. that is about all we have to keep up our spirits for corn meal + pork wont do it + 1/2 rations at that. I'll tell you when a fellow feels like being at home, it is when he has no appetite cold + sick, no good bed, out in the wind all day around a smoky fire, nothing but corn meal + pork to eat, when he wants a good cup of teas + crackers soaked in it, and give his feet a good soaking take a cup of hot ginger tea and go to bed, but such is soldiering sleep with our cloths on the year around. we have been having pretty cold weather but it is a little warmer today. we have one very quaint amusement for some who are skillful and that is boxing one of Co C has 2 pr of boxing gloves so the boys while away some time but we have about enough to do at drilling. I will not write any more today I guess for I have'nt anything worth writing.

Feb 11?   I think I will finish this letter today. last night much to my surprise Lyman H. Gilbert came up with a lot of convalescents + recruits he is quite unwell I dont know what is the matter with him. I am affraid that he wont be worth much again as a soldier in the field. I think he looks about as he did 6 month ago he went to the Surgeons this morning and got some medicine + I hope he will be better soon. I have asked him 40 + more questions about N.B. I wish he [was] well. I should like to spend about 30 days at home before warm weather if I could. he told me about Mrs Caswells death <u>very</u> <u>sudden</u>. you wrote about it at the time. He does not bring much news. he says that Edwin Doane is sick. he heard by way of his wife. I hope that the next mail we get I shall be lucky enough to get some thing. I suppose that you write about every week dont you. I was very glad to see Lyman but wish he was well and I guess he will be better soon. Lyman tells me that he thinks the John F. Dewing place sold or could have been bought for 1700.00. dont you think that it is worth more money than that he says that George Dewing has bought him a place in Spencer. I wonder if he will try and pay for it. Father does Judson pay up any rent or interest will he ever pay for the farm think you. you have'nt said any thing about the Parkman boys lately how is [Henry] Lyman getting along has he got well. I suppose that Charles works hard as usual, but I dont think of much more to write this time and it will soon be time for dress parade I will draw to a close. I am feeling pretty well now. Please remember me to all the friends and write often.

Respectfly Yours
George W. Harwood

No 25   Erins Station Tenn Feb 14th '64

Dear Friends at Home,

I rec'd a letter from you a few days ago No 21 thare are three letters back that I have not got yet this was mailed Feb 1st. Father wished me
to write respecting Alvin Thompson + Jim Cummings. at the fight of
Campbell Station Thompson went to fill his canteen a little ways off from
us about the same time we retreated and the enemis line of battle came up,
and Thompson has not been seen or heard from since. he is probably in the
enemis hands now. that is all any of us know about him. as for Jim Cummings he is Division Teamster the last I heard from him he was in Crab
Orchard. I dont think he is in Tennessee. I havent seen him from more than
4 months I asked his Orderly Sergeant yesterday about him. he said he
was off with a team somewhare but he did'nt know whare. I have but little
or no news to write at this time. thare is rumours here and strongly be-
lieved that we shall go North this week. we hope that we shall. thare are
many reports here about what we are going to do. some say we are going
to our own states to recruit others say that we are going to N York and
have a furlough. be it as it may I hope to see home before long. the report
in camp last night was that "Longstreet" had left but I dont believe that. I
think he will try and take Knoxville before he gives up.

Sunday afternoon

I had to stop writing to do a little writing for the Co concerns, and then the
bugle blew for Divine Services so I attend them as I always do if possible
they were very interesting. we have a very good Chaplain who preaches to
the Brigade he belongs to the 79th New York. he is a small man about as
large + I guess a little larger than Mr Peters of N.B. about the same age I
should judge. I wish you could hear him preach a few times. the Chaplain
that came out with us has gone home I understand he was left back in
Crab Orchard he was'nt very interesting I never thought. Thare is a rumour in camp now that we are going to leave Tenn to go North tomorrow
but I guess we shant I hope we do we certainly shall before long. some
are certain that we are going to our own state and go so far as to say that
the Adjutant General says so. I feel quite certain now that I shall soon have
a chance to see N Brookfield and my dear friends I hope I shall wont

those be happy moments when I relate a part of my past 18 months experience. the thoughts are pleasing to dwell upon. a small mail came in today but none for me. I was somewhat disappointed but I hope I shall soon go to whare the letters come from. I had a little rather talk than write, but I esteem it a great gift to be able to write. thare are three in the Co that cant write a word others can only write thare names. O how should I feel if I could'nt read or write a word. they are gifts unspeakable. such I esteem them for some have no factilty [facility] to learn had they an opportunity, but I will not dwell upon that longer I am quite well. Lyman is here, better than he was a few days ago. write often I shall. Pleas[e] remember me to all the friends. I aint so fast to reenlist as I was a few months ago I begin to think 3 years is enough for me. I get along with all but I dont like the army, so well as <u>home</u> Yours &c &c George W.

No 26   Near Knoxville Tenn Feb 21 '64

Dear Friends at Home

This is a pleasant sabbath day it snowed this morning but is now quite warm + pleasant I have but little news to write at this time but thinking, yes knowing that you would be anxious to hear I will write I have written three before this today one to Mrs Ezra Batcheller. we are now under marching orders and some expect another fight soon we are all hoping still that this Corps will go North and I guess that thare is no doubt but that we shall before long. I have read all the back letters that you have sent. I have been very busy of late more so than usual as Capt is unwell and I have Command of the Co and acting Orderly for the time being thare are various camp rumours about the enemy and their movements we hardly know what to believe but it is pretty certain that thare is something going on. I am glad that the young people are having fine times at home this winter should enjoy being with them very much but Longstreet must be attended to first. I suppose that thare is not much mourning over the loss of the old Hotel. I hear by way of Mrs B [Batcheller] that they are intending to build another or that a Committy have been chosen to look out a good locality for one. I hope that they will put up a good one in a conspicuous place. it will impress the outside appearance of N.B. a good deal. We have had a fortnight of pretty cold weather but it now is going to be warmer I think. if I had time I would write to Allen + Fannie a little seperately but I cant this time for I am in something of a hurry, as my writing will show. I am glad to hear from you so often the oftener the better. Lyman + I have a little singing when we get time we sang anthems this morning. he is quite well but says they dont give us enough to eat and so they dont but we get more than we did a month ago I have recd the Diary after so long a time it is a fine one I think. I also read a Springfield Republican a day or two ago. Lyman + Joe + I tent together now in one of those little shelter tents a pretty small coop for such large chickens. we live on corn meal and are doing well, but I have seen about enough of it 6 days more and our time will be 1/2 out 27th day [August, 1862] we were mustered in as a Co the time will quickly pass and we shall not regret that we <u>went for a soldier</u> I guess but I must say that we have some trying times military disapline is pretty severe 2 men in Co A were court marchelled not long ago their sentences were read to us this morning. one of them is to spend the remander of his time on 1/2 pay and spend 9 months in the service after the Reg is discharged. the other is to loose conciderable pay. I have forgotten how much. do you hear any thing said about the 9 Corps coming back to recruit I think it must be so I have not attended Divine Services as yet today but hope to this afternoon. I have recd some paper[s] of late from Mrs B [Batcheller] + Mrs Cushing and you so that I have had a good amount of reading matter. I do not think of much news that I will write this time write often and I will Remember me to Uncle Jonas + Aunt Lucretia and the rest of the friends. I am quite well and enjoying myself as well as I can under existing circumstances.

Affect- Yours

George W Harwood

The Springfield Republican *was a Massachusetts newspaper. Today it is called* The Republican. *On February 23 George returned to Massachusetts on a furlough and a recruiting assignment. Burrage, page 127. General Grant assumed command of all Union armies on March 12 and ordered the Ninth Corps to Virginia. General Longstreet lingered in eastern Tennessee until he received orders to move to Virginia on April 7. General Sherman organized several armies to begin his Atlanta Campaign in early May.*

PENNSYLVANIA

NEW JERSEY

MARYLAND

DELAWARE

Potomac River

● Spottsylvania Court House, VA

North Anna River

Totopotomoy Creek
● Gaines Mill, Cold Harbor, VA

Richmond, VA ●

VIRGINIA

Chesapeake Bay

Harrison's Landing at
Berkeley Plantation, VA
City Point, VA ●   ●
James River

● Appomattox
Court House, VA   Appomattox River
Farmville, VA ●
Petersburg, VA ●● Union Encampments

There were 5 railroad lines leading into Petersburg:

Southside RR (comes from the west on the south side of the Appomattox River)
Petersburg & Norfolk RR (comes from the southeast to Petersburg)
Petersburg & Weldon RR (comes from the south to Petersburg)
Petersburg & Richmond RR (runs north to Richmond from Petersburg)
City Point RR (runs east from Petersburg toward City Point)

A U.S. Military Railroad also ran around the south
and east side of the Union encampments.

NORTH
CAROLINA

~ Chapter 10 ~

RETURN TO VIRGINIA, OVERLAND CAMPAIGN
May 15 - June 12, 1864

On May 4 George began his trip back to his regiment from a recruiting leave in Boston, Massachusetts. The regiment was in Virginia where it participated in the Battles of the Wilderness and Spotsylvania Court House.

No 1   Near Penn Court Horner Va
                                                          May 15th '64

Dear Friends

      I will write one word and send back by a man that is going to Washington. I joined the Regt this morning and found that they had lost very heavily, and among the friends was Louis Winslow I saw his grave poor boy has gone to rest and many others with whom I used to associate Wheelock is wounded I saw him. you will hear more about us after the fight is over. we are now in front and the bullets fly good Lyman is all right. the boys look hard, and since I left Washington we have seen many wounded and 10,000 prisoners our Regt has lost killed + wounded some 175, about 40 killed. I do not feel much like writing today. you can imagine my feelings perhaps to find the boys in such condition and Louis dead I feel very badly. Lyman helped dig Louis grave and saw that he was buried in good order. his name is marked on the head of a board at the head of his grave I read it. he was shot through the shoulder lived but a short time. I will see to his things the boys have got them and will write more about it some future time if I am spared. good Bye for this time. with live [love] I remain your son + brother   George W Harwood
I dont know as you can read this for I am writing under difficulties pleas[e] remember me to all the friends assure them that I think of home + friends at this time, for the Lost + wounded I can only pray + weep and hope on, hoping that I may be spared to see you on earth, but if not may we meet in that world whare parting is no more + sorrows never come. I feel deeply interested for the future welfare of my friends but I can only pray for you + leave the result with my God. I would like to write more but I dont feel like it now.
                  Yours Aff George W.
          Address me
          Co. E. 36 Regt Mas[s] Vols
          2nd Div 9th Army Corp
          Washington D. C.
write often they will reach me some time tell Uncle David about Louis I

will write him after the fight and give him more particulars if I am spared.

Louis D. Winslow died at Spotsylvania Court House on May 12. He was buried on the battlefield and re-interred in the National Cemetery in Fredericksburg. His father, Uncle David, was my great-great-grandfather.

I have not been able to locate where Penn Court, Horner, Virginia is or was. George's summary of service written in the letter dated September 23, 1864 indicates he landed at Belle Plains and went from there to Fredericksburg and then rejoined his regiment.

Louis Dennis Winslow, 1863
(Tintype in author's collection)

Gravestone in Fredericksburg National
Cemetery, 2012 (Photo by author)

No. 2

Near Spottsylvania Court House Va
May 16th 1864

Dear Friends

Thare is a chance to send a mail so I will write a few lines [I] have only 10 or 15 minutes to do so in. I sent a few lines yesterday by a man who left here perhaps you will get this first. in it I stated that I got to the Regt yesterday morning in front on the skirmish line and found them looking pretty hard many of them have lost friends Louis is among the killed as I wrote more particularly in my other letter I have got his watch and some other things. please tell his Father ask him if he wants his watch sent home or sold. I must close good Bye

George W Harwood

Direct   Co E 36 Reg Mass Vols
                 2nd Div 9 Army Corp
                 Washington D C

Write often I shall get them sometime. I am all right and in good spirits.

[No. 3]   May 19th 1864

Dear Friends

This is lovely day and at this time I am not very busy the boys are building a good strong breast-work now in front. we moved from our old position to this in the night (last). day before yesterday I went on duty as Sergt. of the Skirmishers, had charge of 20 men came out all right. thare is but little news to write we have some fighting every day. every day some are killed or wounded. It so happened that we did'nt leave Boston soon enough into a few days, as they boys had 2 or 3 hard fights before I got back, but we expect more. we are now but a few miles from Spottsylvania Court House Va. in the woods, a very fine pleasant place. At the time that Louis was shot the Regt was laying in line of battle not engaged at the time. he was shot through the right shoulder, so that he lived but about one hour after that I think that he said nothing after he was shot but lay stupid. he was buried near whare he fell in a beautiful pine grove near a gentle brook with many others, and a rough board at the head of his grave with his name in[s]cribed markes the place whare the remains of that dear one lies. Have we not reason to believe that his soul is now at rest and is shining brightly as the stars in heaven. we may mourn his loss here on earth but doubtless he is far happier in his present home. I have got his watch pocket book + Diary which I intend to sent to his Father as soon as I can. 20th   I will write a little more today. thare was a chance to send out a mail this morning I sent a little to Uncle David. this a lovely day. we are now in a nice piece of woods. I have spent a good part of the day writing letters I hope to have a chance to send soon. Lyman, Joe Walker + I tent together. Wheelock is wounded in the foot. I feel somewhat sad but at the same time am in good spirits, hoping for the best, preparing for the worst, trusting that all will be well with me whether living or dieing. Thare is but little news for me to write at this time only to let you know that I am all right. I would not have you worry about me, it would do no good you know. things are much more forward here [spring is further along] than they are in Mass. I suppose that you (Father) are perhaps planting now. Lyman thinks that Farming is the only good business and I dont know but he is right. I tell him I will see in a year from now if nothing happens. that is I will think about it then. have they drafted in Mass yet. if so who goes from N.B. I hope Allen will never think of such a thing as enlisting. if he knows what is best he will keep out of this business. I will write to him in my next I guess if I dont in this. Freeman I had a good deal rather be in N.B. in recruiting service than fight in Virginia. I should like to call up and see Edwin a little while but I will wait a while I guess I will write again in a few days write often.

Yours Aff.

George W Harwood

Edwin was probably Freeman's brother who served in the Massachusetts Forty-second (100 days) Regiment.

May 20th 1864

Brother Ethan [Allen],

     I will write a few lines to you in this letter. I suppose that you are farming very busily now, and traiding doves or rabbits. since I left you I have had some hard times but no worse than I expected as I know of. I have seen many dead and wounded men the past week. it is then I think of home. it is then I ask myself am I prepared to die. I trust I am. [Ethan] Allen how is it with you do you feel that you are prepared for death. you have had a good opportunity to prepare and I hope that you improved it. did you. if not I hope you will. Please write me how you feel about these things. I am well and in good spirits and hope to come out of this campaign safely. I will close for this time. write often.

From your brother

George W Harwood

I believe that this is the 5 letter that I have written you since I left.

May 30th 1864

Dear Friends

We are in the woods on the South side of the Pamonky [Pa-munkey] River said to be 15 miles direct to Richmond, but we shall have to go much farther to get thare. I thought I would commence a letter this morning hoping to have a chance to send soon. I have recd no mail from you since I left. We have had some pretty [hard] marching the past few days. I feel quite weary. my feet as usual are badly blistered. we had orders to be ready to move at 5 this morning but it is now 8 and we have'nt started yet. we are all packed up ready shall probably move in a few moments. I dont know as I have any thing in particular to write of news for we dont know much about what is going on. A mail came in this morning. we get a mail every little while. some of the boys got a paper with the names of the drafted men in N B but I presume that most of these men will pay their commutation money wont they? but it is rough for some of them. I begin to feel quite anxious to hear from you as it has been nearly 1 month since I left. thare are 3 of us N Brookfield boys here Lyman, Joe Walker + I. the rest are played out. I had a letter the other day from Cousin Mary Allen West Troy N.York. We have got a new Chaplain now his name I think is Richardson not a very smart looking man. I havent heard him say much yet. they are skirmishing about 1 mile ahead. I presume that we shall have something to do before long. it will be strange if we dont.
Tuesday morning 31st. We moved a few miles yesterday and are now in line of Battle with goo[d] strong breastworks in front. I have just rec'd a letter from you in which you said that you had got No 2 of mine but said nothing about getting the one I sent from Worcester with 35.00 in it or the one that I sent from Washington the day but one after that I think. have'nt you ever got them? I'd like to know. They are skirmishing in front of us pretty lively at times. I was Sergt of the alarm guard last night. it is very warm + pleasant here, too warm for comfort. We have plenty of hard-bread, sugar + coffee + beef, but my appetite is not very good. I feel old. I have no chance to send those things to Uncle David [Winslow] yet. I hope I shall have soon. you spoke of being done planting the corn is up here all round some 6 or 8 inches looks very well, and thare is considerable of it planted. dont fail to let me know in your next letter whether you rec'd the money I sent from Worcester. have you ever heard anything more from

Uncle David Allen since I left. I suppose that the drafted men feel a little sober dont they. I think I should if I were in their places. 15 months looks long to me, longer now than it did when I was at home. I wish they were over. I suppose you like Lenth for a school teacher dont you? how does Susan Sanderson get along with hers. I shall have to close for this time. I am laying on my back my knees up for a writing desk. my work looks like it I see but I'm tired. write very often. I want them now more than ever. Freeman keep me posted

Aff Yours George W.

During the Overland Campaign, Generals Grant and Lee circled each other to the northeast of Richmond, Virginia. They had just finished pursuing each other across the North Anna River and the Pamunkey River. General Grant had been unable to enter Richmond so he was cutting off access to roads, railroads, and river shipping. Lee was being forced to defend a smaller and smaller perimeter around Richmond. Cousin Mary Allen and Uncle David Allen were relatives of George's mother, Angeline Allen Harwood.

No 6   Gains Hills Vaga [Gaines Mill, Virginia]
                                                                          June 4ᵗʰ 1864

Dear Friends

I will commence a letter to you I understand that that a mail will go tonight or in the morning. we have had a sad fight. yesterday morning we formed a long line of battle and advanced on the enemy ~~our lines were~~ they fell back to their breast works and our line came up within 15 rods we lay on the ground and threw up some breastworks in front of us, and kept it up all day we lost in our Regt 57 killed + wounded Our Orderly was wounded so I have got to act Orderly again. I have not felt at all well for several days. I think I feel a little better this morning. the rebs left last night we used them rough. we have been out all the morning skirmishing Cos F + E men were wounded within 3 feet of me on both sides yesterday several shot dead near me, but a kind Providence spared me, for which I have great reason to be thankful. several of the boys that went home on Recruiting service with me were wounded 1 killed. Leander Bell my re-cruit has got ~~back~~ up with the regt was in the fight yesterday. he is all right. I wish you could look over a battle field you can form no kind of idea. we are in a thick piece of wood and the trees are all cut up. Lyman has got the Rheumatism so that he is quite lame. Some of the 45ᵗʰ Pa. boys found a lot of ~~of~~ silver + gold under some house at front they exchanged silver for greenbacks afterwards 3 dollars in silver for 3 greenback I got 2 silver for 2 greenbacks. it looks good I wish it was at home. I am getting short of writing paper and thare is no chance to buy such things I wish you could send me some by mail either in a newspaper or small package, and a very few stamps. we are a pretty sober lot of fellows I can tell you worn out + dirty. The boys are talking about home today. Capt [James B.] Smith who came home with [us] is in command of the Regt Capt Barker was slightly wounded our old colors got pretty well riddled, that is several holes + torn   I dont think of much more to write this time. a mail came in this morning I expected one from you, but did not get write often for now is the time we want mail.

   the mail is going out now so good by   George W Harwood

George was writing from Gaines Mill describing the second Battle of Cold Harbor the previous day, June 3, 1864. Captain Thaddeus L. Barker was wounded at Gaines Mill.

N7   On the field Va.
                     June 8th 1864

Dear Friends

  I will commence a letter to you we are about 3 miles from Chicahomnany [Chickahominy] River in the woods our skirmishers are out it is very quiet along the lines at present. as I told you in my last I have not felt very well for nearly a fortnight. I think I am a little better but my throat is badly swollen. I think I have had the mumps on one side. We are kept on the move most of the time and are broke of our sleep nights. the boys begin to feel old. I have got Louis things now and do not think it is safe to send them by

General Ulysses S. Grant at his headquarters, Cold Harbor, Virginia (Courtesy Library of Congress)

mail and thare is no other way to send. I am some afraid that something may happen to me so that Uncle David will never get them, but I shall keep them with me for the present and send when it is safe that is the best I can do. I am quite anxious to hear from you and I wish I could know whether you got the money I sent from Worcester. The 15th are about 2 miles from here Smith + DeLand have got back Smith was wounded in the arm or shoulder soon after he got back. I have not time to write much this time for the mail goes out before long our Chaplain is around with some today the first time for a good while. I begin to feel old and lame I guess that this campaign will use me up in some way or other. I feel a good deal as I used to getting the hay out of the meadow or like an old horse all drawed out. It seems as though Id give most anything if I could get home to stay I do want a milk-toast, my appetite is poor hard-tack + boiled-beef day after day. money is no object for a man to go into the Army Id like to give money to get out of it now, but my time is slowly wareing away. I suppose that Freeman has no thoughts of entering the army even if drafted I hope not, nor any other friend of mine for it is to hard for any one. Sergt [J. Hervey] Miller, Louis old tent mate lost an arm in the last fight on the 3rd. Jim Cummings is all right just as ever. he dont seem to worry much. Henry Johnson of the 25th came over here the other day he is some 2 miles from here. thare are a world of troops around here and all busy. these are days of changes among us, but I will not write much more. I want to hear from you oftener and long letters + all the news for now is the time I want such letters they are the only things I can have to comfort me from home. Please remember me to all the friends and except [accept] this letter from your Son + Brother

George W Harwood

No 8   Camp of 36th Mass Vols Va.   June 12th '64

Dear Friends

I rec'd letter No 3 from you last night. you said that you had not heard from me since the 16th. I have written 4 or 5 since then and I think that it is strange that you have not got them. perhaps you have before this. I hope so. you say that the papers are full of war news and that you would send me some if they would come. papers do come the mail goes out and comes in almost every day, both papers + letters. I should like a few papers. I write as often as once a week, and I wish that you would if not of-

tener even if you dont get all mine, for now is the time that I want to hear from home. this is a pleasant Sabbath morning but I shall not have the priviledge of attending Divine Services as I suppose that you will we have a Chaplain but I have never heard him speak in any meeting he has gone to Washington I understand now on some business. he is a Congragation-est, so they say he does not look or act like a very smart man. we are now about 7 or 8 miles from Richmond and about 2 from the Chickahomany River, 15 or 16 from the White House Landing. we are going to the White House Landing in a few days so <u>report says</u> and over [to] the south side of the James River near Petersburg but we dont know any thing about it. I wrote in some of my last letters that I was not very well but I am now a good deal better, but my appetite is rather poor. you notice that I write with a pencil mostly my ink is about played [out] + so is my paper this paper is hardly fit for use. I said something in one letter about sending some paper + wrappers in a newspaper. I think you can I should like it if you could. I have bought seven stamps since I wrote for some, but they wont come[?] a miss here, if you send more. I hope that you will get the letters that I sent along I dont know as thare is any particular news in any of them I spoke of the fight on the 3rd this month [Cold Harbor] 5 of our Co wounded. last night we drew some clothing we have plenty of hard bread + fresh-beef sugar + coffee. I wish we could get some beans + pork I think I should relish that. I asked in one of my letters if you got the money that I sent from Worcester if you did or did not I should thought you would have spoken of it. I should like to know. I wish that you would write often if you dont hear any thing from me. I will send Louis things as soon as I think that it is safe if I live. Over
[new sheet of paper]
It is rather risky carring Louis things around for fear that I may be killed and then perhaps loose them + my own also I have 25 dollars of money beside my watch but if so all right I suppose, money is of no <u>acct</u>. I wish that I could have Freemans + Annas Photographs I should like Allens + Fanni[e] and all the family first rate why cant you send them? they wont cost much. Mary Allen is very anxious that I should send her mine but I cannot at present. she felt pretty sober I should judge by her writing. she wanted me to bare in mind that she had had no Father to look after her + her advantages had been rather poor, compared with some. 22 months ago today I signed the enlistment roll in Mr. Smith's store little did I realize

what I had got to pass through the next 3 years. I cant say that I feel sorry that I ever entered the service at the same time I have gone through what I never want to again and now am whare I have got to go through hardships, to hard perhaps to service but if I live to get home I shall never regret seeing what I have seen it is a school worth everything, but the tuition is high and they are sure to get it out of you. But I leave myself in the hands of an all wise being who is able + I believe willing to protect me under all the circumstance in which I shall be placed and if best ~~will at last~~ I shall meet you all again on Earth. if he has other ways ordered I can only say "thy will be done" if I am to be taken from this world this early in life I feel that my Maker has an all wise plan in so doing, and can I dictate his holy purposes? I suppose that Mr + Mrs Young look natural dont they have you seen them to talk with them any? did they say any thing about seeing me in Lexington about 1 year ago I dont know as I ever saw Fred Harwoods Mother whare has she been living? + whare is Fred? is Aunt Lucretia as well as usual this summer I should that that she would want help now having so much company. have they any one? Please remember me to them. I suppose that Uncle [Jonas] will do all his own work this summer and work on the road + every thing else wont he? Anna in the next newspaper you send me put in a piece of flag-root 6 or 7 inches long will you? I guess that you will think that I have written a good long letter this time + so I have I want one as long + much longer you can put in 2 full sheets as well as not. do write often + long letters. Remember me to all the friends I want to hear from all the family when I can Freeman can keep me posted as well as any.   I remain as ever your

Aff. Son + Brother   George W.

The Regiment was east of Richmond. White House Landing on the Pamunkey River was the former home of General Robert E. Lee's son. It was General Mc-Clellan's headquarters during the Peninsula Campaign in 1862. The Regiment crossed the James River at Harrison's Landing, the site of the Berkeley Plantation, to Prince George Courthouse. The paper used for this letter is very thin and almost transparent. Mary Allen's father, Oshea had died in 1844. Fred Harwood and his mother Abbie Comee Harwood Lincoln were living in Rowe, Massachusetts in 1860. She later moved to Wilton, New Hampshire. His father Jonas Harwood had died in 1840. Flag-root, also known as sweet flag (Acorus calamus) is a native plant used for gastrointestinal problems including loss of appetite.

Freeman R. Doane
(Photo in author's collection)

Anna Mariah Harwood Doane
(Photo in author's collection)

~ Chapter 11 ~

PETERSBURG, VIRGINIA
June 17, 1864 – March 30, 1865

The regiment crossed the James River at Harrison's Landing and was now near City Point, General Grant's headquarters for the Petersburg Campaign. Grant had decided to conduct a siege around Petersburg to continue to weaken General Lee's army and cut the supply lines to Petersburg which also supplied Richmond. For the next eight and a half months there were numerous Union attempts to break the Confederate defensive barriers around Petersburg.

[No. 9]   Two miles from Petersburg Va
                                          June 17ᵗʰ 64

Dear Friends

  As I have a few moments at leasure I will commence a letter to you. I have slept but a few moments or hours for 2 days + nights night before last we marched all night and a part of the day yesterday last night we reached here about 5 in the afternoon and formed a line of battle and supported some of the 2ⁿᵈ Corps who came up in advance of us. they had some pretty warm work. after dark we marched up + down the lines and changed places + dug pits all night so that we got but very little sleep. just before day light our brigade formed a line and advanced on the enemy. the Regt on our right broak + run the right of our Regt fell back but soon rallied again we took their pits and one fort, 6 pieces of artillery several ~~pris~~ hundred of prisoners. we had a warm place for a few moments but our loss was not very heavy, no heavier than mint have been expected, 15 wounded + 3 killed 1 Capt + 1 Sergt + several others, we think will die. Co E ~~lost~~ had 2 slightly wounded not to amount to much, but it was saddening to come back over the field and see the dead + dieing laying on the field, besides the many that they had carried off. we were relieved about noon and are now a little ways back in the woods resting under orders to be ready to move at a moments notice. the ground was almost covered with Guns + equipments blankets knapsacks haversacks &c the rebs had'nt time to take them along. a part of them were asleep. we found in their haversacks cornbread + pork, and so we took breakfast out of them. some of the prisoners seemed glad to be taken and said that they wished this war would end. they had seen enough of it. we can all say that. our Regt may be engaged again before night but a kind providence has spared me thus far. I will finish this some other time.

           June 18ᵗʰ

I understand that they will send out a mail soon so I will finish this. we advanced last night about 1/2 mile and dug some good rifle pits. the men in front have advanced. things look encouraging I think. Lyman is unwell and back with the cook. Bell my recruit is with us and makes a very good soldier. We are now laying in these pits all dirt. you would laugh to see us sometime when we have'nt washed for 3 days. I think that I told you that our Orderly Sergt was wounded on the 3rd so that I have to act Orderly, which keeps me pretty busy, and respondseble for some things which I should not be if we had our Capt + Orderly. Co F Capt is in Command of 2 Cos F + E. I have got to make out my morning report now, which I have'nt done for sometime. my men are scattered so that it will be a good job to do it correctly. I will not write any more this time I am anxious to hear from you, the 5 was the last I heard. we had a mail yesterday but none for me. I am feeling all right covered with dirt. I will write again soon. Remember me to all the friends. Good Bye,

I remain as ever Your Son + Brother

George W Harwood

[Undated fragment, possibly June 17-18, 1864]

I had a good long talk with Lt. Snell yesterday I like him pretty well. I think more of him then any other boy that came from Brookfield. he always comes to see me if we are near each other. he said he had a good time at home, stopped in N Brookfield only one night. I wish we could have been there together. We expect that the 34th Mass will pass through here today they belong to the 24 corps + have been down to Lynchburg Capt Leach is in command of the Regt I went to see him I think I told you in one of my letters to direct your letters to Co E now for I am back in my old Co.

Most Aff Yours

George W. Harwood

After the Lynchburg Campaign in June, the Massachusetts Thirty-fourth went to West Virginia.

Near Petersburg Va

June 19th 64

Dear Sister Anna,

This is a beautiful Sabbath morning. I cannot but think of my home and dear friends this morning instead of getting up in my quiet home and preparing for and attending church. I am laying here on the ground in the dirt behind some rifle pits. we cannot stand up with any safty. yesterday we had a hard time, 1 after another fell dead around me, their dying groans + pale faces are fresh in my mind. ~~some~~ 1 man in our Co dropped dead near me without a sigh - unprepared I fear, and as I think of these things and see the continued train of wounded and dying, being carried to the rear tears start in my eyes in spite of me one moment some have a oath upon their lips the next moment they are in eternity. Oh sad thought they must meet their God unprepared. the bullets and cannon balls are flying fast over my head now while I am writing. amidst such scense [scenes] as these I can only pray for my self, for my companions, for my <u>dear friends</u> far away from such scenes. I would that my Father + Brothers and all my friends would prepare for death while it is yet an accepted time. let us pray for them and each other. I feel sad in haste good bye George

No 10   Near Petersburg Va June 19th 1864

Dear Friends

     I sent a letter home to you this morning, but have just received one from you. We have just been relieved from our exposed position, and are now in the woods a little ways from the City perhaps 1/2 mile. the 17th we made a charge and were exposed to sharp fire nearly all day. yesterday we advanced in line of battle, lost but 1 killed + 1 wounded we were very lucky. we advanced in open field whare the bullets flew thick + fast. 1 man was wounded on my right hand + one on my left not more than 3 feet or 4 from me. they came pretty close to me but did me no harm. one man in my Co was shot through the head. he never so much as groaned or breathed it entered just under his right eye and came out the back side of head. Capt [Amos] Buffum acting as Major was shot through the heart not 2 rods from me. Capt. [James B.] Smith is in Command of the Regt. he ~~came~~ went home on Recruiting Service with us you know. more than 1/2 of the men that went home are either killed or wounded. we have now 4 commissioned Officers. the Adj. 2 Capt 1 Lieut. the rest are away killed wounded or sick. every Co but 1 is under charge of a Sergt and none of them as Orderlies. Co E has 20 guns present. We draw 26 rations. we have in all present + absent sick + wounded 57 one of the largest Cos in the Regt. We feel quite relieved now after being exposed to the fire of the enemy for 2 or 3 days in the hot sun no chance to wash or any thing to come back into the woods whare thare is a spring and wash up, and then get a mail a good long letter from home for me. I feel much better, but I did feel <u>sad very sad</u> this morning before sunrise before we were relieved. I wrote a little to Anna then. the grave of the man that we had killed was about a rod from my feet, blood &c laying around on the ground and sharp firing in front with every prospect of a rough day before us.

It is now about 1/2 past 11 in the forenoon. I presume that some of you are at Church, but such is not my priveledge today. I can only take my testament and read + pray, hoping that I may some day meet with you and attend places of Worship as I used to. rest assured that I have not forgotten the good instructions I received at home in my early days. For a week or two I did not feel at all well but I much better now I feel pretty well and am in good spirits that is concidering the circumstance under which we are placed. I am very glad to know that you received all my letters + the money &c. inasmuch as I sent a letter this morning I will not send this for some days, when I will write a little more if nothing happens I will write often. shall expect you will do the same.

George.

Dear Friends I will finish my letter to you. this is a beautiful morning we are now laying back in these woods whare we came Sunday morning. Sunday night we shoveled all night. yesterday we drew beens + vinegar for the first time since I came back. for dinner today I think we shall have a little rise + molasses. for the first time I am glad to get a change of food. I bought me a piece of liver and had 2 good meals of that. we are having a little battle right now. I saw Snell yesterday he is 1st Lieut in a Negro Regt he could not get a commission in a White [Regiment] when he wanted to. deliver me from such a command. he sais he likes but it dont seem to me that I should enjoy myself in their Company very much I think that I should about as leaves be in my boots as his. I am feeling pretty well now. our advance is pelting away at Petersburg day and night it is in sight of here about 1/2 mile I should think. I rec'd a letter from Wheelock last night he is in a hospital in Alexandria doing well I think by what he said. he was wounded in the foot below the ankle. there is nothing of much importance to write more as I know of. occationaly a stray shot comes over here and wound[s] some one 1 man was killed another wounded near here a few mome[n]ts ago. Good Bye.

I remain as ever your Affect Son + Broth— G. W. Harwood

Captain Amos Buffum was killed June 18, 1864. Burrage, page 213. This letter described the first attack on Petersburg on June 15, 1864.

Near Petersburg Va.   June 21st 1864

Dear Father

I received your letter last night with much pleasure. I was glad that you saw the Major and that he was willing to do something for me. Capt [James B.] Smith is just as willing I saw him this morning and told him what I wanted. he said that they had sent applications in for all vacancies but that there would be some more vacancies in a few days or soon by Promotion and that he would be pleased to recommend me and would. I asked him if I should do any thing more for myself. he said no, I will attend to it myself, and shall be glad to. I understand that whare a Regt is so small, but 2 Officers are allowed to a Co, Capt + 1st Lieut so I feel in hopes that I may get a 1st Lieutenency. I dont want any one to know anything about it at home out of the family and Im shure that they wont know much about it here if I should'nt be successful in getting it. there would be nothing said but I think my chance is good.

Your Aff. Son

George W Harwood

Confederate morning report paper (Image from author's collection)

No 11   Near Petersburg Va   June 22nd 64

I am now on the skirmish line the boys are loading and firing all the time. I have been, but now I think that I will lay low behind my pit for a while and write on a piece of a Rebel Morning Report which one of my boys took from a rebs havesack. now I will go on a reb bullet just came along and threw dirt all over me. I dont know as any of our boys have been wounded this morning. our whole Regt is out here some whare I have got a Capt + 9 men under my charge. I am now in Command of the Co have 19 guns draw 25 rations Lyman is better and took a gun this morning. Yesterday in the afternoon ~~we~~ Gen Potter an Div Genl reviewed our Brigad[e] we went back into an open field out of the way of bullets. he reviewed us first in line of battle then we passed in review by Division front that is 2 Cos front Capt [James B.] Smith told me to take command of the Div. and of course I did so long as there was no Commissioned Officers to do so. Just before dark one of our Co was badly wounded in the bowels ~~by~~ with a stray bullet. he was cooking his supper. I left the fire about 3 minutes before. we dont know when we are safe. when we think we are we are often mistaken. We came out on this skirmish line soon after midnight. we have to relieve our skirmishes in the night it wont do to show our heads in daylight, and they cant show theirs much for we keep on the watch as close as a cat would a mouse. it is great business for man to shoot his fellow man but such is war. I think that our Armics arc both being used up very fast. if I felt shure that the rebs army was being used up as fast as our[s] I should feel confident that this war would [end] before many months to say the least. we draw beens + rise beef + pork coffee + sugar + hard-tack so that we have enough to eat, and we draw whiskey every day, that is have for several days past some times I draw mine + sometimes I dont. thare are times when I think that a little would do me or anyone good. I intend to use reason + good sence about such things. it is said that "there is reason in all things" I dont know as you will be able to read this readily on this paper and I am writing on my Diary and that on my knee, beside that my pencil is'nt a good one and so short that I can only hold it between thumb + fore finger. therse [there is] no chance to buy one here perhaps you can put one in a newspaper I wish you would try it or into a letter it is light you know, if are full of my little words. I had a chance to buy a little stationary a few days ago 12 sheets for 40 cts not good [quality] at that, wrapper 32 cts. per bunch. I guess I wont write any more this time but will get up and shoot for a while for a change but I dont like the change very much and much rather write to my friends than to shoot men.

June 23rd   We were relieved about 2 o'clock this morning and are now a little ways in the rear plenty of bullets are flying around 1 man in the next Co was wounded just now. we had but 2 men in our Regt wounded I think yesterday. it is very warm and the sun is scalding hot. We drew clothing this morning. We have lain here all day behind these pits but we have had to lay low. the bullets come very low. they have given us 50 - 60 rounds of cartridges each today ready for any emergency. The bands are playing it is just about sundown the pleasantest part of the day, the time when I love to think of home, a good home + kind friends no one can fully realize these blessings until they have been away from them and I think that a man ought to be a sailor or soldier in order to see it then. I should think that they were getting excited in front on the skirmish line they seem to be firing in volleys just now, but I guess that they will cool of[f] pretty soon. they (the rebs) charged on us last night about 1/2 past 10 but we let them know that we were "all present or accounted for" I have just finished my supper what do you think I had hard tack fried in fat + coffee. had rice + salt for dinner + beef boiled. it is getting pretty dark tonight so I will draw this to a close for tonight. you see that I have kept a Diary for the past 2 days on this I like to write, especialy home, for I know that you are anxious to hear from me and I am from you should be glad to hear every day or two but good night.   George W.

June 24th '64

Dear Friends, I will write a little more today, to keep a sort of a Diary. I have been over to see Snell in the 4th Div. and several others of my acquantence. We drew some potatoes tonight 2 to a man, I think that we shall [have?] both now. they made a charge on our right this morning took 2 Regts prisoner so they say, it has been very warm today. I have had all my under cloths washed. it is getting so dark that I can hardly see to write more tonight we expect that they will make another charge on our right tonight. We expect a mail tomorrow in the morning I hope to hear from home. mail comes pretty regular. the band is playing.

June 25th.   This is beautiful morning I think that I will finish this letter, although I have nothing of importance to write A sutler came up last night so we got some cheese + lemons and a few such things I got a bottle of ink, but it is the poorest that I ever saw, half water I should think. it did'nt cost but <u>20 cts</u> but it will do to sell to Soldiers. every thing that we Soldiers buy is of the cheapest quality made on purpose to for us. I shall be glad when we can be whare we can have as good as others, but the [U. S.] Sanitary + Christian Commission[s] are doing a good deed for us. Yesterday I went over to the 4th Div. Commissary Department. a particular friend of Louis + mine, of Co H who stays thare, advised me to send those things of Louis home by the [U. S.] Christian Commission. I told him that I had no chance to ~~send~~ do them up, so he offered to do it for me as soon as he could get time. in the course of a week I presume he will start them. he is a good fellow and perfectly reliable, but you need not say any thing to Uncle David about it, for Hills will let me know when he sends them and I will let <u>you</u> know. I feel quite relieved to get these things off my hands. I hope they will reach home safely. This morning 4 of us were down to the brook a few rods back of us washing a bullet came over thare not more than 1 foot from one mans head and went into his coat on the bank. we have some pretty narrow escapes, but they saw that a miss is as good as a mile. I presume that it is so. Jim Cummings of N.B. had 4 bullets holes through his cloths + knapsack in one charge. I presume that we shall have to go to the front again tonight or in the morning. it is uncomfortably hot. Still we are pelting away at Petersburg we dont gain much ground and I begin to think that we shant get Richmond this summer what do you think about it at home. we have some papers here but we dont know all that is going on. I never was so mad with any thing as I be with this ink. I have sent for another bottle is [if] I cant have better I wont have any. I guess that this letter would [won't be] too long enough for you.　　　Yours Aff.

　　　　　　　　　　　　　　　　　　　　　　George W. Harwood

The U.S. Christian Commission was a privately funded organization formed after the first Battle of Bull Run, July 1861, to provide medical and other supplies, recreation and social services, and religious literature for the troops. They supported soldiers in whatever ways they could with letter writing, mailing and other meaningful tasks. Louisa May Alcott was one of their workers. The U.S. Sanitary Commission which began in May 1861 was designed to replace the various Women's Relief organizations that had started forming. It was a civilian organization which provided medical supplies, encouraged healthy nutrition, and sanitary conditions to support wounded soldiers. Elizabeth Blackwell, MD was one of their physicians. George's friend might have been James B. Hills, Massachusetts Thirty-sixth Cos. H & C.

No 12   Camp of 36th Mass. Vols
                                         Near Petersburg Va. June 28 '64

Dear Friends

     I will commence a letter to you but do not intend to finish today. I rec'd 2 papers from you, this morning Boston Journal + Mass Spy was very glad to get them. I see that Gold is worth something about this time. I saw by the paper that in some parts of New England the Crops were not very good. how is it with you? corn, grass, oats &c For the past two days we have been down to the front we were relieved about midnight last night. the last 24 hours we were in a very exposed position on the Skirmish or Picket line. the enemy had a raking flank fire on us all day but as providence would have it they did us but little harm. they also threw Morter Shells so that they burst very near us, wounding some. On our left was the 2nd New York mounted rifles (dismounted men) and when the rebs fired pretty fast it was all their Officers could do to make them stand. if they had run + the rebs should know it. it would lieve [leave] us in a pretty position, but we came out all right. This morning we had presented to us by the Sanitary Commission 3 lemons for a Co. of 26 men. I have all the rations to deal out ~~of~~ Whiskey + all. we also draw dried apple, about 1/2 tea-cup full for 3 days ration. it is no very desirable job to deal out such small quantities. they are so small that all want the <u>largest</u> or at least <u>the whole</u> of his. there are several sutlers near here we can buy cheese + canned fruit those of us who have money many of us have'nt and I'm think that I shall find the bottom of my pocket book before we get paid off again. My dinner has just come which consists of coffee + a piece of boiled beef together with my hard-tack is all I shall have today now I don't think that I shall hurt myself eating today. I have got about sick of boiled beef. I think that it will be quite unhealthy here if we should stay here long, for there are so many dead horses &c that are not properly buried, together with the warm weather, hard duties, loss of sleep bad water &c &c I fear that many of us will sicken. some are playing out now. Whenever I commence to write a letter home I never know when to stop. I could easily write a sheet a day to you and I dont know but I shall yet. I have just bought me a new bottle of ink + some paper so I am right on my write. I hear that Doc. Wellworth is dead + that before dying he found Christ precious to his soul. I am glad to hear that + I would that all my friends would seek the Saviour, now while it is an accepted time. <u>Dear Friends think</u> of these things. I am not feeling quite as well as usual today. my bowels are out of line.   George W.

July 2nd 1864

It has been some days since I commenced this letter I intended to send the day before yesterday but I could not. I have been very busy for a week past. the 29th I wrote as fast as I could making out the Co Muster Rolls + Monthly Report &c which is no small job 30th + 1st we were on the Picket line, 48 hours in the hot sun, <u>scalding hot</u> is enough to sicken anyone if he cant wash and is obliged to smell dead horses + men &c such was our case. they bury men here when they get in a hurry with their arms or legs sticking out. they dont intend to bury them so however. Today I am trying to finish my Muster Rolls I did not the other day I am getting along well. we have drawn from the Sanitary Commission dried-apples sour-crout pear been[s] pickels tomatoes onions &c small quantities very to each man but a taste of <u>each</u> to <u>each</u> I have them all to deal out sometimes I take a fork sometimes spoon. the quantities are so small that a fruit cup will hold enough pickaled peppers for a Co of 27 men. I rec'd a letter from you yesterday I think No 6 I was very glad to get it I was on Picket at the time and that is the place for a man to enjoy a letter or paper. I should be glad to receive a few more papers I got the flag you sent somethings has been out of tune with me for a month I have not felt well much of the time I went to the Surgeons this morning but he had but little medicine except pills I took a few of those. I do duty all the time. the Doc told me to lay off today but I could'nt see it these [Muster] Rolls must be made out sick or well I aint very <u>sick</u> only a little unwell shall come out strait I guess by + by. Please write very often

Very Aft Yours   George W

The three newspapers from home were the Massachusetts Spy *which began during the Revolutionary War and was printed in Worcester,* The Boston Journal, *a daily paper which was absorbed by the* Boston Herald *in 1917, and the* Springfield Republican, *now called* The Republican *and still being published.*

No 13   Near Petersburg Va   July 4th 1864

Dear Friends

      As I am not on duty today and have plenty of time I will write a letter to you although I sent one day before yesterday I finished my Muster Rolls night before last. yesterday we were mustered last night our Regt went on Picket. I was quite sick all day yesterday feel a little better this morning. went to the Surgeon and got excused from Picket. it is much cooler today than usual looks some like rain. The Sanitary Commission is doing considerable for us just now. they have given us, beans, pear, sour-crout, dried-apple, tomatoes, onions, lemons, ale, pickeled-peppers, &c we draw now soft-bread beans, rise, molasses, beef + pork coffee + sugar + Whiskey. Whiskey is now going to be one of the regular army rations, so I hear I think I saw it in the paper. I have no fault to find with ~~the~~ our living now but it dont taste much like home after all. I received a letter from Cousin Ida [Allen] yesterday. I have just been down to the Doc and got some more powders. We have got a Doc. that hardly any one likes he is short and sure acts mad if any one comes to him. he shows some partiality I think. the higher one ranks the better he will use him. he always treats me well, especially since I have been Sergt. he will excuse me when he wont a Private just as sick. one reason is he knows me well and another is I'm Sergt. he is very well acquainted with Henry + Harry [Harwood] and the family. he came from Natick. he studied with Doc Russell. he was at home on a short furlough when I was. I have no news to write in particular. if I have, I cant think of it now. It was very quiet along the lines yesterday last night they kicked up a little row, but it is still today it does not seem much like 4th of July. I should like to know what you are about at this time. 1 year ago I was down in Mississippi marching hard. now we are working hard besieging the City of Petersburg. 14th [months] more + then I hope I can return home, but this kind of life wares on us fast. I am in good flesh and if I were at home whare I could rest + clean up, I should'nt look much worn, but Lyman is quite thin I dont know but he feels about as well as I do most of the time. I have seen Snell several times of late but he has moved within a few days I dont know whare he is now. I have not seen or heard anything from the 1st Mass Heavy Artillery I think that [Nathaniel] Maxwell + George Spooner are in that Regt. the 25th Mass is near here I have seen Henry Johnson, Cutler Barnum is wounded. Henry

Cane [Cain] is in the 21st Mass with us. Freeman spoke of going over to see that Hubbard farm. have you got his terms yet. I should like to know what they are just for the fun of it. I presume that if I live to come home that I shall not make farming my business, of corse I dont know, but I guess I shall have to get me a boot + shoe store, or something else. under cover the sun melts me now. I feel well when it is cloudy but this sun melts me. at once I'm going to tell you what I had for breakfast, Tea soft-bread toasted + butter, boiled onions well seasoned with pep[p]er salt + butter cheese 50 cts per lb. butter 75 cts we can buy canned fruit but I havent any yet. it is pretty high.

George W.

Ida Allen was a cousin on George's mother's side of the family. Henry and Harry Harwood were cousins in his father's family who lived in Natick, Massachusetts. Their father will manufacture the Harwood Baseballs. Henry Cain from Spencer, Massachusetts served with the Massachusetts Twenty-first Regiment.

No. 14   Camp of 36th Mass Vols.
                                           Near Petersburg Va July 6th '64

Dear Friends

I will commence a letter to you this pleasant morning, but do not intend to finish it today. tonight we have to go on Picket I expect. Yesterday morning I rec'd a letter from Uncle Joseph [Harwood]. he is in good spirits I should think by his writing. he is in Jacksonville Ill, working at the Cabinet Making. he is very anxious that I should visit him at my earliest convenience either before or after I am discharged from the U.S. Service. I guess it will be after, but I should like to do so very well sometime. I rec'd 2 Boston Journals day before yesterday with some flag-root in them. you can send some such thing most every time it wont cost any thing and I like to receive them. It is a little cooler this morning than usual. we have very warm weather here as a general thing. I dont see as we are getting to Petersburg very fast we are about the same as we were 2 weeks ago or more, but it must some time. there is no news of importance I think every hour almost some man is brought from the front dead or wounded and here in our camp some one gets hit almost every day by a stray bullet.

July 9th

We came on Picket night before last I recd letter No 7 from you yesterday morning one from G [George H.] Jackson. yesterday in the afternoon there was some disturbance all along the line but I guess it did'nt amount to much. I understand that the 1st Heavy Artillery is in the 2nd Corps joins the 9th on the left it cannot be many miles from here. I suppose that the 15th Mass Regt are all taken prisoners or nearly all their time is about out I think, rather rough on them. I wish that you would send me one of those square rubbers to rub out led [lead] pencil marks I have to use a led-pencil so much. you can send it in a letter or paper free of charges I think. I am full of my wants about this time.

I also received a letter from Mary and Ada Jane Allen yesterday. they are both at home at with their Mother in West Troy Mary works out in some shop I think and boards at home. you tell Anna Jackson that if she dont write in answer to my letter pretty soon I shall write to her again I have been looking for one for 2 weeks from her. I wish that you could see us now as we lay in our pits. we have hardly room to straighten out. Imagine a ditch dug along through a corn field or oat field about 4 ft wide + 4 deep dirt thrown up on the sides and that ditch filled with men as thick as they could lay, the sun scalding in on them + the sand rattling down on them 48 hours, without washing or brushing their cloths and you have our condition at the present time. We dont show our heads above our pits very often. if we do happen to a ball will fly into the bank, perhaps not 2 ft from you. sometimes they go nearer, even through their man. one got his eye on me the other day and Zip, Zip, into the bank went several balls. thats all the good it done. I made as many low bows + kept down.

Sunday Morning July 10th

Dear Friends

I will finish this letter this morning it is very warm and rather uncomfortable. We were relieved from Picket last evening. we lost ~~none~~ no men this last time[?]. I wish that I were at home with you this pleasant morning to go to Church with you. but that cannot be. There are various reports here one is that Lee has sent 30,000 men to Frederick City Md. and going from thare to Baltimore + Washington, but we dont believe any such thing. There have been several new Officers made in our Regt lately one or two Lieuts made Capt + Sergts made 1st Lieuts. one Sergt that came home when I did is 1st Lieut now. he is off wounded. Maj Draper is now Lieut Col. I dont know when my turn will come for Promotion. I hope sometime, but dont say anything about it, for it may be months before I shall get it if <u>ever</u>. I wrote to Mr + Mrs E D Batcheller some time ago but have not received an answer yet. When you break your colt Freeman you can try mine a few times if you will it is pretty young but I guess it wont hurt her. I think that you will find some grit in her if I aint mistaken. if You + Father dont think she is going to be a good, smart, fast, horse I want one that will and will pay the best. Tell Fanni that I will answer her letter when I have a little more time + Ethan also. I receive a letter from you about once in a week, very regular about 4 days after they are mailed. I write oftener nearly twice a week. I write home about as often as any of the boys I guess, because I am aware of your anxiety. I guess Jim Cummings has'nt written home for some time by what I hear. he is a poor boy, fat + tough. he makes a good soldier, just about rough enough for one. I sometimes think that a man is'nt fit for a soldier unless he is in the habit of drinking cheating stealing + other like good [qualities?], but I will not say that. many are of that discription among us + all tends to demoralize. We have just drawn a loaf of soft-bread + I am going to get a little butter and go to eating. Lyman is not very well today I dont know what is the trouble with him. The Doc talks to him as though he thought he was homesick but I guess he isnt. dont say any thing that his folks will hear that I say any thing about him. the Doc tries to bluff him off. tells him he aint very sick. It is now past 2 o'clock in the afternoon I have just been out to the 4th Div Hospital Commissary to see my friend Hills of which I have spoken before, the man who took Louis watch &c. I took dinner with him. we had a good milk toast sody crackers + apple sauce + pickels &c a good dinner for a soldier the Commissary boys live better than the men in the ranks. it is very warm today but a good breeze I must draw this to a close as my sheet is full. I always fill the wrapper full whether it takes 1, 2 or more sheets. Remember me to all + write often.

Aff. Yours George W.

Mary and Ada Jane Allen were cousins on George's mother's side. Their mother was Aunt Lydia Fowler Allen. Uncle Joseph W. Harwood was George's father's brother and lived in Illinois. G [George H.] Jackson and Anna Jackson were also cousins on George's father's side. On July 11, 1864, Confederate General Jubal Early approached the northwest outskirts of Washington City from Maryland. On July 12 at Fort Stevens, he met troop reinforcements who had arrived from Petersburg. On July 13 he was driven back and retreated across the Potomac to Virginia.

No 15   Before Petersburg Va. July 13 '64

Dear Friends

   I will commence a letter home this morning and finish it when I come off Picket. we came out night before last have had a very good time so far except it is very warm. there has been but little firing in front of us. the rebs say they wont fire if we wont they want to change papers [exchange newspapers] with us or trade ~~of~~ tobacco for coffee or cornbread for hard-tack, but all communication with them is strictly forbidden. one man was arrested yesterday and one this morning for meeting half-way to exchange coffee for tobacco they belonged to the 58th Mass just on our right. this morning I have sent a corporal + 2 men off with a man to Brigade HdQuar [Headquarters]. It is scalding hot here in these pits and so dirty that a man can hardly stand it. in the last letter that I got from you there was some stamps I was glad to receive them. I have been looking for some stationary but am in no particular hurry as I have bought a little. I suppose that you have seen by the paper that we draw more pay than we used [to] it dont say very plainly what a Sargt shall have but I think 20.00 that will be much better than 17.00, but money dont go far with now. we shant be likely to get any pay till Sept 1st they say if they dont you will find me sending home for money I have got a little left, [it will] do for the present. I have got something over 2.00 in silver 2 halves that I am going to send home + perhaps my watch also when I get a good chance, and buy me another watch. I like this watch first rate it runs very well. What do you think we had for dinner yesterday – boiled-pork cabbage + potatoes + vinegar small rations however. today we are going to have for dinner beans + pork, pickels + hard-tack. I am laying on my back and writing. we do our writing in most any position that is most handy for us. Lyman didnt come out with us this time. he isnt well. Time moves of slowly with us here on Picket for we can hardly straighten out during the 48 hours, by 7 or 8 in the morning we think it must be most noon. What do think about the Reb's coming up to Baltimore + around thare I hope that it wont amount to much but it dont look just right, does it? I suppose that you Farmers are at their haying very busily. I think I had rather work at haying than lay here in these hot pits.

July 14th   We were relieved last night all is quiet as usual + the Christian Commission or rather an agent has been around in camp today and distributed small articles of clothing + tobacco, soda crackers, lemons &c ~~the~~ reading matter, &c the Sanitary Commission gave us some dried apple, 3/4 of a lb to a man. We had for dinner 1 potatoe a little cabbage + boiled beef. Lyman has gone to the Hospital he went while we were on Picket. I am glad that he has gone on some accts for I think he will be much better off there. I am not feeling quite as well today. my bowels trouble me a good deal this summer, too tight one day too loose the next. I have a good appetite a day or two and then I cant eat a thing hardly for a few days. one day I want pickels + vinegar and every thing, tart, sharp, the next it is the opposite all sugar + sweet stuff.   over

[on a small sheet of paper]

What do [you] think about the rebs coming to Washington. report here this morning is that they are within 4 miles of W[ashington] with a force of 35 to 40,000 I dont feel so much alarmed as some for I believe that Grant knows his business + will manage the affairs so as to bring the War to a speedy close. since I have been writing this another report later is current + that is that we have whipped the Johnnies there in Md. this may be true. We have received no mail today some think that it is on acct of this trouble near Washington I hope they will give us mail for that is next to bread with a soldier I expected a letter from you today and shall look for it next mail. it takes 3 or 4 days for one to come through. the Christian Commission gave of us a sheet of paper + wrapper today. I had some but I thought any little would help a little. I dont think of much more to write this time. I should'nt wonder if I sent home for money in my next letter if I dont see Lyman. he bought a watch. he hadnt any money, was going to send home for a part and pay the rest pay day. I let him have 5.00 till he could send home + get it. the 5.00 dollars came but it was Mass. <u>War money</u> and would [not] pass so he sent it back, expecting to get it today or in a few days ~~but~~ for me, but he has gone I may not see him for some time. Greenback alone are good, some gold + silver, but good Bye

Write often.   Affect. Yours George W.

No 16   Before Petersburg Va.
July 17 '64

Dear Friends

      I received a letter from you a few days ago No 8 with a lead pencil in it, saying that you had sent No 7 with 8 stamps but no stamps on the outside of the letter. it came with a stamp on all right + in due time. This is a beautiful Sabbath evening the band is playing very prettily but give me the soft gentle strains of a malodian I often think of my home on a quiet evening like this after the noise and confusion, eases + perplexities of the day are over between sun set + dark my mind wanders back to my home in old New England that quiet home, kind friends + Oh! how little do you know the sufferings of this war I have just been looking at a wounded man wounded a few minutes ago I think he will die. It is so dark I cant see to follow the line so I think I had better stop for this time.

Monday 18th

Last night we were all ordered out. we expected that the rebs would make an advance but they did not we came back this morning. I dont know as Mr. Hills has sent those things yet but they will come safely they need not worry about them. I am surprised that Louis Hinds is so low. I spoke in my last about 5.00 that I let Lyman have. I have got it. Lyman is at City Point I hear I have 2 letters for him. I am kept pretty busy of late writing &c yesterday I made out the Description lists of 25 men beside a little of every thing else. I write a good many letters. We expect Capt or now Major [Thaddeus L.] Barker here in a few days to take Command. Capt [James B.] Smith has sent for a recommendation for me a commission I hear, but dont say any thing about it till I get it <u>if</u> I do. A man in our Regt was shot through the heart this morning he never knew what hurt him. I received a letter from Jennie Bush this morning I have got my pockets + knapsack full of old letters + Co. papers. I am going to destroy a lot of them today I think. I like to keep some old letters to look at occationally. I suppose that the boys are enlisting in No. Brookfield fast, for 100 days Has Allen enlisted yet, if he knows when he is well off he will stay at home but I think that it would be a good school for him the term of enlistment is short the bounty is some indusement but if I am allowed to express my opinion I should say stay at home <u>little boy</u> time enough when you are old enough. you aint liable to a draft that would make a great difference. if I were coming into the service again I should'nt enlist as a private soldier I have seen to much of that. I find that 3 stripes if you keep on the right side of the Officers + Doctor &c help some. I should like to know how much higher gold + silver is going up, that is all nonsence speculation. Write often

George W Harwood

A melodeon is a type of 19th-century reed organ. Many men from North Brookfield and surrounding towns enlisted with the Massachusetts Forty-second (100 days). Three stripes refers to the insignia of a sergeant and access to an officer's privileges.

No 17   Before Petersburg Va.
                                                   July 22 '64

Dear Friends

     I will commence a letter home this morning. I expected to hear from you this morning as it has been a week today since I had a letter from you. I received a paper from you yesterday morning with some flag-root. I want you should send me ten dollars ($10.00) in the <u>next</u> letter without fail as I shall want to use some soon + I have but little with me. the Government owes me about 50.00 but I cant get that now. I shall be likely to want conciderable money along about this time, or soon. I should send for more this time but I dont like to trust too much at once. perhaps in the next you had better put in 5.00 more. be sure and send Greenbacks as nothing will pass here but them. there is nothing new here as I know of. we keep up our pelting at the old city, which has seemingly little effect. I am feeling pretty well now. we have had a good rain of about 24 hours and we feel greatly refreshed. somehow I dont think of any thing to write this morning. I have been writing all the spare time I have for a day or two making out Sutlers checks &c for the boys. the boys are all in for Sutlers goods now our Sutler has come up and trusts a few dollars to each, ~~th~~ takes it out of their next monthly pay. You spoke about sending some stationary to me some time ago. it has never got here + I dont know as you ever sent it that is all. Now I guess I will finish this letter so that it will go out with the mail this afternoon. I have just finished my dinner of salt-beef + Potatoes. this is a very pleasant day not so warm as usual. George Smith of the 25th Regt is over here now. he says that S. Kemp is either killed or a prisoner as nothing is know[n] of him since the fight at Northe Anna I think. Is thare any thing new going on in + around N.B. + who have enlisted? I suppose that they have enlisted for 100 days before this. I wonder to myself if Allen has gone or will go into the army, when he is'nt liable to draft. I should hate to have him enlist, but it would be a good school for him, if he could only stand the hardships. he would be likely to think of his home + the good easy times he used to have. I often think of home and wish myself there. I dont have so hard times as some for I am in good health most of the time and seem to get along with any thing and every body better than some I look on the bright side of things + make every thing go as pleasantly as I can for my self + others + if they dont go right it is all the same I dont worry much. When we first left home nearly all the Co. were from Monson + Palmer Capt from Monson, 1ˢᵗ Lieut from Palmer. they thought that [they] could have every thing their own way, receive all the Promotions + rule the little squads that came from other places such as N B & Oakham &c they did for a while, but we dont hear much from them now. their Capt Lieut + most of the men are gone. I will not write any more this time I should like that money as soon as I can get it be sure + have greenbacks I dislike to send for money but I shall have to under the present circumstances as I shall be obliged to use conciderable more ~~than~~ Write soon + often. Yours &c   George W. Harwood

Stephen B. Kemp, Massachusetts Twenty-fifth, was wounded and taken prisoner at the Battle of Cold Harbor, June 3, 1864.

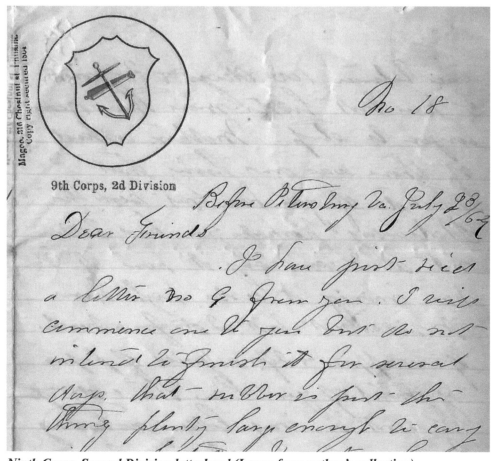

Ninth Corps, Second Division letterhead (Image from author's collection)

No 18   Before Petersburg Va. July 23 '64

Dear Friends

     I have just rec'd a letter No 9 from you. I will commence one to you but do not intend to finish it for several days. that rubber [eraser] is just the thing plenty large enough to cary in my pocket. I sent a letter to you yesterday. I began to think that your letter must have been miscarried but I guess not. I am sorry that things are so dry at home. we have just had a good rain but things are very dry now.

Then Harry has at last concluded to come to war. that is all right but there is some difference between 100 days + 3 years. I have but little more than 1 year longer to stop. Mother asked if there was any thing that I wanted. if you have not sent the Stationary, perhaps you had better not as I can buy it here if I have money it costs high here. it will cost but 2 cts for a bunch of wrappers + 2 for a quire of paper by mail if you leave the ends open. I sent in my letter yesterday for some money. I am about out + shall want some. I have not received my Commission yet but expect it now soon, but dont say anything about it till I get it that will be time enough. when I enlisted I never thought of such a thing. I thought if I became Corpl. I should do well, but my first step was 3rd Sargt. if the next should be 1st Lieut or even 2nd I should think that I had done well when the Corpl. + 1st + 2nd Sargt ~~are~~ now belong to the Co. and came out as such from Camp Wool Worcester, but I will say no more about this at present. if I get Promoted as I expect that is my luck.

Freeman I should like the Doc [Doc's] mare if I were at home but it is a good deal of money to put into a horse, most to much I guess, but I suppose she is smart.   July 26 '64

I guess I will finish this letter this afternoon. I had hoped to hear from you today or some one else but no letter came for me I understand that my papers have come to Hd. Qu. [Head Quarters] they had notice days ago of my appointment as 1st Lieut. it is known through the Regt now that I am to be Lieut many were a good deal surprised knowing that thare were Senior Sargt in the Co. that have been trying to get a commission for some time some say that they never trusted that I was going to have one. they can only say "Bully for you Harwood" go in again for 3 years I suppose but they must be foolish if they think I [am] going to stay in this Service 5 years, that is if they fight all the time. Of corse they all know of my Appointment at home I suppose they have all kinds of remarks to make. I used sometimes to wonder which would get promoted to Corpl first Lyman or I but for some reason or other he did'nt take very well among the men. I have been sick for a few days and have been off duty. I am a little better now.

Good Bye George W.

Harrison (Harry) Harwood, George's cousin, enlisted with the Massachusetts Forty-second (100 days) regiment. George was mustered as a first lieutenant on July 26.

Special Orders No. 125 (Image from author's collection)

Head-Quarters, Ninth Army Corps,
Before Petersburg Va July 28, 1864

Special Orders,
No. 125   (Extract)

x   x   x   x   x

3.   .   The following named enlisted
men are hereby discharged the service
to enable them to receive promotion
Sergt Geo. W. Harwood Co "E" 36th Mass Vols
            To date from July 25th 1864

x   x   x   x
[written over the text sideways]
Paid for Sept Oct Nov & Dec 1864
T. P. Haviland
Paymr. USA

BY COMMAND OF MAJOR GENERAL BURNSIDE:
[signature]
Lewis Richmond
ASSISTANT ADJUTANT GENERAL

A.C.W 2nd Div

Lieutenant George W. Harwood
(Photo from author's collection)

No 19   Before Petersburg Va
                                                            July 29 '64

Dear Friends

      I will answer the letter that I rec'd from you this morning No 10. I was very glad to hear from you. I sent a letter a week ago today asking for 10.00 + 5.00 in the next and I shall want 10.00 more in the next, as I do not draw rations now as I used to but buy them, so I must have money by me. I dont know when the Paymaster will get around. I have got my Commission + have been mustered and assigned to Co E. I could have gone into some other Co if I had wanted to. I wish you would send this money along as soon as possible for I need it. I saw Snell a few days ago and took dinner with him he is not far from here. I think I shall go over there this afternoon. I dont know whether I shall like being Lieut better than Sergt or not but I shall get rid of carrying knapsack + gun. I have got to get a Sword somewhare I have not got one yet nor Straps but the suttler has got the Straps. Im waiting for money, "money makes the horse go" What do the friends say about my Promotion or dont they say any thing about it. Then Harry [Harwood] went as Orderly Sergt. did he? You say that it continues very warm + dry at home. it is so here we have a little rain now + then. I suppose that Andrew [F. Jackson] is all right now if he has got a colt I wish that I was in this service for 100 days instead of 3 years but I dont expect to stay so long as that you know. I have seen about enough of this kind of life. I feel a little homesick today because I am so short ~~of~~ for money. I wish they would pay off. I dont suppose that I shall lay up much more money now [as] Lieut than I should [as] Sergt while we are here in this poor place but I shall have more to eat that I like, something besides hard-tack + pork, although we have been living pretty well of late. I do not think of much more to write this time I have written this in something of a hurry for the mail is about to go out. let me hear from you often. I dont like to call for so much money but it must be I need it now if ever + I see that I have only 2 stamps I wish you would send a few of them also. I must close for the mail is going. Good Bye

                                Respect Yours
                                George W. Harwood
                                Co E 36th Mass Vols

Cousin Andrew F. Jackson, Massachusetts Thirty-fourth, had been wounded and was discharged on May 11, 1863.

No 20   Before Petersburg Va July 31 '64

I sent a letter to you last Friday, but as you will see by the papers, that a Fort about 100 rods on our left, that this Corps ~~that~~ has been undermining for more than a month was blown up yesterday morning soon after daylight all the regts in our brigade were in the charge and we were ordered [to move] but the troops send to relieve us lost their way they intended to relieve us with Darkeys. they relieved our right + left and supposed that we were [relieved] but were not, if we had been we would have been in the charge. at first we gained the two first line of pits but the negroes run and so they [our men] all fell back with great loss. our Brigade is badly cut up. many were killed or wounded those that were taken prisonors were many of them murdered in Cold blood because they were with the Darkeys I feel that it was only the hand of an overruling Providence that spared us from the charge which would have caused a wound or death if nothing worse to many of us. it is sad to see the hundreds of killed + wounded laying between our works + the rebs. they are now out under a flag of truce burying our dead I think that it is cruel to put in white troops with the colored for it is sure death if they take us. we were exposed to the fire some, several were wounded. Joe Walker was hit with a piece of shell below the knee a very bad bruse. he has gone to the Hospital. I feel sad and down spirited this morning. I have seen about enough of this life sometimes I think it would be far better for me ~~to~~ if my Maker would take me home to dwell with him, but perhaps it is wrong to say so, for it is of corse desirable to live while I do live I will try and live so that when death does come I may be ready.
I shall not write a long letter this time. I write so that you may know that I am all right. I rec'd a letter from ~~then~~ Lyman this morning he is in Philadelphia. I will not write any more this time I have not told you much about the fight, for I dont know how much our loss is in either killed wounded, or missing. I was whare I could see most of the battle it look sadding to see such sights + I dont feel like writing any more about it. the enemy loss must have been very <u>heavy </u>also.
I am now in Command of Co I of this Regt. you had better direct your letters to Co I instead of E. I saw Snell day before yesterday I dont know whether [he] was in the fight or not. Write Often

From your Aff Son + brother

George W Harwood

This letter was written after the disastrous engagement in Petersburg on July 30, 1864 which later became known as the Battle of the Crater. The Union Army had tunneled under the picket lines to Confederate defensive works where they placed gunpowder. There were last minute changes in the roles each regiment would play in the advance after the explosion. These decisions changed the orders for the black regiments (USCT). This was probably a contributing factor in George's unit not being relieved as planned. The Massachusetts Thirty-sixth was 100 rods or 550 yards from the line where the explosion took place. George's friend Moses Porter Snell was one of the fourteen recruits from North Brookfield who served with the Massachusetts Thirty-sixth Regiment. He was now an officer with the Thirty-ninth United States Colored Infantry Regiment. In the winter, his regiment left with other USCT for duty further south. First Sergeant Decatur Dorsey was the flag bearer in Snell's regiment at the crater and is one of the few black soldiers to receive the Medal of Honor.

[upside down in top margin]
These 2 stamps wont stick perhaps you can make them
No 21   Before Petersburg Aug 6 '64

Dear Friends,

      I received a letter from you some days ago + the 10.00 which I was very glad to get. there is no news here of much importance that I know of. last night a Fort or something blew up but did no harm I guess although we dont know what it was exactly. We are having very warm weather now, dry and scorching hot we were relieved last night from 2 day Picket duty. the flies and misquotoes are so thick that it hardly pays to try to live. I received a paper from you this morning with the flagg.
[page] 2 this is a great place to live just some of our Commissioned Officers do live fast. I dont suppose that they lay up any thing some of them, and I dont think I can lay up much more money for a few months now then [than] I could drawing Sergt pay and rations from the Government, but money is no object as I know off [of]. thare is some talk of our being paid off but I dont know when it will be. I dont know as I ever worked so hard to write a letter in my life and this is the poorest that I have written for a long time. I am ashamed of this for I can write much better the files [flies] are all over my hands + face. I had a letter from Ida about a week ago. the little town of N B, I suppose is as

[page] 3 just as usual. I saw Snell yesterday he was in the fight last Saturday a week ago to day when the Fort blew up but came out all right he is act Adjutant he likes [it] pretty well I guess. I see him quite often he is always in fine spirits, think[s] a good deal of his position as 1st Lieut. he worked hard for his Commission and I'm glad he got it, but I say deliver me from the Darkeys. I suppose that you have got done haying before this time. Im glad you were so lucky getting the meadowes [done] I should like to come home and stop about 2 weeks to get me some new cloths + sword &c &c but that cannot be at present

[last page]every thing that I want to buy costs very high here. a Valice to cary my things in will cost 16.00 and every thing else accordingly. I have a good deal of writing and one thing + another to do in the Co my time is pretty well occupied. I find I dont have so much time as I used to to lay around. I had as leave have something on my mind as not, if I dont have too much. Father are you going to traiding after haying or going to get a drove of cattle or what are you going to do Does Uncle Washington say any thing about bringing a car load of cattle or horses East now. I will not write any more this time will try + write better next time. Good Bye

Write often + long letters

George W Harwood

On August 5, the Confederates attempted a similar mine explosion under Hare's House. This mine explosion also failed. The Union side of the site was later renamed Fort Stedman. M.P. (Moses Porter) Snell was mustered into the USCT Thirty-ninth as a first lieutenant. on April 16, 1864. He was now Acting Adjutant. All of the officers of black troops were white, therefore a soldier could receive a promotion more quickly if he was willing to serve in a Colored Regiment. Uncle Washington was probably Washington Harwood who was living in Adrian, Michigan.

No 22   Before Petersburg Va Aug 8 '64

Dear Friends,

I recd a letter from you this morning with the 5.00 + stamps. when I first saw the letter I wondered who it was from for the ink (blue) + envelope ~~look~~ looked like home + the hand writing I saw was Freemans so much the more I wondered why Anna did'nt write as usual, but when I opened + read I saw the reason why. I am very glad that they are comfortable. I presume you are pleased a Daughter give her some name that all the family has'nt got. some thing not very familiar would suit my taste but suit yourselves of course. It is now most dark long after sundown. I have just finished my supper, which consisted of biscuit + butter, Doughnuts + apple sauce, cold water. I have drinked no tea or coffee for most a week I think I shall feel better without. I have a cook all by myself, a very good one. I have my milk-toast + boiled[?] dishes quite often. the men are not living very well now. I believe I should die on their living, for I am half sick on mine. it is too warm here for me. I have conciderable Co business to do. when in camp we are in the pits half the time. we are here now, so you see that we are pretty busy most of the time. I wonder if Mary hears from Lyman often. he was in Philadelphia the last I knew. he is lucky to be in the Hospital so much the Doc sticks to it that he is homesick. I have got writing paper + envelopes enough for the present.

Aug 10 '64

I will write a little more today but I dont feel like writing or doing any thing else. I have been laying down most all the forenoon. I am quite un-well just now and have been for several days. I dont know what is the mat-ter with me, but I think I am pretty well worn out, together with a bad Diarrhea which wares upon me very fast instead of waring my usual fresh healthy countenance, I am now frail + poor, weak + sick I have done duty all the time but unless I feel better soon I shall have to lay off for a while I have worked on pluck + good grit for several weeks, still I mean to keep up good spirits. Lieut Col Draper arrived here last night he is looking pretty well concidering what he has gone through this warm weather. An Express box came for Lyman last night. I have'nt opened it but suppose that it is <u>Couf Balsom</u> [cough balsam] I dont know what will be done with it. I dont know but I shall take a <u>few bottles</u> of it for <u>surup</u> [syrup] to put on my bread. my appetite being poor that may help it. I cant send it to him very well. Martha Carruth wrote to [Leander] Bell that Judson Adams was married to <u>Jennie</u> Bush. I suppose she ment <u>Louise</u> + that Charles Kellogg was dead. is there any more news from N. B. later? we had something of a shower here last night but it is very warm + dry now + dusty I see M.P Snell quite often he is feeling well, Act Adj   another sheet, Continued

I am going to have for dinner soft-bread toasted + beet with apple sauce. the water here is quite poor and I think it must be unhealthy to drink. we are advised to drink our whiskey ration every day, some days I do + some

I dont. I dont see how a gill of whiskey is going to hurt a man going through what we do. I wish we could draw ale every day instead. I should like to know what Andrew thinks of doing you say that he does'nt think of making boots much longer. he likes a horse I guess better than I do. I am very fond of one you know. Whare does Ruth Livermore board I dont know as I have heard? Do you know whether Uncle David has rec'd the Diary of Louis yet. I sent it alone [along]. My friend Hills is going to send the watch + pocket book if he has'nt already. It has been reported here that Gen Potter has been relieved of his command, and that Gen Griffin now commands I dont know as it is true. Potter commanded our (the 2nd Div) was relieved on acct of Drunkenness. I should'nt think strange if it was so. I've seen him when he could hardly ride his horse, others say they have seen him fall off. they say he fell of 2 in one day not long ago. I never saw him when I thought he was sober. We have a good deal of Whiskey courage with us, too much, more than people at home are aware of I guess, but I must draw this to a close for this time. I will write a little to Anna personaly. I hope to hear from you very often Remember me to all the friends.　　　Very Aff Yours
　　　George W. Harwood

Anna and Freeman's baby girl was born on August 3, 1864. Mary was Lyman's wife. Judson E. Adams married Harriet L. Bush on August 3, 1864, in North Brookfield. George's cousin Louis was my great grandfather's half-brother. We have a few letters he wrote home but not his diary or pocket book. None of the watches we have are identified as belonging to Louis.

No 23　　　　　　　　　　　　　　Before Petersburg Va Aug 13 '64

This letter is on 4 sheets of paper of varying sizes. The largest is 15.5 x 9.75".
(Image from author's collection)

Dear Friends

I received No 13 from you this morning with 5.00 making 20.00 in all that I have received. the paymaster is here now at these 4th Div and before I finish this letter I presume I shall tell you that we have been paid off. we signed the payrolls yesterday. you need not send any more money, for I have got enough now or shall have in a day or two. You say that Uncle David is getting anxious about Louis things. tell him that they started the 9 of this month. the Christian Commission took them and said that they would go safely through, probably free of charge. Father thinks his taxes are high does he? so are mine larger than his I have to pay. I understand one tenth of my pay [goes] to the Government as tax which is 132.00 a year, 11.00 per month, but I dont care much about that if that will put down the rebellion. I hope Maj Foster will like his new position, but I would'nt swap Commissions with him for a good deal of loot. Do you think that they will have to draft in N B to get the other 8 men. I hope not. I wonder if Edwin has got acquainted with Harry Harwood any yet. I received a good long letter from Anna Jackson this morning, was very glad to here from her. have been expecting to for a long time. I miss Sister Anna hand writing very much. this is the first letter that I have rec'd from home for a long time without her hand writing some whare in the letter. I hope to see it in the next. I am glad that she is getting along well. I suppose you have not named the little one yet. give it a good name that every body has'nt got. when I wrote last I was'nt feeling very well, and I do not now, but I think I am a little better this morning. I am sorry to hear that Mr. Cushing + son are getting along no better. dont you begin to want to hear Mr C- [Cushing] virses[verses] again in the pulpit. I should if I were there I think. How are Uncle + Aunt Harwood [Jonas + Lucretia] now you wrote a few weeks ago that they were not very well. I suppose that you have got done haying by this time. I see by the papers that the hay crop was as large as usual in Mass N. Hampshire + Vermont. do you think yours was as heavy as usual?
Freeman you will please remember [me] to Joe Wheelock. I should be glad to hear from him. our friend Haskell has not made his appearance yet. tell Father I shall expect to see his hand writing in the letters now he has finished haying. he wont have so much to do. I was sorry to hear of N. Dickenson death. I remember riding to Boston with him the morning he left. he was as fast [fit?] as you please + in good spirits.

But Judson Adams got married all on the sly did he? He was long enough about it. I find that in order to fill up one of these larger sheets one must have a good deal to write I hardly ever tire writing home, or get to large a sheet of paper, but I will stop for a while we shall get our pay soon and I shall want to write a few words after that. I have had more writing to do of late and I write so fast that it is not as plain as it mint be. I suppose if I should take more pains it would look better. We have been paid off I got only 2 months pay 40.00. I guess I shall not send any home at present any way, for I may want to buy a suit of cloths + sword &c. I drew the pay for the Co. as they were in the pits and then went up and paid them. there was about 14.00 in all. I did not go out with the Regt the last time for I did'nt feel like it. I have got about 500.00 worth of property in my charge that I am responsable for. I guess I can manage that amount well enough. Well I must go + pay my Sutlers bill I bought a Hat and a few other things when I had no money he wanted me to buy a suit of cloths &c + trust me for those but I could'nt see it in that light. The Government owes me about 35.00 now but I expect that they will take the 25.00 bounty that I have already received. I shall not get the 100.00 for I was in the service only 23 months instead of 24 before I was discharged, then I was mustered for 3 years more from July 26 1864. I can resign most likely if I dont like the business by + by. if I had waited one month more I should have hit it I guess but I dont care a fig if the war will only end. I dont expect to make much money in the service. if I save any thing I shall do better than most of the Officers + Soldiers do. Perhaps you would not be wholly uninterested to know what I had for Dinner. I will tell you, boiled beef + potatoes, beet, onions cabbage soft bread + tea, (pepper, salt + vinegar, sugar &c of course.) a rare dish for us to have togather. It relished well. Soldiers think a good deal of their food, that is about all the comfort they have, eating + sleeping. Wm James Haskell is on his way back to the Regt I understand. he feels a little rough to think he is a private, but he must be for a while at least. I dont think of much more news to write you this time. I expect to hear from you in a few days and then I shall want to write again. There are boys here among us no older or larger than Ethan Allen.
George.
I will commence one of these large sheets but dont know how far I shall go. we draw from the Quartermaster such paper as this every month, to do my Co. business with but I shall appropriate some of it for my private use

as I have a good supply on hand. this is the cheapest + best paper that one can buy for any use. I have'nt got me any sholder straps, sword nor belt as yet. I have an old sword blade that I cary around with [me] when I go on picket. all I have bought is a had [hat] + <u>cord</u>. the cord is all that distinguishes me from a private. I am going to buy me some new cloths when I get around to it. I find that the mail is just going out, but I can finish my letter and send it tomorrow just as well, but I dont know what to do with 3 or 4 Doz. of bottles of [Lyman] <u>Gilberts Cough Balsom</u> on hand I dont believe I can sell them for 5 cts per bottle which will hardly pay the cost. Bell my recruit + I are all that there are left in the Regt now from N Brookfield. he isnt very well + I dont know how long we shall be here. I think I have hung on about as well as any of them the rest have been off in Hospitals long a ago. Our Regt is pretty small now not more than 100[?] Guns I think. my Co. has 13 Guns. I dont think of much more to write I have written now more than I expected to when I commenced but if I close now I can send it out in the mail today. I see he is sorting it over and will go in a moment. I hope to hear from you often. I hope to hear that Anna + the baby are getting along well. I hope that before this reaches you I shall feel better. I certainly shall be better or worse. I feel better than I did in the morning I think. I wonder if Mr. Cushing has written to me yet? I have been expecting a letter from Mr + Mrs E D Batcheller but I dont know but they have forgotten me. this is a dull place, playing cards drinking whiskey wine + ail [ale] &c + smoking is all. some reading but I am short of that just now. write often. Remember me to all the friends &c.

Very Aff. Your George W. Harwood

I will write a little more on this sheet I guess I shall have a full letter. Perhaps, Bucher will think best to charge 3 cts. I have been settleing some of Louis affairs. I have taken 5.00. I think that thare is about 2.00 more oweing to him but the man is off wounded I think. I will try and collect that sometime. you can tell Uncle David that here are 5.00 that I will send for you to give him. tell him that his matters are all ~~strate~~ straight here in the Regt, except 1.50 or 2.00 the pay for a shirt. I dont know how much it is exactly I will settle that in time as soon as the man returns from the Hospital if he ever does. I would have done this before but the boys have been without money untill now. Snell has just been here and wants me to come over and buy a sword + belt + ~~valiase~~ valease that one of those Officers wants to sell. he says that he must sell he has been dismissed from the service lately, for ill conduct. I dont like to pay out 20 or 30 dollars and then send home for more to spend for a livery, at the same time I must have an outfit. it costs something to start in this business as well as any other some can make money at it in the right place. I dont know whether I can or not. I shall try and save some thing. I intended to send this letter in the mail today but I did'nt get around and now it is almost dark so I shall send tomorrow. there is a rumour here that we are to be relieved and go some whare else. Genl Burnside starts for home tomorrow morning I dont know what for on a furlough I presume. I wish we could go North, perhaps we should'nt like it any better but it would be a change if nothing more. write often + I hope to see Anna['s] hand writing in the next. I will close for tonight.   Good Bye. From your Affect son + brother

George W. Harwood

In 1864 the income tax was increased to five percent on incomes between $600 and $5,000, seven and a half percent on incomes between $5,000 and $10,000 and ten percent above $10,000. Edwin Doane (Freeman's brother) and Harrison (Harry) Harwood (George's cousin) enlisted with the Massachusetts Forty-second (100 days) regiment. Sutler trusted me means he bought items on credit. William James Haskell enlisted as a Corporal was promoted to sergeant and then reduced to private, perhaps because of illness. Ethan Allen Harwood, George's brother was now age 16. In all, fourteen men from North Brookfield served with the Massachusetts Thirty-sixth, only two were currently fit to serve. This letter is much longer than most, so it may have needed more than the usual three cents postage. We do not have any of the envelopes or wrappers to be sure. Major General Burnside left on leave and was not given another command during the Civil War.

No 24   Before Petersburg Va. Aug. 17th '64

Dear Friends,

I was relieved last night from 24 hours Picket duty. by the way we moved about 1 mile to the left last Sunday night and are now whare the rebs are more friendly. I took 20 men and went out in front of the Regt, deployed as skirmishers the rebs send out skirmishers the same. We make an agreement with them not to fire at each other and so we can walk around at liberty[?], talk with them and exchange coffee &c for tobacco and some times they will give us Greenbacks for jack knives. I had a poor one and one of the boys went out and left it at the front of a tree that stands about half way between us + them. a reb came up and left a plug of tobacco for it. one of the boys gave me 40 cts for the tobacco. they would come up to the tree and leave some tobacco and corn bread or something of that kind and our boys would go out and get it and leave some coffee hard tack + cheese &c they are on very friendly terms with us and say they dont think this war will last always, but they dont say how they think it will end. I dont think it is going to last long either, neither do I know how it will end. we hear some good news from Sherman + others Butler is doing some thing on our right I hear, but what do you think of these Peace Commissions that we read so much about in the papers of late will they amount to any thing think you? I dont see as they can do any harm any way. I told you in my last [letter] that I had a box of Lymans on hand. Sunday night we had orders to move and so we did about midnight. I opened it and took a couple myself and gave the rest away. I could do no better under these circumstances I have written to Lyman about it. no one wants to buy Cough Balsam this season of the year. we aint apt to have very hard colds. the boys thought that it was a very pleasant drink and on the whole liked the taste. I feel about as I did when I wrote you last about 1/2 sick. have a bad Diarrhea a good deal of pain in my bowels that is unusual for me. sometimes I go to the Doc but he dont seem to help me much if any, but I guess I shall come out right by + by when the weather is cooler I am careful what I eat my appetite is not very good. I had for breakfast this morning warm biscuits + butter, doughnuts + cheese pickels &c cold water is my drink. I have a very good cook I guess I shall have fish + potatoes for dinner. there is a rumour here in camp now that this the 9 Corps is going to Kentucky soon, but I dont know what to think of it. I had a letter from Cousin Harry Harwood a few days ago. he is in Alexandria his Regt [Massachusetts Forty second (100 days)] is doing Provost Guard duty. he says that if the warm weather holds on he shall get enough of soldiering in 100 days. I have answered his letter this morning and am making that my business answering up old back letters this morning I have answered 4 or 5 havent got through yet. I have concluded that I would take a sheet of paper this time large enough to write all I have to say dont you think this a good generous sheet, I do? and dont know as I shall be able to fill it. There is but little news of importance that I know of except what we see in the papers. we have daily papers a day or too [two] after they are printed New York Herald, Philadelphia Enquirer, Washington Morning Chronicle, and several other papers are brought around. I dont believe all that [I] read in the papers. I saw yesterday a man who said that he had seen Burnside baggage and that it was marked Louisville Ky. his horses are at Fortress Monroe so they say. he has gone home I understand. he told some one that the 9th Corps would be all right in a few days, and some one else that the 9th Corps would follow him soon, but we cant tell much about what we hear. he did not tell me any thing about his business. I think it would be more healthy in Ky. then here. the water is much better. what I saw of Kentucky before I liked first rate and we saw just a portion of it. we marched pretty much all through it at different times we were there twice. I should like to see, Mr Youngs people, very well. what I saw of the old folks before I liked them very well. Whare is Lucretia [Young] now the last that you wrote about her, she was in N. Brookfield I think. Cousin Anna [Jackson] writes me that her Mothers [Phebe] health is not very good or that her hands trouble her a good deal with the salt[?] Rheum[atism]. I thought by the way Anna spoke that we had'nt had a very good school or that some thought so, although she said the examination passed off as well as was expected. Susan Sanderson had a good school she thought [she] was thare at the examination and the committee praized it up highly. I understand that they are going to rase some new Regt in Mass. for one year is that so? have you filled your quota in N.B. we think of the poor fellows at home who dont want to come but dont care so much about it ourselves so long as we are in and expect to stay for a while. my cook has just brought my dinner Macerell + Potatoes + Dinner is over and I have got about 2 hours more to write before the mail goes out. A few days ago ~~of~~ one of the boys in Co E found a pretty desent old sword steel scalbard <u>and gave</u> me, so it will do as well as any to go through this rough campaign with. I guess you wont find any fault with this letter with out it is because it is to long I know that the main thing is to have some sence as well as all length. I have written already far too much for politness but I dont stand so much for that when I am writing home and I hardly ever read over my letter after I have written one for I dont have time, unless I am writing to one that I know to be my superior and then I take time. I have not heard from Mr Cushing yet. is he or his family any better? I wrote you not more than 3 days ago I guess it was, telling you that we had got paid off, and that I wasnt going to send home any money this time for I shall have to buy so many things and shant have any too much if I do enough before another pay day. most of the boys got 4 months pay but I got two of mine the day I left home you know and left it all + 1 dollar more but have had a large portion of it sent to me. have you got the 5.00 dollars that I sent to Uncle David [Winslow] and what did he say? has he got the watch yet? I find that I have got nearly to the bottom of this large sheet I dont know but I could fill another, before I have written all Freeman have you broken your colt yet? if you have did you try mine. What has become of the Doc mare? have you got her still? how does Andrew get along with his colt, and does he like it? write often and all the particulars.

Very Resecpt Yours, George W Harwood

The troops had moved closer to the Weldon Railroad, an important supply line for the city of Petersburg. Major General Sherman was in Atlanta, Georgia. Numerous engagements against Lieutenant General John Bell Hood resulted in the fall of Atlanta on September 2, 1864. Major General Benjamin F. Butler's troops were entrenched southeast of Petersburg, preventing any Confederate movement in that direction. Because the Battle of the Crater on July 30 was a disaster, Burnside left on leave in August and was never given another command. When George visited Mr. Daniel Young's people in Kentucky, his wife Lucretia Tomblen Young saw a family resemblance. Lucretia was the granddaughter of Jonas and Lucretia Harwood (George's great-uncle and aunt).

No 25   Near Petersburg Va Aug 23rd '64

Dear Friends

  I received a letter from you a few days ago. we left our old position last Friday and marched down on the left a few miles towards the Weldon rail road. the 5th Corps have taken a portion of it. last Saturday the rebs charged on them to retake it if possible but did not succeed our men killed or wounded a lot of them and took many more prisoners 1000 in one squad 900[or 300] in another. we expected to be attacked any moment and as we advanced we were deployed as skirmishers and marched in line for some ways then we halted and went to throwing up breast works sent out pickets &c the enemy came down to feel of us a little and drove in our pickets wounded 1 man in Co E. they had a hard fight with the rebs here on the groun[d] day before yesterday and when we came the ground was strewed with dead men guns + equipment. The[y] have been picked up now. this is a low damp place, swampy, and thickly wooded. we have had a good deal of rain here lately most every day we have had a hard shower if nothing more. we have been wet through every day for most a week. some of us begin to feel it the sun will scald one hour and the next it will rain hard. it will be all moonlight in the night and in half an hour it will be raining in torrents. Gen'l Meade, Ferrero, Potter and 3 or 4 more have been riding around here yesterday + today we have got some strong works in front and on the whole a very good position I think. I received a paper from you today and a letter from Edwin [Doane, Massachusetts Forty-second (100 days)]. I should like to see him first rate. I guess he likes pretty well. I should judge so by what he said. I received a letter from Uncle David Winslow yesterday I shall answer it in a few day. I am glad to hear that you are getting along so well at home and the little one. Anna, you asked me to send a name, but I guess I will leave that for you to do. Nameing babies aint my business just now, but dont give it a name that the rest of the family have all got for 3 or 4 generations. I like a double name. I could send a dozen names that I like but they mint not suit you such as Harriet Louise &c, but I will not dwell upon the subject. I guess it will be dark before I get through. I have got a very poor position for writing. I am leaning up back against a large pine tree, my portfolio on my knee and my paper dropping down through my fingers every line. I feel tired and lonesome tonight. I hear the band playing in my rear but I dont care any thing for that. it is dark and I cant follow the line so I will stop for tonight. This is a beautiful morning the men are busy fixing up their tents. I am going to have mine fixed up when I get a chance to get an axe. Freeman do you ever go to Worcester when you go again look for some sholder strap <u>barrs</u>. I presume you have see[n] Officers with the barrs only. I want 5 or 6. they will cost 20 or 25 cts each. you can send them in a letter. I cant buy any here I havent got any straps yet. the sutlers dont keep much such stuff. I have got me a pair of good pants. last night I was quite unwell all night and I ~~drempt~~ kept dreaming all the time about home I thought I was at home sick with a fever and mother was taking care of me, up in my room whare I always used to sleep, then I would wake up and find myself laying on some leaves in the woods I would lay and think a while and then go to sleep and begin to dream of home again. I have felt so unwell for a few weeks that I suppose I am a little home sick but I shall get over that soon I hope. I went to the Doc. this morning and got something I dont know what it was. the Doc dont have much medicine here at the front a few pills + powders sometimes a little ligment [liniment?] of some kind.

The sun is scalding hot and I guess we shall have a shower before night. I have written about all I can think of this morning so I will close. Edwin wrote that he had just received a letter from home saying that his Grandmother was dead. Freeman if you can find any of those bars I should like them straps would be to to large to send in a letter but a large bundle will come through safely now. I want to hear from you often and good long letters nothing is so cheering as a letter from home you know that Freeman, especially if a fellow dont feel well.

      Very Aff. Yours

         George W Harwood

The Union took possession of the Weldon Railroad on August 21. Lee was still able to bring supplies north from Wilmington, North Carolina and then around to the west of Petersburg. The Union now had control of most of the railroad lines which supplied Petersburg. Mercy Doane died on August 15, 1864, in North Brookfield. She was the grandmother of Edwin, Freeman and Hubbard Doane.

No 26   Before Petersburg Va Aug 28th '64

Dear Friends

      I received a letter from you a few days ago and was glad to learn that you were getting along so well, + the little ones. Lyman + Haskell have both come back to the Regt they are looking very well. there is no particular news as I know of since I wrote last, which was but a few days ago. I have been quite busy for a day or two, making out the muster rolls and some other Co papers. I have been Brigade Officer of the day for the past 24 hours, have just been relieved there are 7 Regts in our Brigade. perhaps you have never seen any or many military orders so I will send this that you may see how they do business. they dont come and ask you if you will be the <u>Officer of the day,</u> but give you the detail and say nothing. I think I shall send home for Freeman to get me a small trunk or valease, some boots perhaps coat &c and have it come through to Baltimore to our Sutler and let him bring it through to me, but I may alter my mind in a day or two. I can get these things much cheeper at home, and beside that would be a good way to have a box come to me. We are having lovely weather here now, good air most of the time. I think I am feeling a little better than I did. I received a paper from you yesterday with some charcoal in it. I took one spoonful last night. that peice about Gen Burnside being relieved from his Command of the 9th Corps, is not so. I think it has been contradicted in other papers. whoever put that into the paper I guess wasnt thare and dont know the Gen as well as some of us Soldiers do. he was present the day the fight was and done his part to gain a Victory, I believe. You say Father has named the baby Irene that is an old name and rather pretty I like the name Ida Adella pretty well, but Mother used to say that the name was nothing, only behave yourself. I see by Mother letter that Andrew has got a skittish colt. I think they were lucky not to get hurt any worse, but Andrew likes a horse. he will sober it if he drives it as much as he used to his other. if my colt is always going to be as small as Bill [a horse] I think it would be a good Idea to traid her for one of some size dont you. I like her spunk if she is any[thing] like her mother.

Tuesday morning 30th

As I did not finish my letter the other day I will this morning. We are having fine weather, nothing new as I know of. tomorrow we are to be mustered for 2 months more pay. I shall draw 1 Sergt + 1 Lieut I expect. I expect that they will deduct the 25.00 dollars bounty that I received in advance next pay day, as I was not in the Service 2 years before I was discharged and mustered again for <u>3 years more</u> or a <u>sooner dischage</u> but this war will play out before long I think some way. if it dont a man had better be in the Army than at home. I dont think of much more to write this time I guess I havent got my thinking cap on. I saw Porter Snell a few days ago I guess he dont or did'nt know that his little brother in law was dead, for he would have been ~~shure to~~ sure to have spoken of it. Who lives on the corner now whare Mr Hair moved from any one. Andrew + the Forbes boys wont trouble the old lady now by cracking their whips and driving around the corner fast to make her think they are going to tip over any more, but she can see them go by Mr Greens What is Herman mad about? did he think he could get more property if he had them come there to live with him the old folks would die there, but Addison has a soft thing for a soldier but I had about as leave be with the Regt if I had got to do duty and I suppose he has some duty to do. Now I will finish my letter I have been to dinner. I have been thinking about sending for those things I can buy them in Mass much cheaper than I can get them here, but I run some risk in getting them through so I wont send this time. I can get a desent pr of Boots here for 10.00 heavy or double calf upper-half double sole, worth not over 3.00 at home. some think we shall leave to go to Ky soon and if we do, I can get things cheaper if I have the money

Good Bye for this time. I will write again soon
Very Aff. Yours, George W. Harwood

The articles reporting that Major General Burnside had been relieved of his command would in fact be true. Irene Amanda Doane was the third child of Anna (Harwood) and Freeman Doane. M.P. Snell's baby half-brother died on August 17, 1864, at age one of cholera infantum.

No 27   Before Petersburg Va. Aug 31 '64

Dear Friends

 I have pretty much come to the conclusion that I would send for a small trunk or valise, boots coat &c as I shall have to have the things and I have not the money with me and beside I can get them from home much cheaper. I saw our Sutler, Wheelock, and others say that I can get Express boxes through in about 2 weeks. Freeman you have seen Officers trunks about 2 ft long 15 inches wide 18 or 20 inches deep with straps to strap a blanket on top. these that I have seen are black some of our officers have got them that is what I should like. if I cant get one of these, I should like a sole-leather[?] valise not quite as large strictly bound. they are kept in Worcester all ready made for Officers I suppose. they cost 16 dollars here. we have to send to Washington or Baltimore I presume they can be bought their for 8 or 10. I want a pr of heavy calf boots, half double sole, size 9 I dont care whether you buy them ready made or not if they are only good. then I want a bleus or sack coat, you know about how long 3 ft I have just measured, most to F. knees. my arms are a little longer than yours from the top of the sholder 2 ft + 4 inches. they are ready made. you have seen enough of these to know what I want. I take a coat a trifle larger than you across the sholder get one that is a little loose for you, and get a pr of desent 1st Lieut. Sholder straps, 5 or 6 dollars and have them put on. then I want me a sword belt worth from 3 to 5 $, patent leather or any thing. I shall buy me a Good sword belt + pistol sometime perhaps. I have got an old sword now that will do for this campaign I bought me a pr of pants a few days ago. I dont think of any thing else to have you get. you can put in what else you wish or any body else if they have any thing they want to send me. a pr of slippers something like my old ones would come handy, but they aint good enough. there are 40 little things that I should like well enough, but I will let you put in what you please. perhaps Aunt Lucretia [Harwood] or Aunt Phebe [Jackson] or some of them may want to send some little thing. Lymans wife [Mary] or Mrs Haskell [Orrill] or Bells mother [Luzetta] may want to send some small article if there is room, but you need not trouble yourself they will know of it if they want to send. all of these things will make quite a bill but if Father will let you have the money and keep acct of it we will make it all right. let me know what they cost. put the Key into a letter and send * I wish you would send it as soon as you can for we are now laying still and hope to stay here or near here a few weeks. if you think you cant get the things to suit me send the money, but I guess Freeman can get them to suit. he has been in the Army and knows about what I want. Try on the boots and see that they are not 10 I wear about the same size over the instep that you do. send by Adams Express direct the same as you would on a letter, Co I 36 Regt Mass Vols 9th Army Corps Washington D C On one end of the trunk or valice have my name printed after this style no Co letter.

Lt. Geo W. Harwood

36th Regt Mass Vols.

I believe that I have nothing more to write so I will close and get ready to go on Picket tonight. I know that it will be some bother to you to send these things but I should like them first rate and soon as I can get them. if I think of any thing more I will send in day or two. I sent a letter yesterday write soon. this is a fine cool day. little small apples are selling for 3 cts each, watermelons 1.5 dollar[?] each and other things about the same.

Yours &c &c

George W. Harwood

Bleus or sack coat, a working coat or frock, originated in France as bleu de tra-vail. Leander Bell's mother, Luzetta (various spellings), a widow, had re-married in 1857, and was now Luzetta Bell Haskell. The Adams Express Company began in 1854 as a freight and cargo business between Boston and Worcester.

[upside down at the top of the letter]
I have worn my old ill looking rings as long as I want to. I dont care to throw them away after waring them so long so I will send them home I will get another better one when the time comes right.

No 28   Near Petersburg Va. Sept 6 '64

Dear Friends

I received a letter from you day before yesterday. Yesterday I went on Fatigue, 1 Capt, 1 Lieut + 90 men worked on some rifle pits from our

Regt, in rear of our lines. I understand that Genl Grant is afraid that Gen Early will try and flank him, so that when Lee attacks us in front he will attack our rear thus forcing Grant to fall back, ~~and they will~~ so that they will again have possetion of the Weldon Railroad which is of great importance to them, but I think that our Genls have got their eyes + ears open, and will soon be ready [for] a combined attack if they should make one. Orderly [Joseph] Hancock came up from the Hospital a few days ago. he belongs to Co. F, was mustered yesterday as 1ˢᵗ Lieunt. he tents and messes with me so that I am not alone. I find it much pleasanter. he is a man nearly 40 if not quite he is a man of good principles and is good company, and a man who reads a great deal. he brought up a book Entitled "Young's Night Thoughts" perhaps you have seen it. I have commenced it and find it very interesting, blank verse, much like "Popes Essay on man. I find that I can ~~eary~~ carry much more reading matter than I used to when I was in the ranks, for my baggage comes up once a week. I can read one book or books, papers or any thing one week then put it into my valice and take another. I like my Position very well every [thing] thus far has passed of[f] pleasantly. Sunday I had to write all day as busy as I could. I had several Descriptive Lists to make out, and my monthly returns of Clothing, Camp + Garrison Equipage Final Statements &c. I have to send Descriptive Lists to most all the Hospitals in the United States. Final Statements have to be sent to the Adjutant General in Washington. Monthly + Quarterly Returns have to be sent to the Quartermaster General U. S. A. in Washington. I think I shall like this business first rate after I become more acquainted with it so that I understand it better, but there are old Officers enough here that do, and are willing to show me any thing I dont understand. I sent home for a trunk or valice nearly a week ago. I hope it will come through safely + quickly. News came into Camp this morning that Mobile was in our posession now, but I dont know how true it is, nor as it is official. things look a little dark here just now, but I trust that we shall come out right in the end. I had a letter from Andrew a few days ago he spoke about George Harwood. I think he said he was there visiting. does he belong to the Army now? or has he resigned. Andrew says that he has bought his Grandfathers old house. I didnt think the old man would sell his for any money. I rec'd a letter from Harry Harwood yesterday he is in Alexandria still, says that his health is better now the weather is cooler, and so is mine. I have gained in weight lately since the weather has become cooler. we have had some cool nights. we had a Thunder shower last night and it is dull and misty today. Lyman + Haskell tent together now. I call on them quite often. Haskell seems to feel bad to think that he was reduced. almost the first thing he said to me when he came back was "well I suppose that you are an officer now" We saw Snell yesterday he thinks a good deal of his position and most every time I see him he says something about our being Privates one year ago, and so we were. yesterday he said to Haskell, <u>only think, one year George + I were Privates and you Sergeant in the same Company now we are both 1st Lieut and you a Private,</u> rather insulting for him to make such a remark but he didnt think of saying anything out of the way but it made Haskell look down he acted as if it worried him, but dont say any thing for I would not have his wife or any body know that I said any thing about them any way. <u>good, bad, or indifferent</u> I am not in the habit of talking about folks much, and cercan'tly [certainly] not to injure them. Snell + I are very good friends. We are both somewhat demoraliscd in Haskells eyes because we both smoke a little occationaly, to while away a few lonely moments and keep off the <u>blues</u>. I find that I have got no more room so I will close my dinner is nearly ready. Wishing you all success, also peace + happiness through time + eternity. I remain as ever, Affect. Yours

George W. Harwood

The books he was referring to arc Edward Young, Night Thoughts *(1742-45) and Alexander Pope,* Essay on Man *(1733-34). Cousin Andrew F. Jackson served with the Massachusetts Thirty-forth Regiment. George Harwood was probably his cousin George Harwood Jackson. His grandfather George Jackson (1798-1876) lived in West Brookfield. On August 5, Rear Admiral David G. Farragut led Union forces into Mobile Bay, and reportedly said, "Damn the torpedoes, ..., go ahead." Two forts surrendered but the city did not surrender until April 1865.*

Dont send any Stationary for I have a supply. Slip in a few stamps if you have them in next letter.

No 29   Near Weldon Railroad Va. Sept 9 '64

Dear Friend

I expected a letter from you today but was disappointed, so I will commence one to you tonight and wait till tomorrow and see then if I get one. I did think this afternoon that I would go and apply for a furlough to go home and get me an outfit, and beside that I have got to have some money, to pay my board bill if we dont get paid off soon. they owe us two months pay now and [illegible] but I dont think they will pay us off for 2 more after I get paid and get a little start I shall have money enough and intend to lay up conciderable but I have got to have an outfit of clothing &c ahead. it takes a small capitel for a Commissioned Officer to start here in the Army. I hate to send home for money, seeing that I did not send any home the last time, but I havent spent much foolishly. I have bought some things that I needed, hat, pants &c Commissary stores are high it costs conciderable to live. I have said that if I get out of the army with my life, I did'nt care if I did'nt lay up a cent, but I mean to send home several hundred dollars <u>this</u> year. in my next letter you may expect to have a call for <u>money</u>. I sent a letter to Lyman Parkman today I have'nt heard from him since I came in from home the last time. Had another letter from Harry Harwood a day or two ago, perhaps I told you in my last. About 50 men came in + gave themselves up this morning, from the reb lines. they come in most every day. I dont think their cause looks very encouraging just now. the papers this morning state that the villenous John Morgan is now no more. he is killed, his staff captured. many of his little band of Guerrillas killed and prisoners. Our Armies at and around Atlanta Ga are successful of late also at Mobile. things must look dark to them now. we are pressing them hard here around Petersburg.

Sunday 11th.   I received No 17 this morning and another with Hubbards letter in it. I am glad to know that you have got the letter respecting my things. I also hope you will get some good styleish boots, and coat as these will be what I shall want I dont care so much about the cost as I do the quality, as I shall make it all up to you for the things you send and also the money you send. I should like 10.00 in the next letter as I understand that [we] shall not be likely to get our pay for sometime to come. I dont know but Father will think I am calling for a good deal, but while I hold a position like my present one, I intend to dress + live accordingly. I am feeling pretty well now most of the time, except my Disyentary which is a little better. I hope you will send that trunk or valice as soon as possible because I need them now. you say Anna that you wish I had told you what I wanted most, but you can send what you please nuts and such things will keep if food wont there are things enough that I have got to have, Sock, Handkerchiefs &c, but I can get them here. I am sorry that the little ones are so unwell now, + mother also. I hope to hear next time that they are better. I have been quite anxious for the past few days to hear from home. please write as soon as you ~~get this~~ send the valice I had rather Uncle David would make my boots, but say nothing so that Uncle W^m folks will know it. I had rather not wait for either of them to run after the stock and make them. Father why dont you go to Vermont and buy cattle you can do well I think for I understand that stock is not very high there Lt. [Joseph] Hancock had a letter from his son who is living with his Uncle there (Brookfield Vt.) says that his Uncle either bought or sold 2 cows with calves by their side lately for 35.00 each calves + all, and some other cattle at the <u>same rate</u>. I will not write any more this time for this is a busy day with me Every Sunday our baggage + Company books &c come up and we have an unusual amount of business to do. I understand that we are to have Divine Services here today somewhare in the Brigade I intend to attend I havent been to a meeting for a long time. Lyman is tough as a whip. Write often for I love to hear from home better than any or all of my other correspondents, and I have quite a number of them

From your Aff. Son + Brother,   George W. Harwood

Confederate General Morgan led many successful raids against Union troops in Kentucky, Ohio, and Indiana. He was killed on September 4, 1864. Atlanta, Georgia surrendered to General Sherman on September 2, and the evacuation of the city began on September 7, 1864.

Camp of 36th Regt Mass. Vols.
Near Weldon Railroad Va. Sept 13 '64

Dear Brother Ethan [Allen]

    I thought I would commence a letter to you this morning I have just been relieved from Regimental Officer of the day, and now have a little time to write. in fact I have been writing much of the time this morning, respecting my Co. business. I suppose you are attending the High School. I am glad you are, and hear let me give you a few words of advice. I ask nothing for it and hope you will kindly receive it. In my school days I had a good chance to obtain an Education but I deeply regret to say that I did not half improve then. much of the time my mind was somewhare else beside on my books. I see my mistake now, and wish I could respend them. We have a kind Father who is willing, yes anxious to give us a good learning, and now you are attending school let that be your business. learn to <u>read</u> + <u>write</u> well above all else. Arithmetic + Grammer come next.

every day I need them. I will not name over what you ought to study you know yourself. again let me say improve your time. you wont be sorry. And another thing form good habits and live up to them. I hate to see a man loafing around with no business, no high aim in view. Now you are young prepare to live for time + Eternity. You may think this letter short + comprehensive, and not very interesting but the time will come when you will appreciate it. I would write more upon other subjects more interesting but I want to send a few lines to Anna. I will write you again soon and shall expect you to answer them promptly. I am going to take my Company out to drill this afternoon in the manual of arms, and must study Tactics a little first. Remember me to all the friends and write soon. I am pretty well now, am getting fat. I have made some inquiry about George Spooner, but heard nothing from him till Mother wrote me, he was in N.Y. he is no good for a Soldier, too young.   Good Bye

> From your Affectionate Brother
> George W. Harwood

George's brother Ethan Allen turned seventeen on Sept 21, 1864. George R. Spooner was seventeen or eighteen years old when he enlisted with the Massachusetts First Regiment Heavy Artillery.

No 30   Camp of 36th Regt Mass Vols.
                                             Near Weldon R. R. Va. Sept 17 '64

Dear Friends,

It was with the greatest pleasure that I received a letter from you this morning, for I have been somewhat anxious to know whether you succeeded in getting those things that I sent for, and am glad to know that they have started I hope they will reach me safely and in due time. I am sorry Freeman that you were so troubled to find suitible things, perhaps I can do something for you sometime. I will let you know as soon as the things reach me. I am glad that you had such a pleasant time in Springfield. I know I should have enjoyed being there with you. then you like the looks of Genl Burnside do you? he is a good man I think. Father what did you think of him. a good soldier cant help liking such a fatherly old man for their leader. The reb cavalry made a dash yesterday morning and took some of our cattle near Genl. Meade's HdQrs. I dont see how they did it. they also drove in the Pickets in front of the 5th Corps yesterday morning. there is but little news here that I know of. the papers are full of Politics.

What do you think of the Chicago Convention and McClellan. I dont think so much of little <u>Mac</u> as I used to. give me old Abe yet. I think Mr Lincoln will be our next President I hope so, would vote for him if allowed to vote. Tomorrow I shall be 23 I suppose. it dont seem as though I was so old sometimes and at other times it seems as though I was much older. How does Andrew get along with his Wife [Sophia] + Horses? does he keep a dog or gun? I cant think of much news to write this morning so I will let it go till afternoon or tomorrow before I write any more. I have got the <u>key</u> safe if the valise dont come. you did'nt say but I suppose that you paid the Express before it started. Did you have my name + Regt marked on one End of the valise you didnt say anything about it.

Sunday morning 18th

My tentmate Lt. [Joseph] Hancock + I take a daily paper. we have the Philadelphia Enquirer, so we have a chance to keep pretty well posted. At first when I read so much about Cessation of Hostilities, I thought it were possible perhaps to end this war without much more fighting. I think now that it mint be, but I have come to the conclusion that the only way to have an honorable ~~peace~~ lasting peace is to thoroughly Subjugate the rebellious South, put down Copperheadism in the North, totally annihilate Slavery, which is the chief cause of this cruel war then we can have a peace, a lasting peace, with the many precious lives, and much property that it has cost us. I understand by the papers that a draft will be actually enforced in all places whare the quotas have not already been filled by volenteering. I am glad of it not that I want any one to leave his quiet home + family to undergo the fatigues + privations of Camp life on the more exposed position on the battlefield, but that those who have ~~the hardships~~ undergone these hardships for the past 2 or 3 years and are now in the field, may the sooner have a chance to return to their homes. I expect to remain in the service nearly one year more and by that time I hope to see this bloody war ended honorably. (Abe. Lincoln for President Andy Johnson of East Tenn. for Vice President) but I am not going to lecture all Sunday forenoon on the War. I have already written more than I entended to, when I commenced. This is my birthday. if I have'nt forgotten my age I am now 23.

I told Lyman last evening that I was going to reform, or in other words make the most of the time allotted me, or in other words still improve the <u>one talent</u> given me. the daily papers, Military Tackes [tasks?], and Co. business engage most of my time, when I aint writing letters. just now we have a short drill each afternoon of 3/4 of an hour, mostly manuel of Arms. I am now writing with one of Lyman + Haskells Gold pens it is a very good one. they sent to Eddy [in] N.B. and had 1 Doz. sent to them with Extension Holders. I have a good one now, that I have used for more than a year. he is quite anxious to sell me this. he traids as usual, an uneasy fellow, tough as a whip, to appearance. We have been having very fine weather for some time past, but it looks a little like rain this morning. I have written about all I can think of I believe of any interest to you. I have been looking for a letter from Mr Cushing and Mr. E.D. Batchellers folk for a long time and some others I have not heard from. I sometimes think that [they] have entirely forgotten that their friend Harwood still exists. I received a letter a few days ago from Ada Jane Allen she is a very pretty writer and I should judge by her writing that she was a pretty fair scholar, as her letters are tolerably well composed. I dont remember that I ever saw her. I saw her picture once I think. How is Aunt Lucretia this fall? did she send any thing to me? or had'nt she an opportunity. How quickly one year will pass away then my first term of enlistment will have expired. it has been said that our Government intends to hold all Officers (if they need them) 3 years from the time they were last mustered as such, but we dont see it, unless our Regt should enough of it reinlist to hold its organization then thay mint keep enough of us to Officer them, but I dont worry any about that if my health should remain good I may want to stay longer, but I guess our men wont reinlist very much. they dont talk at all like it now. they say they had rather go home and then if they want to they will go in for 1 year and get just as much bounty. I have just finished my Dinner of Apple-dumplen + Doughnuts. now I will finish my letter. I guess you will become weary reading this long letter Government finds one some pretty large sheets of paper to write home on. I am glad Freeman thought to send some small note paper to write to the ladies on, but Good Bye Write often. Yours &c George.

Springfield, Massachusetts, home of the Massachusetts Twenty-seventh, held a huge fair to honor the regiment when it returned home in September, 1864. Major General Burnside was one of the speakers. The Beefsteak Raid was September 14-16, when Confederate troops went behind Union lines and captured over 2,000 cattle. The Democratic Convention in Chicago, August 29-31, nominated General McClellan for President. Not all soldiers were able to vote in the Presidential election of 1864. Ada Jane Allen was a cousin on George's mother's side of the family.

No 31   Camp of 36th Regt Mass. Vols.

Near Weldon R. R. Va Sept 23rd '64

Dear Friends

I was very glad to receive a letter from you this morning also the money, which I so much needed. we some expect to get our pay soon but it is uncertain if I knew we should I can [get] along, a little more would come in play. I will write again in a few days I shall expect Father to write next time. I wish you would put my silver chain into the next letter I have got a good hook to put on it. you wish me to write a sort of History of myself since my enlistment. I could if I had my old Dossier and time [to] fill a large book. I will in this letter write a few particulars all that will be necessary I think. if you can get the needed information from it do so if not I will try and be more minute about it. You spoke of having Mr Knight or Earl copy this but I do not want they should copy this while for I have not spent time to write it as I should by this you may be able to give any needed information, but dont have this copied

I enlisted Aug. 12th /62, joined the 36th Regt. Mass. Vols. and was mustered into the U.S. Service Aug 27th /62. We left Worcester Sept 2nd took the Steamer that night in Boston and reached Washington D.C. the 10th. we marched on through Md. and joined the 3rd Brigade 1st Div 9 Army Corps at Antietam Sept 20th and marched with the Corps to Falmouth Va. were held in reserve at the first fight at Fredcricksburg Dec 13th/62 We did Picket duty on the Rappahannock River opposite Fredericksburg till early in March when we left the Army of the Potomac, went to Newport News whare we remained 3 weeks, then took a Steamer for Baltimore went by rail to Parkersburg Va. via Fredericks City Harpers Ferry &c at Parkersburg we took Transports down the river Ohio, landed at Covington Ky took the cars and went to Lexington. we remained here doing Provost Duty 10 days. we then marched on to Camp Dick Robinson stayed about 1 month and go on through Ky. to Columbia, Jamestown to Lebenon [Lebanon]. at this place we took the cars to Louisville crossed over the river on the Ferry to Jeffersonville Ind. went by rail to Cairo Ill. and the Steamer down the Miss River and up the Yazoo some 12 miles to Milldale Miss. we marched up to the rear of Vicksburg and remained there through the siege till its surrender July 4th/63, then we marched to Jackson and were again engaged with the enemy July 16th I was wounded. the rebs evacuated this place on the 17th after tareing up several miles of Railroad. we marched back through clouds of dust + no water. we again took Steamers at Milldale Near the first of Aug. for Cairo + the cars to Cincinnati Ohio, crossed over to Covington Ky. we encamped here a short time, took the cars to Nicholasville Ky. marched from here to Crab Orchard. Sept 10th /63 we started our long + wearisome march over the Cumberland Mountains and after 15 days of hard marching we reached Morristown Tenn, then to Knoxville and encamped a few days. when we marched back to Moristown + Bulls Gap and to Blue Springs whare we had a brisk fight with our enemy. we followed them through Greenville, up the Tenn. + Va. R.R. as far as Rheatown. we then returned to Knoxville remained but a few days. when the Regiment marched to Lenoir Station, I was ordered to Greenville Tenn. with a recruiting party. after 3 weeks I rejoined my Regt at Lenoir Station on the 14th of Nov. we marched to the Loudon bridge here we were attacked by the enemy and forced back to Knoxville. we made a stand at Lenoir and Campbell Station the 16 of Nov. here I was wounded. we fell back to Knoxville that night then it was that the siege of Knoxville commenced. we were constantly under fire 21 days, poorly clothed and on 1/4 rations. after the siege we marched to Blains Cross Roads. here I was appointed Sergt Jan 1st 1864. Jan 16 we marched to Strawberry Plains. on the 24 we were obliged to fall back to Knoxville closely follow[ed] and fired upon by the rebs. we encamped 6 miles West of Knoxville at Erins Station. on the 15 of Feb. we marched back to Knoxville, and worked on the Fortifications on the 25 of Feb the Regt started for Strawberry Plains, I for Massachusetts with a Recruiting Party. took the cars at K[noxville]. and came via Chattanoogga, Knashville, Louisville, crossed over to Jeffersonville, through Indianapolis, Cleaveland, Buffalo + so on home. remained at home and Boston till the 4th day of May/64. reached Washington the 5th to Alexandria the 6th left here the 11 on a Transport landed at Belle Plains the 12. 13 we marched on to Fredericksburg Va. and on till we joined the Regt May 15th in a fight and we have been under the enemies fire almost constantly ever since. We have marched nights and fought days, through rain + shine have been engaged in several distinct fights at North Anna, Cold Harbor. charge on the 17 of June support on the 18 Continuous siege since. If I had time and thought it necessary I could give a more distinct Idia [idea] of my Sojourn in the South, but I understand that they only want the dates of my enlistment, of my Promotions and the Battles I have been in their Dates + places, &c I was Promoted to Lieut July 26 was mustered then. if you can not get all the information you need out of this or my old Dairies [diaries], write me again and let me know what particular point you lack in. We have been in one continuous fight properly speaking ever since the 17 of June. I have been under fire + in skirmishes many other times not worthy of mention. I have said nothing of our poor fare, hardships, nor any sufferings, it is needless.

Va	Fredericksburg	Dec 13th 1862
Miss	Vicksburg	July 4 1863
	Jackson	" 16 "
Tenn	Blue Springs	Oct 10th 63
	Campbell Station	Nov 16th 1863
	Siege of Knoxville	till 8th of Dec 1863
Va	Spottsylvania	May 15th 1864
	North Anna	" 25th "
	Cold Harbor	June 3rd 1864
	Charge on the works of Petersburg	June 17th
	Support of an advance	" 18th
	Siege of Petersburg from that day to this.	

12 Distinct Battles as many skirmishes that do not come to mind, nor are they worthy of any mention.

George W.

No 31 I think   Near Weldon R Road Va   Sept 30/64

Dear Friends

    I received a letter from you + Rosetta this morning and will answer this now if I have time. we are all packed up + have been for 2 or 3 days. I shall not write a long letter for I dont like to write on my knees thare has been fighting on our right + left + we dont know what will come next. things are very uncertain here now. I saw Snell yesterday. We have not got our pay yet and dont hear so much about it now. I am afraid we shant at present. I hope we shall for I want the money to use. we are having very fine weather here now. we hear good news from the right. [Major General] Butler a few prisoners came in this morning. I understand that the troops are all packed up the whole line from here to City Point. I dont feel like writing much this morning my thoughts are somewhere else I guess. I should like to know how Father thinks now is the time for me to get Promoted. I wish he would explain it to me. <u>I dont see it.</u> I suppose Aunt Lucie looks natural, dont she? I should like to see Uncle Washington pretty well but should rather see Uncle Joseph. Ann [Anna?] said that [Ethan] Allen had got the Western fever what does he want to do there, or dont he know. I intend to go West on a visit after this war is over, + I think it will end soon if Lincoln is elected President and I guess he will be. I think you will hear of some great movement down here in Va. soon but what they will be I dont know every body is expecting something we had orders to be ready to move at 7 this morning but we are here yet, all ready. I presume we shall go now before night. I intended to write to [cousins] George + Anna Jackson today but I guess I shant, then I am going to write to D W Knight. when we get settled down again I shall have to [be] very busy in making out my monthly + quarterly returns of Ordnance + Ordnance Stores, Clothing, Camp + Garrison Equipage, &c &c. I usually write long letters especially home but I shall make this some shorter under the present circumstances. dont worry if you dont hear for some days again for we may be on the move and its not be very convenient to write. rest assured that all will be well there may be a fight + there may be not. I am not anxious to fight but I want to see this thing ended. if we must fight so be it. there was something of a fight on our left last night and the wounded are now being brought in. I will not write any more now perhaps I will before the mail goes out add a few words. I remain as ever your Aff. Son + Brother.

George W. Harwood

George's cousin Rosetta Harwood, the daughter of Uncle Washington and Aunt Lucie, lived in Michigan. Uncle Joseph W. Harwood lived in Illinois. From September 29 to October 2, the Union moved towards the railroad on the south side of Petersburg. There were engagements at several farms. General Parke's Ninth Corps was on Squirrel Level Road. The Massachusetts Thirty-sixth was engaged at Peebles' and Pegram's Farms. At the same time, Butler's Army of the James was directed to attack Richmond from the south at New Market Heights.

No 32   Near Weldon R R Va
                                          Oct 3 '64

Dear Friends,

    I will write you a few words to let you know that I am all right as
yet we advanced on the 30th Sept. but were badly repulsed and fell back in
confusion. we have lost between 20 + 30 or 40 all killed wounded + missing. Lyman is killed. Haskell is wounded. Lyman was wounded under the
right arm I saw him fall it was on the top of a little knoll as we were
falling back. I ran back with another man and got him out of a warm place.
we brought him back a little ways and laid him beside a house. the rebs
char[ged] upon us. I was the last to leave him the rebs were in sight and
the bullets flew thick and fast around me. I had not time to take even his
diary, nor dying request for I knew he must die. I think he had no money
with him. Haskell got off he was wounded in the thigh not dangerous I
think please tell his wife [Orril]. yesterday we made another advance. we
found the body of Lyman whare I left him. he had been stripped of every
thing. some thought it was not him he was black + bloated, but I knew him
by some scars on his hands &c and he was just whare I left him +
wounded in the same place. I saw him properly buried this morning we
are now as it were in the midst of a fight and I cannot write much. I have
written a few lines to his wife + will write her again soon if spared through
this present struggle, Haskells also. we were in the warmest place that day
I ever saw men fell thick and fast. yesterday the rebs threw a shell in to us
+ killed or wounded 12 at once in our pits. it is sad to be here but so it is
we have not seen all yet. Bell + Cummings are all right so far. I remember
reading a Psalm the morning before I went into the fight, that reads thus,
Thousands shall fall by the side + 10 thousands at thy right hand, but it
shall not come nigh thee. that ran through my head all that day even in the
hottest of it it came to my mind. I feel that I have great reason to be thankful that I have been spared thus far let us pray for life + victory. I will
write again soon if I can. my dearest friends here in the Army are being
taken from me one by one. should it not stimulate me to be near my Saviour.

    Affec Yours
    George W.

No 33   Camp of 36th Mass. Vols.
                             Near Weldon R R Va. Oct 9/64

Dear Friends,

        I received a letter from you last Friday on Picket and have not had time to answer till now. I was relieved last night. the rebs are very social and peasable. we made an agreement not to fire on each other on Picket. my post whare I put up was whare I left Lyman after he was wounded + whare he died. I saw the spot whare he was shot whare he died + whare I buried him. I miss him a good deal as we used to associate a great deal together you know. This is Sunday a very pleasant but cool + windy day most to cold to write much this morning. I recd the chain all right. I see that Anna is disposed to make fun of it, but when I get rich perhaps I shall buy a better one. I recd a paper this morning with chain in it. After a long time we have got our pay up to the first of Sept. I recd 135.50 Lieut pay from the 26th of July to the 1 of Sept I think I shall send 50. home in this letter and if I want any more I can send home + get it. I have got some bills to pay out of it. Mother asked how my shirts were they ware very well but shrink some being washed + boiled so much they will do for undershirts, this winter and I can buy some more by + by if I choose. we are having pretty cool weather just now a <u>cold snap</u>. I have got me a Cavelry Over-Coat coller reaches my hat cape comes down to my hands. we have been on duty pretty constantly lately, since the fight last Friday + week ago, but I have come out all right I believe. Bell had a ball go through his pants + coat that is coming pretty near he is a pretty good soldier I think. I heard from Haskell a few days ago he was getting along well was in good spirits then. I am trying to settle up Lymans affairs, have written to his wife twice. there is but little news as I know of, that is of much importance, plenty of Camp rumors as usual. I should like to be at home when Edwin comes home I should like to see him + Harry Harwood also, but there is about 10 1/2 months longer for me. then I hope providence permitting to see you all if not before, but life is uncertain especialy so here in the Army. when I look around to see the companions that left N Brookfield with me I dont find them they are all gone. Lyman + Louis are dead Haskell, Walker + Wheelock are wounded. by the way whare is Wheelock? is he at home now. Jim Cummings is all right. This is a cold raw day and I guess I shant write any more letters. I should not have written this to

you but I knew you would feel a great anxiety for me consequently I felt
it my duty to write you. enclosed you will find a green back 50 dollar bill.
if I want more money I will send for it. I find that my pay is much more
and my expenses much greater than when I was in the ranks. it was so cold
that I put up my pen + ink and took my pencil + put on my gloves. I have
got to get me a new pair before long as cold weather is coming on. We feel
quite releaved to get our pay and the boys are living pretty high. I'll bet
that it will cost them some of them as much to live for a while as it will
me. in some Regts they gamble stroangly but this is not so bad as some
most of the men are married and have families they of corse nead to send
their money home. my family dont need much but I may want some,
should I live to get home. I think we have got to have some more hard
fighting. should I fall in battle or die of disease I feel that all will be well. I
mean to be ~~fath~~ feathful [faithful] in duty while I am spared. I am glad to
hear from home so often. Freeman tell Hubbard that I will answer his letter as soon as I have time. I must of corse answer my female correspondents first. I dont know as I will write any more this time Remember me
to the friends + write often. I have got to go on Picket again tomorrow
morning I expect. it takes about 40 men + 1 Lieut. has charge of them. the
sun has at last come out and I think it will be warmer. it makes me think of
going chestnuting in the fall or picking apples or digging potatoes these
cold windy autumn days The boys are thinking their time is most out 10
months and a bit they say.

Good Bye from your Son + Brother
George W Harwood

*Edwin Doane and Harry Harwood completed their service in the Massachusetts
Forty-second (100 days) on November 11.*

Camp of 36th Regt Mass Vols
Oct 12/64

Brother Allen

      Here is a pretty little watch that I will send home by way of Capt
[Edwin A.] Morse he is going home tomorrow and will cary it for me. it
wants about 2.00 dollars laid out on it and then I think it will be a good
one if you want the use of it you can get it repaired. when I come I will
pay for the repairing It will look well, cleaned it up. it would be hard to

detect it from a good gold one. My old Gold pen I want to save I have broken the Holder. I presume that Anna will like it to use I have got me a new one. this watch would do to go with the chain that I let Anna Jackson have. show it to her sometime. if she will keep school this winter some whare she may have it, or next summer. He will leave the box at Reed + Adams Worcester Mass   Yours &c George W.

[on the back of the letter]

Lt Col [William F.] Draper is also going home they went out in the 25 Mass have been in 3 years and think that is about long enough. I should think so. when I have been here 3 years that will do for me. there [they] are two [of] the best ~~of the~~ Officers in the Regt.   George.

[Addressed to:]   Ethan Harwood
                              Present

[No 34]   Camp of 36th Regt. Mass. Vols.
                                            Near Weldon R Road Va Oct 12/64

Dear Friends

        As I am not very busy this afternoon I will pen a few lines to you. There was an Order issued not long ago from the war department that all Officers after having served for a period of 3 years can resign + go home. Some of our Officers went out in the 25th Mass and were commissioned in this two of them are now going Col Draper + Capt Morse. The later [latter] lives in Worcester these are two of the best of Officers Col is about 24 + Capt 22. I am going to send a Watch + pen &c by Capt. + he will leave it with Reed + Adams Main St Worcester. you will have a chance to send down wont you by some one if you aint going yourself. he starts tomorrow and will be there before this letter reaches you. Call for a Package left there for George Harwood. The Watch is one that I traided for + if I lose it, I shant be mined entirely I think. I think it will be a good one pay-out about 2 dollars perhaps Allen will want to cary it to the parties this winter. I think that Anna will like the Gold pen to write with. it is what I call a good one rather limber. I am now using a steel one the first letter that I have written with one for a long time + I guess the last. I have a good gold one now. This is a beautiful day, cool + clear. Every thing of Nature seems lovely but the rebs are in front scarsly out of sight, but they dont worry me very badly. I am going on Picket again in a few days and will have a chance to see them. News came last night that Sheridan had won another brilliant Victory captured 11 pieces of artillery 300 prisoners, baggage trains and Ambulances &c &c, good.

I met a Sergt the other day in the 38th Wisconsin Regt. who asked if there was anyone in the 36th Mass who came from Brookfield or Brimfield someone told him that there was a Harwood from Brookfield so he came to me He is Nathan Proutys son of Brimfield not a very stout looking man, tall and thin. I was glad to meet him. he has just come out + is in this Corps I dont Remember the Brigade or Div. but I can find him. I am expecting every day to hear from Lymans Wife do you know whether she has written to me or not. I have got Lymans business settled I think pretty much + what is Mr Cushing about that he dont write to me + Eva D + C. I should like to hear from them at the same time I have about all I can to attend to. I have got out of postage stamps and I dont know whare I can get any. I wish you would slip in a few. Have you ever got the 50.00 dollars that I sent in my last No 33 I think it was, you can draw interest on that without paying taxes on it. Father if you think it would be more profitable to traid that colt off and buy another when I come do so act your own pleasure. I think she will have spunk enough but perhaps not sise to back it up. are you going to Winter Bill [a horse] or kill him. I suppose he is about played out. let me hear from you individualy sometime when it is convenient. Wont you? I dont think of much more news to write this time I write so often that I must keep you pretty well posted. Col [Sumner] Carruth of the 35th Mass has been absent sick for sometime. he came up a few days ago. we are in the same Brigade. Do you ever hear from Uncle Joseph. he has not written to me for some time I think I wrote him last. When is Edwins time out I have forgotten I had a letter from Jennie Bush yesterday She didnt seem to speak as though Louise had got a very pleasant home, but dont say any thing from me. she says about as she expected. We are going to fall in at 5 o'clock tonight and hear a few words from Lt Col Draper. we all hate to have him go but dont blame at all I should go if I were in his place I think. There will be one or two vacancies in the Capt when they leave but no sight for me yet for there are several Lieuts Senior to me. It begins to cloud up now and I should'nt wonder if it rained some about tomorrow How is business now in N Brookfield good as ever? how do they get along with the new Union Store. do they like it any better. I guess I will draw this to a close I will write again in a few days if nothing happens

Very Respect Yours
George W. Harwood

The victory at the Battle of Tom's Brook on October 9 was part of Major General Philip H. Sheridan's campaign to secure the Shenandoah Valley for the Union and provide a source of food for troops and animals. Nathan Prouty's son was Albert S. Prouty, serving with the Wisconsin Thirty-eighth. Edwin Doane was serving with the Massachusetts Forty-second (100 days) and was discharged on November 11.

Camp of 36th Regt. Mass. Vols.
near Poplar Grove Church Va Oct 17/64

Dear Father

As I sit in my tent alone this pleasant evening thinking of my home and the future of my life, and meditating on the past. The question very naturaly arrises in my mind what do you intend to do? what branch of labor do you intend to pursue? being a minor when I enlisted, I of course had no permanent business on hand, neither had I fully settled in my mind what I would do. I think you have expressed to me a desire that I should follow Farming. is that your mind now? It has always been my desire (as perhaps you know) to be engaged in some traid, some merchantile business, and to this day I think I should like something of that nature, say a Boot + Shoe Store, or even a Grocery Store. Oweing to the very unsettled condition of our Country at the present time, it is hard to make much calculations on the future, but I thought it not wholly improper to consult you, to ask your opinion upon the matter. 10 months and a little more Providence permitting I hope to return to my home, to private life, and at once engage in some business. if success attends me, I shall then have a few Hundred dollars at my command enough perhaps to commence a small business with a good Partner with equil capital.

When I first began to talk about enlisting you hesitated to give your consent. perhaps you thought that the influences that would surround me would be injurious to me. perhaps through fear that I should never return. why you hesitated I know not. my motives for enlisting were purely patriotic, a high sense of duty promped me to do so. I felt it my duty to offer my services feeble though they are to my Country to help put down this vile rebellion, and never in my sober honest moments have I regretted the action I took at that time, perelous though this may be, degrading as the surrounding influences tend to be. the feeling that one is in the performance of duty more than repays him, and in the performance of this duty have I not earned for myself a character worthy of imitation? have I not won for myself a title worthy the respect of common people, a title which I and my friends in after years can look upon with some degree of satisfaction. I have arisen from the rank as a private to my present position without the help of widely known + highly influential men, in less than two years, while many a man left our old camp in Worcester a Sergt and having used all the means in their power, with the aid of their influential friends are Sergts. still.

I commenced this for a business letter but I find that I varied conciderbly from my intention. I have spoken ~~upon~~ about these things, not that I wish to exact praise for myself, far from that, but I have mentioned them that you might rightly consider my past and present career.

Let me hear from you when convenient perhaps you would like to advise respecting my future plans. I know that it [is] a good ways ahead to mak[e] much calculations on. the changes may be great before that time. I remain as ever

>Your Aff Son
>George W. Harwood

[No 35] Camp of 36th Regt. Mass. Vols.
near Poplar Grove Church Va   Oct 17/64

Dear Friends,

I received a letter from you a few days ago [on the] 15th and was very glad to see Fathers hand writing again. this is a very fine day quite warm + pleasant. there is no news of importance as I know of only that there is to be a Review this afternoon. Secretary [of War] Stanton is going to visit us they say. I do not hear any thing from Lymans Wife as yet. I had a letter from Haskell this morning he is in Alexandria Va. doing well he says. I was very glad to hear from him for I have some 50.00 dollars worth of Gold pens + Holders &c belonging to him + Lyman, besides I am collecting some small bills due them. I think that there is an order issued that a few furloughs will be granted and the men are all talking about home. I dont think many will be granted at present. if I thought I could get one I would try it, but my business at home is not very urgent. I think that some of you asked me if I were sure that it was Lymans body that I buried I think I am. I feel that there is no doubt about it. It seems sad to be obliged to leave one as I was obliged to leave ~~one as~~ Lyman but I was obliged to do so at that time. I should hardly dare to stop so long again the bullets fell thick and fast on all sides of me. surely we have reason to be thankful that an all wise Providence saw fit to prolong my life yet a little while. Why it is that one is taken + another left is more than we can tell. We have Divine Services now on the Sabbath. our Chaplain Mr Richardson is an elderly man but we like him much. he has preached to us the two past Sundays. he seems to take an interest in our affairs willing to do any thing that he can for any of the Officers + men Yesterday he brought around some religious papers also some small books. I took one to read and thought I would sent it to Sister Fannie. Yesterday was a pleasant quiet day. how forcibly did that little hymn come to mind. ~~day of all the~~

> "Day of all the week the best
> Emblem of Eternal rest"

I had a chance to sell my Silver watch chain a few days ago for 2.50 after I had broken it now I want you to send my large watch and I ought to have a gold hook + slide on but no matter for that. when the boys are full of money you can sell any thing you have. I have had more than a Doz. chances to sell my watch I can take 25.00 any time perhaps 30.00 but I dont want to sell I intend to send it home sometime. by the way have you got the watch + pen I sent home by Capt Morse to Reed + Adams [in] Worcester. Tomorrow morning I go on Picket again. I hope I shall have as pleasant time as I did before I go on 1 in 4 days thus spending 1/4 of my time on Picket have a good chance to read &c. the Col. Comdg Brigade found it necessary to put a stop to gambling has issued an order to that effect. gambling has been carried on to a great extent in some Regts but not so bad in ours. Genl. Potter Comdg this Div. acknowledges this ~~to~~ Regt to be the best in the Div. aint that a compliment for us. we have got some new colors. I hope we shant loose them as some have. I dont know as I have much more that I will write this afternoon. I write so often that a lengthy letter will not be expected from me every time. it is most time to go out to the Review I hope you will continue to write often oftener than once a week if convenient.

> Very Respectfully Yours
> George W. Harwood

The words to the hymn are from John Newton, "Safely through another week"
found in the Trinity Psalter Hymnal. The regiment received a new set of flags to
replace their original set which had been damaged.

No 36   Camp of 36th Regt Mass Vols
                                 near Poplar Grove Church Va.   Oct 21/64

Dear Friends

  I received a letter from you this morning No 23 was very glad as I always am to hear that you were all well, and that my money reached you safely. next pay day if nothing happens I will send you 2 of them. News came last night that Sherman had gained another brilliant victory. I did not learn many of the particulars. there is nothing new as I know of since I wrote you last. we are having fine but cool weather here now. You said something about their having Lymans body sent home. I suppose that it can be done now. I think if I were in their places I should want to do so. I some times think if I should chance to fall it would be my wish that my body be sent home and have funeral services as though I had died there. I have been expecting to hear from Mary or some of them respecting Lymans effects. I know he had made his will but he did not tell me anything more. he said nothing when I carried him off. when I laid him down he asked me to put a knapsack or something under his head. I did so. you say that Dea. Moore is going to write me to you? I should be glad to hear from him I have not heard from Mr Cushing or Batcheller yet. I am quite surprised that business is so dull in "Town" I hardly understand why it should be. I rather wonder that Andrew dont find a better partner to do business with than I think Henry Forbes is. I suppose that he knows his own business best. I think my colt must look rather comical in the harness does'nt she? I should like very well to be at home this winter and drive her or something else. I wish that Freeman could come out and see Edwin and both of them come down and see me. I dont know whether it would be possible or not. I should like very much to see you I dont believe Ed. will go home to stop long, do you? I should like to see him a few moments I think almost as much of Edwin as I should if he were my Brother.

Now I am going to tell you about a Family that live between our Picket line + the enemies. he, his wife + 3 little girls. he says that he wants to be nutril [neutral] that is he dont want to take up on either side. we watch him + so do the rebs. one of them shot at him a few days ago. he is free to converse but is quite guarded in his speach, has got a cow + calf and 2 dogs + a few hens + cats. he says that he was well pleased with the Government as it was. he never owned a slave in his life. he used to hire any one he could no matter whether black or white it was all the same with him. he speaks about the Southern Confusion, for such he declares it is, that they are about played out in his honest opinion. we have a Vidett post at his house and every day I am on Picket I go out and talk with him. I understand that they have advanced our skirmish line up since I was on Picket up to the corner of his Barn. how should you like to have a large army on either side of your house, digging your mowings all up for rifle pits pulling down all the fences, + chopping all your choise fruit + ornimental trees, such is his case. it is very much as though our line of pits run along the edge of the woods on the South side of your house + the foot of the Bond-hill on the North. we have now moved up so as to take in your hens + barn our pits run along our line the same as from the corner of the woods next the lower mowing to the N E corner of your barn just back of the house through the garden, then back of the barn back to the first ridge up the hill forming something like a letter A. he has a good well of water. the rebs line runs about the same as at the foot of the Bond-hill in sight of each other, their line of breast works + forts &c is about the same as from Demon [Damon?] Knights down through the hollow to the meadows ours the other side of the woods from Mr Hair up through the whistleberry pasture to the Dean place. I guess I have told you enough about our position but what I was going to say was that the old man has to stay at home. I dont know but I have written more than you will care to read about the corner of the woods + barn but I can picture in my mind just how I could run a line there very much like ours. we have a large Fort in front of the house in the woods the rebs one the other side, a very unpleasant position for the women, if we should open about 7 or 8 pieces of Artillery on each side. ours is Fort Fisher I dont hear much about the Sergeant place I suppose that you want to sell it still, do you? it could be fixed up so as to become a desirable place for one wishing to live near the village. Freeman do you traid watches any more. I do once in a while I sent one home + had another since if I had the old brass one here in running order I could dispose of it for about 50.00.

Do Mr. Woods folks say much about Lymans death? of course the[y] feel sad I miss him a great deal, for we used to meet often. he used to have a gold pen or watch to show me always Haskell writes me that he had between 16 + 17 dollars in his pocket + that he had him-self some 20.00 they were in Co. Haskell lost his pocket book + all his little notes. I have sold about 2 Doz gold pens + holders for them, have got now 60.00 that belong to them I am going to send Haskell soon.

Genls Grant Meade + staffs just went along and Crawford + staff also I saw Snell + shook hands with him. he had on a monkey jacket red sash + white gloves. he looked slick enough. I must have me a dress coat + sash + new sword &c &c. I should wonder if Genl. Grant + the rest kicked up a fuss again before long they stopped and examined Fort Fisher it was then I spoke to Snell. he always calls for me when he comes around + seems glad to see me. "then poor Lyman is gone," was about all he had time to say. It is almost noon. I have spent most of this fore noon talking and trying to write this letter. send me occationaly a Worcester Spy that gives the news near home.

Good Bye let me hear all the news. all about the young people. who is going to be married + who wants to be &c &c

I remain + ever

Yours Aff

George W. Harwood

On September 2, General Sherman took possession of Atlanta, Georgia. After eliminating Confederate troops from the area, he began his now famous "March to the Sea" in November. There were several farmhouses near Confederate Fort McRae. George was probably describing the farmhouse of either the Peebles or Pegram family which was surrounded by Union troops. Union Fort Fisher is southwest of Petersburg. I have not discovered what whistleberries are. Perhaps it is a local name for a common berry or possibly an heirloom variety of apple. Lyman Gilbert's mother was Jerusha A. Wood. Lyman lived with a Wood family in the 1850 Census, perhaps his aunt and uncle, as his father had died when he was young. The Worcester Spy *is the newspaper from Worcester, Massachusetts. A vidette is a mounted sentry placed in advance of the pickets.*

No 37   Camp of 36th Mass Vols
                                             [undated, probably October 26, 1864]

Dear Friends

In haste I pen you a few lines. we are now under marching orders 40 rounds of cartridges 6 days rations. it is very probable that we shall start for another left flank movement tonight. I had a letter from Haskell this morning. I have been selling some pens for him since he was wounded. I settled up with him today sent him 55.30 by mail today. I am glad to get that off my hands I have settled Lymans affairs and have 5.10 cts left I should like to know why I dont hear from Mary or George or some of them. this is a very fine day. I presume you will hear of fighting in this neighborhood soon but dont worry. I will write again soon. if we dont move I shall go on Picket tomorrow. we have drills 2 each day + dress parade besides. I have got so I like a battallion first rate. I have nothing in particular to write this time only to let you know that we are on the move, and if you dont hear from me for a week or 2 you wont worry. I commenced writing on the back side of this sheet I find come to turn it, but it is all the same. I wrote to Daniel Knight yesterday I have been thinking about it for a long time. we have just got orders to be ready to move at dark. it is now about 5 and the mail is about to go out so I will close + pack up.

Good Bye for this time

Very Aff Yours

George W Harwood

I have been trying to [trade] watches all the afternoon but I have not yet. I hope we shant go into a fight and get defeated for it will hurt Lincoln for the Presidency, wont it? but I feel confident of success. I trust in my maker and him alone, especially in times like these.

George was waiting to hear from Lyman H. Gilbert's widow, Mary and her brother George P. Doane. He has written to Daniel Knight, who was the publisher of the local newspaper and had requested the details of George's enlistment and service.

No 38   Camp of 36th Regt Mass Vols
                         near Poplar Grove Church Va Oct 30/64

Dear Friends

I wrote you about the middle of last week that we were about to make another move and so we did. we moved to the left, I should think 2 miles the 2nd a part of the 5th + 9th Corps. I suppose that it will be called a reconnoscence in force. I dont see as we accomplished much. I dont think we were oblidged to fall back our loss was small. the negroes went in bravely. We came back Friday night to our old camp and pitched our tents again in good order. Yesterday morning I went on Picket again in the same old place. last night a reb. came in or rather about 3 oclock this morning. he was a young man about my age said he had been in the Army about 1 month was conscripted from N Carolina and that he had made up his mind never to fight on that side. he also said that his brother older was then on Vidett would come in but dare not for if he should'nt succeed they would surely kill him. When I saw him, I said to him the first thing how are you Johnnie? he look up and laughing saluted me, said he was all right now he thought. I askcd him if he had got lost. he said he hoped he was found now. I asked him a few questions and sent him to Brigade HdQtr under guard he was thinly dressed ~~and~~ he told me that the rebs laid pretty short. there were a few shots fired yesterday but did no harm. we all have to keep awakc all night. I saw Snell yesterday he said he would do any thing he could to get ~~his~~ Lymans body homc. it will be a bad job to did [dig] him up for he would scent [smell] so and has no coffin you know, but I think it can be done, but I dont think Louis body could be found now. it is 40 or 50 miles from here in a large forest near or some whare within a few miles of Spottsylvania Court House. The 36th + 21st have been consolidated and arc now known as the 36th the old 36th has been consolidated into 7 Cos the 21 into 3 Cos. my company that is the Company I command Co I is about to be broken up. I expect to go back to Co E. I am about to turn over my Ordnance + Ordnance Stores, Clothing, Camp + Garrison Equipage. I am very busy making my returns + Muster rolls. We are to be mustered tomorrow forenoon We expect Adj Genl Schooler [William Schouler] of Boston to call on us tomorrow sometime. The other day several of the men fell out thinking that we were going into a fight and thought they would shirk it one of Co E has been sitting up on a rail today, others do [illegible] duty, 1 a Sergt has got to do Privates duty for privates pay for 60 days for punishment, another a Private in Co C has never been in a fight yet always managed to shirk out. this time he has got to take a severe punishment. he is to be bucked + gaged 3 hours his Company are to pass by him in single file and each spit upon him. after that he is to be marched around camp with the word <u>Coward</u> printed in large letters on a board fasened to his back. I think I had rather run my risk among the bullets a little while, but as it happened we didnt get into a fight at all and that shames them all the more. Another man in another Regt. has all his back pay that is due him stopped and he [was] drummed out of Camp with the word Coward on his back then to be sent to the dry tortugas for 5 years hard labor. how is that for punishment? You say that Freeman is talking about coming out to see me if he comes to Washington I should be very glad indeed to see him. I hope he will come. Now I must tell you what a fine time I had with my shirt this morning. I put on my clean one, and found that by washing it had shrunk so much that I could'nt button it around the neck into an inch certain the sleaves are several inches to short. I worked away till I got it round my neck but it chocked awfuly. it stopped the circulation of blood so that I turned black + blue + every other color. I was oblidged to cut it open in the back but my paper colar covers it. I am getting so large that I shall have to get my things all made for me soon, if I keep on. I weigh about 190 lbs. that is good weight, isnt it? We have had Divine Services today as usual with now on the Sabbath most all attend and lend a very attentive listening ear. Orderly White of Co. I. came back a day or two ago he was wounded at Spottsylvania he has the appointment of Lt for more than a year but has [not] been able to get mustered till now he hopes to. he used to preach some before he came into the Army, and has been speaking to large assemblies at home of late spoke to us this evening, in very eloquent + appropriate language. he is a noble man a brave Christian Soldier. we listened with deep interest as our comrad assured us that there ~~were~~ are those at home who take a deep interest in the soldier beside those who have a near relative or a dear friend there, but I find that my sheet is nearly full. I recd a letter from you Friday with the watch cord all right but as it happened I have a good chain now. tell Allen he had better get the watch fixed. I will pay the bill whatever it is + he may cary it. it did not cost me very high. I presume I shall have 2 or 3 more before the week is out. Write often Very aff yours George W Harwood

The Battle referred to here was Burgess Mill, October 27-28, 1864, also known as First Hatcher's Run or Boydton Plank Road. The Union was unsuccessful in capturing the Confederate position or severing the supply line at the railroad. Louis Winslow's body was one of the first to be re-interred after the war. He was moved from his burial location near Spotsylvania Court House to the National Cemetery in Fredericksburg in 1866. There are also headstones for Louis and Lyman in the North Brookfield cemetery. The bucked and gagged punishment meant placing a stick across a man's mouth like a bit for a horse, tying it in place and tying his arms around another stick between his bent knees or behind his back. The Dry Tortugas are in Key West, Florida. Fort Jefferson was under construction there from 1846-1875. It was built to protect the shipping lanes into the Gulf of Mexico.

[No. 39]   Camp of 36th Regt Mass Vols
                                                        Nov 7/64

Dear Friends

As I am not very busy this afternoon I will write you a few line to let you know that I am all right. Freeman Started for home Sunday morning I presume that he has got home before this I feel very anxious to hear from him. It was hard for me to bid him <u>Good Bye,</u> for I wanted he should stay with me longer I love him as an [my] own Brother. none could [be] kinder to me than he has been. I enjoyed his visit very much. we succeed in getting Lyman body with out much trouble at last I should like to be present at the funeral as I presume they will have one. Of course he will tell you all the news about here. the fighting on our right the night before he left I understand was the rebs charging on our Picket line they succeeded in taking some prisoners but we took as many of theres, so that they did not make much by the operation. I have command of Co. D. now. I received a letter from Mrs E D B- [Batcheller] the morning before Freeman left. I think I have no news in particular to write. it is raining today. my old House leaks some but that is nothing. Lt [Joseph] Hancock is on Picket today. I shall have to go tomorrow or next day. I received a letter from Haskell today. I sent him $55.30 sometime ago but he did not get it, I see by his letter. I am sorry he is at home now I suppose. I should like pretty well to get a short furlough. I told Freeman about the Photographs I wanted I hope I shall get them. I suppose Freeman can tell you all the news so I will not write any more this time. I felt very badly to see Freeman start for home, but we cannot always be togather. write often tell Fannie I will write her when I get a little more time.
                              Very Aff Yours
                              George W Harwood

Freeman Doane came to Petersburg and retrieved the body of Lyman H. Gilbert. It was buried in Walnut Grove Cemetery, North Brookfield. Younger sister Fannie's birthday was November 3, she was now nine years old.

No 40   Camp of 36th Regt Mass Vols
                                              Nov 11/64

Dear Friends

    I rec'd a letter from you this morning and was as usual very glad to get it, a welcome message from home. I expect to hear from Freeman tomorrow or next day. I went on Picket yesterday morning and came off this morning. after I came in Lt [Joseph] Hancock asked me to go down and have our Pictures taken, so I went after keeping awake all last night. I had one taken in my own cloths sitting, and then put on his dress coat and sword + sash and had one taken standing. they are both pretty good ones. I will send them home and I want you should have 1/2 Doz Photographs of each kind taken from them and send to me. I want to give them to some of my friends. Col Draper said he would give his in exchange for each of us line Officers and would be glad to, perhaps I will send him one. if Mary Gilbert rearly wants one you may give her one. I wish you would have this

George Washington Harwood. This may be one of the seated poses described in this letter. (Photo from author's collection)

taken as soon as possible, will you Freeman. I am so fat that it sticks right out of me. I told the artist that I would sit and have one taken in my natural easy position Lt [Joseph] Hancock said that was Harwood all over. I think so to. Anna you say that you would like to see me for you have a great many things you would like to say to me. I should like to see you and talk, but inasmuch as we cannot at present, why not write all any thing that you would like to <u>ask</u> I will try and answer and be glad to. I am feeling pretty well now I should like to get a furlough by + by but dont know as I can. what do you think of these pictures? do you call them good ones or not. I think they are pretty good ones, considering that I sat up last night in the open air. show them to the friends and see what they say to them. 4 Deserters came in last night and say that there are more that would like to. I should like a Box but I dont think it best to send one just now for it is very uncertain whare we shall be in 1 month. when you see Edwin Doane tell him to write to me, for I want to hear from him. We are having very fine weather here now but it is most time for the rainy season I suppose. I understand that Lincoln is to be our next President I hope he is. I will not write any more this time let me hear from you soon. I remain as ever Yours Respect.   George W Harwood Lt. Co D

I am going to put on about 2 stamps I presume it will take about 6.

President Lincoln was elected to his second term on November 8, 1864.

Nov. 13th 1864

Dear Sister Fannie

  I suppose you have been looking for a letter from me for some time, but I dont think I can write one that you can read. I guess Anna will have to read it for you. I am very much obliged to you for those chestnuts that you sent me. I have eaten them all up. the chaplain gave me some little books this morning I will send one or both to you now I have read them. this is a short letter but I will try and write more next time.

Good By

George

The letter begins in block printing and switches to cursive for Anna to read to Fannie.

No 41   Camp of 36th Regt Mass Vols

Nov 16/64

Dear Friends

  I received a paper from you this morning and a letter from Haskell. I expected to have heard from Freeman some days ago as he told me that he thought he should put a letter in for me in Washington. I have felt quite anxious to hear from him to know that he got home safely &c. I now take it for granted that he did as Haskell wrote me that he + Walker + Wheelock were all present at the funeral. I wish I could have been there also. I suppose most of you went. yesterday I rec'd a paper from Mrs Ezra D.

[Batcheller]. I answered her letter last evening yesterday I pulled down my house or rather had my men do it for me, and built it up again much better. I have now got a very convenient house, warm + lovly. I feel quite at home here now, but I have had the blues for a few days past. every thing dont work to suit me, always. if it did I should apply for a leave of Absence for a few days and visit you. I presume I could get this leave if I could make it appear that I [had] good reasons for so doing. as I told the Maj. that I had reasons good enough but I wasnt going to tell him what they were he said that he would approve it, but there are so many in now ahead [of me] that I shall have to wait awhile at any rate. I guess I will not finish this letter this morning. I will wait till tomorrow and see if I do not hear from Freeman. I shall have to go on Picket again tomorrow I expect. have you got my pictures yet if so how do you like them? I suppose that Mr Abel Harwood is in N. B. now is he not. I should like to see him pretty well for I dont know as I remember how he looks. I think I shall go out and see him + Uncle Joseph Washington [Harwood] + Aunt Anna Moriah &c after I get out of this service. dont you think it will pay. if I dont come home by + by I want Father to get a pass and come out and see me. I think it will pay him well. I was very glad to see Freeman and felt sorry to have him go away. I have felt quite anxious since lest he should not reach home safely. We have had orders to fix up our Tents suitible for Winter Quarters. I dont believe we shall stay here all winter. by the way Maj. [Thaddeus L.] Barker has been mustered Lt. Col. , Capt [James B.] Smith Maj. + 1ˢᵗ Lt [Philip G.]Woodward as Capt., Capt [Henry S.] Burrage who went over to see the rebs the day before Freeman came here, has been dismissed [from] the service of the United States, a sad mistake in Burrage. Im sorry for him for it will worry him, a minister Lieut [Joseph] Hancock could not be mustered as there is no vacancy as yet, nor Sergt Perly [George A. Perley] Friday Morning   I have waited for a letter now 3 or 4 days but have got none so I will write. I came of[f] Picket this morning. this is a splendid morning they are talking some about a move here just now. I dont know much about it Burnside came here night before last and went back to Washington yesterday I dont know what he came for, some say that he came to take Command + some say he was only on a little business. I did not see him. I am very sorry that I did not get a letter from you this morning I most always get one from you on Friday + I have not heard from Freeman most 2 weeks since he left here. I fear something has happened to him. I have just heard that Genls Grant + Burnside have gone to Washington on Special Business. Lt Snell came over to see me day before yesterday in the afternoon. Lt. [Joseph] Hancock was on Picket. Snell staid with me to supper and quite a while in the evening. I like him pretty well, much better than I used to. he is the best friend I have in the Army. some of the time I feel quite lonely, and if I dont hear from home about such a day I have the blues. I have not heard from home quite [paper torn] as usual. I dont hear any thing about being paid off yet and I have got but a few dollars left Uncle Sam owes me about $300.00 but that dont do me any good I guess you had better put in say $10.00 for fear I should want to use some. We expected to get our pay long before this but they are behind as usual, all the more when I get it. I am getting pretty anxious to come home on a furlough and I should not think very strange if I made an application before long I think that before the winter is out I shall have a chance to come. I dont know as I feel like writing much more this morning kept awake all night last night. be sure and write often

Saturday morning

I have just rec'd No 27 from home. I am very glad to learn that Freeman + the body got home so safely. I wish I could have been present at the funeral. I also received a letter from Ada [Ida ?] Allen this morning saying that Aunt Louisa was there. It is raining hard this forenoon but I feel quite contented as my house is new and dont leak as it did when F- [Freeman] was here + I have got a letter or two to think of. I dread the cold winter on some accts, for wood is not very plenty here and we have a good deal of Picket duty to do in an open field whare the wind has full sweap across [letter incomplete, paper is torn]

Mr. Abel Harwood was George's great uncle visiting from Bloomington, Illinois. His father's brothers and a sister, Uncle Joseph Harwood, Uncle Washington Harwood, and Aunt Anna Moriah Harwood Lothrop also moved out west to Illinois and Michigan. The remaining three of his father's six siblings, Harrison Harwood, Phebe Harwood Jackson and Dolly P. Harwood Winslow, lived in Massachusetts. Major General Burnside visited the Petersburg headquarters in November hoping to ask for a new assignment. He was unable to meet with General Grant. They both left for Washington but not together as George presumed.

No 42   Camp of 36th Regt Mass Vols
                                                        Nov 25/64

Dear Friends
        I received a letter from you this morning 1 from Ida [Allen], a
paper from Edwin [Doane]. I like the looks of these pictures first rate I
understand [from] you that you are going to send some different ones do
I? I will keep these till then and then I will send them back if the other
ones are as good Ida said that her father said he saw my picture in the
shop that I sent home, and he hardly knew me I looked so old. I thought
they were good ones. if the Artist cannot take them as they are have him
take 1/2 Doz of the one he can take the most perfect, which I should think
would be the sitting one. I should like first rate to have Father have his
mothers [+] the rest taken so that I have them to look at. I got one from
Hubbard a few days ago Yesterday was Thanksgiving I came of[f] Picket
in the morning and we played ball &c through the day. I had nothing unusual for dinner Beef-Stake + Potatoes Parsnep + Onions Bread + butter +
apple sauce Apple pie, meat-pie + cheese + plum pudding, &c. I suppose
you had a pleasant time at home. You say that Bells brother is going to
send a box. I dont know hardly what I do want I guess nothing in particular. I dont think of any thing now. have you said any thing to Uncle David
about his having a Sash? Freeman I keep my same cook I like him well.
the man who cooked for [Capt. Henry S.] Burrage cooks for Capt Fairbanks [John B. Fairbank] now. I understand that they are going to try and
have Capt Burrage reinstated. I hope they will succeed. [Lt. Joseph] Hancock cannot get mustered as Capt at present. I am now in Commmand of
Co D the Co that Burrage belongs [belonged] to. Lt Emery is 1st Lt and belongs to that Co but is on Special services now, as commissary he has
gone home on a furlough. Lt Osburn did not start till the next morning
after you did. Freeman did you get any of those small bars at Washington
I have not heard you say any thing about it. I like those Pictures of yours
first rate and if they will stay in an Album I dont care whether you send
others in exchange for these or not. I dont see any signs of our being paid
off till the 4 month are due us. I have got 2.25 left. I think I told you in my
last letter that you had better put in 10.00. I think that there [are] more
signs of a move now then there was I have got another little watch now
just like the one I sent home and you could hardly tell the difference. Free-

man do you think the pictures that I sent home look savage? dont they look as I did when you were [here]? I look very different now nothing but a mustache. Freeman I guess you must have put a stamp on Idas letter? I hardly know what more I have to write. Father I see by your last letter that you have sold the Plain. one night I was thinking about that piece of woods and thought it would more than pay to cut every thing off except the Pines and draw to market the woods of Pines would be worth more without this wood then it is now isnt that so? now you had better sell the meadows and you will have a very pretty farm, plenty large enough Does Mr [Uncle] Abel Harwood look as he did the last time you saw him. I dont remember how he looked. We have very fine weather here now it did rain 3 days in succession but is now quite pleasant rather cool night + morning. I would like to know whether Edwin + Father measured with their boots on or in stocking feet. I dont know as I have any thing more in particular to write so I will close as it is about dinner time. Ever Aff Yours [George Harwood] [letter incomplete, the paper has been cut off leaving part of his signature]

Leander Bell's brother was Alonzo.

No 43   Camp of 36th Regt Mass Vols
                                         Nov 28/64

Dear Friends

        I will commence a letter home this afternoon but do not intend to finish it. in the first place I will tell you about our Thanksgiving supper that was issued to us Friday night. 1 chicken to 2 Officers + so Capts [Philip G.]Woodward + [Joseph A.]Marshall Lt [Joseph] Hancock + myself thought we would sup together, ~~we had~~ on Saturday. We had chicken Plum pudding, three kinds of pie + cheese bread + butter, pickel &c. we had a fine time and in the evening we had Oysters. Freeman you know that large cook house where we used to eat on the whole [when you were here] we had a very pleasant time

Friday morning   It has been sometime since I commenced this letter, and I will try and finish it now. we have moved since I commenced this. we are now in Fort Rice nearly opposite Petersburg. we can see the City. they fire here, a good deal. Freeman perhaps you will remember the last night you stayed with me there was a good deal of firing on our right. the rebs charged on our Picket line and captured some of them. We are there now. it is a pretty good place but rather exposed. I received letter No 29 from you and one from Ed. [Edwin?] with his picture I was very glad to get the 5.00 you sent for I had not got a cent left. I dont see any signs of getting our pay till we get the 4 months I am as blue as a wh[e]t stone this morning and dont feel like writing and cannot write or that it can be read hardly. I shall be obliged to send home for money to pay my board with till we get paid off then I shall have enough. it looks like rain but I dont know as it will. I wish they would pay off every 2 months, but it will all come sometime I guess. there is no news of much importance as I know of here. we have got a good view of the Picket line for a mile each way. I do not feel like writing this morning and so I shall not write much of a letter but next time I will try and write more and better Father I should like to hear from you, and I want your picture + mothers. it is a good thing to get your pay of M. Bartlett if you have to take old horses. Write soon + often.

Very Aff Yours

George

The Johnnies shelled us good just before dinner they have got good range of us but have done no harm thus far. 1 shell struck within 12 ft of the Adj tent went into the ground more than 6 ft. the Adj thought he had better leave, but our Artillry soon silenced them. this is a very exposed place, but I guess the duty will not be very hard

No 44   Fort Rice Va Dec 10/64

Dear Friends,

Yesterday morning I received a letter from you. I like that Photograph very well and think I will send it back and have some more like it. when are you going to send the Album with your pictures or before. I guess it will come the quickest and safest by mail if Mrs Bell sends a box to Leander and you can put in any thing all right. I came off Picket last night we are having a cold snap about this time it snowed last night some. We are going to have a fight here or some where near here, before long if nothing happens but I guess we shall not have a hand in it, for we are in this fort a very good place when all is quiet but the Johnnies throw some shells pretty near here. I have got a minnie ball that came down through my tent a few days ago and came very near my hat. Lt [Joseph] Hancock + I were playing Bak gommon [backgammon] it went between us but nearer me. it was warm when I took it up. I told Lt. that I would put that into my pocket, when he told me that it was for me. I should feel pretty well if I could only get my pay. I dont see any signs of that yet, and if I dont have any money I shant have it to spend shall I? no great loss without some small gain. Lieut Hancock wants to know if I am doing this writing by the job. he says he should judge so by the way I scratch. I dont seem to have much news to write this time I have written home so frequently of late. I shall not write a very long letter this time. I feel very sorry to lose Aunt Lucretia but we could not expect the old Lady to remain with us always? What will Uncle Jonas do now sell his farm and go and live with Mr Tamblin [Tomblen]. if that farm was not quite so large I should like to own it myself. I dont know but farming is about as good business as any but I like to be where there is more going on. What does Charles K. have to say now a days now Lincoln is our President. Stoddard could'nt see having him for President again. did you show him my last Pictures. if so what did he think of them. I got a jolly letter from Jennie Bush this morning. I should judge that she was feeling pretty well do you know Mary Dean of Oakham she is with her I believe I will close for this time. we can hear the roar of the distant cannon, peal on peal afar. I should like those pictures as soon as you can get them conveniently. I will write again soon it takes just about 5.00 p[e]r week to pay my board Father you dont think Uncle Jonas farm would be quite the thing for me do you? I dont think it is a very good one. Good bye Write often

This from Your Soldier Son + Brother   George W Harwood

Great Aunt Lucretia Winslow Harwood died on November 28, 1864, age seventy eight. Mr. Orin A. Tomblen was the son-in-law to Aunt Lucretia and Uncle Jonas. He married their daughter Rebekah. Of Jonas and Lucretia's eight children, only two were in Massachusetts, six had moved out west.

No 45   Fort Rice Va   Dec 16/64

Dear Friends

I received letter No 31 a few days ago and 32 today. I have received the 3 letters with 5.00 dollars in each. was very glad to get it, but dont see any signs of getting our pay yet, so I shall want about 5.00 more each week that will just pay my board. there are some measures being taken now to have the Officers pay raised. I hope they will the more the better dont you say so? I was very glad to see Fathers hand writing again for I had almost forgotten how it looked. should like to see it oftener. I should like to see Mr Abel Harwoods + Wifes Photographs. I have almost forgotten how he looked + have never seen his Wife. I suppose his daughter Mary has not got married yet has she? a pretty good looking Young lady. [torn bottom edge of the paper]

I am about to have me a house built 10 ft long 6 ft wide all in one room no garret, no cellar, Parlor, sitting room bedroom Kitchen all in one, chimney at one end with the door + bunk in the back side. There is a report here tonight that Genl Thomas has whipped Genl Hood up good in E. Tenn. capturing 1500 men 17 pieces of Artillery &c &c and that Genl Sherman is doing a big thing somewhare. I expect that Sherman will do something before he gets through. We expected that there would be something of a move here but they only made a reconnassince on the left a few days ago. Every thing is quiet now. the Johnnies opened on us a little this afternoon but we soon put them to silence with our artillery it is quite interesting to look of[f] from this Fort and see just whare our shells burst and whare all the rebs do also. they come whizzing over and plunge into the ground some six or eight ft and then burst throwing the dirt in every direction. some of them burst in the air and then you have got to look out for your head for the [torn bottom edge of the paper]

There is a report here that all who enlisted in 1862 when we enlisted under that call and got so small a bounty that they will be mustered out 3 months before their term of service expire, but I dont believe that, and another that the 36th are going to Baltimore to do guard duty. Col Bowen [Henry Bowman] is there a Maj in the Regular service and wants us, but that is all nonsense. I could tell these rumors all night and that is all the good it would do. I should like first rate to come home and spend a few weeks but I cannot very well + as I have no business to attend to I will not think of it. 8 months + a few as the boys say and then good bye Uncle Sam. I dont think I shall care to stop any longer till after I have tried something else, but it is just about lazy life enough for me. I had rather have some responsibilities on my hand than work hard for a living did Mother[?] [torn bottom edge of the paper]

Now I am going to retire as it is high time no good bed stands invitingly before me, but in its stead a bunk of boards + a blanket to cover me, no stairs to go up, no doors to lock by the way the sutler had some 300.00 worth of goods taken from him last night by some unknown evil disposed person. Joe Walker came up yesterday Capt [Stephen C.] Warriners

Brother also he is a young fellow no larger or much older then Allen, <u>no business here? so young</u>. now good night, not quite yet I have got to write a few words more. We have not got that Box yet I guess it is not quite time. The boys sing most every evening and how good it sounds but it makes me almost feel homesick the same time we used to sing at home. I dont try to sing at all now Lyman is gone. we used to sing "We are going home," "Heaven is my home" &c but we shall sing together no more on earth. I hope we may be [letter incomplete, paper torn]

General Sherman was near Savannah, Georgia by December 10, 1864, near the end of the March to the Sea. General George H. Thomas defeated General John B. Hood at the Battle of Nashville,Tennessee on December 15-16, 1864.

Fort Rice Va

Dec 17/64

Dear Brother Allen

  I will write a few lines to you in this letter I have nothing in particular to write. I am having my house built today I have to look after that some I have not much else to do this is a lazy life to lead some days I have to be pretty busy writing or something of that sort, but no hard work so I am as fat as a pig fat and clumsy. I presume you could trip me down but you could never jerk me down a fellow the other day took hold of me who is used to wrastling but after twiching on me about 1/2 hour said that there was no fun in that for that was science against strength so gave it up. Can that old horse trot any that Father has got. when I come home I want a horse that is able to cary me on his back, that is the best exercise a man can take. I mean to follow that more when I get home. Do you want to know what kind of a pipe I have got it is made of earth in the shape of a turkeys foot holding an egg and in the same color toe nails are there all perfect. the egg is just the color of a turkey egg This is a very warm day. the ground is not frozen at all.

Write again

Yours &c

George W.

The pipe George was describing was probably a meerschaum pipe.

No 46   Fort Rice before Petersburg Va
                                              December 21 1864

Dear Friends

     I received a letter from you yesterday morning with 4 of my Photo-graphs I cant say I like them very well for I dont call them very good. they look just as though I smelt a skunk. I like the one sitting pretty well and I would like 1/2 Doz of them. Mother I would like well enough to give Aunts Caroline + and Martha one well enough but there will not be enough of the sitting ones + the standing one[s] are not good enough they dont look at all like me, so I guess they will have to wait till some other time I have nothing in particular to write this morning I wrote only a few days ago and about all I could think of. We have had a hard rain and it has not cleared off yet. We have got a good house so we dont care much about the weather only that it is very bad for the Pickets. I dont see as they are even going to pay us off again. we dont hear any thing about it. I received a Springfield Republican this morning. I like to get that paper for it is the best one that I know of. I guess I will hold on and not scratch quite so fast as I am in no great hurry, and I may want to read it myself before I send it and I should hate to have it as bad as Uncle Washingtons [Harwood] was when he took down the name of a person who wanted the Doc. I have heard Father tell the story, he could'nt read it himself. It is rather amusing to go along and see some of these tents, where the boys have dug down a foot or two to keep warmer and have a fire place &c this rain has filled some of there tents 1 foot high with water. they will get up on their bunks and think of home. As Joe Walker said this morning when his tent was full of mud + water and he sitting on a little stool, "this aint much like Mass" there is no firing on the Picket line today for the pits are most of them knee deep with mud + water on both sides so that out [our] men + the Rebs are both standing up on the banks looking at each other and no doubt wishing this War was over. President Davis is said to be very sick [but] is living I shall have to draw this letter to a close pretty soon as I have got to make out a report of all the alterations in my Co during the year 1864, and they want it this afternoon so I shall have to hurry and do that. let me hear from you often I like to hear as often as I have of late 2 a week. if you have not sent any money since the 5.00 Freeman sent I would like some more it would be well to put in 5.00 every week till I get paid off.

Afternoon   the mail has gone out and I have not got this letter ready, but there is another day coming. it is quite cool and damp, just such an afternoon as we are'nt apt to enjoy very much especialy in the army. I dont know but I might as well give you a scetch about our Chaplains. the 21st Mass had a chaplain Sevens, and we had one Richardson neither of them were mustered but when consolidated Richardson got mustered. He is an old man too old for this business and stays back in the Hospital comes up on Sunday and preaches and gives a few papers when pleasant. that is all we see of him Sevens stays with the Regt and shares in all the marches goes to the Tents and see if the boys want any thing give us more books + papers beside articles of clothing and does everything that he can for the men both temperaly + spiritualy. the men signed a paper ~~polightly~~ politely asking him [Richardson] to resign and give Sevens the chaplainsy but he took no notice of that and so the Officer gave him another but as yet he has taken no steps in that direction, but has reported Chaplain Sevens as a citizen doing mischief in the Regt, trying to buy the boys, and get him out. Sevens has gone home now but will return we expect. such is the state of feelings with our Chaplains, but then dont say any thing about it from me. Chaplain Sevens is a younger man, perhaps I will show you his Photograph he has promised it to me. I saw Capt Warriners Picture last evening his Brother has got it. it looks just like him exactly I wish he was here with us now. Freeman did I tell you about sending Wm J Haskell $55.00 + over by mail when he was in Alexandria and he never got it. I had another letter from him yesterday but he says he never has got it, so that speculating with Lyman didnt amount to much. he must have lost 75. dollars by it in all. I sold 1 1/2 Doz of their pens and that is how I came to owe him that amount I dont know but that he will be mad if I dont pay it over again but I guess he will get over it. I have got the best of it, if he should ever cauget[?] into law. George W.

Aunts Caroline and Martha Ann were George's mother's sisters.

No 47   Fort Rice before Petersburg Va
                                               December 23/64

Dear Friends
        I received a letter from you this morning with your Photographs & one of mine in it also the box came to [Leander] Bell + I. I am very much

pleased with my Album + Handkercheif + my Photographs look so much better in the Album. I think the pictures of those little boys + F + A [George R, Elmer F, Freeman + Anna] are compleat but I dont think my Photographs are very good. who did you give the other one to, Ed [Edwin?] or Hubbard they dont look as well as I should like to give them I should like to give one to Aunts Caroline + Martha but I dont think these look well enough I will send one for Aunt <u>Caroline</u> I guess there wont be many to see it there. when will the other 1/2 Doz of mine be done sitting. I like them much better. I wrote a letter to you calling for more <u>money</u>, that seems to be the cry out here among all. the Government owes me about 450.00. When I commenced this letter I had something in particular that I wanted to write but I dont think of it now. I should like to be at home a little while about this time and drive my colt a little. I shouldnt think Edwin would be contented to work in that mill it is a lonesome place I think. I wonder if Lucy Gilbert lives at home this winter. she is a very pretty Girl I think. I should like to see Sarah Damon or Austin now. does she look as she did when a little girl? or dont you know? I believe she used to be pretty. Freeman will my colt rear up when you start off, or have'nt you learned her that yet. I could hardly think how it happened that you sent me two papers for I know that Anna wrote on one and Freeman on the other, but it is a good Idea to send enough I find I think that is the best paper we can get here in the Army for everything is in it. Bell is very much pleased with his box I guess it is reported here th[at] Genl Meade has issued an order that enlisted men shall not wear boots only cavalry, and that any box sent to enlisted men and liquor or boots are taken out and sutlers are not going to be allowed to sell to men any boots, for all that about 1/2 the men ware boots and nothing is said, so Bell was lucky in having it directed to me.

Saturday Afternoon

You would laugh if you could see us turn out a little while ago the pickets commenced firing by full volleys, but it was only at a flock of wild Geese that were flying over both sides opened at once it was amusing to see how quickly the men put on their accoutermits [accoutrements]. This is a pretty cold day. I have been down to the Sutlers and bought me a new vest + pr of Drawers. the Vest that I now ware I bought 1 year ago and have worn it every day since cost 5.00. I bough[t] a very nice one today for 7.50. an Officer can get trusted for as much as he pleases, some have run up bills to the amount of 100.00, mine is about 30.00. this is good winter weather these cold night the Johnys desert fast one night 70 men came in on our Div line every night they come in. War news is good Genl Sherman is doing the good thing I think. I dont think of much more to write this time. I will write again soon. George.

Freeman and Anna Doane's boys were Georgie (George R.) age four and Elmer age two and a half. General Sherman occupied Savannah, Georgia on December 21 at the end of the March to the Sea. In January he moved north to Charleston, South Carolina.

No 48   Fort Rice before Petersburg Va.
                                              Camp of 36th Mass Vols
                                                      Dec 30/64

Dear Friends

     I received No 35 from you this morning with 5.00 dollars. I was just out of money and was very glad indeed to get it. Please send the same Amount in your next. When did you send No 34 I dont know but I have made a mistake in setting down the Nos as I have rec'd them I can't find 34 among them. did you send a letter between the one containing F + A [Freeman & Anna's] Photographs and the one with the 5.00 dollars if you have I have not got it there was just a week difference between these two. Have you sent my sitting Photographs yet or aint the[y] ready. Anna You spoke of the excelent Sermons you heard that day (Christmas) from Rev Mr. Manning I can tell you what I did that day. Our old Chaplain preached to us about 20 minutes. Instead of Attending Church I had my Co out + inspected them Guns + Accoutriments Knapsacks + all. Spent the rest of the day in reading + writing. I have had a good many of letters to write + the Muster + Payrolls to make out beside the Returns of Ordnance + Ordnance Stores, also of Camp + Garrison Equipage, of late and expect soon to have some Invoices + Receipts to make out of both Ordnance + Camp + Garrison soon. as Lieut [Joseph] Hancock is expecting to be mustered as Capt soon and will take Co. D, I expect I shall take Co F but dont know. Day-before Yesterday the rebs opened on us + we replied with our Artillery. You better believe that there was music for some hours they wounded 2 of our men. yesterday they shot one of our Cooks through the Arm, when he was serving out coffee to the men on Picket. That is all the men we have lost since we came here. Christmas Eve, M.P. Snell came out to see me, took supper and spent the evening till 9 o'clock then he got on his horse and went <u>home</u>. he <u>lives</u> about 2 miles from here he is one of the best friends I have in the Army, he is smart. We like to talk over the old times together when he + I were Privates trudging along with our Knapsacks + Guns. We called it hard then + so it was, but we laugh at our hardships now as though we had none. I find that the best way to get along in the Army or at home even is to look on the bright side of every thing if there is any, and keep cool if things dont go just right at all times. there are times when I dont have much to do, and I have been looking into the French language some, the Phonographic short hand writing some + this afternoon I have been doing some problems in Square Root. I dont know what to pitch into for improvement, (<u>what would you</u>) if I had a Book of Surveying or Book Keeping I would try them. I hear from [cousin] Anna B Jackson quite often I like to correspond with her for she is an excellent correperson [corresponder?]. she says that George [Jackson] is going to Boston to work with his Uncle Charles. I hope he will do well and have no doubt he will for he is steady - minds his own business. I have not heard from Uncle Joseph [Harwood] for a long time I think I shall write to him some. Freeman is Carlton DeLand exchanged or parolled? how does he look after his imprisonment? as usual. You say that it is good sleighing in B. there is no snow here but it looks like snow some this afternoon. Freeman name over some of the boys that belong to that Co. in N B + Oakham. I should like to be there to see them drill a few of the first times. Mother do you go down to see Aunt Caroline any this winter. how do they get along this Winter do they have work or help from the Town. Allen do you ride out with the Girls any this Winter or are you afraid of getting the mitting I dont believe I should be as bashful as I used to be. I was afraid of getting the mitting or something else I suppose. my bump of contioss is pretty large I expect[?]. Freeman tell Hubbard that I will write him in a few days I ought to have done so long ago but I havnt forgotten him. I take him out and look at him in my Album with Ida. Every one admires the looks of my family that is F + A. [Freeman & Anna] on one side the boys [Georgie & Elmer] on the other. they think Anna looks a little like me but I cant see it. I guess I have written about all I can think of, all that I have time to write. I some times laugh to my self when I think of some of the old Maids in N B that is that are going to be, when this civil war is over they must put in a ticket. I wonder what Mr. Woods folks think of <u>Mankind</u> on the whole, but I cant stop to dwell. I ha'nt got long to tarry, so I will hurry on before the mail goes + leaves my letter behind. Write often. I should be glad to see Fathers hand writing again. I have a man in my Co by the name of Wheeler. he is Cousin to Ellen Goodnow of Baldwinville. he says she is married her Husband is or was in the Army. I believe he is at home now she wants me to write to her but I have no time to write to Married Women. so Good Bye for this time Remember me to all the friends Let me hear from you Eathan [Ethan Allen] + send 5.00 dollars in the next letter. Please axcept this with the best wishes of your ever Aff. Son + Brother

George W. Harwood

I have written my name so many times of late that I can put it on now about as quick as I could with a chi[?]   [on a separate piece of paper]
Saturday Morning   After all my hurry yesterday I did not send this letter so I will add a word. We were mustered this morning for 2 months more pay. I dont know as we shall ever get it. it is now raining or rather hailing I guess it will snow before it gets through. You ought to have seen me jump up this morning an hour or two before light. there was some trouble in the Picket line a little below us we supposed that the rebs were charging on our Picket line, but it died away I dont know what the trouble was, but my boots carried 200 lbs out of my little shanty very quickly. This being the last day of 1864 I will wish you all "A Happy New Year"

George

Anna B. and George Jackson were brother and sister. They were George's cousins. At this time Uncle Joseph W. Harwood was living in Illinois. Carlton M. DeLand served with the Massachusetts Fifteenth and Massachusetts Twentieth Regiments. Mitting is an act of coming together or a gathering (Merriam-Webster.com).

No 49   Fort Rice before Petersburg Va
                                              January 6th 1865

Dear Friends

        I received No 36 from you this morning + a paper. I was very glad indeed to get it. we are hoping to get our pay about the 20th of this month. I think that Freeman said that you would send some more money with my picture I presume that they are on the road by this time if you did send some. I that [think?] that will be enough unless you hear from me again. It has rained hard all the afternoon. this forenoon I went down to Hancocks Station about 3/4 of a mile from here to see a man hung for Desertion It was a sad sight to see a man follow his own rude coffin to the gallows as he did. he looked as though he had been crying I think he had + he plead not guilty till the last. I dont know the circumstances so I will not attempt to tell. ~~Capt~~ Maj [James B.] Smith is Provost Marchell, he + the chaplain went up on the platform with him the chaplain knelt + prayed then tied a handkerchief over his face. soon he was hanging in the air. I took one last long lingering look and then turned from that sad place. I dont know as I am anxious to see another such case. I presume that it was a just punishment however but I dont pretend to be judge.

I dont know when I have had such a good hearty laugh as I did this morning when I read about the christmas tree, and Aunt Dolly's presents. I know her temper so well that I could'nt help laughing as loud as I could hollor. Capt [Joseph] Hancock looked at me and wanted to know what on earth pleased me so I had to tell him. he grinned. he is almost as old as my Father and much grayer. I should like to have been there and heard her sputter but I guess I have said already to much. Now I will commence again I had to stop and read your letter over again + have a good laugh about Dear Morse + Aunt D[olly] + familes presents. now I will tell you what is going on in the tents around now. I am all alone this evening writing in one of the tents nearby is one of my men whistling + shaking some bones. in the first tent on my left are 4 Officers playing cards. in the tent behind that some of the men are praying + singing I can hear all this planely. in other tents near by the men are telling stories + amusing themselves most any way. perhaps I have told you that there is quite an interest felt among the men now, on the subject of religion. I am now in Comd. of Co F of this Regt. so you will direct so for a while. Capt [Joseph] Hancock has filled [Capt. Henry S.] Burrage place. there are now no vacancies for captaincy The Capt of F is on the staff so I take it being senior Lt present, should there be another vacancy I presume

If I could get it before the Regt has less than 6 months to serve I can be mustered for the unexpired term of the Regt Service but if not I shall have to stay three Years longer + I dont think I shall stop for Promotion would you. I think I had rather come home 1st Lieut at the end of 3 years than stay 3 more for a Captaincy or even Major. a great title dont amount to much. I often think of what Henry Harwood said that he had rather be a live coward than a dead hero but I dont know as it will be any more cowardly to come home after doing ones duty, than it is not to do it at all. I should have been very glad to have remained with Co D the rest of my time out but that could not be, but I have the pleasure of knowing that the men of D were satisfied with me for the Orderly + several of the men told me that I had not one enemy in the Co + that they wished I could stay with them the rest of the 8 months but I have got a very good Company now + all appear to be well satisfied. I have a good Co clerk in this company so I dont have so much writing to do myself.

Saturday morn.

I did not finish my letter last evening so I will write more this morning it has cleared of very pleasant + windy the mud is drying up very fast. We have drills now of 1 hour a day in the Manuel of Arms there are days when I dont have much to do. I spend much of my time in reading + writing. Mother you said you wished I would not smoke, but you did not speak quick enough for I left of[f] some time ago of my own accord. It is not a very Gentlemanly habit besides expensive There is an agent of some Christian commission here in camp + left some papers + other things for the boys. I dont feel so much like writing this morning as I did last night, but I guess I have written all the news of any value. I guess I have never told you the names of some of the Forts around here on our left are Forts Hell + Damnation. On our write [right] are the Seven Sisters + others in front the rebs have got plenty of them but I dont know what they are called some bad name I presume. there are some things about this life that I like but I believe I shall be glad to get home again. Freeman I judge that you see Abbie Babbit often in the Shop. she is a very pretty Girl if she only belonged to some other family I should think she was prettier It dont take long to get acquainted with her. I presume I could speak to her now. I dont know as I feel much more important now than I did when an enlisted man. perhaps it would be proper to remember me to her in return. Ask her if she will give me one of her pictures now if I will come home + get it. just for fun, tell her I told you to but I find I have filled this large sheet so I will close Write often as usual.

Very Aff Yours,
George W Harwood

No 50

Fort Rice Va
Jan 11th 1865

Dear Friends

I received No 37 this morning with those Photographs I like them pretty well. I believe I have got every letter you have sent I recd 36 about a week ago. Edwin write in that Past letter that he had not got that letter I sent him yet. some evil disposed person must know my hand writing and want to play it on one of us. Anna did you ever get a letter I sent to you about the 1st of the month I dont know what day. We expect to be paid off about the 20th of this month. I dont know whether it is best to trust a hundred or two of dollars by mail or not. I dont like to keep it by me very well. I shall have quite an amount I expect + I dont want to loose it or spend it for nothing. Father what would advise. perhaps I can get a check I dont know. I came of Picket last night it rained hard all the time I was out and the pits were full of Water so that both Yanks + Johnnies were obliged to get up on the banks and look at each other very sympathisingly, talked back + forth very friendly. one said he should like to see Jeff Davis + Abe Lincoln hung up on that tree, that stood between us. another spoke up let us all go home, but it has cleared of now and is quite pleasant but rather muddy

Friday Morning.   I rec'd 38 this morning. I dont know as we shall get our pay now but I hope we shall. Freeman I wish you would write in your next letter how much I owe you, that is how much you have paid out for me + sent me, so that I can pay you next time I get my pay. I am sorry that you + the little ones are so poorly now. I dont seem to have much news to write just now if I have I cant think of it. What do you think of sending Genl [Benjamin] Butler home to Lowell Mass. I wish they would send me home.

Afternoon   I guess I will finish my letter now I have had some game of chicken with one of the other Lieuts so if I dont hurry I shall be behind the mail again as I have been a good many times. I have got a few old Atlantic monthlys + Harpers Magazine &c to read so I shall have enough to do for the present. I should think it strange if Edwin did'nt get that letter at all should'nt you? This is a very warm day a man is very comfortable working in his shirt sleeves. can you tell me Mary Ann Earls Husband name I have forgotten. Do you remember who Mary Loevring[?] married she lives in the same town Prescott I think it is Do you ever hear any thing from Mr Underwood people I wonder if Sarah is married yet. do you know whare Nat Powers is. I might ask a thousand other questions do has George Jackson gone to Boston yet Anna [B. Jackson] wrote that he was going. I hope Freeman + his children will be better before you write again I have been thinking about getting me a furlough but I dont know as it will pay it will cost me at least $150.00 to go + come + spend what I shall be likely to. if I come I shall buy me a dress coat + sword &c. only 7 months + a few longer or sooner [illegible] as the boys say.

good Bye   George W Harwood

Mary Ann Parkman Earle was the widow of Leander M. Earle, Jr.

No 51   Fort Rice before Petersburg Va
Jan 19th 1865

Dear Friends

    I will commence a letter home this morning but have not much time just now as I am Officer of the day and am about to call for a party to clean up the Fort some. Capt [Joseph] Hancock started for Milford Mass this morning on 20 days leave of Absence, also Capt Davidson, Lt Field (A.R.D[?].M.) of Clinton and about 7 or 8 enlisted men I shall apply for a leave of 20 days in 2 or 3 weeks I think. I am hoping to month is out but perhaps not. see the Pay-Master before the I shall have to have about 10.00 more from home I think so you will please send it in your next. It will cost me something to come home + get me a new sword + some other things I shall want, but if I can get a leave I shall. I have got to give some good reason but I dont know what it will be. if I should'nt get my pay before I start or at Washington or Boston, I should feel cheap. I almost wanted to send my old sword home by Capt Hancock + let him get me a new one but then I perhaps I should come myself. What do you think will it pay or not, if I knew for certain that I should live to come home in 7 months in health, I would'nt come now any way, but life is uncertain. Snell was over to see me a few days ago. he dont seem to think that we shall not have much more hard fighting. he some expects to get a leave + visit N.B. if he does I presume you will see him. I rec'd a letter from Hubbard a few days ago with a line from you, F[reeman]. I am going to send a line Freeman to [cousin] Ida [Allen]and send in this letter you will please give it to her or Uncle Alvin [Allen] dont tell him whare you got it for I have not signed my name. I presume she will know my writing but no matter perhaps I will tell you some time what is in it

Friday Morning

I did not finish this letter as I was pretty busy and besides I expected to hear from you this morning but am disappointed so I will finish this and send it along + write again when I hear from you. I received a letter from George H Jackson this morning he is in Boston, says he is having a good time. Freeman I wish you would come out here now and spend the 20 days that Capt Hancock is going to be Absent. We would have a good time. I have got a large tent + 3 1/2 Woolen Blanket + 3 Rubbers + Greatcoat, plenty of men to bring all my wood + chop it. a good Company clerk to do all my writing so I dont have very much to do just now unless I have a mind to + you know I'm to lazy for that. I am as fat as a pig. I guess I shall have to come home + see you for I want to see how old Mass looks again in the Winter I think I can get a leave the Last of this month or rather the first of next about the 10 day but I dont know if I do some of those old horses will have to take it for I dont go on foot much. I'm to fat for that I have got me a good Waltham Watch now. I am afraid that some of you are sick as I most always get a letter from you on Friday when you write on Sunday but I hope not. There is no news of any importance as I know of. there is a good deal of talk about Blair going to Richmond but I dont know as it will amount to much. a good many seem to think that this War will end in less than 6 months + that the[re] will be but very little more fighting &c, but it is hard telling what will be. we may have a hard Spring Campaign but I hope not. What do you think of it North? do you see the beginning of the end? all the daily papers seem to talk favorably I think. we get them here every day. I will not write any more now perhaps I will add another line before the mail goes.

Most Aff Yours

George W. Harwood

Uncle Alvin Allen was George's mother's brother. His daughter was Ida. Francis P. Blair, Sr. was a journalist and a personal friend of both President Lincoln and President Davis. He travelled to Richmond, Virginia in January 1865 hoping to begin peace talks.

No 52   Fort Rice before Petersburg Va
                                                    Jan 22 :65

Dear Friends

     I received a letter from you this morning with thaes [those] barrs that went to the 38, that was a big thing. I think I sent a letter to you day before yesterday. Who is this Hammond Goodrich. Is he Aunt Lydia's Husband, Son. I think you told me about him before. That letter that Henry Macomber wrote to the prettiest Girl in N.B. is fine for some of them isnt it do you know of any body that is going to write to him in return. that is one way to get correspondents, I think but I dont think I shall try that way. I dont sign my right name to such documents. I know of another young man who wrote in the same way to the prettiest young lady in the City of Oakham. they have had no Answers as yet. Yesterday it rained hard all day + was cold but today it does not rain but is damp + very muddy cold + disagreeable. No Divine Services, so unpleasant These barrs are just the thing I have got them in my straps. I guess I will send a picture of my tent mate Capt [Joseph] Hancock it is spoiled but you can see the face he gave it to me. he is going to get a good one for me when he comes back They have got me on Regimental Officer of the day, again today but I dont have much to do except keep the peace   Tuesday Afternoon Now I guess I will finish my letter so that you will get it about next Saturday. I think I told you in my last letter that we did not expect to get our pay now for a month or more + that I shall want a little more of green paper called <u>money</u>. I wish you would put in say $5.00 in each letter or every week till further Order (using the military phrase). If I should get a leave of Absence to visit Mass. do you want I should take my Negro along + leave him with you. I have such a chap 16 years old. he says he will stay with till he is 21 if I want but I dont suppose I shall keep him long. he has been with Soldiers most too long. he will lie. last evening they commenced their everlasting shelling after dark and kept it up most all night they are rather uneasy today. The report among us today is that we have taken Fort Darling but I dont know as it is official. One can hear about any thing he wants to. The Rebs call the loss of Fort Fisher a blessing in disguise. the New York Herald says that if we should take Richmond there would be the greatest Jubilee among them ever known, that is among the sesesh. I think there would be some rejoicing in the North dont you?

Mother you asked if I had got any new shirts I have and ware the old ones for undershirts this winter if I should come home I should take them with me + leave them. they would be of service to some of you there but will soon be of none to me. I have got some other things I should like to leave at home, my sword for one thing. I keep talking about coming home I presume I shall not come at all till my time is out with Uncle Sam, that would be about my luck but I should like to drive my colt a few times in a sleigh this winter. Our boys fixed up their Picket Posts in good shape so that they were almost as comfortable as tents but they proved to be too good for they got so careless + negligent that one of the Brigade Staff ordered them pulled down. We are required to keep a most vigilant watch especialy during the night + more especialy in very dark nights, no sleeping is allowed. I guess we are more wakefull than the Rebs but they are so tricky that we dare not risk them. All communication with the enemy is strictly forbidden, for all that they talk back + forth about as much as they want to. every night about midnight the Johnnies will holler Yank, what time is it? our boys will answer them they will say all right Yank, let us go to sleep. The pickets seem to be on very friendly terms. one of our news-boys went over to their picket line and sold ~~him~~ them some paper. they let him come back but it is risky I should not suffer him to go over, if I were in charge of the line. I dont allow much talking either, black-guarding has played out, I tell them.

Now I guess I will draw this letter to a close + write to Ed[win] or some body else. I dont get much news here, except War news + I suppose you get all that + perhaps more, so I will not spend my time ~~talking~~ writing about that. I think that Genl Butler is the smartest man in the crowd + will come out top of the heep if they investigate his matters.

Most Aff. Yours

George W. Harwood

Henry Macomber from Oakham served with the Massachusetts Thirty-sixth. Confederate Fort Darling on Drewry's Bluff was on the James River protecting Richmond from the south. Fort Fisher in Wilmington, North Carolina protected the harbor and provided safe cover for blockade runners. It was a major supply line for the Wilmington and Weldon Railroad, which ran north to Petersburg and Richmond. The Union captured the fort on January 15. General Benjamin Butler had been relieved of command on January 8 because of his failure in the first battle of Fort Fisher, December. 23-27. Blackguarding is an obsolete term for using mean or abusive language (Merriam-webster.com).

No 53   Camp of 36ᵗʰ Regt Mass Vols
Fort Rice before Petersburg Va
Jan 29 :1865

Dear Friends

     I rec'd a letter from you yesterday morning. Was pleased to learn that you were all well as usual. This is Sunday afternoon. we had preaching this forenoon + afternoon the first time I remember of having two meetings in one day for a long time. I attended them both. the boys have got a little chapel built that will hold about 50 it seemed good to meet together and have a chaplain preach to us. I have had so much to do or an excuse so that I have not attended many of the meetings except Sundays. I had a letter from Capt H[ancock] this morning he is at home all right, drew his pay in Washington on the way home. when he comes back I think I shall apply for a leave that will be about the middle of Feb. I am quite anxious to test the sleighing for myself. you all say that it is fine I dont doubt it much. I guess some of those young ladies want to ride after my colt. I want she (my colt) should become acquainted with the sight of Eves fair daughters. I rec'd a letter from George Jackson a few days ago. I guess he is having a pretty good time by the way he writes. there is but little here that is new I presume that you have got the letter that I sent last week begging as usual for more money if you have not sent it I wish you would. I've got a musical chap for a Darkey he is fixing up my fire now and at the same time whistling. he is quite anxious to learn to read so I am learning him he knows all his letters and can pronounce small words, spell Dog cat man &c &c I presume that all this is very interesting to you. he tents with my Co. cook. Ada [Jane] Allen says that Mary talks of going to NB. in the Spring to open a Millinary Shop. she says that if Mary comes she shall to. she is living in Williamstown. I guess that Macomber has not heard any thing from the prettiest Girl in NB. yet I like to ask him once in a while who the prettiest girls in NB is. he will color up and say he dont know, is pretty sure to begin to talk about something else. Lt. M.P. Snell was over to see me yesterday, had a Capt with him but I have forgotten his name, a Michigan man. had some friends in Adrian [Michigan] said he [they?] had seen Mr. Lathrop [Lothrop]. he belongs to the 5ᵗʰ corps old Genl. Meade used to command that Corps, + I'm down on him as bad as they are on Burn-side so I have a good many arguments with them but always part good friends. I see that the [Worcester] Spy [newspaper] you sent me is down on

Genl Butler pretty hard and a good many other papers, but I dont see the use of every body coming down on a man just because he happened to make a mistake that is just the way all the world over. if a man happens to be successful, papers will all blow for him and exalt him as it were to the skys but should he take one step downward, or not come up to somebody's high expectations, public opinion is against him + all help kick him down ward I should think for the sake of making a bad matter worse. Freemen do you know whether Edwin has got the last letter I sent him about a week ago I think it was.   Monday afternoon

I will finish this letter now I guess. I drilled my Co this morning the first time for a long time I usually let the Sergt do it Jim my boy is greasing my boots now he says he wants to go home to Mass with me when the Regt time is out if he dont before says he can work on a farm or tend cattle + horses he used to drive an Omnibus I think he said before he run away from his Master in Ky. he says he is willing to do any thing I want him to + if I had any thing for him to do I would take him home with me + perhaps I shall. I have not fully discussed what I shall do for a living providing I live to come home. I guess I shall team it or rather have someone to drive my Team I shall pitch into some thing I guess my head will do what my hand cant or dont want to.

Our Pickets are on very friendly terms the rebs say that we shall have peace in 40 days. wood is pretty scarce here now + there was several large trees between the two picket lines so they proposed to come over with us + chop those trees and divide the wood I just now heard a man say that they had put up a flag of truce + where [were] chopping those trees now they sent over a woman + child a few days ago under a flag of truce our Div Provost Marshall Maj [James B.] Smith of our Regt. sent over a large bundle of orders to the Rebs a few days ago stating how we use their deserters + it is thought that many will come over I will not write any more this time. I hope I may be able to visit you in less than a month but dont know as I can. We are having very fine weather here now pleasant but cool no snow. I went into their prayer meeting last eve it was full about 50 several Officers.

Very Aff Yours George W.

Aunt Lydia Allen, and cousins Ada Jane Allen, and Mary Allen lived in Williamstown in 1860. Samuel Lothrop married George's Aunt Anna Moriah (Mariah) Harwood. They were in Adrian, Michigan. Peace in forty days from January 29 would be March 10.

Jan 30 :65

Brother Ethan

I dont see your hand writing every week as I told you. cant you write with that pen or do you have some thing else to do. how is the old horse fit for a trot if I come home by + by some old horse will have to take it you may bet if I am well as I am now. I shall try and find Lt Nichols of the 37 they are not far from here I believe. How many times have you got the mitting this winter? I have been lucky from the fact that there are few women here + they all use tobacco I suppose. I'm down on Southern Women for that if nothing else. You think you are pretty smart on a scuffle but I have got a boy 16 that can take you down every time. he is good at fighting. Write often

G. Harwood

[Paper is torn, some text is missing.]

Second Lieutenant Samuel E. Nickols was in the Massachusetts Thirty-seventh Regiment.

No 54

Camp of 36th Mass Vols
Fort Rice (before Petersburg) Va
Feb 5th 1865

Dear Friends

This is Sunday Morning. I will write a few lines as I am not particularly engaged. I am Officer of the day as usual. There are some rumours here this morning that there is going to be a move round on the left again but I dont know how true they are or whether they have any just ground for such rumours I have seen nothing very exciting as yet. I rec'd a letter from you yesterday with 10.00 all right. I dont know whether I had better send for any more or not I shall want I presume a good deal more if I dont come home + if I do I shall have to have some to get to Washington with. I cant get a furlough for more than a week to come if I do then, on the whole I will not send for any this time I expect Capt [Joseph] Hancock home about Thursday I presume he will have enough they paid him about 600.00 They owe me almost $600.00 but I have got some big bills to pay out of it. I have got my mind about mad[e] up to come home if I can possibly. I want to get me a few things that I ought to have I can get them here but they will cost more. There dont seem to be much news of importance here it is pretty much the same thing over + over, except a little excitement now and then. We have strict orders to have no communication with the enemy. some Officers allow it, by laying themselves liable to a dismissal or some other punishment others dont like to allow it I am one of that kind and a few nights ago I was on Picket and gave orders to have no communication with the enemy, that is trading for those were the orders I rec'd from the Brig Officer of the day at 10 o'clock that evening I missed some of my men + found out their names and watched them come in from the enemy's lines at that late hour. I suppose they had been trading with the rebs but they would not tell me what their business was but told me some out-rageous lies. I knew that they had no business there so I put them under arrest + they are there now waiting a Court Marshall 4 in number. it will be nothing very serious only stop a part of their pay perhaps. the Charge is Disobedience of Orders. Speceficulars in this that Private so + so did leave their post on the picket line on the night of the 31st of Jan and go toward the line of the enemy for the supposed purpose of trading in violation to positive order to have no communication with the enemy. Army Regulations say that a man leaving his post without leave shall suffer Death or such other punishment as shall be inflicted by the sentence of a Court-Marshall.

[Page was cut off at top.]   [undated]

Hear [? word cut off] our old Chaplain out side talking I guess he is going to have a meeting so I will go to that. do you forget to No your letters now or dont you count I notice that the last two were not numbered. I think I have numbered all mine. What do you think about this War's ever coming to a close, some of our ablest men seem to think that it will certainly close before many months. Vice President Stephens it seems has gone back to Richmond [from the Hampton Roads Conference, Feb. 3, 1865] I dont believe that he or [illegible] [Francis P.] Blair [Sr.] will do much good running <u>back + to</u> as my Grand-father used to say. I dont suppose that either of them have the authority to state on what terms either Government will settle the thing I understand that Stephens says they must have Slavery, but that they cant have. I came out to fight for the Slave all the Christians in the North have been praying for years that God would turn + overturn and set the bondmen free + now he is doing it, isnt he. how much so ever we want this war to end, we want it to be ended for the good of the people both North + South + certainly Slavery is a curse to all. the drum beats for Divine Services so I will go to meeting and finish this when I get through. we have a little Chapel that will hold 50 or more + it is comparitively comfortable

[Page was cut off at top.]

I cant say that I fancy a steel-pen very much I dont write much with one + never any letters that I care any thing how they look. I hope to be with you for a few days if nothing more [illegible]. Joe Walker has experienced religion out here he thinks often speaks out in the meetings they say I dont go very often except Sundays as I am on duty or at my tent doing something. I guess I will not write any more this time You need not look for me till you see me in Town.

Most Aff Yours George W. Harwood

Lt. 36th Mass. Vols

The Hampton Roads Conference was held on February 3, 1865 to discuss terms for ending the war. It was proposed by Francis P. Blair, Sr. after visiting President Davis. The Union was represented by President Lincoln, and Secretary of State William H. Seward. The Confederacy was represented by Vice-President Alexander H. Stephens, Senator Robert M.T. Hunter and Assistant Secretary of War John A. Campbell. The conference was not a success.

No 55

Camp of 36th Mass Vols

Fort Rice before Petersburg Va

Feb 9th 1865

Dear Friends

I received a letter from you this morning I was very glad to receive it as I always am, also to receive the Money. I have sent in a furlough and it is going up to Brigade this morning I hope to have it accepted but I dont know if it comes back as I expect I can start for NB about next monday or Tuesday, but dont look for me too much for I may not come. it is going to be a pretty expensive job but I can get some clothing that I want and shall have to get me a sword and perhaps barr + sash, dress coat &c &c I received a letter from Mr. Cushing a few days ago but if I can come home I shall not answer it but if I cant I shall by + by. I am feeling pretty well and begin to feel anxious to see home for a few days perhaps I shall conclude to reinlist. I received Photographs from Ada [Jane] + Mary Allen, they look a little alike, but not much as I expected they did. we are having fine Weather here but rather cool I am not going to write a long letter this time for I hope to be able to talk with you soon + not write it all. I am in a hurry this morning as you will see by my writing it is about as bad as Mr Cushings or Capt [Henry S.] Burrage they always write on the jump. Freeman I want you should drive my colt some so that she will know what it is to do something. I am going to leave my Colored Populate with Capt [Joseph] Hancock. I have got several other letters to write so I will not stop to write any longer this time. in about a week from now if nothing happens and all prospers I shall be with you for a short time.

I remain as ever

Yours Aff

George W. Harwood

Populate could mean people, his servant (boy), his cook, and his company clerk.

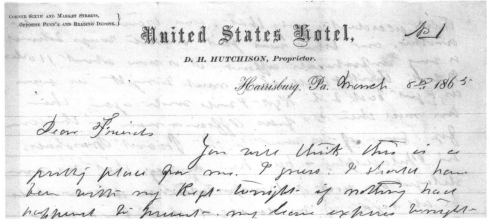

Harrisburg Hotel, March 8, 1865 letter (Image from author's collection)

Corner Sixth and Market Streets,
    Opposite Penn'a and Reading Depots.}   No 1

United States Hotel

D. H. HUTCHISON, Proprietor.

Harrisburg, Pa. March 8th 1865

Dear Friends
    You will think this is a pretty place for me I guess. I should have been with my Regt tonight if nothing had happened to prevent. my leave expires tonight We came through to Philadelphia without trouble but could go

no further, as the Susquihanna river is full of floating ice so we went to the Continental Hotel + put up till this afternoon + then found that we might have to stay in the City several days more, at an expense of 4.50 per day, so we concluded to go by the way of Harrisburg. it is about 125 miles out of our way, but probably the cheapest + quickest was for us under the present circumstances. we arrived here at 6 this evening we shall leave for Baltimore at 2 1/2 tomorrow morning. I expect to get to the Regt on Friday night. the Engine gave out 2 or 3 times coming from Philadelphia here perhaps you saw by the paper that an accident happened near Bristol 5 men killed + 40 wounded all or nearly all paroled prisoners, going home on furloughs. I dont know the particulars of this accident only that one train ran into another. our train was just a little ways behind a very unfortunate affair. it is now about 11 o'clock I dont think I shall sleep much tonight as soon as I get back to the Regt I will write again there are more than 50 of us Officers + men in the same fix. some of us went to the Provost Marshalls in Philadelphia + had him certify that we were delayed on acct of transportation so that we shall be all right if we dont get there for a week I presume. this has been a pretty expensive + not very pleasant trip for me so far since I left home I lost my valice in New York but I found it again in a few hours, but every thing seems to work wrong end first with me. I felt the worst to leave home this time then I ever have before, but I guess I did not show it much I did not intend to at any rate. now I will go into the barbers shop + have my mustache shaved off. the bar-room is a pretty place to write a letter. I should think this was a pretty good Hotel by the looks. good night I hope I shall have no more trouble in getting to the Regt. write soon

Aff Yours

George W. Harwood

On March 7, 1865, two express trains of the Pennsylvania Railroad, on the Philadelphia to Trenton north bound line collided at 2:30 a.m. Five soldiers on furlough and a fireman were killed. Weiser, page 24.

No 2   Camp of 36th Regt. Mass. Vols.

Fort Rice (before Petersburg) Va

March 12/65

Dear Friends,

  I arrived at my Regt on Friday night 2 days behind time, but that is all right I guess. Yesterday forenoon we had a Battallion drill in the afternoon Guard mounting &c, very different from the quiet scens of home. I found all the Officers + men in fine spirits, meeting or rather apparently glad to see me. last evening I attended the prayer class meeting, had a very pleasant time. this is Sunday morning. I almost wish myself at home whare I was one week ago. I expect however to attend Divine Services today. it is now almost time for our Regimental Inspection which comes off at 10 o'clock. Yesterday I paid up my bills my Sutlers bill was $80.00. I sold both my watches now I wish I had my old brass one from home. I find that I have more money left then I expected to have, about $74.00. We are having very fine weather here warm and pleasant   it is muddy in places but not very bad. I see no reason why this Army cannot move before long, but I dont see any signs of it at present I suppose they are waiting for Genl. Sherman Genl. Sheriden did a good thing when he captured so much of Genl. Early's Army.

Our Col. is trying to bring this Regt into better discipline. he says that the men are too familiar with their men. here after they are not expected to associate very much with their men + the men are ordered to salute all their Officers, but I dont think I shall be told who to associate with if I am I shall do as I please about heeding it. I have got to go on Picket tonight I was on Picket last sunday night + if I have as pleasant trip this time as I did then I shant feel very bad I hope the time will fly as quickly. I saw Dr. Fisk + Mr George Forbes of E Brookfield at Fortress Monroe they came down as far as City Point to visit the front. I some expect they will come up + see me. It is now most time to go on Picket so I will not stop to write much more. let me hear from you very often. Remember me to the friends. I suppose Uncle Bartletts folks are feeling pretty badly about the death of their little boy, but the poor little fellow is better off now I hope. My Valice got into a crowd several times coming out + broke that bottle of Mr Spooners in spite of me. I could'nt possibly take it in my pockets for they were all too full. I am sorry that it is broken but I cannot help it. I find that George [Spooner] is some 10 miles from here but I should have tried to find him + I may now. You can tell Mr Spooner how it is if you please.

Good Bye

George W. Harwood

In early 1865 Confederate General Jubal Early still had troops in the Shenandoah Valley. On March 2, Union General George Custer, under General Sheridan, routed these remaining troops and captured many of them, resulting in the final en-

gagement in the Shenandoah Valley. City Point was the location of General Grant's headquarters on the James River near Petersburg. Uncle Elias and Aunt Caroline Allen Bartlett's son Oshea A. died March 6, 1865, of typhoid fever, age fourteen.

No 3   Camp of 36th Regt Mass Vols.
                                            Fort Rice before Petersburg Va
                                            March 17/65

Dear Friends

I have been here with my Regt just one week tonight, but have not had a letter from home or any whare else as yet. I have been looking for a letter from you for a day or two. I think it will shurely come tomorrow. I shall not send this letter till then. We are having more duty to do now than before I went home. we drill an hour in the forenoon + an hour in the afternoon + have a school for Officers in the evening. Day before yesterday we had orders to pack up and be ready for a move at a moment's notice. we packed up but did not move. it is very evident that there will be a move in this vicinity before long, but I am unable to settle in my mind at what point the attack will be made. it has been rumoured that a part of this Army is going to support Sheridan but that we have no good foundation for. it has been reported here in camp today that Sheridan ~~was~~ is within 15 miles of Richmond and still another that he is within a few hours ride of our extreme left. this however is hardly probable. I see no reason why this Army cannot move very soon unless they are waiting for Genl Sherman or Sheridan to co-operate with them. I flatter myself that this Spring and Summer campaign will end the most of our hard fighting. I should like to see the end of this re-bellion. I should like to be in the service at its close. If I rightly understand the territory now in the enemy's hands + their limited means to fill up their thinned ranks or even cloth and feed their present Army, it looks to me like uphill work, enough to discourage them. they must by this time read their in-evitable doom with gloom + dispondency. Deserters come in nearly every night on our Brigade they all tell the same doleful stories, which we have every reason to believe to some extent are true. Now it is past roll-call about time to retire my humble bed of pine boards is ready I suppose to receive me. that shell that came into my tent while I was at home is under my bunk now it weighs 32 lbs. a pretty little ball to be throwing through the air, is'nt it? I hope they will remember hereafter that they are careless things to play with and keep them at home. I hear the troops cheering in the rear I am inclined to think that they have just heard some good news. I wish I knew for they cheer so loudly.

Saturday afternoon: I received a letter + paper from you this morning. was very glad indeed to hear from you. I had a good drill this forenoon. I had 2 Cos. Capt [Joseph] Hancock is Officer of the day, so I took his + drilled in the skirmish. We have no drill this afternoon. the weather is warm + the ground dry. I trade watches some, day before yesterday I had 3 different ones. I had none in the morning + none at night. I have one now. I wish that Snell had come home home while I was there, but it is all the same now. a few furloughs are being granted now. What do you think about our Vice President Andy Johnson getting drunk at the Inauguration. that dont look just right does it? I thought he was a different man than that. it seems almost as warm as Summer here now real dusty + dry, but it may rain in 2 days and be very muddy the sacred soil of Virginia will do for those who like it but I cant say that I like it any better than I do old New England, but I suppose it is all because "Thare is no place like home." I like my sword first rate all who see it call it a little beauty + cheap at the price I gave for it. I guess it will do me for 6 months. The Orderly Sergt of Co E used to be foreman of the out of door work at the State Alms house in Monson, the job that you say Ed has taken. I should think it might be a good place. You dont suppose that Oshea death will kill Uncle Elias do you? but I will draw this to a close hoping to hear from you often I remain as ever   Your Aff. Son + Brother

George W

General Sherman was in North Carolina. March 7-10 he captured Kinston at the battle of Wyse Fork. On March 16 he approached Averasboro, south of Raleigh but was held back by General Johnston's troops. Confederate troops retreated temporarily. Major General Sheridan rejoined the Army of the Potomac in the Siege of Petersburg before the Battle of Five Forks on April 1, 1865. Edwin F. Doane was listed as a farmer at the State Alms House in Monson, Massachusetts, Census 1870.

No 4   Camp of 36th Regt Mass Vols
Fort Rice before Petersburg Va
March 24 /65

Dear Friends

      I received a letter from you this morning I was very glad to hear from you again. We are having a good deal of wind here now. the wind has blown hard for nearly a week, most all of the chimneys have blown off, but mine is all right. I have got a little dirt or some thing in my eye, and it pains me all the time most since last night I can hardly follow my lines. Dont you think that the War news is good taking every thing into acct. The papers say that President Lincoln thinks there will be but very little more fighting. 15 deserters came in to our Brigade a few nights ago. they say that they are about played out. Sherman + Schofield are said to be doing great things. I shall stop writing till my eye feels better.

Friday evening.   my eye feel much better this evening, so I will re-sume my writing. I have found several very interesting books to read lately. one Rose Clark by Fannie [Fanny] Fern a beautiful thing Romantic yet Reli-gious. should you ever come across it I know you would be interested in reading it. (especially Mother + Anna) another is the Color Bearer, [by] Francis A. Clary Sergt of the 31st Mass Vols killed at Port Hudson. beside these I have borrowed several Magazins + papers. I think a good deal of Pe-tersons Ladis [Ladies] maternal Magazine, monthly terms 2.00 a year. it is well worth it. Every one feels very hopeful just now that this war will soon cease, some say within one month others say that before the 4th of July, oth-ers say that they hope to celebrate the fourth in Mass. but I fear that the end is not so near. I do think if we can rely on what the papers say that our terms of service will see at least the beginning of the end 5 months more only. I should like to be in the service at its close. wont that be a glorious time, when we go marching home. Freeman you say that Uncle Wm folks were coming up to see me Sunday night ~~had~~ if Uncle David had not gone down there to sing, but I am afraid that they would have lost their journey or wasted rather late. I was on duty that night, got very little sleep, it was not very tedious however.

Saturday forenoon.   We were aroused this morning at 4 o'clock by a charge on our right nearly in front of Meads Station. the rebs drove in our Pickets + I think took one of our Forts, but I understand that we retook all the ground we lost + ~~that the~~ some prisoners. the enemy's loss in killed + wounded is said to be quite heavy. heavy Artillery firing and also musketry, it filled the air with one continual roar of thunder + shells. We fell in + stacked arms. it lasted from 4 to 8 in fact it has not wholy ceased yet As I find out more about it I will write more particularly.

Until then Adieu

George W.

(over)

There are various rumors as to the number of prisoners taken this morning. it is thought that we have not seen the last of it yet they have been having a fight on our extreme left since. We are now under marching orders. I will write again soon. we took somewhere from 2500 to 5000. they took Gen McLaughin prisoners. our loss is not said to be very heavy you will see it in the papers I presume, more correct than I am able to give it now. I will write again soon. Providence permitting

George W.

General Sherman was moving north on the Carolina Campaign. Lieutenant General John M. Schofield under Sherman was moving inland from the coast of North Carolina. Digital copies of the two books he was reading are available at the Internet Archive, Rose Clark *by Fanny Fern,1856, https://archive.org/details/roseclark00ferngoog* The Color-bearer *by Francis A. Clary, 1864, https://archive.org/details/colorbearerfranc01amer Peterson published the* Ladies' National Magazine *beginning in 1842. George may be referring to Uncles William Allen and either David Allen or David L. Winslow who met for an evening of singing. Meade Station was on the eastern side of the Petersburg lines; this engagement took place just before the Battle of Fort Stedman on the western end of the line, on March 25. General Napoleon Bonaparte McLaughlin (McLoughlin) was captured at the Battle of Fort Stedman. He was released in April.*

No 5

Camp of 36th Regt Mass Vols
Fort Rice before Petersburg Va
March 30th 1865

Dear Friends,

I have just received No 3 from you. You say that Father has got into office I saw it in the paper sometime ago but never thought to speak of it. then he thinks that my last letter was the best I have ever sent home, perhaps it was. I suppose that there was more war about it. I suppose you have read long before this all about the fight on the 25th. our loss is said to be about 800 while that of the enemy is about 5,000. this includes killed, wounded + prisoners. President Lincoln, Genl's Grant, Sherman, Sheridan + others held a council of War at City Point a few days ago. Genl Sheridan started with his Army + a part of this Yesterday morning for the left. he will be very likely to cut the South-side R. R. + so cut off their supplies, also form a connection with Shermans Army. The 34th Mass. have gone with him. they have been up in the [Shenandoah] valley or with the Army of the James of late. Within two weeks we may look for hard bloody battles, perhaps the most desperate that have ever been fought during the war. I have but little doubt as to the success. I am so confident that Victory will be ours. we may [have] met with defeats for a while, perhaps we may even expect them, but the end of this rebellion is not very far distant. We are expecting an attack on our lines in our immediate front. we fell in last night at a falts [false] alarm, at 10 o'clock but soon retired again. our things are nearly all packed up. we are looking for them tomorrow morning, if they should come, there will be some bloody work I assure you. it is now past role-call so I will go to bed + finish this some other time. ~~George~~ Charles Davis is not more than 1/2 mile from me + has been all winter I did not know it till yesterday. I have not seen him yet one of the Monson boys have. he sent word that he would come + see me. he did not know that I was here. he is in the 1st Connecticut [Heavy] Artillery right in sight of us. I mean to see him before long.

Friday Morning   we were rousted early this morning and ordered to be ready, but it was raining so we did not go. perhaps we should not have gone if it had been pleasant. the Artillery has commenced on the left now it has stopped raining. I dont think we shall leave here today. Has Andrew found a job yet or dont you know. I have been thinking for a long time I would write to Mr Cushing + Mrs Batcheller but I have not taken the time yet. I dont find any thing new to write in particular the same thing day after day. I am pretty busy just now making out my returns of Ordnance + Ordnance stores, also Clothing, Camp + Garrison Equipage, monthly return of Company. I will not stop to write any more this time but will write again in a few days if nothing happens. Remember me to all the friends + write often Do you know whare Uncle Joseph is now?

Aff Yours

George W.

The Confederates' final attack of the war was March 25 against Union Fort Stedman. Initially they captured the Fort, but the Union re-took it. President Lincoln was at City Point from the end of March until the fall of Petersburg. He met with General Grant, General Sherman and Rear Admiral Porter to discuss the ending of the war. His meetings are depicted in the 1868 painting Peacemakers *by George P.A. Healy, which is in the White House art collection. Uncle Joseph W. Harwood lived in both Illinois and Wisconsin.*

~ Chapter 12 ~

PETERSBURG, FARMVILLE, CITY POINT, VIRGINIA
April 4 - 29, 1865

First Federal wagon train entering Petersburg   ***(Courtesy Library of Congress)***

No 6   On the march April 4th/65

Dear Friends,

      You will see by this heading that I am in Fort Rice no longer. the 9th Corps took Petersburg Sunday the 2nd Genl [Edward O. C.] Ord entered Richmond the same day with Negro troops the Rebel Genl [A. P.] Hill is killed. we took a great many prisoners. I dont know how many but you will see by the papers a more correct 'acct' than I can give. We started yesterday morning from Petersburg towards Lynchburg. We halted last night about 10 miles from P[etersburg]. We have now halted for dinner. The men are all in fine spirits. We did not lose any men in taking Petersburg. Our Regt was left in Fort Rice. Gen [John G.] Parke made his HdQrs there during the fight + requested that we sho[u]ld stay for a kind of guard, Provost Guard. I had charge of a part of the line halting skeedadlers. I packed up all my things + put them in the teams except my Over-Coat + Haversack but I have picked up a woolen Blanket + tent now Lieut Wright of Co F has come up now, so I have turned over my Command to him + am now in Command of Co E, my old Co. Capt Fairbaks [John B. Fairbank] is adj Maj so you will direct to Co E I cannot give you a correct acct of our doings this past week, for there are so many many rumours. I can only say that Glorious Victories have attended our Armies. President Lincoln came over into Petersburg with us. Oh! how the boys did cheer. I wish I could see you now + tell you all about it but but I cannot and time will not permit me to write it. all is confusion the men cheering at the prisoners that are marching past us. the Rebs are all broken up + Sheridan is making horrid works with them You will see it all in the papers so I will not write much about it. when I come home I will tell you. You have no Idea how the men felt, so gay + happy. these are the brightest days we ever saw, Individualy + as a nation There is much that I want to write but time will not permit. The streets of Petersburg were lined with Darkeys so glad to see us. They could'nt do enough for us giving us water + tobacco. one Young Negro lady came out with tobacco + gave to the boys she handed me the last hand I made her a polite by she saw that I was a commissioned officer. you ought to have seen her whirl + run, so pleased at a by + smile. I will add a few lines before I send this if I have time. I received a letter from Lizzie Gilbert this morning.   Aff.

George W.

The sides of the road are lined with blankets Tents Knapsacks haversack[s] + clothing.

Wednesday 6th.   The mail goes out this morning. I say [saw] George Spooner this morning he is well looking finely, says he dont care any thing about that medicine I lost. We are now about 30 miles from P. [Petersburg] on the South Side R.R. bound for Burkville [Burkeville]. We had a good long hard march yesterday. I stood it well, my stood it well my load is not so heavy. I dont have to cary my Knapsack or rations. I presume you are very anxious to hear from me. I should have sent this before but no mail has gone out for a few days, nor come in either. Our Wagon train is 17 miles long 6 mules or horses to a wagon then there is several batteries along with us. I saw Charles Davis the day before we left Petersburg. every thing seems to be working for our good. we all feel hopeful that the end draweth near. I will not stop to write any more this time. but let me hear from you often Remember + direct to Co E.

George W Harwood

Confederate General A.P. Hill was killed when the Union broke through the Confederate line on April 2. Petersburg fell on April 2. On April 3 George's regiment accompanied President Lincoln into Petersburg, the beginning of the Union occupation of that city and of Richmond. They then moved southwest towards Lynchburg in pursuit of General Lee's retreating Confederate army. Richmond fell on April 2-3 and President Davis fled the city. When General Grant's troops reached Farmville on April 7, he began exchanging letters of surrender with General Lee. The formal surrender was at Appomattox Court House on Sunday April 9, 1865.

No 7   Farmville Va Apr 11/65

Dear Friends

I am now sitting at my window in the third story of the principle Hotel in this place. Our Col is Provost Marshall of the Town. Gen Lee has surrended his Army to Grant 30,000 prisoners. This morning Genls Grant, Ord + several others with their staffs came into this place stopped at this Hotel One of the staff told me that this War was about ended that in the course of 2 months I should probably have a chance to go home for those where time is out in the fall of 65 would be likely to be disbanded first, (by the way I am acquainted with a few of the staff officers that is the reason I come to talk with them.) I dont much expect ever to go into another hard fight we are doing provost duty now for a while in this place. I think I shall like it much better than marching.

Wednesday Morning.   I understand that a mail will go out this morning so I will finish this letter. Gen Meade has come into the place + he + his staff now occupy the Hotel so we have taken quarters in another building. Gen Sheridan passed through here yesterday The 6th Corps is passing through here to the rear this fighting is now nearly over. the time is not far from here when we can return to our own homes + again persue business of a different character I long for that glad day to come, though I do not consider my life in that danger that I did 2 weeks ago. will there not be joy in old Mass when her sons come marching home Victorious, not as they went away with 1000 strong but very thin ranks of 200 or 300. doubtless many homes will be filled with sadness at the one or more vacant chairs, but let this be their consolation they have given their lives in a noble cause. I know that it would do you good to hear our bands play, the men cheer. last evening we had a concert or rather negro minstral perform- ance in the Hotel. they painted about a Doz of the boys. the citizens in this place are nearly all red-hot Rebs. they are Mad to hear our soldiers cheer so + that suits us all the better, but the Negrous are all so happy they will do any thing for us that we can ask one of them mended my boots this morning. I understand that the people at home are having a regular drink over these Victories some of us here do. that is one way to express this joy. I shall have to begin to think of some business for myself to pursue. I never desire[?] any thing yet at home. I have earned a position here in the Army but I dont propose to make this my business. I guess I shall better cheer for one week at least but I have not time to write any more this time as the mail is about to go out.

Very Aff Yours

George W Harwood

The Provost Marshal was responsible for maintaining order and carrying out other policing functions. In Farmville they were issuing paroles to the Confeder- ate soldiers. The Historical Marker on the site of the hotel states:

SITE OF THE RANDOLPH HOUSE

"Here stood the hotel where General U.S. Grant made his headquarters April 7, 1865, and opened correspondence with General R.E. Lee which terminated in the surrender of the Army of Northern Virginia at Appomat- tox Court House two days later. From the porch of the Randolph House, Grant reviewed segments of his army — the last wartime review. The hotel was erected in 1859, and included Morton's Tavern built in 1798. The hotel collapsed during restoration in 1964. This marker was erected by Joseph E. Wood, last proprietor of the Randolph House."

No 8   Farmville Va Apl 12/65

Dear Friends

Although I have just sent a letter to you, I will commence another and send when I have a chance. The mail does not go very regularly now for a lit- tle while. Troops are passing through this place now + the bands are all playing. they are bound some of them for Richmond some Petersburg I suppose. I understand that the 5th + 24th Corps are going to Richmond to do duty there. some say they are going home very soon but I dont think it would do to disband to much of our Army at once. there is work yet to do. perhaps Gen Sherman will want more help. if not I should think that we should have to send some troops down to Texas. Our Government is about ready to fight with Foreign nations if they see fit England has not used us just right since this war commenced you know! but I think that our late Victories will change the feelings of other nation[s] somewhat, for we have shown that we can put down a rebellion in our own land. I think that our Government will ever after this be stronger and more united than ever before. I do not feel sorry that I enlisted at all, though I have passed through many unpleasant seasons but it has been a school well worth attending. Thousands of dollars would not pay the tuition. The more I think of it the more I feel glad that I have made that advancement that I have, having made this advancement may make some difference with my after life

Friday morning.   after several days of dull rainy weather it has cleared off and is very fair + pleasant. There are Thousands of Reb prisoners in this place some have been paroled some are being paroled now Capt Fairbanks [John B. Fairbank] is Assistant Provost Marshall + is paroling as fast as he can has got 2 or 3 clerks. We give each one days rations. They are going to their homes as fast as they can. some of them seem to be glad and willing others are little more stubborn. most of the citizens in this place are strong rebs, but say that we have whipped them. I wish you could see the amount of Tobacco that there is in this place. The boys have all they want now. some of our boys who are cigar makers have a chance to make their own cigars now. The is a Female Seminary here in this place 120 girls. I have not seen many of them. they are shy as foxes. The lady who runs this house + lives down below is a very fine woman I should judge she has 5 children all small. There are several old Gentlemen in this place who have invited us to call on them at any time, come and stay all night, willing to give us the best they have. There are 100's of Negroes hanging round the streets doing nothing want something to do. we set them to work cleaning off the sidewalk after the rain for it was muddy. I have got a little chap to work for me. he works for his board sometimes I think that I shall get home by the 4th of July but I dont much expect to get home before my 3 years are out shall be pretty will [illegible] to get home then. I wish I knew what to go to doing then I guess I am too lazy to work much

Saturday Morning.   I received a letter from you yesterday, so I will write a little more and and send it. I should think that Father would have his hands full this summer to attend to all his business. I think that Judson Adams has done pretty well to pay so much but I guess he worked pretty hard last Winter. I have been thinking for a few days past that I would go out + visit Uncle Washington, [Uncle] Joseph, Mr [Oramel] Rugg + [Uncle] Abel Harwood &c when this war is over or when my time is out, and if I like I will find a job if not go back home again. I should like to see how Mr [Uncle] Abel Harwood is situated. I have been thinking for some time that I would write to Uncle Joseph but I dont know as I shall. I understand that there has been an order sent for our Regt to go to City Point to guard Commissary stores from the [City] Point to Burkville that will be a good job but I am afraid that we shall not go, but still we hope to. I like here in this place pretty well but I dont suppose we shall remain here long. I guess I told you that my darky Jim that I had when I was at home ran away just before I left Petersburg but I have got another now Simon is his name the first thing I see in the morning when I wake up is my boy blaking [blacking] my boots. he sleeps with my cook but comes to my room early every morning + slicks things up for me. I wish you could see the little girls here about Fannie size put a pail of water on their heads and cary off. they dont pretend to cary anything in their hands or tout it as they call it. Our Baggage is coming up tonight I understand that that they are on the road. if so I shall dress up and go to Church tomorrow, but I will not stop to write any more this time for I sent a letter to you a few days ago + will write again soon. I guess you had better send a few postage samps [stamps] for I have got short + I see that there is no chance to get them here at present

Aff. Yours

George W.

General Sherman headed to Raleigh, North Carolina. President Davis is fleeing to Greensboro, North Carolina. The war in Texas ended June 19 when Major General Gordon Granger brought the news of the surrender at Appomattox to Galveston, and the announcement of the Emancipation Proclamation, which was issued January 1, 1863. Juneteenth continues to be celebrated as Independence Day or Freedom Day for formerly enslaved people. In June 2021 the day became a Federal holiday. The Farmville Female Seminary Association, established in 1839 is now Longwood University. Family members George would like to visit were: Great-uncle

Abel Harwood and his brother-in-law, Great-uncle Oramel Rugg, in Bloomington, Illinois. Uncle Washington Harwood was near Adrian, Michigan. Uncle Joseph W. Harwood was in either Jacksonville or Dixon City, Illinois.

No 9   Farmville Va. Apl 17/65

Dear Friends

I have just been relieved from duty. I have had charge of the Rebel prisoners. I have drawn and issued more than 150 rations I could not help thinking how badly they used our prisoners, + if they were in our places how badly they would be likely to treat us, but I have no heart to misuse any of them. We treat them as well as we do our own men. News reached us last night of the assassination of President Lincoln, [and the attack on] Secretary [of State] Seward + son sad sad affair. Every Officer + man + even the citizens in this place are filled with the highest indignation. You cannot imagine what a sensation it has created and will create throughout the land. We have lost a dear friend, the South have lost their <u>best</u> friend + they know it. our Vice President is as unlike him as Black from White we learn tonight that there is great hopes of Seward's recovering. I hope that will prove true. I understand that they have taken this Booth who shot Lincoln. I dont know what punishment can be inflicted upon him that will be severe enough, hanging is to good so is shooting. We are taught in the Bible that our Heavenly Father does all things well, and for our best good, but I fear that too many of us fail to realize it at the present time. I dont know as I ever felt so indignant in my life, yet at the same time sad. perhaps it is all right I hope it + try to feel so. it seems as though his faithful services were needed now more than ever. It is hard telling what Johnson will do but let us hope for the best, and trust in an ever over ruling providence and all will be well. I saw Snell today he said that this assassination was next to the crucifixion of Christ I think he was more than half right, but I have been thinking tonight that perhaps we have trusted to much to our President and not enough in our God, and for that reason he has suffered this affliction to be brought upon us, using this means to bring us nearer to himself. viewing it in this light should we <u>not use</u> it as a means of bringing us into closer communion with our blessed Saviour should we not trust more fully in him who has the rule over us. I know for one I have thought to much of this life + not enough of the life which is to come. I fear it has been to true of us as a Nation. I had hoped that our President would live to see the end of this conflict and enjoy the blessings of a redeemed country, yet many years. though he has passed away from earth, his name will live after him, and will be handed down to future generations like that of Washingtons + others, for the Noble deeds he has done. I will not fill my whole sheet upon this subject though I would like to fill a Doz if I could only find words to express my mind, but above all things else we have the consolation that our lamented President was prepared to meet his God. he has lived a good life, a life worthy of imitation and is now I trust at rest. though he is dead to us he will yet live throughout the endless ages of eternity, + his name will live in history for ages yet to come. Yesterday I attended Church all day. it seemed the most like sunday that it has for a long time. as I sat in my room looking out of the window I could not help think how Nature itself seemed to say that it was the Sabbath, for every thing was so quiet so lovely. the birds sang never so sweetly. my mind wandered back to my home, so far away. I could imagine how you all looked Oh! how I longed to be with you We do not expect to remain here in this place many days longer I understand that we are ordered to Burkville soon. no one knows whare we shall go to from there. We hear that there is good news from Sherman but no particulars as yet. Capt [Henry S.] Burrage has been reenstated and is now on Gen Curtis's staff our Brigade Commander. he is looking finely + had a good deal of news to tell. I shall be glad when my 3 years expire though I sometimes think I should like to follow the military service through life.

Tuesday Morning.　　　The boys are putting up our Flag this morning across the street. there is a man in the place about 50 I should judge who tore down the Union Flag when this rebellion broke out and threatened to burn the building if they put out other. they say that when they get our flag up they are going to make the man cheer whether he wants to or not. I hope they will. There is our old Col here, who was Col of a Malithia [Militia] Regt when this war broke out. he resigned and being an old man they let him remain at home in charge of a Depot. he is in his glory now. we have every reason to believe he is a good Union man. I received a Springfield Republican last mail. We do not get our mail every day since we have been here Our Brigade is going to have a concert in the Hall of the Hotel this evening I dont [know] whether I shall go or not guess I shall. they are going to paint up about a Doz of our Musicians and comical fellows and call them Negro Minstrals it will do for a change I suppose.　　　　　　　　　　　　　[unsigned]

The Assassination Plot targeted three men, President Lincoln, Secretary of State Seward and Vice-President Johnson. Lincoln was killed by John Wilkes Booth. William F. Seward, his son Frederick, and a nurse were wounded by Lewis Powell. George Atzerodt failed to follow through on his assignment to assassinate Johnson. The Springfield Republican *was a Massachusetts newspaper.*

I sent for stamps in my last letter but I dont care so much about them now + can get them here.

No 10   City Point Va. Apl 22/65

Dear Friends

We left Farmville yesterday morning we reached Burkville last night a distance of 18 miles. We took the cars there for this place got here a little before light, this morning. We expect to start tomorrow or next day for Washington, for what purpose we do not know. they are ordering back to their Regt all the sick that are able to move. the Surgeons tell them that they will get discharged quicker with their Regt then in a hospital. The 9th Corps is all ordered to W-[Washington] We have it from good authority that the 62 [1862] men are to be discharged or furloughed to report in case of emergency. We are all hoping that we shall get out of the service some way the quicker the better. all are anxious to try civil life again. I should'nt be surprised if you saw me at home in the course of 3 or 4 weeks. May 1st the Government will owe me 4 month pay, making about 500.00 for me. I am getting short of money now and I wish you would send me about 10.00, as quickly as convenient. I hope that will last till get paid off I bought a pr of pants today so that it redused my small pile much smaller. Freeman ask Charles Bush if he still wants me to bring my Negro for a Hostler. I have got a good one now about 20 [illegible] smart. he told me he wanted one, and if I should come in a month or two I can bring him I think he will suit him I know. I wish you could see the Artillery here that we took from the Rebs. I was surprised to see how destitute the Rebs were all their mules + horses were poor the men said that they had not had any thing but corn for several days. the citizens at Farmville had lost every thing most no seed to plant no teams to do it with, no nothing. We all sadly lament the death of our late President. I have been reading the Washington Chronicle today. I see that there were women connected with his Assassination. they are worse than an armed fox. I hope you will not think that I flatter myself too much that I shall get out of service much if any before my time is out for fear I shall get disappointed. I think that the fighting is pretty much over, and my pay is good but I will gladly take less pay, and lead a more civilized life. I dont know what I shall do when I get home. most of the boys say they wont do any thing but visit for 6 months perhaps it will be so with me but I doubt it some. We do not learn that Gen Johnson [Johnston] has surrendered yet but it is expected every day that he will. When he + Gen Smith surrender the thing is about done, except cleaning out the copperheads in the North which is very important. I did not hear much of it when I was at home yet I know that such feelings do exist in the North. I will not write a long letter this time. I simply write to let you know that I am all right. I received letter No 5 from [you] + a Springfield Republican a few days ago, a pretty short letter I called that 1/2 sheet. could'nt you find anything more to write? but good Bye

George W. Harwood

A military railroad ran around the southern side of the Union occupied area south of Petersburg. It was a major supply line for the regiments. The regiments took the railroad cars to City Point, on the eastern end, General Grant's headquarters. The Union troops camped in Washington and Alexandria, Virginia for the Grand Review on May 23-24. The 1862 men had served most of their three years and were eligible for discharge. Mary Surratt's boarding house was the location where the assassinations were planned.

No 11   City Point Va. Apl 29/65

Dear Friends,

Our Regt left here several days ago but 3 Cos. of us are left to load the Div wagon train we shall probably leave here in 2 or 3 days at least. There is no news of much importance of late except that Gen Johnston has surrendered to Grant. Gen Sherman made a sad mistake. he was at one time the most popular Gen we had, but is now far from it. Grant is the man. There has been an order issued from the War Department that all Officers in the U.S. Service shall wear a strip of black crape around their left arm and on their sword for 6 months 100 guns were fired here yesterday in the afternoon in honor of Johnstons surrender. Capt [Joseph] Hancock + Lt [George A.] Perley went up to Richmond + back yesterday they say that they were well paid for going. I should like first rate to go myself. We are having pretty dry weather here quite dusty. I suppose you are about getting ready to plant I imagine I see Father with a pair of old horses + steers. A good many of the boys think that we are going to be mustered out soon, but I hardly think we shall for 4 month, then our time will be out. I dont see what they want of us all now for I think that most if not all the fighting is over. I really hope it is. it is said that Booth was shot in Port Royal. I sent home in my last letter for more money I thought that 10.00 would be all I should want but I find that we shall not get our Pay quite as quick as I then thought we should and should like a little more. I have not got any mail for a week. our Corps being at Washington, our mail stops there. I expect that there will be a stack of letters for me when I get them. I will write again when I get some where beside this place. I dont like to write on my knee very well + I have no news in particular to write. Father what are you going to do with that Colt this summer she ought to have a good pasture + see if she wont grow a little.

Aff Yours

George W.

On April 26, General Johnston surrendered to General Sherman near Raleigh, North Carolina. The arrangements and terms Sherman offered Johnston have been a source of controversy ever since. John Wilkes Booth died of a gunshot wound at Garret's farm near Port Royal, Virginia on April 26, 1865.

~ *EPILOGUE* ~

VIRGINIA, WASHINGTON CITY, HOME

~ Chapter 13 ~

ALEXANDRIA, WASHINGTON, MUSTERED OUT
May 6 - June 9, 1865

Sunday morning I have just been relieved from Guard I have the advantage of you. Mail goes here Sunday as well as any day.

No 12   Near Alexandria Virginia
                                               [Saturday] May 6th 1865

Dear Friends

　　　We arrived here a few days ago. I think I wrote in my last letter that 3 Cos of us were going to remain at City Point for a few days to load the Wagon train. After waiting several days they concluded to send the train the overland rout, so we took a Steamer Manhatten + landed at Alexandria. We are encamped a very little ways from Fort Lyon in an orchard of Apple + Peach trees. After ~~we left~~ the Regt left I think the day before we started some Colored troops were brought out to discharge their pieces into a bank but some of them fired to high and came over into our Camp. We all hugged the ground. they hit 2 of Co "K" 21st one of them died in 10 minutes he had served nearly 4 years been through every thing and was Setting upon going home in a few days, so he did but not alive he was at once embalmed and sent home that next morning. his Co. felt very badly about it, so we all did. Today Myron Sherman and a Glassmore boy came over to see Bell they told me that Sam Maxwell was with them in Fort Williams about 1 1/2 miles from here. When I come up to the Regt I found 7 letters for me, 2 from home. the next day 3 more came 2 more from home. the 10.00 came all safe. I dont see any prospect of our being paid off for a while probably not till we get mustered out. I shall want to use some as I shall have to get a few new things in order to look as well as any body, (as Col [Thaddeus L.]Barker says he wants this Regt to look as well as any body's) We are drilling and preparing for a Grand Review and perhaps march through Washington, then we shall probably be mustered out if that should take till the first of June I shall want to use 30.00. I see no one here of whom I would like to borrow, so I wish you would send it. I shall probably have enough by + by to pay it back. Freeman now business is so dull I would like to have you come out + see me again. You do not have to have a pass now to go from Washington to Alexandria and we are not more than 2 or 3 miles from the City. What do you think will you come and bring my watch and some money. I have sold my watch or rather traided it for a large pistol a shooter I intend to bring that home with me. Capt [John B.] Fairbank + I have got a large wall tent and have pretty good times. Capt is going to be on a Court Marshall which sits on Monday I think. I was very much pleased with those Photographs you sent me they look very natural now if I had Fannie I should have the Family. I guess you had better have hers taken like the ones Allen + I had. it will only cost 50 cts I wish I could get it. I am am Lt of the guard today so I will not stop to write any more tonight I can finish it in the morning before the mail goes out. is'nt almost remarkable that I have been so well since I came into the service have not been sick but little and then not so as to be sent to a hospital, have received 2 slight wounds but not enough to be sent off to a hospital, and the Rebs have not taken me prisoner yet though they came very near it 2 or 3 times. Mount Vernon is but 5 or 6 miles from here a good many of the Officers have been down there. I intend to go in a few days. Capt Fairbank has got a horse keeping I guess I can get that. they say that it pays well. Fort Washington is on the opposite side of the River We saw them both when we came up the River a few days ago. Fairfax Semenary is but a little ways from here. I feel pretty well contented here in this camp. it does'nt seem as though I was far from home, certainly not from civilization. a good many of the boys are more anxious than ever to get home now they have been thinking about it so long and hearing so much said about it of late. I too am quite anxious but shall not feel very bad if I have to remain here till August probably our duty will not be very severe + my pay is pretty good if I could only get it. I think since it has been raised it amounts to about 140.00 per month. that is much more than I should be able to earn at home, unless I should get into some pretty profitable business. I have no idea yet what I shall pitch into. I dont know but I shall try and buy out Charles Bush, but it is pretty risky so long as I dont understand the business at all. I dont believe I could go Farming I was not cut out for farming I know. Joe Walker is Corpl. now. Joe Wheelock is trying to get a Pension I hear. Capt is about to make out some papers to enable him to. is he so very lame I did'nt suppose he would be. We did not suppose at the time that it was very bad. I think now that some would have got over it much quicker than he did. There is but little war news of late of much importance in fact the fighting is about played out. The most interesting news now is the Capture and information of the Assassinators it seems by the papers that there are something like a hundred of them connected with it among them Jeff Davis 100,000.00 Reward offered for his capture. I hope they will succeed in capturing him if not the rest, but I have written a long letter and will close. Most Aff. Yours George W. Harwood

Sam Maxwell served with the Massachusetts Fourth. Fort Lyon was in Alexandria, Virginia. It was destroyed by a gunpowder explosion on June 9, 1865. Fort Williams in Alexandria, Virginia was one of the forts providing a defense around the city of Washington. A Grand Review of troops was held in Washington on May 23-24 down Pennsylvania Avenue. There was a Grand Review for United States Colored Troops (USCT) in Harrisburg, Pennsylvania on November 14, 1865. Charles Bush was a stable keeper. A reward of $100,000 was offered for the capture of Confederate President Davis.

No 13   Camp of 36th Regt Mass Vols
                                         Near Alexandria Va May 11/65

Dear Friends

    I received another letter this morning with 10.00 You say that Mrs Lovering is doing Uncle Jonas work now do you know where Sarah is now. I have not thought of her for a long time. I was intending to go down to Mount Vernon today but I am Officer of the day so I shall have to put it off. Sam Maxwell came over to see me a few days ago. They are about 1 1/2 miles from here. I wish Allen could come out and see me but I dont suppose it would pay to take him from School beside I may get home in 2 or 3 weeks some Maine Regt are going pretty soon if they have not already gone also Pa. troops are about to start I dont know as we shall have that Review that was talked about. I see by the papers that Genls Wilson and Stoneman are both after Jeff [Davis] and it is thought that he will not be able to escape. We are laying here in Camp as when I wrote last drilling about 3 hours a day. the boys have great times in the cool of the day playing ball, kicking foot ball, leaping frog &c. the Officers had a game of ball at 4 old cat last night about 12 of us. we were all catching all knocking. It was pretty cool yesterday but is much warmer today pretty warm. I see by the papers this morning that all officers are to get 3 months pay proper making for me $150.00 extra for remaining in service till the end of war. virtuely the war is ended and we shall soon come home. I have no reason to regret that I have passed through 3 years of hardships + privations. the satisfaction of being able to say hereafter that I helped restore this nation to peace + prosperity is enough of itself, to pay me and the experience of a soldier life is clear gain. I will not write a long letter this time as I have no news.

Most Aff. George W.

From late March until mid-May, Major General George Stoneman destroyed all property and materials from Knoxville, Tennessee through North Carolina, southwestern Virginia and into Georgia. Stoneman's raid ended when President Davis was captured. Brigadier General James Wilson conducted a similar raid and led the unit which captured President Davis. Old Cat is a variation of baseball or rounders played with fewer than nine players per team.

No 14   Camp 36th Mass Vols
Near Alexandria Va May 26/65

Dear Friends

        I received a letter from you last night. I will write a [to] you a short one now we are making out our Muster-out roll + other paper now we shall probably be at home the last of next week soon after the first of June. the men will all get their pay when they are mustered out. the Officers will have to wait a few weeks to prove certificates of non indebtedness. if I had remained a Sergt I should have got about $150.00 [illegible] when mustered out now I shall have to wait a few weeks and get about $900.00 or 10,000.00 [sic 1,000], that is the difference you need not send any more money to me now for I saw Fortin Walker & son in Washington and said they had money enough offered to lend me 20.00 so I took it. When I get home I shall want a 100.00 or more to use till I settle with the Government I suppose a suit of cloths such as I shall want will cost from $75. to 100 dollars. [Leander] Bell is going to be transferred to the 21st and remain awhile I dont know as I have written you that. Mr Spark, Stoddard + Alonzo Bell came out and staid with me from Saturday afternoon till Monday morning. I was very glad indeed to see them they were at the [Grand] Review Tuesday + Wednesday We marched over to Washington Monday Morning. I got a pass and went round the City in the evening. the Review passed of splendidly. I suppose you have read an exact acct of it before this. We are all highly pleased to think that we shall so soon become Citizens again. I presume we shall have to go to Readville or Gallopps Island and stay a few days after we get into Mass, but I hope to be with you a week from Sunday, possibly not quite so quick perhaps you had better not write after Sunday or Monday of next week. You will get this letter about that time. it is raining today. I will not write any more this time perhaps I may before I come home. I dont know whether we shall go home on the cars or Steamer

Ever Aff Yours

G.W. Harwood

Tuesday, May 23, Meade's Army of the Potomac including the Ninth Corps paraded. On Wednesday, May 24 Sherman's Armies of the Tennessee and Georgia paraded at the Grand Review. Readville was a military camp in Hyde Park (Dedham) Massachusetts. Gallops [also Gallups] Island was a military camp in Boston Harbor.

No 15

Camp 36th Regt Mass Vols

Near Alexandria Va.

June 1st 1865

Dear Friends

I will drop a line to you this splendid morning. our Muster out rolls + discharges are finished. we were hoping to start for home tomorrow but shall not I guess probably not till next Monday. I am in a pucker now, to know what to do with my boy or Man (21 years) I like him first rate. he is as stout as an ox + not a lazy bone in him. when I tell him to do any thing I know it will be done. he was brought up on a farm. if I knew I should cary on a farm myself by + by I should surely take him along with me. I guess I shall as it is, so you need not be surprised if you see him come with me. if you dont want I should keep him at home I will dispose of him in a few days. if I do fetch him he can have a bed made in the back chamber or my bed room. I know that Father is very much opposed to the color but if he could have him on the farm a month he would keep him, the year round I presume. he is bright and understands himself, and good disposition The first thing I shall do when I get into Mass will be to go home and get some money I presume we shall have to stay at Readville a week or two before we get mustered out, and paid off. the Chaplain is trying to put my certificate of non indebtedness now. I have not made up my mind what to do when I get home yet, visit with you for a week or two I guess, go a fishing perhaps. I will not write more this time. You may look for me and My servant also. I may not stay any longer than I did the last time I was there unless you get me to having or something on the farm.

Very Aff Yours

George W.

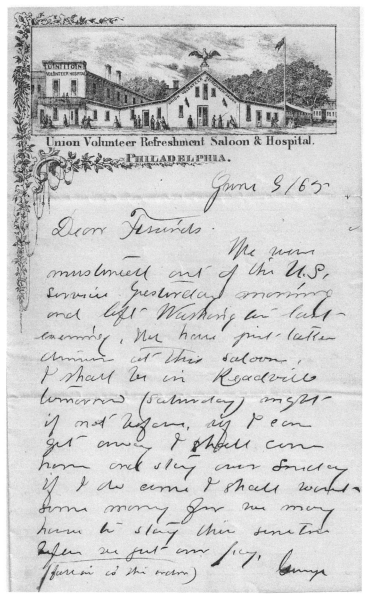

Union Volunteer Refreshment Saloon & Hospital, June 9, 1865 letter (Image from author's collection)

June 9/65

Dear Friends,

We were mustered out of the U.S. Service yesterday morning and left Washington last evening. We have just taken dinner at this saloon. I shall be in Readville tomorrow (Saturday) night if not before. if I can get away I shall come home and stay over Sunday if I do come I shall want some money for we may have to stay there some time before we get our pay.

(furious is the order)   George

The regiment arrived in Readville on June 10, went to Worcester, Massachusetts for a reception, returned to Readville, received their pay, and were discharged from the service on June 19. Bowen, page 562.

~ Chapter 14 ~

AFTER THE WAR
November 1865 – June 1920

Washington D.C.
Nov 4 1865

Lt. G. W. Harwood
    Dear Sir
        I have pursued your case on <u>claimed</u> so far and the inclosed indicates you will please answer the wants required & return the whole to me - that is the "Yellow paper" & the answers & I will close it up for you. All you have got to do is to make affidavit before Justice that said stores were unavoidably lost, stating how they were lost.
        Please do this & send it to me at N.Y. City I shall be there in about 10 days.

                    Most Truly Yours
                    John F. Severance

Affidavit for items lost in the final days of leaving Alexandria, mustering out in Washington, and final discharge in Readville.

After the war George went to Bloomington, Illinois to visit his great-uncle Abel Harwood and his great-aunt Mary Batcheller Harwood. There he met and married their daughter, his second cousin, Mary N. Harwood. He initially went into business with Uncle Abel and later when they both moved to Champaign-Urbana, Illinois, he was a resident agent for the General Insurance Agency.

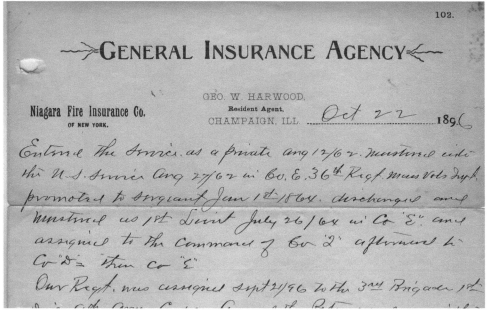

Letter from George W. Harwood to Loyal Legion, Chicago
(Image from author's collection)

Oct 22 1896

Entered the Service, as a private Aug 12/62. Mustered into the U.S. Service Aug 27/62 in Co. E. 36th Regt. Mass Vols Inft, promoted to Sergeant Jan 1st 1864, discharged and mustered as 1st Lieut July 26/64 in Co "E," and assigned to the command of Co "I" afterward to Co "D" then Co "E" Our Regt. was assigned Sept 21/96 [62] to the 3rd Brigade 1st Div. 9th Army Corps – Army of the Potomac – was in the battle of Fredericksburg Va. Dec 13/62, spent about a month at Newport News, then taken to Ky – and in June 63 went to Vicksburg Miss, was in battles of Vicksburg July 63 Jackson Miss July 12th 63 – received a flesh wound in right leg - the 12th returned to Ky in Aug. & in Sept over Cumberland Gap into East Tenn. all through that Campaign in battles of Blue Springs Oct 10/63, at Lenoir Station Nov 15/63, Campbell Station Nov 16/63 then received a flesh wound in neck, in siege of Knoxville Nov 17 to Dec 2/63 – in March 64 returned to Washington DC & re-entered the Army of the Potomac, was in Boston Mass from March to May 15/64 on recruiting service, and so missed the battles of the Wilderness & Spottselvania. Was with them then to Appomattox. Was in battles of No Anna May 23/64 Cold Harbor June 2/64. Near Petersburg Va. Known to us as "shamed house battle" June 15/64 – Norfork [Norfolk] R.R. June 18/64, Jerusalem plankroad June 22/64. Mine affair, "Elliot Salient" in "Crater" July 30/64 – at Pregram [Pegram] farm Sept 30/64, Petersburg Va Apr 4/64 [Apr 4/65]– in the Pits & on skirmish line from May 64 to April 65 under fire most of the time – Was in 9th Army Corps all through the Service

Copy sent to	Geo. W. Harwood
Roswell H. Mason	Late 1st Lieut Co E. 36. Regt. Mass Vols Inft
Loyal Legion	
20 McGinn Bldg	
Chicago	

George W. Harwood was a member of the Military Order Loyal Legion United States (MOLLUS), a veterans' organization for officers. He belonged to the Colonel Nodine Post in Illinois as he lived in Bloomington and then Champaign, Illinois after the war.

George and his wife Mary visited North Brookfield periodically over the years. While on a visit in June 1920, George died. He is buried in North Brookfield and also recognized on a monument in the family plot established by Abel Harwood in Bloomington, Illinois. Mary moved to North Brookfield and spent her final years with sister-in-law Frances Harwood Cummings. She died in 1924 and is also buried in North Brookfield and recognized on the monument in Bloomington, llinois. They had no children.

GEORGE WASHINGTON HARWOOD.

First Lieutenant Thirty-sixth Massachusetts Infantry,
United States Volunteers.
Died at Brookline [North Brookfield], Massachusetts,
June 6, 1920.

THE following sketch of the life of the late George W. Harwood is compiled, in the main, from a tribute by Dr. Charles B. Johnson, of Champaign:

"I wonder if this community fully realizes what it has lost in the death of George Harwood? I can but think it does.

"Those who knew him best realized that he had a very high sense of right and justice, and that he fully lived up to his ideal of both.

"With possibly one or two exceptions he had been in business longer than any other man in our city, and in all that time, perhaps, no one had been a party to more transactions than he. Nevertheless, in all of these business matters with which he had to do, no man can say truthfully that George Harwood wronged him.

"Indeed, so just and fair-minded was he in his ideals and in all his dealings that it had come to be the custom for scores of our citizens to go to him for counsel and advice, and in most instances the advice given would be followed to the letter.

"What a record! What a reputation to leave behind as a priceless legacy to his friends! Furthermore, George Harwood was a great moral force in the community. Modest, kindly, instinctively a gentleman, he wielded a quiet influence for good that many a noisy, wordy enthusiast might well envy.

"George Harwood holds a fine record as a Civil War soldier. His regiment, the 36th Massachusetts, was attached to the Army of the Potomac, and this means much; for everyone familiar with Civil War history realizes what the Army of the Potomac was up against. During the Vicksburg campaign in 1863 the Ninth Corps was temporarily transferred to that field of action and there rendered most important and valuable service, taking part in the battles at Vicksburg and at Jackson, Miss., where Lieut. Harwood was wounded, July 12, 1863 — thence to Kentucky and East Tennessee, through that campaign, in the battles of Blue Springs, Lenore Station and Campbell Station, in which action Lieut. Harwood was again wounded, Nov. 16, 1863 — thence to the Siege of Knoxville, Tenn., and in March, 1864, returned to Washington, D. C, and re-entered the Army of the Potomac. With his regiment, Lieut. Harwood served three years and did not quit the service till the last enemy of his country had surrendered. He enlisted as a private and won a First Lieutenancy through meritorious service. Colonel Nodine Post will miss him. Indeed, all Civil War veterans who knew him will mourn the loss of their fallen comrade.

"But perhaps George Harwood will be missed nowhere more than in the First Presbyterian church of this city, wherein he had for a great many years given most efficient service as Clerk of the session. Finally, it is not too much to say that everyone recognized in George Harwood the very highest type of the Christian gentleman."

He was elected a Companion of the Military Order of the Loyal Legion of the United States through the Commandery of the State of Illinois, May 7, 1908, Insignia No. 15701. His Companions will miss the presence of a man so courtly and loyal.

> EDWARD BAILEY,
> STEPHEN ALFRED FORBES,
> CHARLES ALBERT KILER,
> *Committee.*

Military Order of the Loyal Legion of the United States (MOLLUS).
Commandery of the State of Illinois, pages D-591-593.

APPENDIX I
Massachusetts Thirty-sixth Regimental Chronology
Battles and engagements are in bold

1862

August — George W. Harwood enlists, regiment mustered and trained at Camp Wool, Worcester, Massachusetts

September — Received flags from mayor of Worcester, train to Boston, steamer to Washington, steamer Potomac River to Leesboro, Maryland, Antietam, joined Third Brigade (Welsh), First Division, Ninth Army Corps

October — Pleasant Valley, Maryland, Frederick, Point of Rocks, Lovettsville, Falmouth, Virginia

November — Camp Fisher, Camp Forbes

December — **Battle of Fredericksburg,** Virginia, camped across the Rappahannock River

1863

January — In camp near Falmouth, Virginia

February — Train to Aquia Landing, steamer South America, Potomac River to Chesapeake Bay to Fortress Monroe, Newport News campground at Newport Creek

March — Steamer Kennebec to Baltimore, train across West Virginia to Cumberland, Piedmont, Parkersburg, steamer Bostonia on Ohio River to Cincinnati, Ohio, crossed Ohio River to Covington, Kentucky, train to Lexington, Kentucky

April — Department of the Ohio, First Division (Willcox), train from Lexington, Kentucky to Cincinnati, Ohio, return to Lexington, Nicholasville, Camp Dick Robinson, some to Harrodsburg, Danville, Camp Dick Robinson, to Lancaster, Stanford

May	To Hustonville, Middleburgh on the Green River, Liberty, Neatsville, Columbia, Glasgow, Gradyville, Breedingsville, back to Columbia, through Adair County with prisoners
June	To Jamestown, Lebanon, Louisville, Kentucky, across Ohio River to Jeffersonville, and Cairo, Illinois, pass Seymour and Sandoval, arrive Cairo, Illinois, steamer Meteor to Milldale, Mississippi
July	Day after Battle of Gettysburg, Vicksburg surrenders ending the **Siege of Vicksburg**, corps to Jackson, Mississippi, **Siege of Jackson**, corps to Canton, Mississippi, back to Snyder's Bluff, return to Milldale, Mississippi
August	Steamer Hiawatha, Cairo, Illinois, train to Cincinnati, Ohio, Covington, Kentucky, reassigned to Burnside, Army of the Ohio, train to Camp Nelson, Nicholasville, Crab Orchard, Kentucky
September	To East Tennessee through Cumberland Gap, Morristown, Bulls Gap, Knoxville
October	**Battle of Blue Springs**, Greenville, Rheatown, back to Knoxville, regiment to Loudon, Harwood back to Greenville for recruiting duty, winter quarters at Lenoir Station
November	Lenoir Station, **Battle of Campbell's Station**, retreat to Knoxville, **Battle of Fort Sanders**
December	**Knoxville Siege** ends

1864

January	Blair's Cross Roads, George W. Harwood made sergeant, Strawberry Plains, back to Knoxville, Erin's Station
February	Near Knoxville, to Strawberry Plains, George W. Harwood home to Massachusetts on recruiting leave
March	Grant made General in Chief, regiment left Knoxville
April	Knoxville, Cumberland Gap to Nicholasville, Kentucky,

	train to Annapolis, Maryland, assigned to Army of the Potomac, First Brigade, Second Division, Major Draper, to Alexandria, Fairfax Court House, Bristow, Catlett's Station, Bealton
May	Rapidan River, **Battle of the Wilderness,** Chancellorsville, **Battle of Spotsylvania Court House,** George W. Harwood rejoins regiment, Po River, North Anna River (twice), Pamunkey River
June	**Second Battle of Cold Harbor (Bethesda Church)**, Gaines Mill, to White House Landing, cross James River, to Prince George Courthouse, near Harrison's Landing, to Petersburg, **charge on Confederate works at Petersburg**, to Weldon Railroad, George W. Harwood appointed first lieutenant
July	George W. Harwood commissioned first lieutenant, to Poplar-Grove Church, **Battle of the Crater**
August	To Weldon Railroad, remained in this area until the end of September
September	**Battle of Poplar Grove (Spring) Church**, Virginia, **Battle of Pegram's Farm**
October	To Boisscau House at Pegram's Farm, to Hatcher's Run and back to Pegram's Farm
November - February	Consolidate to seven companies, left Pegram's Farm for Fort Rice
1865	
March	On leave to Massachusetts
April	To Petersburg, at Black and White's Station, to Nottoway Court House, to Jutter's Station, to Burkesville, Rice's Station, to Farmville, Massachusetts Thirty-sixth in charge of prisoners, regiment leaves, steamer Vidette from City Point to Alexandria, Virginia, George W. Harwood stays behind

May   Grand Review in Washington, regiment camped in Alexandria, Virginia

June   Mustered out at Alexandria, Virginia, recruits and enlisted men transfer to Massachusetts Fifty-sixth, arrived Readville, Massachusetts, reception for regiment in Worcester, returned to Readville, received pay and dismissed.

APPENDIX II
Family Genealogies

People mentioned in the letters are in **bold.**

HARWOOD FAMILY

Major Peter Harwood 1740-1805 and Phebe Prouty 1744-1811
m 1763

Children of Major Peter Harwood and Phebe Prouty (eleven in all)

George Washington Harwood	**Jonas Harwood**
1779-1860	1784-1872
m 1807	m 1808
Anna Bisco	**Lucretia Winslow**
1780-1849	1787-1864

Children of George Washington Harwood and Anna Bisco (ten in all)

Anna M	**Washington**	**George**	**Harrison**	Phebe P	**Dolly Powers**	**Joseph W**
1809-1875	1811-1876	1813-1897	1814-1882	1816-1868	1820-1897	1823-?
m 1831	m(1)unknown	m 1837	m 1840	m unknown	m 1849	m(1) 1847
Samuel	**Laura**	**Angeline**	Adeline	**William C**	**David L**	Mary
Lothrop	**Jennings**	**Allen**	Greenwood	**Jackson**	**Winslow**	Mason
1806-1867	m(2) 1856	1818-1868	1819-1902	1820-1901	1808-1880	m(2) 1857
	Lucie Anne Lane					Cordelia Selfridge
	Rosetta	**Anna M**	**Henry G**	**Andrew F**	children of see	
	1841-?	1839-1868	1841-1914	1842-1912	WINSLOW family	
	plus 3	**George W**	Harrison/**Harry**	**George H**		
		1841-1920	1842-1918	1843-1914		
		Ethan Allen	plus 3	**Anna B**		
		1847-1917		1846-1928		
		Frances A (Fannie)		plus 2		
		1855-1932				

Children of Jonas Harwood and Lucretia Winslow (eight in all)

Rebekah D	Jonas	**Abel**	Frances E
1811-1897	1812-1840	1814-1891	1830-1856
m 1833	m 1836	m(1) 1841	m 1852
Orin A Tomblen	**Abbie** Comee	Mary D Batcheller	**Oramel A Rugg**
1807-1866	m2 I S Lincoln	1821-1856	1824-1888?
|	|	m(2) 1858	
Lucretia	**Fred**	Isabella D Boyd	
1833-1871	1839-1870	1831-1902	
m 1857		|	
Daniel P Young		**Mary N**	
1832-1878		1842-1924 (plus ten more)	

ALLEN FAMILY

Alvan Allen 1784-1840 and Mehetable/Mehitabel Goodnow 1783-1838
m 1809

Children of Alvan Allen and Mehetable Goodnow (eight in all)

Caroline	Oshea	**David** G	**Angeline**	**Alvan**	**Martha Ann**	Mehitabel
1810-1871	1812-1844	1815/16-1898	1818-1868	1821-1901	1823-1869	1826/28-1855
m 1839+	m unknown	m 1838	m 1837	m 1842	m unknown	m 1843
his 2nd	**Lydia**	Mary	**George**	**Louisa**	Smith?	**William M**
Elias	**Fowler**	**Barnes**	**Harwood**	**Smith**		**Allen**
Bartlett	1820?-?	1812/14?-?	1813-1897	1825-1911		Wm. (m2) 1856
1808-1869	|		|	|		**Anna L Bartlett**
|	**Ada Jane**		children of	**Ida E** (Adelia)		1822-1888
(five plus)	1841/2-1901		see	1846-1887		(5 children)
Oshea A	**Mary**		HARWOOD	**Ethan Alvin**		
1851-1865	1845-1885		Family	1854-		

Angeline Allen was born Angelina, Alvan Allen (1821-1901) was known as Alvin.

WINSLOW FAMILY

David L Winslow 1810-1880
m (1) 1837 Mercy Hinkley Dexter 1815-1847
m (2) 1849 **Dolly Powers Harwood** 1820-1897

Children of **David L** and Mercy H Dexter (three in all)
Louis Dennis
1839-1864

Children of **David L** and **Dolly P Harwood** (six in all)
David Frank 1853-1925
m 1889
Edith Lord
1863-1947
Janet M Lebourveau Drake descended from David Frank Winslow

DOANE/DOAN FAMILY

Joseph Doan (1767-1829) and **Mercy Doane (**1778-1864)
m 1798

Children of Joseph Doan & Mercy Doane		(probably nine children in all)
Harriet	**William F**	Roland F
1799-1875	1805-1890	1808-1891
(m) unknown	(m) 1827	(m) 1831
Welcome Doane/Done	Mary P Shedd	Amanda Shedd
1798-1881	1806-1883	1808–1889

Children of Harriet and Welcome (eight in all)
Josiah M 1844-1906
(m) 1863
Mary Ann Steele (Polly)
1843-1922

Children of **William F** Doane and Mary P Shedd (six in all)

Mary	**George P**
1838-1923	1840-1925
(m1)1862 **Lyman Gilbert**	(m) 1868 Julia F Harrington
(m2)1864 Josiah Frank Hebard	

Children of Roland F Doane and Amanda Shedd (eight in all)

Freeman R	**Hubbard S**	**Edwin**	**Eunice A**	**Ellen R**
1837-1910	1839-1914	1841-1904	1843-1871	1848-1918?
(m 1) 1859		m 1879	m 1863	m 1869
Anna M Harwood		**Emeline Pike**	**John D Lamson**	**Ethan Allen Harwood**
1839-1868		1859-1901	1838-1899	1847-1917
|		|	|	|
George R 1860-1925		6 children	2 children	1 child

Elmer F 1862-1888
Irene A 1864-1873
Albion H 1867- 1938 (m)1894 Mary Adna Varney 1872-1942

Children of Albion H Doane and Mary Adna Varney
Frances C 1898-1996 (m) 1939 Kenneth Martin 1907-1989, no children
plus two brothers
Frances inherited the letters

APPENDIX III
Bibliography

There are numerous printed resources for the Civil War. This list includes the ones which I found were particularly helpful. The majority of the sources listed here are the digital ones, which are more difficult to identify and locate.

Advertisements for horse remedies. *Horse Review* 32, 2 (1905): page 762 (digital).
https://www.google.com/books/edition/The_Horse_Review/6q4QAQAA-MAAJ?hl=en&gbpv=0.

American Battlefield Trust. https://www.battlefields.org/. Online database, formerly Civilwar.org
> "This day in the Civil War,"
> https://www.battlefields.org/learn/articles/day-civil-war.
> This is the best place to find what happened by date or location.

> Georgia's Blue and Gray Trail,
> https://www.battlefields.org/visit/heritage-sites/blue-and-gray-trail.

Ancestry. https://www.ancestry.com/. Online database, subscription required.
> Fold3 by Ancestry. https://www.fold3.com/. Online database. © 2021, formerly Civil War Archive.com, and Historical Data Systems.

Bearss, Edwin C. and J. Parker Hills. *Receding tide: Vicksburg and Gettysburg: the campaigns that changed the Civil War*. Washington, D.C.: National Geographic Society, 2010.

Bowen, James Lorenzo. *Massachusetts in the War, 1861-1865*. Springfield, Mass: Clark W. Bryan and Company 1889 (digital).
https://www.google.com/books/edition/Massachusetts_in_the_War_1861_1865/4_lYAAAAMAAJ?hl=en.

Burrage, Henry S., editor. *History of the Thirty Sixth Regiment Massachusetts Volunteers*. Rockwell and Churchill, 1884 (digital).
https://play.google.com/books/reader?id=ADpAAAAAYAAJ&pg=GBS.PP4.

Double, S. M. "Forever with the Lord." Dadmun, J. W. *The New Revival Melodies a collection of some of the most popular hymns and tunes adapted to all occasions of social worship*. Boston, J. P. Magee, 1860. page 23. (digital).
https://www.google.com/books/edition/The_New_Revival_Melodies/I18CHSyvjNYC?hl=en&gbpv=0.

FamilySearch. https://www.familysearch.org/en/, Online database, © 2021 by Intellectual Reserve, Inc. A service provided by The Church of Jesus Christ of Latter-day Saints.

FamilySearch. United States Civil War Soldiers Index, 1861-1865, https://www.familysearch.org/search/collection/1910717.

Find a Grave®. https://www.findagrave.com/, Online database © 2021.

Hess, Earl J. *The Knoxville Campaign: Burnside and Longstreet in East Tennessee*. Knoxville: University of Tennessee Press, 2012.

Library of Congress. https://www.loc.gov/, Online database, extensive resource for photos and maps.
Pictures and Maps, https://www.loc.gov/pictures/collection/civwar, (this is a good place to begin)
American Civil War Sesquicentennial Web Archive, https://www.loc.gov/collections/american-civil-war-sesquicentennial-web-archive/,
Prints and Photos Division, https://www.loc.gov/photos/, (search Civil War).

Marvel, William. *Burnside*. Chapel Hill: University of North Carolina Press, 1991, (a positive biography of Gen. Ambrose Burnside).

Marvin, Abijah P. *A History of Worcester in the War of the Rebellion*. Worcester: Published by the author, 1870 (digital and paper) includes section on Massachusetts Thirty-sixth.
https://www.google.com/books/edition/History_of_Worcester_in_the_War_of_the_R/IbATAAAAYAAJ?hl=en.

Massachusetts Adjutant General's Office. *Massachusetts soldiers, sailors, and marines in the Civil War*. Printed at Norwood, Mass. 1931-37 (printed and digital) multiple volumes.
        https://www.ancestry.com/search/collections/29987/,
(Ancestry.com is the easiest to use)
        https://archives.lib.state.ma.us/handle/2452/50883,
        https://catalog.hathitrust.org/Record/100123717.

Massachusetts Civil War Research Center. http://www.massachusettscivil-war.com/, Online database © 1999 – 2021.

Military Order of the Loyal Legion of the United States (MOLLUS). Commandery of the State of Illinois. *Memorials of Deceased Companions of the Commandery of the State of Illinois from January 1, 1912 to December 31, 1922*. Wilmington, North Carolina, Broadfoot Publishing Company, 1993. (originally published in three volumes 1901-1922) pages D 591-593. (digital)
https://archive.org/details/memdeccompillinois03furnrich/page/590/mode/2up.

Miller, Donald L. *Vicksburg: Grant's Campaign that broke the Confederacy*. New York: Simon & Schuster, 2019.

National Park Service. American Battlefield Protection Program (ABPP) https://www.nps.gov/orgs/2287/index.htm . Online database.

National Park Service. Soldiers and Sailors Database, https://www.nps.gov/civilwar/soldiers-and-sailors-database.htm. Online database.

Newton, John. "Safely through another week." *Trinity Psalter Hymnal*. https://hymnary.org/text/safely_through_another_week.

Rhea, Gordon C. *Cold Harbor: Grant and Lee, May 26-June 3, 1864*. Baton Rouge: Louisiana State University Press, 2002.

Schouler, William. *A History of Massachusetts in the Civil War*. Boston: E.P. Dutton & Company, 1868-71, two volumes (digital) (also titled *A History of Massachusetts in the Rebellion*).
Volume 1 https://www.google.com/books/edition/A_History_of_Massachusetts_in_the_Civil/Ocd3AAAAMAAJ?hl=en.

Volume 2, (Volume 2 page 659 has quota number for North Brookfield) https://www.google.com/books/edition/A_History_of_Massachusetts_in_t he_Civil/HMp3AAAAMAAJ?hl=en.

Temple, Josiah Howard. *History of North Brookfield. North Brookfield, Massachusetts*. Published by the Town of North Brookfield, 1887, reprinted Salem: Higginson Book Company, 1987 (printed and digital) (page 300 gives quota figures for the town). https://www.google.com/books/edition/History_of_North_Brookfield_Ma ssachusett/rHmAAAAAIAAJ?hl=en&gbpv=0.

The Siege of Petersburg Online (covers entire Petersburg campaign). https://www.beyondthecrater.com/. © 2008–2021.

Town of North Brookfield. *A Historical Record of the Soldiers and Sailors of North Brookfield. North Brookfield.* Published by the Town, 1886 (printed and digital available in Ancestry.com) Each town compiled this publication for the Massachusetts Soldiers, Sailors and Marines set.

United States. War Department. *The War of the Rebellion: a compilation of the Official Records of the Union and Confederate Armies.* Washington: Government. Printing Office, 1880-1901
(Also known as the Official Records or OR). 1894-1922.
https://ehistory.osu.edu/books/official-records at Ohio State, incomplete but good keyword search.
http://collections.library.cornell.edu/moa_new/waro.html, at Cornell, complete.

Weiser, Eugene. *The Pennsylvania Railroad: A Brief Look in Time*. N.p.: Lulu.com, 2013, page 24. (digital) https://www.google.com/books/edition/The_Pennsylvania_Railroad_A_Br ief_Look_i/hrAXBAAAQBAJ?hl=en&gbpv=1&printsec=frontcover.

~ Acknowledgements ~

I would like to acknowledge and thank the many people who have helped make this dream a reality. It is never possible to thank everyone but here are some of the people who made a special contribution.

First of course is the family of George W. Harwood and his great niece, Frances Doane Martin, who preserved the letters and lovingly gave them to my family to cherish. Next are my parents John W. and Marion E. Lebourveau who copied them to share with their three daughters.

Mark Gleusing, Needham History Center and Museum, asked us to present a program on our travels. Thom Gilbert introduced us to the General Lander Civil War Roundtable of Lynn where Nadine Mironchuk and others encouraged us to publish a book. Brandon Avery and Jim Buzzell, North Brookfield Historical Society, arranged for us to speak at the Haston Free Public Library. Dana Zaiser and others at the Olde Colony Civil War Round Table in Dedham invited us to speak and offered support for publishing. Donald L. Miller, of Lafayette College, in Easton, Pennsylvania read some of the letters and was encouraging.

Judy Putnam, Meg Weekes and Derry Allen have hosted us on our travels and cheered us on at every step, desiring to see a book of the letters. Diane and Stuart Myers shared their experience publishing a Civil War memoir. Stuart R. Christie, of the Dedham Historical Society and Museum, shared his insights about publishing and identified George's hat as belonging to an officer. Rose Doherty has been extremely helpful and supportive as I learned more about the process of writing, editing and publishing. She also suggested the title for this book.

There were numerous librarians and National Park rangers who assisted us. I would especially like to thank E. Tyson Bolles, of the Wellesley Free Library, for introducing us to the OR, officially known as *The War of the Rebellion: a compilation of the Official Records of the Union and Confederate Armies*. We don't know everyone's name but are forever indebted to you for guiding us along the way.

The team assembled by Damianos Publishing has been wonderful to work with. Thank you, Lynne Damianos, Brett Peruzzi, Lisa Thompson and Rob Levine.

My family, my sisters and their families, Mardy and Peter Shapland, Sujoy Spencer and Richard Thorlakson, Greg, Alli, Michi, Elaine and Steve have encouraged us as well. Last but by no means least, I must thank my husband David E. Drake for sharing my interest in the letters and planning out the many trips we took to visit the places where they were written. He was invaluable in re-reading the original letters. I could not have done this without his partnership. Finally, to Hattie, Piper, Gemma, Harrison, Zack and Lava, this book is for you.

~ About the Author ~

Janet M. "Jan" Drake graduated from Needham High School in Massachusetts, Hobart and William Smith Colleges in New York with a bachelor's degree in Chemistry, and Simmons University in Massachusetts, with a master's degree in Library Science. She is a retired librarian who worked in university, corporate and public libraries. Drake has had a lifelong interest in history. Her first job in high school was working for an antiques dealer.

When she is not traveling and discovering the history of new places, she enjoys gardening, reading and music.